Parali

Paraliterary

The Making of Bad Readers in Postwar America

MERVE EMRE

The University of Chicago Press

CHICAGO AND LONDON

PUBLICATION OF THIS BOOK HAS BEEN AIDED BY A GRANT
FROM THE BEVINGTON FUND.

The University of Chicago Press, Chicago 60637
The University of Chicago Press, Ltd., London
© 2017 by Merve Emre
Published 2017
Printed in the United States of America

26 25 24 23 22 21 20 19 18 17   1 2 3 4 5

ISBN-13: 978-0-226-47383-3 (cloth)
ISBN-13: 978-0-226-47397-0 (paper)
ISBN-13: 978-0-226-47402-1 (e-book)
DOI: 10.7208/chicago/9780226474021.001.0001

Library of Congress Cataloging-in-Publication Data

Names: Emre, Merve, author.
Title: Paraliterary : the making of
bad readers in postwar America / Merve Emre.
Description: Chicago ; London : The University of Chicago Press, 2017. |
Includes bibliographical references and index.
Identifiers: LCCN 2017016749 | ISBN 9780226473833 (cloth : alk. paper) |
ISBN 9780226473970 (pbk. : alk. paper) | ISBN 9780226474021 (e-book)
Subjects: LCSH: Books and reading—United States—History—
20th century. | Books and reading—United States—Sociological aspects. |
Literature and society—United States. | Reading—Philosophy. |
Communication in international relations—United States. |
United States—Intellectual life—20th century.
Classification: LCC Z1003.2 .E48 2017 | DDC 028/.909730904—dc23
LC record available at https://lccn.loc.gov/2017016749

♾ This paper meets the requirements of ANSI/NISO Z39.48-1992
(Permanence of Paper).

For Gulus and Hasan Berk,
in memoriam

Contents

Pop Quiz

Select four answers to the question what should a reader be to be a good reader:

1. The reader should identify himself or herself with the hero or heroine.
2. The reader should identify himself or herself with the hero or heroine.
3. The reader should concentrate on the socio-economic angle.
4. The reader should prefer a story with action and dialogue to one with none.
5. The reader should have seen the book in a movie.
6. The reader should be a budding author.
7. The reader should have imagination.
8. The reader should have memory.
9. The reader should have a dictionary.
10. The reader should have some artistic sense.

VLADIMIR NABOKOV, "Good Readers and Good Writers" (1948)[1]

GOOD READER, BAD READER

Quizzing the students in his European literature class at Cornell on their reading habits, the Russian-American novelist Vladimir Nabokov observed in 1948, "The students leaned heavily on emotional identification, action, and the social-economic or historical angle. Of course, as you have guessed, the good reader is one who has imagination, memory, a dictionary, and some artistic sense." On one level, Nabokov was airing a teacher's frustration at how American readers had failed to cultivate key practices of aesthetic appreciation. While Nabokov was busy scrutinizing and cataloging literary devices, his American students were frittering away their time trying to feel what fictional characters felt. On another level, however, Nabokov was making a subtle argument about the reading practices that had arisen alongside other changes in the United States just after World War II: not only the growing prominence of book clubs and Hollywood adaptations but also the vast array of literacy programs that imagined an increasingly intimate relationship between a "social-economic or historical angle" of reading and nationally marked practices of "identification," "dialogue," and "action" undertaken by readers.

Although his pop quiz registers his disdain for readers who deprioritized aesthetics, Nabokov himself was no stranger to such institutional projects of reading. In 1947, he had asked his good friend Edmund Wilson to recommend him to the State Department as a Russian broadcaster of American literature at the Voice of America (VOA)—a job he lost to his more charismatic cousin, Nicolas Nabokov, who would later become the secretary general of the Congress of Cultural Freedom (CCF). "Good old Nika got the job which had been promised to me," he grumbled to Wilson.[2] Installed at Cornell less than one year after the VOA denied him a job reading literature over the radio to Russian audiences, Nabokov had suggestively titled the introductory lecture to his European literature class "Good Readers and Good Writers." Yet what seemed to lend the lecture both its revelatory and its judgmental force was precisely its intimation of all the "bad" readers who lurked outside the literature classroom, fiddling with the dials on their radios or attending mass readings sponsored by the CCF. These were the readers who in Nabokov's view had made reading into both a problem for teachers of literature like himself and a tremendously powerful activity—one that had the potential to shape international histories of identification, dialogue, and action outside the confines of the literature classroom.

Nabokov's alignment of "good" readers with the aesthetic sensibilities of "good" writers would go on to become one of the most commonly promoted identities of American fiction after World War II.[3] Never before had so many people aspired to engage with literary texts as serious works of art, armed with an autonomous set of rules governing what they read, how they read, and to what ends. Whether as exceptional students, who went on to become professional writers, editors, publishers, teachers, or scholars of literature, or merely dutiful ones who would scatter into the workforce after graduation, the imprint of the good reader was often treated as a wholesale remaking of whatever reading habits had come before and a defense against those that might come after. And although he had pegged his students as mostly bad readers, Nabokov's pop quiz, widely cited and circulated in introductory literature classes to this day, suggests the extraordinary degree to which literary culture would go on to naturalize the figure of the good reader—once hailed as the "close reader" by the New Critics, later as the "critical reader" by literary theorists—as its privileged reading subject.[4]

Yet whatever name he went by, the good reader's cultural elevation always relied on his oppositional relationship to the curiously undifferentiated mass of bad readers, who struck Nabokov—and have struck many teachers and literary scholars since—as a kind of irritating background noise; always already present and unworthy of any serious or systematic consideration. Indeed, Nabokov's lecture seemed custom designed to bolster a general disdain for bad readers in US academia. Poet Edouard Roditi noted in 1947 that "curious high-brow prejudices make many of us neglect our good writers who have gained popularity with bad readers."[5] Columbia professor William York Tindall, in his 1959 guide to reading modernist literature, argued that a "great artist" was one who "found the exact way to say what he saw. If the way he found shuts bad readers out, they must try to become better."[6] For Kenneth Burke, an "overwhelming array of bad readers" was responsible for perpetuating the "practicality shibboleth" of reading: a widespread belief in the "kinds of action" that literature could "stimulate" in "political and economic situations."[7] Such pragmatism all but ensured that the artistic merits of "good books" would "pale into insignificance." Walter Kaufmann bemoaned "the future of the humanities" when, in 1977, it appeared that this future had been bequeathed to "bad readers," while the monthly magazine *College Teacher* instructed "bad readers" to steer clear of serious literature and limit their efforts to "menu reading, cookbooks, 'how to' manuals, comic books, advertisements, magazines, newspapers, and simple novels."[8] Of course, such sweeping indictments raise more questions than they answer. Who were these bad readers? Where had they come from? What did they want out of reading? And what, exactly, made them so bad in the first place?

This book is about bad readers and the institutions that spawned them in postwar America. By bad readers, I mean individuals socialized into the practices of readerly identification, emotion, action, and interaction that Nabokov decried; practices rooted in a political culture that insisted on "Something to Be Done" by literature, as the poet Conrad Aiken put it so bluntly in a 1956 letter to President Dwight D. Eisenhower.[9] As literary historians have demonstrated, the midcentury United States witnessed a dramatic shift away from reading literature in elite academic institutions and toward institutions that stressed literature's communicative and public value in a rapidly internationalizing world.[10] This book's central claim is that this shift also consolidated new practices of reading literary texts that posited a strong, disciplined, and habitual relationship between aesthetic representation and readers' lived experiences of public communication—a relationship located not exclusively or even primarily in the national production of literary fiction but in international acts of speech, gesture, perception, consumption, and face-to-face interaction. Absent any theoretical account of how reading and international communicative practices came to overlap with one another, it is all too easy to dismiss reading that does not look like Nabokov's good reading as merely imitative, emotional, information seeking, faddish, escapist, propagandist, or otherwise unworthy of critical attention in its own right—as the genetically "middlebrow" or "mass cultural" antithesis to the university's highly specialized literacy projects.[11] To do so is to fail to grapple with the historically contingent production of specific kinds of bad and good readers, whose matter-of-fact opposition to one other—and, more implicitly, their definition through one another—was negotiated in more materially and imaginatively complex ways than the terms *good* and *bad* could ever convey.

Nowhere was this shift in reading practices more apparent than in institutions of international communication, where American literature played a crucial role in helping national and international readers alike acclimate to the rise of American power in the lead-up to World War II and to the perpetually anxious state of Cold War liberalism in the years that followed.[12] At the same time that American universities appeared to be churning out good readers by the hundreds, one could also observe the rising social prominence of hundreds of thousands of bad readers conscripted by the nation as disciplined international communicators, whether in the social spaces of Nicolas Nabokov's VOA, diplomatic and ambassadorial missions, private and public cultural exchange programs, multinational corporations, international magazines, or global activist groups. The institutions of literacy cultivation, which I bring together across the chapters of this book, are intriguing not only for the sheer novelty of their political and international conscription of American reading publics. (Although I will confess my delight at excavating histories from unexplored archives that are surprising, counterintuitive, and often bizarre.) Instead, these institutions strike me as exemplary for how people trained to read under their auspices began to imagine that reading literature might, quite literally, change the world: how it would emotionally move and ethically instruct the nation's political adversaries, how it would educate and improve its allies, and how it would transform readers into living, breathing representatives of the culture that produced them. By my account, "bad readers" were not born; they were made. And their creation helped devise enduring strategies for how people could use literature to learn to speak, feel, perceive, and interact with others throughout the postwar period.

While I seek to fill the conceptual gap left by bad readers in the history of postwar literature, the central purpose of this study is not simply to anatomize the various techniques and aesthetic forms of bad reading. Nor is it to match distinct varieties of reading to their specific institutional origins.

Rather, this book ultimately aims to analyze the kinds of citizens—the internationalized subjects—that practices of bad reading aspired to produce; and to show how these literate subjects used reading to navigate a political climate that championed liberal individualism, on the one hand, while establishing unprecedented forms of institutional oversight, on the other. It argues that these subjects' diverse and often overlapping genres of reading—properly "literary" novels but also "how to" manuals, advertisements, magazines, newspapers, simple novels, and bureaucratic documents—formed a rich textual ecology whose national and geographic limits literary scholars and cultural historians are only just beginning to map.

Another way of marking the difference between good and bad readers is to turn to the critical idiom of the literary and its codification in the literary institutions of midcentury America. One common recasting of Nabokov's good reader was as the properly "literary reader": the exemplary subject of the school whose lectoral techniques and choice of textual objects mirrored literature's cultural construction as an autonomous discipline. Yet just as good readers required bad readers to prop up their sense of social distinction, so too did the category of literature require something outside itself to stabilize its cultural construction. If, as one critic insists, "the core of a thing called literature" is simply "what people in literature departments do," then it would seem impossible to grasp the pressurized formation or the structural integrity of this core without understanding what people outside of literature departments did (and continue to do) with literary texts.[13] And as the example of Nabokov's desired if unrealized VOA gig suggests, neither literature departments nor universities are closed systems; the people who flit into and out of these institutional spaces often do double—and sometimes triple and quadruple—duty as readers, writers, and human actors in many different social contexts. There is no reason, then, to assume that people's methods of reading can or should remain constant throughout the situational twists and turns of their day-to-day lives. If the good reader is framed as the properly literary reader and his privileged spaces are literature departments, this book proposes we think of Nabokov's bad readers not as "unliterary," "subliterary," or "nonliterary readers," but as paraliterary ones, forged in the political, economic, and civic institutions that orbited literature departments throughout the postwar period.

My title, *Paraliterary: The Making of Bad Readers in Postwar America*, will take on both historical and literary significance as this book progresses. For now, should the term *paraliterary* conjure up such unpleasant etymological bedfellows as *paramilitary* or *parasite*, these associations are nonetheless instructive. Like a paramilitary group, which borrows its training techniques from the military but adapts them to different ends, or a parasite, which lives beside and feeds off of its host, paraliterary readers exist alongside and in dialogue with the institutions of literature. More specifically, they count in their ranks many of the same actors—readers as well as writers—who, when airlifted out of American literature departments after World War II and placed in internationally minded contexts of reading American fiction, started to embrace apparently inscrutable ethical and practical dispositions toward literature. Each chapter of this book thus concerns readers—some famous but many not—who were trained by their new institutional contexts to treat literary texts as repositories of "typical situations, roles, possible trains of events, [and] schemes of action," to recall Bernard Lahire's extensive catalog of how people read once reading and producing literature is no longer treated as an autonomous enterprise.[14] *Paraliterary* is about how these strange, but no less systematic or meticulously considered, methods of reading came to shape the constellation of aesthetic and communicative practices within which postwar American literature flourished. At the same time, it is an account of how American literature made its mark on the world in strange and unappreciated ways: not through the triumphal denationalization or subnationalization of literary production, as so many transnational or comparative critics would have it, but through distinctly international institutions of literary socialization, at home and in the world at large.[15]

PARALITERARY: GENRES, INSTITUTIONS, READERS

How does one become a paraliterary reader? We are overwhelmingly familiar with the equipment that goes into the making of good readers: close reading, critical reading, depth reading; the canon, the curriculum, the literature seminar. But what texts and institutional spaces account for the creation of bad readers? To understand how people read in institutions adjacent to literature departments, *Paraliterary* articulates a theory of literary socialization that accounts for the distinctive types of genres that people read in tandem with literary works. From elocution primers to conduct books, advertisements, consumer guides, scientific treatises, intelligence reports, and bureaucratic archives, the written artifacts of modern institutions offer surprisingly perceptive commentaries on how one can and should read literature as a properly internationalized subject. If these various nonliterary subgenres once helped to frame literature's pragmatic uses for their readers, they now constitute the archival materials that lend to my study of reading its local and historical specificity. In this sense, *Paraliterary* offers a pointed rejoinder to recent positivist polemics about the uses of literature and more impressionistic appeals to reading as ethically nurturing, evolutionarily encoded, or "vividly human."[16]

Yet this is not to dismiss the questions that such studies about reading raise, only to ask that we develop a more precise method for answering questions that, at first glance, may seem deceptively simple. What if, under certain circumstances, literature could teach us how to imitate fictional characters? What would such imitation look or sound like? Which authors and texts would lend themselves to imitation? Where would it take place? How would imitation be taught? Similarly, what if reading could, in a non-naïve and nontrivial sense, teach us how to feel or amplify certain feelings? Which feelings would we learn to feel? How long would they last? What if reading could motivate actions among its readers that transcended the realm of the imaginary? In more self-reflexive terms, in this book I pinpoint how we—in the most capacious sense of that word—learn to do things with literature and literary historicism that exceed the habits and dispositions of successful literary scholars.

Let me begin, however, somewhat conservatively, as Nabokov suggests his good reader ought, with a dictionary. Tracking the various and evolving meanings of the term *paraliterary*—as a genre, a reading practice, and an institutional domain—offers a general framework for the argument that will unfold at length in the pages to follow: from the early twentieth century through the 1970s, delegitimated attitudes toward reading literature thrived in institutions oriented to international communication. Take, for instance, an imposing 1974 research report published by the Prague-based Radio Free Europe (RFE), a government-run American broadcasting institution. The report, which assessed a series of techniques for teaching citizens of both the United States and the Soviet bloc how to read American novels, curiously prefaced its instruction with a meditation on what the authors deemed "paraliterary works."[17] "In a serious culture great events are followed by an abundance of paraliterary works," the report's authors claimed. "These take the form of memoirs or personal diaries of outstanding personalities, biographies of leaders, studies of diplomats, collections of documents, and—last but not least—feature reports." As the authors imagined it, a reader could sift through the "abundance of paraliterary works" generated by a "serious culture" to better equip herself to read that culture's "literary works." While this suggestion would have prompted Nabokov, Tindall, Burke, Kaufmann, and like-minded readers to rise up and protest, others would have simply accepted the RFE's recommendation as an inevitability of modern textual culture. "Novels today have neither the wish nor the ability to make a contribution to 'literature': the nature of modern society demands a slough of paraliterature to wallow in," observed the British poet Sebastian Barker in a spirit of anti-American book-ish malaise.[18] Note Barker's use of scare quotes around "literature," as if to indicate that the term was nothing more than a figment of the cultural imag-ination, an imminently unstable construct. From the point of view of liter-ary history, it seems significant that the term *paraliterary* did not arise until the "literary" appeared to have coalesced as a cultural category, only to fall immediately into crisis due to the "nature of modern society": the rational-ization of everyday life, the failure of liberal pluralism, and the intensifying stakes of geopolitical struggle. At least, these were the conditions under which the RFE urged the reading of memoirs, diaries, biographies, diplomatic stud-ies, bureaucratic archives, and feature reports as primers for engaging with literary texts.

The RFE was by no means unique in its invitation to readerly prepara-tion through paraliterary works. Consider a similar exhortation found in a slim 1975 dispatch titled "Reading Research in the Socialist Countries," published by the American Center for Library Science and Methodology as a manual for colleges, libraries, and federal communications bureaucracies. More explicitly than RFE's guide, "Reading Research" analyzed the social and cultural stakes of preparing oneself to read "belles lettres" by initially un-dertaking a careful evaluation of the "paraliterary genres." While the "com-mon feature" of "all documents, diaries, memoirs, reminiscences, and also epistolography" was a "lack of the 'literary aspect,'" the authors contended that these texts' lack of literariness was only "important from the point of view of the theory of literature." Indeed, once the learned habits of literary theory were checked at the door, readers not only could read paraliterary texts without feeling the pinpricks of low cultural shame but also could also use paraliterary texts to train themselves to transcend the "literariness" of literature, paradoxical though the notion may seem to us today. By bracket-ing a "theory of literature" that privileged the disinterested appreciation of aesthetic forms or the production of interpretive discourse, the reader who had first cut her teeth on bureaucratic documents, diaries, reports, reminis-cences, and studies could transform belles lettres into a model for how to lead what the authors touted as an "authentically real human life." Or to echo the description of a popular class on literature and communication offered by the University of Michigan in 1975, reading "across a range of literary and paraliterary forms" would show students how the "accomplishments of the 'great' novel" could be "adapted to the more specialized cultural needs" of the time.[19]

The descriptions of paraliterary works provided in these reports prefigure what cultural critics have often said about the "banal" textual objects produced and archived by political, economic, and civic institutions since the 1930s: that as the typical "written material of self-documenting social settings," they were "unobtrusive" and "naturally occurring."[20] For New Historicists, paraliterary texts were "traces" that verified an inaccessible historical or cultural context, but they always played second fiddle to the properly literary object itself.[21] Yet while these genres were proffered to their readers as portals to a more "authentically real human life," their apparently unmediated presentation belied a highly particularized project of literacy education underwritten by a multitude of invisible factors: the institutions that produced and distributed paraliterary and literary texts in tandem; the archives that registered an expanding geography of literacy; the Cold War entanglements that positioned VOA, RFE, and other similar institutions at the heart of international literary socialization. Indeed, once we begin to account for the far-flung material and historical contingencies of reading in this expanding field of texts, we can see how the various paraliterary "works," "genres," and "forms" produced by "a serious culture" (American culture) after "great events" (World War II) were, in fact, framed to suggest a more useful and timely way of reading literature than what a theory of properly literary reading had to offer.

But how was this scene of reading organized and what did it hope to accomplish? By attending to these reports more closely, we see that descriptions of paraliterary works all shared an explicit commitment to nonfictional representation and reference. Paraliterary works were meant to be read as factual, historically accurate narratives. Or to borrow the terminology deployed by John Frow, Catherine Gallagher, and other theorists of fictionality, these narratives unsettled fiction's stylized "discontinuities" between "discourse about a character"—what the narrator stated about a politician, bureaucrat, or memoirist—and the politician, bureaucrat, or memoirist's own role as a "producer of language" or "enunciator."[22] Here the narrator and the enunciator were often one and the same. Intimately bound up with the nonfictional status of these paraliterary texts, then, was their emphasis on chronicling the speech, behavior, and comportment of individuals whose social roles were defined by visible and self-reflexive acts of public communication: political icons, national leaders, diplomats, and other such "outstanding personalities." To prime one's reading of literary fiction with paraliterary works was to direct one's attention to the embodied and socially mediated schemes of action narrated therein; actions like speech, gesture, perception, and interaction that could be—and, in fact, had been—performed by real people in historically consequential circumstances. Rather than an insistence on genre differentiation, which Mary Poovey has shown was key to the separation of literary from "nonliterary" culture in the nineteenth century, here the invitation was to genre confusion.[23] The promise that belles lettres could thus be read as encoding publicly communicative schemes of action instantiated one of the more visible and aggressive resurrections of what Deidre Lynch has characterized as a "bygone rhetorical culture in which words served pragmatic, social ends."[24] To tweak an earlier observation about properly literary reading as what people in literary institutions do, we could conclude that paraliterary reading—defined here by the cultivation of publicly oriented schemes of action, a weakened commitment to fictionality, a newfound attentiveness to the political temporalities of texts, and the juggling of distinct documentary genres—became what people in paraliterary institutions did with texts.

Equally important, however, was that paraliterary reading coalesced as a form of reading capable of producing a self-governing and communicatively adept international subject. The gradual convergence of international relations, reading methods, and subject formation can be seen in a 1979 United Nations Economic, Social, and Cultural Organization (UNESCO) "Cultural" report, which insisted that training readers to attend to literature's "paraliterary features" was the key to "introducing self-management to the cultural sphere."[25] As we will see, the alignment of reading literature with disciplined practices of internationalized "self-management" emerged as a clarion call that was answered by bureaucrats and literary scholars alike. In one of the earliest studies of postwar American fiction to treat it as a distinct disciplinary field, literary scholar Warner Berthoff classed the literature of the period as transmitting "a whole paraliterary class of messages to the age."[26] Going against the grain of professional literary criticism, Leslie Fiedler, at a controversial 1981 meeting of the English Institute on world literature and communication, encouraged "paraliterary reading" as an entry point to regulating and promoting "irresponsible fantasy, shameful concupiscence, and shameful tears and laughter" to unite readers around the globe.[27] And today, while the richly polyvalent origins of "paraliterary" have yielded to narrower uses of the word—as a modifier for unappreciated literary genres (as in Samuel Delaney's discussion of science fiction) or unsung literary professional roles (like Rosalind Krauss's description of the work performed by editors)—the very flexibility of its reclamation points back in time to how an unusual range of genres, social settings, and reading subjects were first brought together at a distance from the institutions of professional literary study.[28] By attending to the past, we can begin to see not only that contemporary concerns with paraliterary reading were also postwar ones, but that they came into being through the era in response to a specific set of sociohistorical pressures. Chief among them was the pressure on ordinary citizens to communicate with one another in the constitution of an internationally minded public sphere.

CONSCRIPTED READERS AND INTERNATIONAL RELATIONS

While the fascinating etymological evolution of the paraliterary offers one frame for this book, my primary interest is in how distinct, but historically interconnected, institutions of international relations imagined the relationship between paraliterary reading and the production of international subjects. I have argued that the shift from reading paraliterary works produced by institutions to reading literature more broadly was propelled by a confusion of genres. As variously nonfictional subgenres—lecture transcripts, elocution primers, conduct books, publicity stills, advertisements, consumer guides, financial instruments, magazines, journals, intelligence reports, bureaucratic files—collided with the expressive forms of literature, complicated modes of reading emerged as simply untutored scenes of literacy: reading imitatively (chapter 1), reading emotionally (chapter 2), reading faddishly (chapter 3), reading for information (chapter 4), reading like a bureaucrat (chapter 5), and reading like a revolutionary (chapter 6). While the relatively autonomous forms of reading that cohered throughout the period—close reading, critical reading, depth reading—have been treated by scholars as historically contingent practices, paraliterary reading emerged as a grubby and residual mess of activity perpetuated by a mass of "heretical readers," as Pierre Bourdieu once dubbed the reading subjects who "take liberties with the norms and forms imposed by the guardians of the text."[29] Yet from the 1930s to the 1970s, as Armando Petrucci has shown, the dizzying rise of institutions of international mass communications and the sheer volume of texts they produced and circulated made it impossible to ignore the heteronomous attitudes toward literature embraced by readers conscripted by the state and acting in the service of the nation.[30]

So why have these institutions and the readers they tapped for projects of international communication not received their due? It is not for their lack of historical importance. Paraliterary reading existed long before the mid-1970s work of RFE and UNESCO. My examples here reflect one codification of the idea, not its origins, which this book first locates in interwar discourses of US international relations and traces through its efflorescence in the decades following World War II. The history of American internationalism during this period is well charted. For many, it begins on a rather definitive note with Henry Luce's 1941 *Life* magazine editorial "the American Century"—the most widely cited rallying call for American empire—and seesaws for the next thirty years between the liberal establishment politics of the (early) Truman administration, Kennedy, and Johnson and the realpolitik containment strategies of the (later) Truman administration, Eisenhower, and Nixon.[31] Overwhelmingly, however, these decades witnessed a shift away from enmity and conflict toward what Christina Klein has called a "global imaginary of integration," propped up by concerns about "cooperation," "mutuality," and "community."[32] Whether in the form of written documents or physical acts, it was "ordinary trade, travel, communication, and intercourse between people" that the State Department identified in a 1953 Office of Public Communications bulletin as the key to creating a reading public that extended across the Atlantic and Pacific Oceans.[33]

By and large, however, the literary historical interest in international relations remains narrowly focused, whatever decade, administration, institution, or policy one chooses to investigate, and strikingly removed from the realm of "ordinary" "intercourse" (or discourse) that was central to the period.[34] For scholars, the main interpretative predicament is one of exposing covert artistic influences: how did the state, acting through the State Department, the Central Intelligence Agency (CIA), the Rockefeller and the Ford Foundations, exercise power in the world and how did its exercise of power leave an enduring mark on the aesthetic qualities of literature? The standard critical narrative is one of surreptitious coercion and writerly resistance through the production of sophisticated formal allegories for state control. This is an idea aptly expressed by Michael Walzer, who argues that the state must first be "personified," "symbolized," and "imagined" in order to be critiqued—a critique that must likewise take place on the level of narrative character, symbol, and other imaginary features of the text.[35] But critiqued by whom and for what audiences? Who, precisely, was reading and decoding these representations of state power? And what did the knowledge produced by critique set out to accomplish?

To ask these questions is not to find concrete answers. Rather, it is to realize how a narrowly politicized version of reading and writing critique dominates interpretive practices today. It is also to realize how profoundly the retrospective projection of these reading practices into the past has limited narratives of the relationship between institutional power and international literary culture. What has been left out of most thinking about the internationalization of American literature is that neither its production nor its reception cleaved to the practices of reading literary form as symptomatic of broader political conditions, at least not in any generalizable or uniform way. While several accounts of American internationalism and its expansion of midcentury reading publics have been written as of late, most revisit or expand the argument staked out by Frances Stonor Saunders, in *The Cultural Cold War: The CIA of Arts and Letters* (1999), that American arts and letters brandished a "High Cultural" ethos that valorized abstraction, allegory, autopoesis, experimentalism, and modernist difficulty over and above other modes of communication: entertainment, emotional stimulation, information gathering, publicity seeking, and more.[36] While the latter modes of reading have received better treatment in accounts of the Arts Projects of the New Deal and the middlebrow cultural institutions of the 1920s (libraries, museums, theaters), their influence is limited to the earlier, more nationally insulated decades of literary history.[37] One would imagine, then, that the burgeoning reading publics for American arts and letters had to be socialized into the same close, critical, and artistically sensitive practices of hermeneutic engagement that critics today use to read those histories, although there is little evidence to support this kind of widespread continuity between writers and international readers.

The alliance between high cultural autonomy and international reading practices, derived from a narrow sample of artists and writers, tends to take for granted the marginality of ordinary discourse: the expressive language produced by students, career diplomats, tourists, spies, ambassadors, businessmen, soldiers, and revolutionaries. Yet these were the majority of the figures tasked with trade, travel, communication, and intercourse—of all kinds—as well as building cooperation, mutuality, and community. This book makes these figures and their social production visible. Or rather, it restores these figures in aggregate to the visibility they once enjoyed alongside the individual geniuses of literary fame and fortune. At the same time, this book shows how even those individual geniuses and the abstract, allegorical, experimental, or difficult literary fiction they produced had to engage in alternative modes of reading—Mary McCarthy's propagandistic reading, F. O. Matthiessen and Sylvia Plath's passionate reading, the Beats and Erica Jong's faddish reading, William Faulkner and Richard Wright's bureaucratic reading, John A. Williams's revolutionary reading—that they could not readily square with their professional identities as writers or critics of fiction. Even good readers, and writers, had to be bad sometimes.

One of the larger aims of this book, then, is to unpack a related strand of literary internationalism that remains undertheorized: an older, more persistent connection that both historical figures and contemporary critics have posited between literary aesthetics (and communicative acts) and the representational work performed by literary work (and communicative acts). In the case of readers conscripted into projects of international communication, more powerful and power seeking than any one institution or program was the idea that the expressive actions of any particular individual, addressed to any particular audience at any particular time, could come to stand in for the cultural or political qualities of an entire nation. Thus by the twenty-first century, it was possible for Brian Edwards and Dilip Gaonkar to identify as the defining object of global American studies the equivalence between "the figure of the American abroad" and the "figure of America or American forms abroad."[38] The assumption that the histories of these two "figures" were one and the same—let alone the idea that they should be connected at all—is itself a central conceptual problem that this book addresses. The paraliterary practices of conscripted readers, I argue, helped to stabilize the textual logics by which the widely accepted, if sometimes overhasty, embrace of metonymy— the imaginative scaling up from the symbolic expressions of individual texts or subjects to the representational politics of the nation—became the most important discursive strategy for claiming American literature's international public value. At a moment when literary studies have, for the most part, moved away from literary internationalism into either transnational spaces or subnational social institutions, this book revives the idea of literary culture as a series of ongoing, uneven negotiations about what "class of messages" (to echo Warner Berthoff) internationally circulated readers and texts could transmit to reading publics around the world.

WELL-SOCIALIZED READERS

Despite the recent barrage of scholarship that claims to have devised new methodologies of reading today, in the grand scheme of things neither our scholarly reading practices nor the objects we choose to read have changed very much. This is a fact I will reflect on in the conclusion of the book. For now, however, it is enough to point out that the aesthetic forms of literary texts and the individual authors who produce them remain, with some notable exceptions, our critical bread and butter, as does our impulse to produce interpretive readings of these texts for a professionalized academic readership. Even the boldest and most inspiring interventions made by recent critics of reading—that we are "postcritical," that we can read "at the surface" of

texts, that aesthetic forms can organize "political forms," that reading can promote an ethics of "self-binding"—sometimes seem more eager to legitimize a
particular ethical subject position than to parse specific practices of reading.[39]
That is, they aspire to present the reader as a particular kind of human being
in the world, but without first elaborating how a historically and institutionally contingent, explicitly mediated, and public technique of reading results in
the creation of that particular kind of human being. As such, scholarly investi-
gations of readers' social practices and ethical dispositions remain hemmed in
by critics' own unwillingness to abandon more radically their proclivities for
reading as literary critics do.

Paraliterary examines how other people learn to do things with literary
texts. In my first chapter, "Reading as Imitation," I will consider how learning to talk about a book converges with the idea of learning to speak like a
book, an argument that pairs novels with the paraliterary genre of the public
lecture, both performed and printed. The institutional mediation of reading as
imitation leans on an imaginary logic that equates reading with speaking—a
model of literary reception whose intimate, if conflicted, relationship to high
modernist aesthetics sharpens after World War II. In my second chapter, I
measure the overlap between reading and feeling, or learning to read in order to learn how to feel. The more we know about techniques of sentimental
reading, the less susceptible they seem to critiques of feeling's irrationality,
embodiment, or purely affective nature. From the somatic reading exercises
enacted in international American literature courses to the publicity stills of
American authors printed by cultural diplomacy programs, the idea that feeling could be produced by and communicated through the bodies and bodily
activities of people reading literature spread like wildfire. My third chapter
analyzes touristic consumption as a nationalized form of communication
through its central figure of readerly address—the brand name—which links
literary texts to corporate-institutional ones, only to encourage the conflation
of reading brands within literature and reading literary texts as American
branded commodities. In my fourth chapter, I probe the military, geographic,
and scientific community's insistence on reading the photographs printed and
distributed in international magazines as speaking ethnographic facts—an
imaginary performance of oral communication that spurred the idea that
people's exteriors could be read for national information in the same fashion
that characters' exteriors could be written into fiction. In my final chapters, I
show how claims about fictional representation, reading, and the truth-value
of communication—as encapsulated by the imperative to "speak the truth"
about the nation—played out in the cases of failed institutions in which actors'

fantasies about what reading literature could accomplish in the world outpaced their social realities. In all my chapters, I trace the literary-historical arc of what looks like bad reading through a theory of paraliterary texts and institutions, one that seeks not only to revise our understanding of postwar American fiction's forms but also our contemporary habits of studying reading.

Paraliterary does many things, but one thing it does not do is rehearse an explicit critique of American political power in the world, either in its militaristic (i.e., "hard") or ideological (i.e., "soft") manifestations. Many scholars have already generated excellent critical histories of American geopolitical literature, yet that is not my primary goal in analyzing models of reading.[40] This book instead merges reception history, literary sociology, discourse theory, and literary criticism to reconstruct an idea about the role that literature has played—and continues to play—in the international public sphere. Good readers and writers, critics, agents, and publishers, as well as leaders, politicians, and other outstanding public personalities, may all insist on the importance of literature, but they do so in ways that are not easily separable from one another. What my analysis of paraliterary readers shows is that we, as critics, must proudly claim the bad readers as our own if we wish to make claims about reading at all.

CHAPTER ONE

Reading as Imitation

No man, excepting in burlesque, should impersonate a woman's part. Impersonation is not reading. And no woman should attempt to impersonate a man, if by impersonation, you mean actually striving to get at the real tone and manner of a male, because she only makes coarseness of it.

NATIONAL ASSOCIATION OF ELOCUTIONISTS (1905)[1]

I'm incapable of writing at length about anyone except an American, so it's not only a question of being out of touch with the native speech but of being out of touch with the native subject matter.

MARY MCCARTHY (1971)[2]

LITERARY IMPERSONATION

"Expatriate writing, a potpourri of the avant-garde and the decadent, has almost faded away."[3] So proclaimed critic and novelist Mary McCarthy in a 1972 essay titled "A Guide to Exiles, Expatriates, and Internal Émigrés," tolling the bell for an international literary tradition that had long captivated late nineteenth- and early twentieth-century American reading publics. Considered alongside the imminent terror of the Soviet Union's ascendancy, the rising body count in Vietnam, and her recent stint as a United States Information Agency (USIA) lecturer in Eastern Europe, McCarthy believed that reading the expatriate novels of the past was akin to smelling a bowl of old "potpourri"—sweet but useless. Readers had developed a distaste for the tradition's once attractive and now decaying features: its carefully cultivated cosmopolitanism, its elite discourses of aesthetic autonomy, and worst of all, the self-indulgent figure of the expatriate, whom McCarthy described sarcastically as "an artist or person who thinks he is artistic." The ultimate offense of writing and reading expatriate novels, she posited, was to valorize literary production as the creation of "a work of art" detached from the historical realities of modernity; a work of art preoccupied with the construction of a deeply solipsistic and apolitical interiority at the very moment when literature and its readers needed to look outward, to strengthen their "atrophying power to communicate" with others.[4]

Given her indictment of expatriate writing, it makes sense that McCarthy would name Henry James as the long-dead father of all expatriate fiction. A committed expatriate for more than twenty-five years and a pivotal figure in the shift from nineteenth-century realism to twentieth-century experiments in novelistic interiority, James had "set the themes once and for all." "Everything that followed," McCarthy observed, "was a mere variation, however grotesque," from the poetry of Gertrude Stein and T. S. Eliot to the novels of H.D., F. Scott Fitzgerald, Ernest Hemingway, Djuna Barnes, and Henry Miller. Presumably, McCarthy counted herself as part of this genealogy. In 1961, she had relocated to Paris with her fourth husband, James R. West, a cultural attaché with the United States Foreign Service, and had published her first and only expatriate novel *Birds of America* (1971) exactly a decade later. "A Guide to Exiles, Expatriates, and Internal Émigrés," written just one year after *Birds of America* failed to find an enthusiastic audience among American readers, betrayed her fierce and perplexing irritation with the literary tradition whose life-span she had tried to prolong. Expatriate fiction, McCarthy concluded with her signature snark, evinced "a certain Jackie-and-Ari color-supplement flavor." Characters went abroad "to lead the beautiful life in one form or another" by "impersonating figures in a work of art—something few people dare to do at home."

But how precisely do works of art give rise to studied practices of impersonation? And why is "impersonating figures in a work of art" something "few people"—not characters—would only "dare" to do away from home? McCarthy's oddly contemporaneous invocation of the "Jackie-and-Ari color-supplement flavor" of expatriate fiction suggests that James's influence wasn't limited to the literary characters of the twentieth century but a curiously embodied fact of American public and political life: that his works of art had somehow come to shape the practices, rituals, and lifestyles of the rich and famous over half a century after his death in 1916. Contrary to McCarthy's proclamation of the fading out of expatriate fiction, James's legacy was not dressed down in avant-garde or decadent literature's fading tropes but dolled up in Jackie O's powder-pink Chanel traveling suit and pillbox hat for all the world to see. And although the acerbic quality of McCarthy's tone may suggest Jackie O's ditzy obliviousness to James as her stylistic predecessor, this, too, is misleading. During her time in Washington, DC, Kennedy had pointedly stacked James's novels in the White House library as part of her attempt to bring high culture to Cold War America—one model for how to live the beautiful life amid the ugly glare of Soviet-era geopolitics.[5] Yet even before she was rearranging the first family's textual furniture, Kennedy was

McCarthy's near contemporary at Vassar College in Poughkeepsie, New York, where both women had read James's novels in the classroom and dorm room and concluded that he was their favorite American writer.[6] While these two public figures had pursued wildly incomparable paths after graduation—Jackie to Paris, where she wrote her European travelogue *One Special Summer* (1974), and Mary to the *New Republic* in New York—as readers and imitators of James's expatriate fictions, their literary education had shared a common point of departure: the institution of the women's college.

Indeed, it was at institutions like Vassar, as well as Vassar's sister colleges Smith, Bryn Mawr, Radcliffe, and Mount Holyoke, that reading Henry James gave rise to enduring practices of what I call literary impersonation: a strategy of fictional mimesis that turned on a series of unconventional assumptions about the relationship between reading subjects and their textual objects. By "literary impersonation," I do not mean the "performance of impersonation" within literature: a formulation that many critics have invoked quite loosely to describe a wide range of fictional tropes, from narrative vocalization to mimicry, imposture, personification, forgery, and fraud.[7] I mean, rather, the uncanny convergence of literary discourse with real speech acts: utterances that have taken place in richly specified and, to a certain extent, historically recoverable contexts. Literary impersonation asserts the portability between textual properties of the novel and formal properties of speech, gesture, and face-to-face interaction—what McCarthy called the "power of communication" in her dismissal of James's novels. As Benjamin Lee and other sociolinguistics have argued, the interplay between literary discourse (i.e., how people talk about literary representations) and the performativity of speech (i.e., how speech instantiates an action or constructs a subject position) offers a unique nexus from which to examine how literature can shape the formation of social relationships and the individuals who participate in them. Both linguistic performativity and literary discourse, Lee writes, "utilize a shared 'fashion of speaking' about subjectivity that is created by the structural relations among . . . speaking, thinking, and feeling."[8] Literary impersonation reveals a set of readerly logics by which a literary device (like dialogue or narrative interiority) can come to shape lived practices of communication (like speech) across vast expanses of space and time. If reading literature can mediate between literary production and the production of speaking subjects, it does so through a set of unorthodox reading practices that flourished within the institutions of the women's college.

Allow me to orient this claim in more historically specific terms, as it offers this book's first inroads into a prehistory of international communication from the beginning of the twentieth century to its midcentury efflorescence. This chapter suggests that a certain "fashion of speaking" about James's novels and a certain fashion of speaking emerged as twinned components of what women's colleges touted as the first systematic "experiments in international living": the earliest attempts to institute highly regimented and repetitive practices of international communication during the interwar period.[9] There's no good reason why any of the tens of millions of students who have participated in these experiments in international living over the last half century, or even the university administrators and educators who have organized them, should know about the literary historical origins of these massively popular sociolinguistic training programs. By the time McCarthy was writing in the 1970s, study abroad programs, as they are commonly referred to today, were already ensnared in a vast and sprawling network of government-issued texts that discussed "the benefits of study abroad" for college students. In these pamphlets, brochures, conference proceedings, and conduct guides, the benefits enumerated were seldom literary and overwhelmingly social and political: the spread of "friendship," "goodwill," "understanding," and underpinning it all, "communication."[10] These benefits, however, cut both ways. For administrators at the State Department and USIA, students served as ideal national-institutional subjects for international communication projects, no matter what the project's specific purpose was. After all, who more amenable to the imposition of carefully crafted speech and behavioral protocols than full-time learners? Who more willing to embrace with cheerful studiousness their teachers' instructions to say and do certain things and not others?

This point was made early on by educators John A. Garraty and Walter Adams in *A Guide to Study Abroad* (1962), a conduct manual that featured a brusque and bellicose introduction by then-vice-president Lyndon B. Johnson. Reprinted every year until 1977 and widely championed by Dr. Paul R. Conroy, USIA chief of professional training, as essential reading for all college students, *A Guide to Study Abroad* emphasized that "students make excellent 'ambassadors,'" for they are "intelligent, eager, curious, purposeful, energetic, and (being young) attractive."[11] While it was "human for the natives of any country to resent the mere tourist who is idling away his time, often frivolously," the strictly regimented and demanding activities of students tended "to attract sympathy and respect" (12). According to the authors, who aspired to "make the world our campus," there was no better way for students to attract the natives' sympathy and respect than by staging scenes of reading.[12] The *Guide* thus instructed all students to pack a "Six Inch Library" that would include a map of the United States, a "college American history textbook," Richard B. Morris's *Basic Documents of American History*, and D. C. Doyle's *The United States Political System and How It Works*. Students who wanted to be "really well-armed ambassadors" were encouraged to pair the hard facts and figures contained in maps, textbooks, and documents with "a collection of your own favorite paperbacks to lend or give to people you meet" (61). Yet even the construction of one's personal literary arsenal had to follow certain guidelines. "Take books that have some literary stature, of course, but not simply those that you know are highly regarded," the *Guide* cautioned. "Literary stature," a function of cultural prestige, always came second to the student's performance of literary discourse: her ability to communicate, through her impassioned advocacy, a deep knowledge of and personal affection for her books of choice. "There is no better way to gain the respect of foreigners both for yourself and for your country," the authors crowed, "than to talk about a good book that you know well and about which you are enthusiastic" (62).

In the *Guide*'s mingling of textual objects and genres, we can identify the same processes of readerly preparation that my introduction teased out of international communications initiatives like Radio Free Europe. But a very different view of the relationship between reading literature and the power of communication emerges if we look back at the longer history of these experiments in international living. Although various branches of the federal government worked hard to co-opt students as young and attractive communicative subjects—the most titillating chapter in the guide is titled "Sexual Communication"—the history of international literary socialization dates back to the early twentieth-century women's college, a far cry from the board rooms and back offices of Washington, DC. In the bucolic college towns of Bryn Mawr, Pennsylvania and Northampton, Massachusetts, administrators, teachers, and students first debated the communicative practices of international living—a debate set off by none other than Henry James, the progenitor of all expatriate fiction. While James was not interested in students as political actors, at least not as explicitly as the State Department or USIA in the 1950s, he was similarly preoccupied with the problems and possibilities of international communication and its relationship to a national literary culture. Indeed, it was during his 1905 American lecture tour that he debuted "The Question of Our Speech," a prickly critique of the communicative habits of American women, which he first delivered as a commencement address at Bryn Mawr and which was subsequently reprinted in every major magazine and newspaper in the United States.[13] The lecture provoked widespread public outcry across the nation for its unflattering comparison of America's "young ladies'" speech—indistinct from "the grunting, the squealing, the barking or the roaring of animals"—to their European counterparts (46). The failure of women to exercise proper aesthetic discrimination in their practices of communication, James postulated, would lead to the careening cultural decline of the United States in the twentieth century. The scandal that resulted from his lecture tour was unprecedented but not unproductive. By the early 1920s, the lecture's reception had given rise to various programs of speech pedagogy for young women, most notably, the first experiments in international living, which originated at Smith College and spread rapidly to other women's institutions before attracting the attention of the US government and its communications bureaucracies after World War II.

More rigorously than midcentury government bureaucrats, James's lecture elucidated an ambitious theory of literature's social and pragmatic uses, one opposed to both McCarthy's pooh-poohing of expatriate fiction and modernist literary studies' continued association of James with aesthetic autonomy.[14] The lecture, both by virtue of its style and its genre, insists that literary writers and the novels they produced were uniquely positioned to help transform international communication itself into an aesthetic form that could bestow "literary stature" onto the speakers themselves. In a memorable scene in "The Question of Our Speech," James portrayed the speech of American women as "our transported maiden, our unrescued Andromeda," abandoned to her own devices in "the international concert of culture"—a "poor dear distracted organ" waiting to be saved from aesthetic ruin and cultural condemnation by one who had mastered the distinctions between "form and the absence of form" (52). While it would be improper to read James's melodrama without a sense of humor, his audiences were ready to take him at his word as the aesthetic savior of American speech and communication, or the "cosmopolitan patriot," in the words of one critic, whose finely honed mastery of literary form could discipline the speech of his female readers.[15] Like the attractive and industrious students addressed in the *Guide*, the young ladies housed within the women's college were to emerge in the national public sphere as "excellent 'ambassadors'" for James's literary aesthetics and, thus, excellent representatives to communicate the nation's linguistic and cultural singularity in the international public sphere. Decades before government-sponsored *Kulturkampf* would propel thousands of students across the Atlantic and Pacific oceans, equipped with guides to help them "communicate fluently" with international audiences, James's fictions had already laid the blueprint for how international communication ought to look—and sound—in the earliest phase of its national development (71).

That the first tentative and testy steps toward overlaying reading practices and international communication should take place in the women's college is no coincidence. The historical claim that anchors this chapter to my broader argument about the paraliterary is that the reading practices of the women's college and their relationship to the performativity of speech stood in stark contrast to the practices of proper literary reading that flourished outside of its four walls—particularly in the elite male institutions of higher education, where the "literary" loomed as a social category that excluded readers based on their class and gender identities. I am not claiming, of course, that the practices of literary impersonation that orbited James's novels were exclusive to the women's college. Nor do I mean to suggest that practices of literary impersonation remained completely unchanged from James to the 1970s, as McCarthy does when she links James to Jacqueline Kennedy Onassis in "A Guide to Exiles, Expatriates, and Internal Émigrés." Rather, the women's college materialized as the physical space where unacknowledged and even disparaged approaches to reading, communication, and nationalized concepts of gender produced a remarkably consistent set of norms that shaped face-to-face interactions between American subjects and their interlocutors. The persistence of these norms over time served as both a source of inspiration and a point of departure for the readers and writers who fell under the auspices of the women's college: not only writers like McCarthy, Kennedy, H.D., and Gertrude Stein, whom I will touch on in the pages to follow, but thousands of lesser known readers, some of whose writings about reading—their letters, diary entries, and class notes—help us more concretely examine the historical convergence of literature and spoken communication.

While I argue that James and his early twentieth-century readers were eager to imagine literary aesthetics as exercising elocutionary authority over young women, a novelist like McCarthy, writing under the aegis of the women's college in the latter half of the twentieth century, sought to unburden herself from the lingering institutional influence of the Master. I begin and conclude this chapter with McCarthy because her uneasy, even defensive, relationship to the institutional practices of her past reveals both their perseverance and their limitations. McCarthy's diatribe against expatriate writing and its uninspired production of both Jamesian novels and Jamesian "people"—two different approaches to literary impersonation that I will juxtapose throughout my argument here—unfolds not only as a problem of speech aesthetics but as a problem of political representation. The argument of her oft-cited essay "Ideas and the Novel: Henry James and Some Others" (1980), in which McCarthy advocates for the socially conscious "novel of ideas" over James's "pure work of art," hinges on these two genres' competing representations of speech's communicative purposes. "James's people," she argued, were prone to "endlessly discuss and analyze" without ever discussing "the subjects that people in society usually do."[16] Rather, his expatriates enjoyed "constantly telling each other how intelligent they [were]" through "allusion" and "murmured, indistinct evocation." Compared to the straightforwardly muscular statements of political ideology compelled by the novel of ideas and federal institutions alike, Jamesian speech seemed desperately, even pathetically, ill-suited to McCarthy's tumultuous times. Its ability to connect high modernist literature to the political ideologies of the nation-state appeared weak at best and dangerously impotent at worst—a sentiment that was shared by McCarthy and a large number of government agents alike. In the final section of this chapter, I examine how the convergence of James's "indistinct" aesthetic of speech with McCarthy's penchant for politically representative straight talk troubles the production of her novel *Birds of America*, the story of a Cold War international education program gone terribly awry. Despite both McCarthy's and the US government's attempt to overwrite James's legacy, his aesthetic of speech—as well as the tradition of the expatriate novel—remained an ineradicable part of the readerly paradigm that would organize international communication in the postwar period, clearing the communicative channels by which fiction would shape embodied practices of expression around the world. The reception of expatriate novels among American readers thus drives the first part of my critical narrative of reading practices, institutions, and communication from the prewar period to the literary production of the midcentury and beyond.

"ESSENTIALLY AMERICAN INSTITUTIONS": LADIES' CLUBS AND COLLEGES

When Henry James stepped foot onto American soil for the first time in nearly half a century, he found himself surrounded by women. The year was 1904 and James, ever the dogged expatriate, had subsidized his return to America through a six-month speaking tour jointly organized by the Pond Lecture Bureau and a loose national consortium of what James called "ladies' culture clubs." By all accounts, the speaking tour constituted one of the most highly publicized literary spectacles in American history, notable for the hundreds, even thousands, of female readers who flocked on a nightly basis to the Master's bully pulpit. For his part, James regarded this fanfare with sardonic detachment and in a letter to Edmund Gosse complained about the dreadful monotony of lecturing to the "essentially American Institutions known as

Ladies' Clubs which swarm all over the country."[17] He griped, "[T]he leap is taken, is being renewed; I repeat the horrid act at Chicago, Indianapolis, St. Louis, San Francisco, and later on in New York—have already done so at Philadelphia....At Bryn Mawr to 700 people (by way of a *little* circle)."[18] But despite James's anxious, even feigned, reluctance to play to his *"little"* crowds, his popularity only grew among readers as the tour progressed. "Women Lionize Henry James!" roared the Chicago Inter-Ocean's report of March 12, 1905 and *Harper's* editor Elizabeth Jordan, upon making an early exit from a lecture in Rye, New York, to beat a well-heeled stampede of fans, noted from a distance "the Conceivable Appetite of the Ladies for Words of Wisdom from H.J."[19]

Reconstructing the "Conceivable Appetite of the Ladies" for H.J. will in turn reveal how the logic of literary impersonation was, first and foremost, a matter of gendered literacy practices that gradually assumed national importance and international dimensions. Despite James's dismissive quotation marks, "ladies' culture clubs" encompassed a well-funded network of organizations that stretched from Cambridge, Massachusetts, to Los Angeles, California: private salons sponsored by James's Gilded Age benefactresses, city-wide book clubs chaired by middle-class female readers, and prestigious women's colleges, like Smith, Bryn Mawr, or the Packer Collegiate Institute of Brooklyn—all stops on James's itinerary. An integral part of the early twentieth-century public sphere, ladies' culture clubs offered middle- and upper-class female readers access to relatively progressive practices of self-acculturation and community formation through shared scenes of literary discourse: table talks, roll calls, book reports, and debates. For women who did not have access to the linguistic and symbolic capital of higher education, as was the case for many members of the Conversation Club of Dubuque, Iowa, ladies' culture clubs enabled the work of "the university [to take place] in our homes," by demanding that "the learned, inspired minds" of literature "come to us."[20] For women who had enjoyed the benefits of a college education, these self-organized groups represented a middle way for social engagement that transcended the privacy of the domestic sphere but stopped short of full-on political mobilization: demanding inheritance rights, for instance, or marching for suffrage. Hosting a speaker like James, a literary celebrity whose serialized novels and short stories were read and revered by club members, helped authenticate the shared practices of literacy that female readers had designed to suit their aspirations for—and their limited access to—cultural mobility. Indeed, few events could make a group of readers more immediately visible as an influential social institution than having one of the writers whose work had motivated the group's existence literally "come to us."

No doubt the "Ladies" were not the readers with whom James was more intimately and respectfully familiar: "'Boston Brahmin' litterateurs" like Charles Eliot Norton and James Russell Lowell, as well as the overwhelmingly male, college-educated readers of the *Atlantic* and the *North American Review* in which James's novels were published.[21] Yet despite his disparaging attitude toward his fans, James was nevertheless drawn to the clubs as a unique opportunity to see "the people (conspicuously!)" and observe their "manners as perhaps one would not have done otherwise," he reported to Gosse.[22] Given the youthful blush of naïveté that characterizes so many of James's female protagonists—Daisy Miller in *Daisy Miller* (1879), Isabel Archer in *The Portrait of a Lady* (1881), Verena Tarrant in *The Bostonians* (1886), Maisie Farange in *What Maisie Knew* (1897), or Maggie Verver in *The Golden Bowl* (1904)—it is not surprising that he expressed a particular interest in the women who populated single-sex institutions of higher education: the college girls and recent graduates whom he would single out in his writings as "young ladies" and the "large and apparently growing class of not specially occupied single women" in the United States.[23] Eschewing both the workforce and the responsibilities of marriage and motherhood, young middle- and upper-class ladies boasted no other occupation but learning: that is, learning how to transform themselves into full-fledged, mature ladies. They thus served as particularly receptive pupils for James's words of wisdom, as well as character types in their own right. "The prototype of Daisy Miller is with us now," announced the president of the Twentieth Century Club of Illinois when introducing James to his audience of "intellectual, charming diplomatic Chicago women."[24] While many of these women had started their lives as "frank, impulsive Chicago girls," the president narrated, they had had the good fortune to read *Daisy Miller* just in time to receive it as a cautionary tale that distinguished advisable from inadvisable female conduct. If a 1905 *Chicago Daily Tribune* interview with James is to be believed, James went so far as to isolate his individual literary creations from the throngs of young ladies that attended his lectures. "He was to recall later," reported the *Daily Tribune*, "that he had noticed a face in the crowd that was remarkably reminiscent of Daisy Miller's, but he was not sure—it was so long since he had seen her. One other face arrested his attention—the countenance of a girl who looked as if she might know all that Maisie knew and volumes more."[25] When asked whether he was inclined to identify his characters with his audience members and readers, James replied munificently, "Perhaps every woman here is a Daisy Miller."

Whether or not James uttered these precise words, the *Tribune* article nevertheless suggests that, for his readers, James's imaginative labors as a novelist encoded a broader literary socialization project: a disciplinary regime that aligned young female readers with the Master's aesthetic creation of "the young lady." By reading James's novels and attending his lectures, a young lady's consciousness could undergo a startling epistemological transformation, clueing her into "all that Maisie knew and volumes more." Here it seems telling that Maisie's quest for knowledge guides her to a similar context of learning as James's readers and equips her with a similar purpose. She, too, "dream[s] of lectures at an institution," an institution whose only specification is that it is "literally strewn with subjects."[26] Like Maisie, these "literal" subjects to scholastic discipline were young women whose chief aim was to learn to conceive of themselves as aesthetic subjects by first becoming institutional subjects of the women's college. And like Maisie, they were all in pursuit of a self-consciousness that would allow them to convert their unformed childhood impressions into a refined aesthetic consciousness. Yet as both the *Tribune* article and *What Maisie Knew* suggest, the precise content of Maisie's interiorized knowledge was not nearly as important as the forms through which her knowingness was communicated to others. Her epistemological transformation was legible not exclusively or even predominantly in her mind but on her "countenance," the exterior, expressive, and observable signs of a developed interiority written, as it were, all over her face. What mattered for James's readers, then, was a very particular logic of identification: a pragmatic investment in a fictional character's exoteric and seemingly imitable behavior—her "charming, diplomatic" visage, her "face" modeled after a work of art—rather than an unobservable psychological melding of minds between reader and character. To his reading publics, then, James had returned to America not just as a successful writer of expatriate fiction but also as an instructor of young ladies' communicative behavior—a role that his fellow expatriate and champion of modernist autonomy T. S. Eliot, in an essay titled "The Aims of Education," would gloss dismissively as the "paraliterary occupation" of "teaching and lecturing."[27]

Ladies' culture clubs were not the only "essentially American Institutions" to encourage all the single ladies to cultivate a specifically pragmatic investment in the communicative behaviors of literary characters. More important for James were the reading practices of the women's college, where his expatriate fictions often served an adjacent function to middle-class social conduct books, perhaps the most popular genre among women at the turn of the century. Late nineteenth- and early twentieth-century accounts of literacy abound with examples of female students reading James to learn how to alter or adjust their behavior to achieve positive social ends. In a letter to her family written in 1887, Vassar student Louisa Poppenheim instructed her mother to let Louisa's little sister read "only the new novels by Henry James and W. D. Howells, who write the latest and most fashionable novels and whose works every cultivated person must read. But when she reads them let her be sure that she does not spend all her time on the story. . . . Now a day the old-fashioned love story is not the topic of the day, the nineteenth century is an analytical age and traits or characters are clothed as people and these people are worked into novels. With this point in view she will be able to read novels with some good results."[28] Assuming the same didactic tone in the *Smith College Monthly* in 1900, junior English major Tirzah Snell Smith proposed that "the feminine cast" of James's mind enabled him "to portray that intricate creature, the feminine intellect, with admirable exactness."[29] In a strange turn, however, she argued that James's novels were a must-read for any student who aspired to craft her feminized "self-expression" with the same degree of artful precision displayed by his novels. By reading *The Portrait of a Lady*, Smith contended, an attentive reader could learn how to "reveal personality on the basis of gender" by repeatedly performing a series of acts—speaking, gesturing, bodily posturing—which, over time, would impress others as naturally female traits. More subtly than Poppenheim's fashion-forward instructions on how to read "traits or characters" to achieve "good results," Smith's article grasped at a theory of gender performativity *avant la lettre*: a model of reading literature in which the interiority of fictional discourse and the exteriority of communication converged to produce the intricacies of the "feminine intellect." We can see a similar grasping in Bryn Mawr alumna H.D.'s partially autobiographical novel *Hermione* (1927), in which the narrator recalls with no small degree of irony how her classmates tended to "play hide-and-seek behind Henry James"—hiding and seeking the "theoretically feminine (of the period)" in their vocalized mimicry of James's characters' psychological insights in English classrooms and after-hours gossip sessions alike.[30]

Considered alongside the literary discourses of the ladies' culture clubs, the "analytic age" of reading literature in women's institutions of higher education upends many of our assumptions about reading in the early twentieth century and reading James's brand of high modernism in particular. As early as 1918, career academics in the United States and the United Kingdom had begun to treat James as the point for departure for the "art-novel," a prohibitively dense and difficult text that laid claim to aesthetic autonomy as the defining feature of "the literary." It was in James that the art-novel found its "most persuasive spokesman," asserts Mark McGurl; and it was with James that the properly literary novel, through both its difficult aesthetic forms and its institutionalized practices of reception, like close reading, began to assert itself against the genres of mass culture.[31] Although this historical narrative continues to dominate studies of the twentieth-century novel today, it nevertheless jettisons the many ideologies of reading that different readers brought to James's novels and thus to serious literary fiction more generally: the assertion of an easy and fashionable equivalence between "people" and "characters"; the desire to read novels with "good results" for both interior and exterior development; the intimate relationship between techniques of reading and the performative nature of gender. As the archives of the "American Institutions" of female education and literacy socialization show, there existed a prolific tradition of novel reading that simply was not assimilable by critical paradigms of literary fiction as an autonomous field of aesthetic production, defined against the sense of social and material usefulness that marked readings of the daily newspaper or a woman's conduct manual. By understanding how the pragmatic and performative reading practices of young ladies were defined by and through more avowedly literary practices of novel reading, we can begin to appreciate how the institution of the women's college emerged as a historically contingent social formation, one defined by a set of unappreciated, yet systematic, reading practices.

SPEAKING LIKE A BOOK

We may now begin to appreciate why James's lecture "The Question of Our Speech" was so important for braiding together these institutionally specific reading practices with a nationalized understanding of female speech and, subsequently, international communication. Perhaps the most explicit and unusual premise of "The Question of Our Speech" was that speech's double nature—speech as a represented feature of literature, on the one hand, and speech as an act of utterance, on the other—could bridge the ontological divide between James's fictional characters and his female readers. In an interview with the *New York Herald* undertaken at the outset of his speaking tour, James proposed that speech was "one's art, one's craft."[32] Speech's duality offered his readers a unique opportunity not only to create their own works of art but also to serve as their own artworks—the closest many of them would come to producing something stylistically akin to James's novels. As he further explained to his interviewer Florence Brooks, speech's aesthetic possibilities particularly warranted the attentions of female speakers like her for reasons that transcended purely aesthetic concerns. Men, he observed, and would note again and more forcefully in *The American Scene* (1907), had unceremoniously vacated the realm of culture by the twentieth century, choosing instead to immerse themselves in the pursuit of political and economic power. This had left women to set the tone for the everyday practices of communication and interaction that constituted the social realm. "First among" all social mandates, James claimed, was "the unwritten law that a lady shall speak as a lady," for her speech not only "secured the dignity and integrity" of her character, it also shaped the overall quality of the nation's socio-institutional relationships: the irreducibly complex and granular mechanics of individual behavior that, when taken in aggregate, scaled up to form a "coherent culture." "The question of our relations with each other," James continued, "are made possible, are registered, are verily constituted, by our speech, and are successful . . . in proportion as our speech is worthy of its great human and social function" (62).

But not all was well on the American scene, where the women James had interacted with in the early months of his lecture tour betrayed "a sublime unconsciousness of speech as the premiere art of life" (45). Young ladies "spoke badly," James complained, which is to say they spoke in "a mere helpless slobber of disconnected vowel noises," which represented "the weakest and cheapest attempt at human expression" that he claimed to have ever encountered (49). According to James, the aesthetic unconsciousness of women had graver effects on the United States than it would have had on comparable European nations, which, as Christopher Looby has suggested, "experienced their coherence as a matter of racial and ethnic similarity, religious orthodoxy, population concentration, geographic definition, massive and dense structures of inherited customary practices, and highly articulated historical self-representations."[33] The United States had only its shared language and nothing more. The failure of aesthetic discrimination in speech among America's women portended certain cultural doom for the nation as a whole.

Yet there is every reason to be more suspicious than Looby is of James's expeditious shift from the vocalizations of individual speakers to what Looby calls "voicing America," an example, as I noted in my introduction, of the overhasty jump from American figures to the figure of America. Note how exaggerated the performative link is that James draws between women's speech and the national culture forged through the act of speaking; as if, by the twentieth century, the aesthetics of female speech were the sole causal determinants of how all American institutions were constituted. Note also that this emphasis on performative speech and social structure prefaced James's own performance of speaking during the commencement address he delivered at Bryn Mawr at the invitation of President M. Carey Thomas, a renowned suffragette and philologist. The lecture, as Erving Goffman has observed, models a supremely reflexive genre of speech, insofar as it provides the speaker an opportunity "to purposively impart a coherent chapter of information" that "cannot avoid its application to [its own] occasion of communication."[34] Such recursivity seems especially acute and self-interested when, like James, a speaker lectures on the art of speaking. The speaker cannot avoid practicing what he preaches (i.e., speech) or preaching what he practices (i.e., endorsing his speech as the standard for aesthetically discriminating speech). Nowhere is the reflexive footing of James's Bryn Mawr lecture more apparent than in his alleged off-script shout-out to his Bryn Mawr audience: "What you young ladies should do is imitate! Don't be afraid to imitate!"[35] Thus, while his occupation as a lecturer implicitly stabilized James's position as the imitative object of study, his injunction to his female audiences to "imitate" explicitly linked his speech to their speech; his utterances modeled the tone, syntax, grammar, and diction—the aesthetic—that simultaneously inaugurated and marked the character type of the young lady. By extension, then, James's speech not only impersonated the speech of the young lady in a kind of proto-drag performance, it also enacted within the institution of the women's college the "national use of vocal sound" that would arise from a feminized act of speaking (48).

Equally important for James's pedagogy, then, was the indistinguishability of his speaking style—his "use of vocal sound"—and his style as a novelist. "The Question of Our Speech" was, above all, an exercise in speaking like a book, insofar as it luxuriated in the aesthetic hallmarks of James's high modernism: his vacillation between first-person and third-person omniscient and limited points of view, his centripetal hypotaxis, his ambiguous antecedents, his psychological realism. So while the lecture opened with somewhat perfunctory praise for the "ideals" that the young ladies before him had "so happily pursued in these beautiful conditions" of higher education, James quickly drew attention to—and thus began to enact—the speech education he believed his audience was so desperately lacking. "No explicit, no separate, no adequate plea [for speech] will be likely to have ranged itself under any of your customary heads of commencement," he claimed; and absent such a plea, "the educative process cannot be thought of as at all even beginning" (43). The thorniness of the sentences here—try, if you will, speaking that last one aloud—are typical of late-period James, from the layering of negative intensifiers to the separation and confusion of subject that distances his "plea" for speech education from "itself." Within the lecture, the transition from straightforward and ceremonial praise to what Mary McCarthy would later characterize as James's "murmured, indistinct evolution" instantiated the educative process, miming the syntactical structures that characterized and constituted feminized speech. Crucially, James offered no candid indictment of American women here; to speak so directly would have been to speak in an unladylike manner, unworthy of imitation. Instead, his aesthetic contortions allowed him to criticize women's speech by performing the inverse of direct criticism: the crafted, self-conscious style of address that he aligned with speaking like a lady and, by his own exaggerated performative logic, speaking as a representative American.

Taken together, the reading practices of James's audience members, the genre conventions of the lecture, and the lecture's style facilitated a remarkable strategy of literary impersonation. Listeners and readers could not only learn to speak like a book—a novel written by Henry James—but they could also transform their acts of spoken communications into nationally representative works of art; at least, this was the lecture's most grandiose and narcissistic promise. Yet as I suggested earlier, literary impersonation took two forms: the production of Jamesian people and the production of Jamesian novels, both of which arose from within the very institutions of literacy—the women's colleges—in which James had performed his act of speech education. Comparing the fictive scenarios of feminized speech in Jamesian novels to the actual protocols of speech reformation designed in the wake of "The Question of Our Speech" will show different ways in which the logics of literary impersonation were detached from their contexts of origin and emerged as a generalized case of paraliterary reading—what Mrs. Humphrey Ward, one of James's hosts on his lecture tour, rapturously called the "endless" "resources of mere imitation" that arose from "Henry James speaking."[36]

In the case of Jamesian novels, the confluence of literary impersonation, gender, and institutional setting appears as early as 1905, in the opening lines of Radcliffe graduate Gertrude Stein's underappreciated novella *Fernhurst, or The History of Philip Redfern: A Student of the Nature of Women*. Drafted in the months before and after James's commencement speech had gained national notoriety, the novella dramatizes an intrafaculty love triangle at Fernhurst (a thinly veiled Bryn Mawr) between Philip Redfern, a visiting speaker and "student of the nature of women," a female English professor, and the school's dean (a stand-in for James's host, M. Carey Thomas). Given the historical coincidence of Stein's writing of *Fernhurst* with James's lecture tour, not to mention Stein's preoccupation with James as a model for her international literary ambitions, it is likely that she had "The Question of Our

Speech" in mind when she penned the tongue-in-cheek opening lines of the novella, a parodic guide to the practice of publicly addressing large groups of women. "A guest of honor so custom demands begins an address with praise and humor and speaking to the ideals of the audience clothes the laudation in the technical language of the hearer's profession," the narrator intones. "It is known that post prandial attention must be fished with this bait and only slowly rises to interest and labor. So the selected bandar-log begins his imitating chatter with the praise of repetition and a learned lady delights her audience with a phrase and bids them rejoice in their imperfections."[37] More akin to a badly written conduct guide than a novel, the difficulty of *Fernhurst*—and one of the reasons it is rarely discussed in Stein criticism—is its apparently subliterary quality as "autobiographical" or "historical" writing.[38] Yet reading it alongside the discourses of literary impersonation lodged in the women's college reveals how *Fernhurst* parodies the performative transformation of literature's female readers into literature's male writers and vice versa, rendering it a Jamesian novel in a more specific sense than Stein's contemporary critics have realized.

Setting aside the explicit thematic or biographical resonances between *Fernhurst* and "The Question of Our Speech," of which there are many, I want to linger on how Stein's generic "guest of honor" impersonates James's performative strategies of address to a tee. While the speaker begins with "praise and humor," he also "clothes the laudation in the technical language" of the audience in order to cultivate not only their "interest" but also their "labor." At first, the invocation of labor may seem out of place in listening to a lecture, which we tend to think of as a relatively passive act of reception. Yet the next sentence clarifies that the audience's labor is in fact the work of imitating the guest speaker's imitation of them. After the guest begins his "imitating chatter with the praise of repetition"—think of James's call to young ladies to "imitate!" him in order to learn how to be young ladies—a "learned lady" in attendance takes her cue from the speaker and "delights her audience with a phrase." The imitation of imitation encourages the audience of ladies to "rejoice in their imperfections," allowing the self-reflexivity of the lecture to do the work of linguistic admonition. So densely nested is this scene of spoken communication that it is easy to lose sight of who is doing the speaking or the imitating at any given moment: the speaker, the learned lady, or the audience. Of course, this is precisely the point of literary impersonation, at least as James had modeled it at Bryn Mawr only months before.

Crucially, however, Stein's literary impersonation of James's performativity in the style of *Fernhurst* is not identical to the imitation of speech thematized therein. While Stein's paratactic style bears little resemblance to

James's contorted clauses, it is precisely the difference between the two that allows for the figure of the female speaker to emerge out of the male guest of honor. The "selected bandar-log" who begins the address is grammatically displaced (through a single conjunctive "and") as the subject of the sentence by the learned lady, who is in turn herself displaced (through a second conjunctive "and"), leaving the subject of the final clause ("and bids them rejoice in their imperfections") ambiguous. Who bids the audience to rejoice? The bandar-log or the learned lady? Could it possibly be both? On the level of the sentence, then, Stein's style formally reconfigures the male subject as a female impersonator, much like how, on the level of the lecture, James enacts his own linguistic metamorphosis into a female speaker through his literary/speech aesthetic. Thus, although no literary work could be "more unlike the work of Henry James than the work of Miss Stein," as one early reviewer of *Fernhurst* noted, her "murmuring people" did bear an uncanny resemblance to "James's people who not only talk, but live while they talk."[39] Like James, the "great master of conversation," Stein yoked literary style to the performativity of speech to create "living, moving 'situations' " of institutional discourse. That she does so in a notably different stylistic register is a testament to the important gap between impersonation and "mere imitation," a gap that was soon to close in the public sphere.

Like H.D. writing in *Hermione* about "playing hide-and-seek behind Henry James," Stein stands out as an especially discerning student of James's style of address, as well as a savvy parodist of his performative strategies. Her act of literary impersonation in *Fernhurst* emerged in sharp contrast to the tendency of more literal-minded readers to overlook the ironic self-awareness in James's lecture: for instance, his knowingly reflexive joke in "The Question of Our Speech" that "if slang were permitted me here," he would happily wear "so impudent a 'mug' " (46). And yet many of the readers who read reprinted versions of the speech, now detached from its original communicative context by newspapers and magazines, criticized James for what they took to be his utter lack of self-awareness. Both the mass-mediated reading public, as represented in the op-ed pages of the *New York Times*, *Boston Evening Transcript*, *Harper's Weekly*, the *North American Review*, the *Nation*, and *Munsey's Magazine*, as well as professional educators writing in the *Public Speaking Review*, *American Education*, and the *Educator Journal*, agreed that James's lecture betrayed his lack of stylistic self-awareness. If imitated, critics warned, the syntactical inscrutability of James's novelistic style would do irrevocable damage to the national character of American English and America in the world. Although negatively intended, the public's equation of James's novelistic style with the speech of Americans and the figure of America had the paradoxical effect of strengthening the link he had first asserted between the two at Bryn Mawr. The *Philadelphia Dispatch* worried that "the alleged English Henry James uses in his books will doubtless be reinforced when the public reads what he said at Bryn Mawr."[40] Hundreds of readers wrote to the editors of the *New York Times* threatening to boycott James's novels to counter his unwarranted influence over the young ladies of America. "Mr. James should think twice before he slaughters wholesale American speech as he does," warned one such patriotic reader. "There are still Americans who try to wade through his books, (though many eschew them through a love for pure English and a dislike of inverted sentences), and . . . his disdain of his own country may lessen his income of good American dollars."[41] Weighing in from another institution of higher education, the chair of Yale University's English department, Thomas R. Lounsbury, even went so far as to prophesy "the death of spontaneity" now that "ignorant formalism and affected precision of language are prized more than the racy idiomatic speech of the man on the street."[42]

Unlike H.D. and Stein, more literal readers of James's address were most concerned with the wholesale production of Jamesian people as national representatives, a process they conceived of as a straightforward matter of readerly imitation writ large. And while this process had its roots partially in the reading practices of the women's college, once the media outrage died down, the cultural investment in literary impersonation inspired the construction of new institutions that explicitly wed reading James to practices of speech pedagogy and subject formation. On December 16, 1906, the *New York Times* ran a front-page article announcing, "A Movement to Reform the Speaking of English: W. D. Howells, Henry James, and Others Interested in Newly-formed Society to Study Spoken English with a View to Correcting Careless, Slipshod Utterance."[43] The Society for the Study of Spoken English issued as its mission statement an aesthetic imperative that hewed closely to James's call to imitation at Bryn Mawr: "Lend to the rhyme of the poet the beauty of thy voice."[44] Along with Howells and James, who were named the society's "leading instigators" by *Harper's Weekly*, the organization counted in its ranks a bevy of New York socialites, Lounsbury, and Charles W. Eliot, the president of Harvard University. (The last two personnel additions would place James's teachings firmly into the elite orbit of male higher education and into institutional spaces that would remain off limits to female readers until 1970.) After a preliminary meeting at the Academy of Fine Arts in New York, during which founding member Bishop Henry C. Potter called on "public speakers of all kinds, actors, teachers, lecturers, and others" to "lead the reform," the society began distributing a published anthology of speaking exercises to primary schools on the East Coast.[45] Opening with rhymes from Mother Goose, progressing to poems by William Blake, Robert Louis Stevenson, and Sidney Lanier, and culminating in longer passages from novels by James and Howells, the exercise book promised to cultivate "a soft, low voice, an excellent thing in women."[46] The organization of the exercise book—its serial presentation of vocal drills, its emphasis on vocal recitation, and its implied teleology of speech's aesthetic "progress" from rhyme to poem to novel—regimented the performative dimension of literary impersonation in the form of a reproducible, broadly circulated curriculum of study. Even outside the physical spaces of women's colleges or ladies' culture clubs, the society's aspiration was to produce large quantities of Jamesian people with some modicum of efficiency. The society's rationalization of literary impersonation thus marked an important turning point in both the institutionalization of literary aesthetics in lived practices of communication, as well as an ideology of reading as imitation.

Today, the comparison between Stein and the society also signals a telling blind spot in what counts as properly literary reading for literary historians. Given the cultural and social marginality typically attributed to female readers and the institutions of literacy education they inhabited, the examples I have traversed so far show that female readers often produced discourses about literary texts closer to what we might call critical interpretation than more explicitly "literary" approaches to reading in the early twentieth century. Consider Poppenheim, Smith, Stein, and H.D.'s intricate theorizations of the relationship between speech, gender, and James's literary style alongside the reading practices of one "successful literary man," featured in an anecdote from the *New York Times Book Review*. "A year and a half ago a successful literary man in New York was asked in an interview for his opinion of Mr. James's work," reported the *Times* in June 1907, a year and a half after James's lecture had eroded his reputation in the United States. No great fan of James, the anonymous literary man answered the reporter "by opening the first volume of *The Golden Bowl* and reading sentence after sentence from it, only pausing to inquire of the waiting reporter what in the name of common sense it all meant. The reporter copied out the sentences in question and they appeared later in his 'story.'"[47] One is hard pressed to think of anything as embarrassing as this scene of bad reading: quite literally, inept or incompetent reading which refuses to grasp for meaning of any kind. Even worse, perhaps, is the reporter's dutiful willingness to replicate faithfully this scene of reading in his "story" as not only an indictment of James's style but also an endorsement of an anonymous, and thus universal, sense of what a "literary" reader values. Yet far from reinforcing the distinction between serious and unserious readers, or good and bad forms of textual engagement, the comparison between female readers and successful literary men shows how literary impersonation, in its variously textual, embodied, and performative manifestations, is by no means an unsystematic or fanciful approach to reading fiction—two terms that, in the history of literary criticism, are often aligned with women. Rather, the novels, the texts, and the discursive activities that underwrite literary impersonation reveal how the fictionally mimetic production of feminized subjects and institutional protocols relies on a complex inter-articulation of the relationship between reading and speaking, communication and representation. The fact that reading James would soon take on an international dimension, as I will now show, only adds depth to the conceptual development and the historical lineage of literary impersonation.

SPEAKING BACK TO THE FUTURE

So far, the nationalized understanding of feminized speech that I developed in the last section has rested on James's seemingly exaggerated link between the speech of American women and a national-institutional culture. And yet there was a more fully developed historical reason for his choice, one that became clear when James abdicated his leadership role at the Society for the Study of Spoken English and returned to England at the end of 1908. For the members of the society who remained behind, speech reformation seemed increasingly impossible given the sheer social and linguistic pluralism that overwhelmed an apparently enclosed national public sphere. This was a point that James had insisted on in "The Question of Our Speech," primarily through the story he narrated to his audiences of the "*vox Americana*." In contrast to "the French, the Germans, the Italians, the English perhaps in particular, and maybe other people, Occidental and Oriental" whose speech had developed through "comparison with that of other nations," the "*vox Americana*" had begun her life as an "unfriended heroine" (45). Unable to secure her "unique linguistic position" in the "international concert of culture," she had grown dangerously vulnerable to the "high modernism of the conditions now surrounding, on this continent, the practice of our language" (52). No matter where she turned, this metonymic heroine found her aesthetic aspirations thwarted by the barbarians at the gates of American literary culture, "the American common school, the American newspaper, and the American Dutchman and Dago" (53); or in slightly more descriptive (and less offensive) terms, the expansion of primary education to the lower classes, the rise of mass-mediated publishing, and the influx of immigrants to the United States in the nineteenth century. Taken together, these sociolinguistic conditions had besieged the *vox Americana*, overrunning her with the regionally specific accents and slangy neologisms that defied a coherent aesthetic standard for nationalized speech. Thus she had lost her place in the international system of language before she had ever had a chance to secure it properly. As such, she had little choice, James suggested, but to seek recourse in new and undiluted institutions of language training, institutions that made it possible to travel back in time and space, undoing the cultural pluralism of the twentieth century to claim a place for American English in the world.

What might it mean for an institution to give readers the power to travel through time and space? If that question seems ludicrous on its face, this is only because the concept of institutional time, which Eric Hayot has described as "an institution's rhythm and relationship to historical development," remains woefully unappreciated when it comes to literary historiography.[48] Although institutions exist in specific periods and places, the mere historicity of their existence offers no guarantee that the protocols, habits, or norms organized under their roofs sync up with their contemporary surroundings. Yet the assumption of a presentist correlation between an institution's practices and its proverbial "outside" is the default position of nearly all sociohistorically inclined literary criticism, whether that "outside" is defined by the overarching structures of the state, capitalism, or technology. If James's epic-chivalric narrative of the *vox Americana* teaches us anything, it is that the heroic figure destined to save American women from the hulking brutes of modernity had to be immune to the present-day linguistic conditions of the American public sphere. Instead of armor, a linguistic savior had to possess what James described to *Harper's* editor Elizabeth Jordan as an "antediluvian" aesthetic sensibility: the ability to cast everything—people, characters, institutions—in the "mellow light of the old world."[49]

Inhabiting the "old world" required traveling not only through time (a literal impossibility) but also through space to a continent untouched by pluralism (a real possibility). The fantasy of space-time travel was one that Elizabeth Jordan would encourage James to develop in eight articles serialized in *Harper's* from 1906 to 1907, now divided into two longer essays: "The Speech of American Women" and "The Manners of American Women."[50] A substantial portion of both essays was devoted to "the one group to which some cultivation of the sense of speech" was "more or less imputable": "the body of American [women] exposed to the influence of various parts of the social order across the sea" (97). Unlike the "beasts" of Bryn Mawr who found it "easier to snort or neigh, to growl or to 'meaow'" than to speak in well-wrought sentences, American women who had immersed themselves in old world living enjoyed the salutary aesthetic effects of "acquaintance with *trained* populations" (98, italics in original). All of James's examples of American women speaking well came from languorous picnics in the European countryside and similar scenes of naturalistic immersion, far removed from the built structures of institutions of higher education. The rustic magic of space-time travel required a curious inversion of the pastoral mode, whereby noisy female barnyard animals were confined to schools, where they might diligently snort and neigh over newspapers and novels, while more aesthetically attuned humans wandered through the fields learning "imitation and conformity" from primitive scenes of language acculturation (97). Only in the total absence of any competing institutions of literacy socialization could James make his influence felt, wielding his "old world" sensibilities to rescue the *vox Americana* from her modern imprisonment by linguistic variety.

That the "absent educative force" for reforming women's speech should be so explicitly opposed to institutionalized literacy education proved crucial to the subsequent dislocation of discourses of literary impersonation from the national to the international scene, from reading in school to lived experiences outside of its confines. "We are confirmed hermits," claimed a 1908 article in the *New York Times*, following a series of interviews with disgruntled English teachers in New York City who had tested the society's curricular guidelines and drill books and found them lacking.[51] "Our women ... still have much to learn in the ways of social conduct from the best types of European womanhood," lamented a subsequent opinion piece in an otherwise tepid review of James's articles for *Harper's*. "We perceive dimly through the smoke of Mr. James's own literary torch," the writer continued, "that there are 'Europeanized' American women who have pretty good manners."[52] And while James's work continued to inspire readers to publish dozens of textbooks on speech training—*The Sounds of Spoken English: A Manual of Ear Training for English Students* (1906), *The Pronunciation of English by Foreigners* (1907), *A Tract on the Present State of English Pronunciation* (1913), *Educational Dramatics* (1917), and many more—these too noted the disadvantages of national insularity. Drawing a parallel between speech and music training, Katherine Jewell Everts, author of the Jamesian drill book *Vocal Expressions* (1911), analogized American women to concert pianists who had to "expatriate themselves" in order to "spend laborious years in study and practice."[53] Less extreme than James's insistence on a totalizing temporal and spatial break from the American scene, Everts's call for an elaborate program of retraining nevertheless imagined that some spatiotemporal distance from national institutions of literacy could break women's old aesthetic habits and instill new ones in their place.

In one sense, it is surprising that the cultural preoccupation with women's speech continued for as long as it did. Histories of feminism often look to the interwar period for the origins of the shift from the aesthetically preoccupied "young lady" to a more politically and internationally involved female reading subject: the wartime activist, the suffragette, the volunteer nurse. Even James had chaired the American Volunteer Motor Ambulance Corps in France from March 1915 until his death in February 1916, overseeing the nursing work of hundreds of female volunteers from Smith and Bryn Mawr on the front line.[54] Yet the performative discourse of the "young lady as Beautiful Soul" remained an imaginative fixture of the women's college, more vividly anachronistic now that the teaching of femininity stood out as a conservative relic from the pre-Progressive Era.[55] Paradoxically, the out-of-sync-ness of the women's college had the effect of lodging James's premodern and anti-institutional fantasies of literacy education even deeper into the sociological consciousness of male administrators, particularly those eager to reclaim the figure of the aestheticized "young lady" as the antithesis to the politicized New Woman. For evidence, one needs look no further than the 1917 Harvard Classics reissue of James's *The Portrait of a Lady*, edited by Smith College president William Allan Neilson and selected for inclusion in the series by founding member of the Society for the Study of Spoken English, Charles W. Eliot. Dictatorially instructing a new generation of female readers to take James's fictional young lady "on his own terms or not at all," Neilson introduced the novel's new edition by promising "a specific lesson for the American girl" if she read as a good student ought, by attending to the aesthetically ennobling practices of a "lady's refined and exquisite expression" that made "no concession to 'what the public wants.'"[56] Whether the "public" in this case was James's turn-of-the-century reading publics or the politicized feminist publics of Neilson's time, the message to the female reader remained equally conservative.

What may seem like a crotchety old man baiting female readers in the introduction to *Portrait* actually positioned Neilson as a pivotal figure for retrograde articulations of female subjectivity, picking up in 1917 where James had left off in 1908. A former English professor at Bryn Mawr and Radcliffe,

Neilson occupied the institutional-administrative nexus that the society had failed to secure, with one foot planted in the elite literary company of James, Eliot, and Howells, and the other in the cultivation of literate female subjects, whom he referred to as the "gentlewomen" of Smith College. As he declared in his inaugural address, his administration intended to walk a fine line between promoting equal rights and opportunities for women and seeing to "the regulation of the whole matter of women's conduct."[57] Such institutional regulation required winding back the clock on the passage of time, a challenge that Neilson undertook from 1922 to 1924 by replicating James's 1905 lecture tour and peddling an address titled "The Need for Better English" to New York City public schools and East Coast culture clubs. Faithfully imitating both the lecture format of "The Question of Our Speech" as well as James's central theme ("to obey through imitation"), Neilson warned his audiences that "a harsh or squeaking voice may make a person who is otherwise attractive very unpleasant; and many a beautiful woman loses her charm when she begins to speak."[58] In Neilson, the teacher, the administrator, and the literary Master (via his imitation of James) came together in a single figure. Intriguingly, however, he offered his audiences not a throwback to James's premodern idylls of anti-institutional immersion but a journey back to the future of speech pedagogy that the society had sought to institutionalize before the war—one step forward, two steps back in time.

Nearly a decade before teaching texts like John Dewey's *Experience and Education* (1938) asserted the importance of communicative experience in education, Neilson's discursive creation of a time lag in the literacy teachings of the women's college linked the gendered reading practices of the prewar generation with the progressive pedagogical tools and positions of a younger group of social actors. Even if he did not fully appreciate the impossibility of the temporal journey envisioned by James in his lecture tour, Neilson's Janus-faced teachings do seem to have absorbed James's more logistically viable arguments about transatlantic displacement as experiential education. It's hard to imagine, for instance, that Neilson didn't have James in mind when he designed the first Junior Year Abroad (JYA) programs for Smith's "gentlewomen"—the earliest "experiments in international living" conducted under the watchful eye of a university administration. The program's emphasis on speech education represented a departure from existing rituals of upper-class tourism like the Grand Tour, which were motivated by international consumption as a market of socioeconomic distinction; an opportunity for women to learn to discriminate between "the rights and wrongs of caps and hats, dresses and ribbons," according to Emma Hart

Willard, founder of the Troy Female Seminary in upstate New York.[59] Yet the program's "experimental" structure of "living"—thirty to forty students would reside with host families in Paris and take classes at the Sorbonne— nevertheless suggests the crucial role that extracurricular interactions and social communications would play in Neilson's vision of international sub- ject formation. Contrary to both Alice Kaplan and Whitney Walton's obser- vations about the rigorous academics of the program, classroom education was not high at all on Neilson's list of priorities.[60] Most classes were "survey courses" taught in English intermingled with only the most basic French. ("There will be no question of doing . . . Mathematics of Science there," Neilson informed a curious parent.)[61] As Sally Goodell, an aspiring graduate student in French literature, observed in a critical letter to Neilson, she had "heard the professors say" that classes were intended "to show no way in which we may pursue knowledge."[62] Goodell's letter, hyperbolic though it may seem in its accusations of teacherly anti-intellectualism, indicates that a subtler instruction informs the program's design, one geared less toward propagating the disciplinary knowledge of higher education and more to- ward disciplining the communicative lifestyle of the female subject.

"Lifestyle" is a relatively new word—it only enters the English lexicon in 1915—but one whose compound nature ("life" plus "style") perfectly cap- tures the convergence of lived social experiences with aesthetic sensibilities. Here that convergence plays out not within the four walls of the school or the boundaries of the nation-state but against the international backdrop of the "old world," which permits the radical retrojection of space-time into literacy education. As Neilson explained to all Smith students before they departed for France, their goal "was not to live as Americans in Paris but to conform to your hostess's idea of decorum and learn what it is to be a *jeune fille.*"[63] Indeed, the figure of the *jeune fille*—in literal translation, a young lady, but also a characterological darling of French conservative thought in the interwar period—mapped nicely onto the institutional belatedness of the American women's college in more ways than one. A sheltered, virginal, obedient girl who aspired to neither the political nor the economic self- possession of the Progressive Era American woman, the *jeune fille* presented an enduring model of bourgeois feminine subjectivity. Her upper-class po- sitioning was reinforced largely through her carefully proscribed reading and writing practices. Appropriately, she was familiar to most American readers as a literary character. Consider the "ideal *jeune fille* of foreign fic- tion," James's Pansy Osmond from *The Portrait of a Lady*.[64] Pansy may not have been the first *jeune fille* to appear in print in America—that honor already belonged to Aurora Church, the heroine of James's short story "The Pension Beaurepas" (1879)—but by 1922, Pansy was easily the most recognizable. Like Pansy, a *jeune fille* "would be frank and gay, and yet have not walked alone, nor have received letters from men, nor have been taken to the theater to see the comedy of manners." The *jeune fille* would embody the "blank page" of an unsullied discursive past as a character incapable of imitating the communicative forms she might have encountered in suggestive letters or lower-class theatrical performances. As such, Neilson hoped that teaching his students to impersonate the *jeune fille*'s blankness and subsequent discursive creation would help countermand the fact that "American girls did not enjoy a good reputation" around the world.[65] Such experiments in international living, he announced to his co-coordinator Helene Cattanes, would succeed only "if the reputation of the American girl were improving on the French market."

The word *reputation* may conjure up images of young girls tugging silvery flasks from garter belts outside the Moulin Rouge, but the "market" that Neilson had in mind more closely resembled the quasi-metaphorical system of value that Pierre Bourdieu describes as a linguistic market, a rigid hierarchy in which stylistically marked speech acts are mapped onto relative positions of social and cultural capital. Accordingly, the program's day-to-day experiments in international living were all staged communicative events reflexively attuned to gendered practices of speech: organized teas as opportunities to make "small talk" with the *femmes du monde*, evening soirees for conversations with preselected French beaux, shopping excursions which limited all shop talk to formal registers of French. Speech cultivation, in other words, held the key to transforming the American girl into a linguistic identity with purchasing power on an international market. "I can't say that my year abroad did any good commercially but—and it is that 'but' that tells the story," testified participant Elizabeth Murphy in 1935. "Additional poise, self-confidence, a certain *je ne sais quoi* brought back from France have proved decided assets."[66] While we may find ourselves drawn to Murphy's breezy "*je ne sais quoi*" as evidence of her newfound sociolinguistic elevation, what seems more telling is her inverted disavowal of the program's commercial value ("I can't say that my year abroad did any good commercially") and the metalinguistic commentary that interrupts it. In refusing to articulate the economic value of her year abroad (what "good" it did), Murphy draws attention to how her use of the word *but* ("that 'but'") linguistically encodes the program's aesthetic value. Like James's characteristic "but" dialogues, which encrypt rather than elucidate his speaker's thoughts

("But I sometimes wonder—!" interjects Milly in *The Wings of the Dove*, and Maisie often trails off with "But I mean . . ."), the "but" that metacommunicatively relays Murphy's narrative of transformation is evidence of the program's ability to speak back to the future—vocative proof of her transformation into the young lady of the past.

From young ladies reading James's novels to James's impersonation of young ladies to young ladies' impersonation of the Jamesian *jeune fille*, the logic of literary impersonation connects some of the most influential models of reading for women in interwar institutions of literacy education. To recover the fascination with impersonation is not only to recover these institutionally specific practices of reading but also to pay sustained aesthetic attention to the unusual products of women's reading practices: letters, testimonials, magazine articles, and the other paraliterary genres that transpose and fix stylized verbal activity as textual form. Reading these texts not only tells us new things about the immediate social or linguistic concerns of ordinary female readers. It also helps us see the novels that were produced by the minority of female readers in these institutional contexts with fresh eyes, not as straightforward allegories of their conditions of production but as interdiscursive engagements with international speech protocols. It is to these novels and their fraught status as "literature" that I now turn.

ARTISTS OF LIFE

What happens when one generation's readers and lifestyle models become the next generation's writers? How do the various strands of literary impersonation that I have stitched together so far—its relationship to speech acts, gender performances, institutional time, and international setting—influence not just literary reception but literary production? In the case of the first participants in the experiments in international living, the answer is a rather straightforward one, insofar as we can track a rather direct path from study abroad programs in women's colleges to the appearance of the mass-cultural genre of study abroad fiction. "There is so much to tell," wrote program participant Hilda Donahue in 1927 to David A. Robertson, assistant director of the American Council of Education and a former professor of contemporary literature at the University of Chicago. "I am so enthusiastic about everything I have done that at times I think if I had the talent of a writer I should write a book, 'An American University Student Abroad'—etc. I am sure there is material for a 'best seller.'"[67] Per Donahue's enthusiasm about "everything" she has "done," we can observe in the production and marketing of many of these novels a commitment to experiential mimesis over and above literary representation. That is, we can track an insistent claim on the part of writers, publishers, and marketers that these stories were produced directly from life and thus eschewed many of the stylized or imaginative features that characterized literature as such. While Donahue seems to have resisted the urge to put pen to paper precisely because of her lack of literary talent, other participants turned to ghostwriters and collaborators to help transform the paraliterary materials of their diary entries and letters home into best-selling "novels from life." In 1938, young adult writer Alice Ross Colver helped alumna Charlotte Lockwood produce *Adventure for a Song: Sheila's Junior Year Abroad*, a novel whose popularity among female readers—it was, as Donahue predicted, a "best seller"—paved the way for postwar study-abroad fare like Rosamund and Judy du Jardin's *Junior Year Abroad* (1960) and Jacqueline and Lee Bouvier's exquisite picture book *One Special Summer* (1974). In addition to their programmatic settings, what all of these texts had in common was their allegedly faithful replication of discursive events, not only in the form of letters embedded into the novel but also in the word-for-word transcriptions of drawing room conversations, dances, and shopping excursions, replete with their own metacommunicative commentaries. ("No slang, remember," one protagonist chides herself and a friend as they prepare to attend an afternoon tea party. "Repression is our motto today" [89].) In fact, as one author explained, the demand for any apparently literary labor in the production of the novel was obviated by the fact that these young women were, by virtue of their discursive self-stylization, "artists of life." They "quickened my imagination," she wrote, and lent "a framework of authentic detail to [the] story."[68]

Yet if the programs and practices of the women's college had succeeded in producing Jamesian people, these people had not succeeded in producing Jamesian novels, at least not formally or stylistically speaking. Gone was the detailed consideration of the expatriate novel as a work of art and its elaborate discursive relationship to literary impersonation as an adjacent art form. In its place were narratives framed by their authorial teams as women's conduct fictions: peppy and moralizing tales about travel, style, and romance whose purpose was imitation and imitation alone, not aesthetic distinction. "I hope this book will inspire many other young Americans to emulate 'Sheila's' adventure and that the facts incorporated here may be a contributing element of enlightenment and assistance," wrote Colver in the introduction to *Adventure for a Song* (xi). Although her appeal may seem like mere wishful thinking or a savvy marketing ploy, her emphasis on the "book" as a collaborative medium for the communication of "facts" geared toward "enlightenment and assistance" prefigures more sophisticated accounts of literature's role in the conflictual social and political relations of reading, imitation, and communication that emerged after World War II.

One place to find these more sophisticated accounts is in the work of Mary McCarthy, with whom I began this chapter. I now return to her fraught history of reading and writing as an institutional subject to show what happens when the aesthetics of literary impersonation and the postwar politics of international communication collide. Recall McCarthy's conviction that expatriate writing was on the decline, just one year after she had published her own expatriate novel *Birds of America*. Her misgivings about the tradition, however, originated nearly a decade earlier, when she had started drafting *Birds of America* while suffering from an unprecedented case of writer's block. According to her biographer Frances Kiernan, McCarthy was still smarting from negative reviews of her novel *The Group* (1963). The most vicious of these reviews came from the pen of Norman Mailer, who lambasted what most other critics had praised as *The Group*'s good social realism: McCarthy's taxonomic narration of the postgraduate lives of eight Vassar alumnae who work unconventional and dissatisfying jobs, dabble in politics and psychoanalysis, and fall in and out of love in New York City. Yet for Mailer, *The Group*'s mass appeal was precisely what confirmed its status as a "trivial lady writer's novel," one whose scorn for Vassar and its subjects did a great disservice to the "dream of self-transcendence" animating the women's college during the interwar period.[69] The price for McCarthy's institutional "*trahison*," Mailer claimed, was not economic—*The Group* had sold rather well—but aesthetic, as reflected in the flatness of the novel's characters, its clichéd urban setting, and its aborted narrative of feminist activity. One could not even call *The Group* a novel, but merely a book that "squatted on the Grand Avenue of the Novel like a shabby little boutique." One way to reframe Mailer's rather harsh judgment, as well as to connect it to the longer tradition of women's writing as experiential mimesis, is to observe more neutrally that *The Group* simply refused to engage with the reflexive aesthetic discourses of the traditional Novel. Rather, McCarthy had produced something akin to a series of sociological case studies that, when grouped together, qualitatively confirmed a hypothesis she had first formulated in a 1951 essay, that "the statistical fate of the Vassar girl" was to end up as "one of two persons—the housewife or matron, the yearner or regretter."[70]

In response to Mailer's critique of her prose style, McCarthy intended *Birds of America* to be something else entirely: a total departure not only from the institutional world of female higher education but also a Novel (with a capital *N*) that proclaimed its own distance from the "lady writer's novel" on the level of form and style. In a letter to her friend Hannah Arendt, McCarthy described her new book as a "traditional novel," which she had elsewhere called "the pure novel, the quintessential novel," a "formal, priestly exercise whose first great celebrant was James."[71] *Birds of America* thus introduces us to one of the formal, priestly expatriates: McCarthy's protagonist Peter Levi, who self-consciously explores the workings of his "inner self" while spending a year abroad at the Sorbonne (288). Peter Levi is also a boy, an aspect of his characterization that may seem trivial to us, but that was crucial to McCarthy. As she further explained to Arendt, she had conceived of Peter as the antithesis of the girls in *The Group*; the two offered her a "Scylla and Charybdis pairing" that she hoped would dissociate her from both the subjects of the women's college as well as its association with "trivial" women's writing. If the simple fact of Peter's gender would free her from the long institutional reach of the Vassar girl, it would also allow her to assert the masculinized transcendence of the aesthetic (as Mailer had coded it in his review of *The Group*) over the merely mimetic depiction of the life she had once lived as a female student. Yet the more diligently McCarthy tried to imitate the Jamesian novel in the present, both thematically and stylistically, the more she found herself "sagging with doubts and apprehension" about the Novel as a literary genre. "I've just finished the first section of it, which ought to make me cheerful," she wrote to Arendt about *Birds of America*, concluding, "But the traditional novel, which this is, is so undermined that one feels as if one were working in a house marked for demolition."

Returning to the decades in which McCarthy was writing will help to historicize her anxiety about the demolition of James's house of fiction, both in the institution of the women's college and in the form of the traditional novel. In the 1950s and 1960s, the United States had reached the height of its involvement in the Cold War, and the problem of communication was no longer framed primarily or even partially in the aestheticizing terms of the interwar period but rather in political ones. From the newly established disciplines of rhetorical humanism and mass communication studies to anthropological research on sociality, the production of individual speech acts and the production of international political power were irrevocably linked, insofar as every act of international communication now doubled as a potentially consequential act of national-institutional representation. Consider, as historian Slava Gerovitch has, the sheer number of new terms for Cold War practices of orality, ranging from *ideological speech* to *official speech, Communist speech, authentic speech, real talk,* and *permissible speech*. The word *communication,* once exclusively reserved for the analysis of speech acts, now extended to all forms of "verbal and equivalently non-verbal expression."[72] (Recall the chapter in *A Guide to Study Abroad* titled "Sexual Communication.") Such a breathtaking expansion of communication's purview helped to enact a crucial metadiscursive shift: the emergence of a public sphere in which all forms of discourse—speech but also the written word, photography, advertisements, cybernetic code, public opinion polls, and every other form of mass-mediated interaction, including literature—were metaphorized as embodied acts of face-to-face interaction. (As in Dick Tuck's oft-cited concession speech when he lost the race for California state senator in 1966: "The people have spoken, the bastards.") If the writers and administrators of the interwar period had worked overtime to institutionalize the equivalence between the fictive discourse represented in texts and speech acts, one could now take for granted the slippage between the literary and the communicative as a matter of national political urgency.

Thus when the State Department, the Department of Education, and college administrators began to interrogate international education programs, their misgivings often turned on the political fragility of both these programs' aesthetic discourses and the fact of their gender composition. Aesthetic discourse and gender composition were over hastily aligned with each other in conversations about education policy, as both women and the aestheticizing cult of femininity they had supposedly perpetuated came under fire for emasculating the nation's communication initiatives. (It did not help that the number of women who participated in international education initiatives almost tripled the number of men.) In a 1967 roundtable sponsored by the United States Board of Foreign Scholarships, Education, and World Affairs, assistant secretary of state and former Columbia University professor Charles Frankel expressed as much when he proclaimed that "the entire field of educational and cultural exchange has suffered from certain minor but debilitating maladies." The most obvious malady was not material—a problem of space, funding, personnel—but discursive. Everyone "talked about the field" as if it were "just a splendid sort of thing," Frankel recalled. "It is green; the trees are beautiful; the flowers are lovely. How could anything be bad about it? How could anything be in danger? The second thing is that this field is looked at, if I may say so, in a slightly—ladies, forgive me—feminine sort of way. That is to say, intellectual and cultural exchange is considered a very nice thing for people to engage in because it broadens the mind, elicits the emotions, gets people to really know each other."[73]

The transcript of Frankel's comments reveals, among other things, his apologetically unapologetic sexism, made even more unpalatable by the jaunty comparison he draws between a gardener cultivating an aesthetically pleasing floral garden, replete with beautiful trees and lovely flowers, and the "feminine sort of way" in which program participants cultivate their minds, their emotions, and their relationships. Today, it may not surprise us that a policymaker in the 1960s would deploy such unimaginative tropes to dismiss the aesthetics of communication as a "misleading ladies' club kind of truth." Such a dismissal was part and parcel of what sociologist Talcott Parsons had identified as early as 1947 as the "compulsory masculinity" of the emergent Cold War culture.[74] Indeed, Frankel was hardly the first government administrator or the only man to express such reservations, which had entered conversations about education and international communication in the 1950s. "Moving a finishing school to Paris does not make it an institution of higher learning," complained John Garraty and Walter Adams in their 1959 book *From Main Street to Left Bank*.[75] Meanwhile *Esquire* lampooned the "junior year abroad girls": those mock "innocent Smithies" who felt no sense of liberal political responsibility but aspired only to lure hapless French and Italian men into casual trysts to help them bolster their language skills.[76] As we have seen from the example of *The Guide to Study Abroad*, the antidote to such frivolity was reading the right kinds of books and talking about them in the right kinds of ways. And "literary stature" was not high on the list of priorities for successful international literary discourse.

Frankel's language of feminine evasion and aesthetic "disease" or decay prefigures McCarthy's reservations about the expatriate novel and its politically impotent status as decadent potpourri, a point of view that even she had begun to embrace about halfway through her writing of *Birds of America*. To wit, we can read the novel's formal unevenness, much remarked upon but unanalyzed by its critics, as registering the competing pressures McCarthy faced as an institutionally plural subject.[77] There was, on the one hand, her waning desire to escape the influence of the women's college and seek refuge in the masculinized and properly literary Novel. And there was, on the other, her waxing belief that neither the traditional Novel nor literary-aesthetic discourse in general had anything to offer the mode of political representation she had been more recently socialized into as a lecturer on American literature for the USIA.

In this light, we might begin to parse more rigorously Helen Vendler's suspicion that in order to write *Birds of America*, McCarthy had to "divide herself"—and the novel—"in two."[78] One part tells the story of Peter, son of an itinerant Italian Jew and an Ohio Wasp, who aspires to "give his country a hand abroad" (106). Peter places this political responsibility above the frivolous trappings of self-stylization and acculturation sought by girls from "Smith or Wellesley or Swarthmore or Antioch or some other upper-middle-class school" (63). Yet he also frets about whether his exceptional manner of self-presentation is "truly representative," and, as such, finds himself grappling with the incommensurability between his specific acts of communication and the scaled-up discourses of national representation. If Peter acted as a "quality export, he might create a little good will for his country, which was badly in need of it," McCarthy's narrator muses, but Peter fears that his representative function will be limited by the very "quality" of his communication. "If Peter was true to himself, nobody could be misled," the narrator notes rather dryly, "for nobody could suppose that such an unusual boy was a standard American product" (107).

While one could laud McCarthy for rightly and humorously indicting one of the central ironies of Cold War communication policies, she is quick to undercut her novel's tongue-in-cheek metadiscourse. Insofar as *Birds of America* has a plot, it turns on a series of lectures (or monologues) delivered by Peter on the virtues of Ivory soap, Frigidaires, single-breasted turkeys, mass tourism, democracy, and Peter's genetically multicultural and migratory upbringing. Such lectures are always voiced as presentist political or ideological speech, a prime example of Warner Berthoff's "paraliterary class of messages to the age" enfolded into the form of the novel. That is, every lecture either describes itself as a political "argument" or a statement of political "authority," and, perhaps more subtly, cites or recontextualizes popular government slogans about communication—"give the country a hand abroad," "create a little good will"—to reinforce the novel's interdiscursive engagement with the myriad pamphlets, conduct manuals, guides, and conference proceedings that recapitulate government communications protocols. Based on this framing, one could be forgiven for treating Peter as a fictive mouthpiece for McCarthy herself, who tellingly had titled her USIA lectures on the novel of ideas "The Fact in Fiction." Or rather, as Vendler phrases it in her review, Peter is presented as "a fantasy of what Miss McCarthy might be if she were an adolescent in the 1970s": a reflexively masculinized political and paraliterary (rather than aesthetic and literary) subject constituted by a genre of nationally representative speech defined by its persistent opposition to the "cold smug little voice" of the "Smith girl" abroad (236).

In contrast, *Birds of America*'s earlier and better half features Peter's mother: "the fair Rosamund" (22), a "feckless and dreamy harpsichordist" (42) and "real American [girl]" (50), whose interior world remains a mystery to Peter but is offered up to the reader through her soft-spoken, inverted speech and free indirect discourse. If McCarthy had confessed her ambivalence about James's influence on the novel's first half to Arendt, reviewers also noted the anachronistic Jamesian features of her style. Hilton Kramer dismissed Rosamund as an "overcultivated cipher," while *Vogue* observed that *Birds of America*'s opening chapters seemed like an "exercise in the mode of fiction Mary McCarthy has always said she despised: 'the ladies' magazine story.'"[79] One is inclined, then, to flip Vendler's biographical alliances between character type and institutional temporality. As the American girl of James's making, Rosamund is quietly enshrined in the belated institutional time of literary impersonation, while Peter loudly shores up the compulsory masculinity of her present-day liberal representation.

But perhaps it might be both more accurate and more useful to understand McCarthy's act of literary impersonation, like Stein's, as complicating any easy division between male/female and past/present. "Being abroad makes you conscious of the whole imitative side of human behavior," Peter writes to his mother in a long first-person epistolary chapter wedged into the middle of the novel (138). The chapter presents a strange formal shift away from the third-person omniscience of the Rosamund section and a generic shift away from the Novel. The letter is framed by McCarthy as a textual approximation of Peter's speech (he claims that he is writing as he is speaking), yet Peter does not voice the reported speech of his later political monologues. The formal transition that the genre of the letter stages, then, inverts the transition that we observed in Stein's *Fernhurst*. Whereas Stein stages the male bandar-log's grammatical slippage into a female imitator, McCarthy turns the female imitator into the male bandar-log over the course of *Birds of America*. The epistle, located right in the middle of the narrative, suspends Peter somewhere in between the two. He exists as both a feminized imitator of the Novel and a masculinized political ideologue, a writer and a speaker, an institutional subject beholden to James's past and McCarthy's present—in short, both a literary and paraliterary actor.

INSTITUTIONAL TIME WARPS

In a 2002 episode of the television show *The Sopranos*, Meadow Soprano, the Columbia College educated, upper-middle-class daughter of New Jersey mob boss Tony Soprano, tries to persuade her mother to let her study in Paris for a semester. "What, Mom, you've never heard of the restorative nature of travel?" snaps Meadow. "Read Henry James. Why does every college have a junior year abroad if there isn't a need for it?"[80] We could see Meadow's injunction to her mother to read Henry James as a sassy compression of the history of literary impersonation that I have theorized throughout this chapter, so rapidly does she connect James's novels to her school's study abroad program to the physically (and we can speculate, aesthetically) "restorative" nature of travel. Indeed, the historical trajectory she impresses upon her mother could pass through even more literary impersonators than the readers and writers I have focused on so far. A larger pantheon of such stylish figures could include Ann Landers, the syndicated advice columnist who invoked James's educated women when doling out her own words of wisdom to college-aged girls; Cybill Shepherd, the college-aged actress who played the lead in the 1974 film adaptation of *Daisy Miller*; Princess Soraya, the former wife of the Shah of Iran, who attempted to translate, produce, and star in James's 1877 novel *The American*; and even the novelist Cynthia Ozick, who while writing *Foreign Bodies* (2010), a gender-bending, study abroad retelling of James's 1903 novel *The Ambassadors*, confessed that in 1950, at the age of twenty-two, she had "become Henry James."

But Meadow's statement may also give us pause. From the point of view of historicist or contextualist criticism, doesn't it seem a tad reckless to move so rapidly across an entire century, holding only the institution constant? Doesn't it seem equally strange, in a discipline that persists in orienting its criticism to authors and texts, that a literary historical argument should pay so much attention to ordinary people? And so many people at that? The kinds of people who James once described in the New York Edition's preface to *The Portrait of a Lady* as "much smaller female fry" than either literary characters or their creators?

By way of conclusion, I want to revisit the question of institutional time but approach it from a slightly different angle, as a determinant of the objects of literary criticism. The immediate upshot of studying bad reading practices is that we can add more people to the mix—or rather, the infinitely rich textual activities that these people engage in. To do so is to alter not just the scale but also the structure of literary sociology. By interlacing institutional time, generational time, and the temporality of face-to-face interaction, as Anthony Giddens has persuasively encouraged scholars of modernity to do, we can locate in human actors the paradoxically suprahuman persistence of certain features of both literary discourse (like genre conventions) and speech. But we can also begin, in a more rigorously historicist way to expand the spatial and temporal axes of literary criticism. "Temporality is bound up with human agency and so is spatiality," Giddens observes.[81] Across both time and space, constancy is more prevalent than change. Indeed, the "capability of social systems to 'stretch' across time and space, rather than being localized" in one moment or place is made possible only through their reproduction by "knowledgeable human agents"; the source of "all fixity and the source of all change." The discursive activities of human agents must coexist as objects of analysis alongside both institutional structures and literary objects. Only in this way can readers speak next to their books. And only in this way can books speak through their readers.

CHAPTER TWO

Reading as Feeling

"I love you" needs my own language.

SYLVIA PLATH (1957)[1]

To discuss the effectiveness of a program of cultural exchange in developing good international relations is to raise at once the question of whether familiarity breeds love or contempt.

ROBERT SPILLER, "American Studies Abroad" (1967)[2]

FEELING RULES

The first poem in Ted Hughes's anthology *Birthday Letters* (1998) is titled "Fulbright Scholars," and it unreliably memorializes Hughes's 1956 reading of a news photograph of the American participants in the prestigious Fulbright Program. Among them is the writer Sylvia Plath, Hughes's soon-to-be wife. Quickly bypassing the photograph's caption, the poem's speaker imagines that he may have lingered on Plath's face with the tentative, yet admiring, hesitance of an anthropologist trying to make up his mind about an envoy from a newly discovered and distant civilization. "Maybe I noticed you," he muses, "Maybe I weighed you up, feeling unlikely. / Noted your long hair, loose waves— / Your Veronica Lake bang. Not what it hid. / It would appear blond. And your grin / Your exaggerated American / Grin for the camera, the judges, the strangers, the frighteners."[3] The halting study of Plath that opens "Fulbright Scholars," shifting as it does between reading as a proleptic projection of intimacy and reading as a critical assessment of national representation, cautiously entwines the two ways in which Hughes will come to know his Sylvia. There is the "real" Plath that Hughes, and only Hughes, will soon find hidden behind the Hollywood sheen of her blond "Veronica Lake bang." But there is also her "grin," the "exaggerated American / Grin" of the Fulbright scholar that is ominously capitalized and enjambed, and thus does double duty as both a descriptive detail and a communicative imperative directed to Plath: "Grin for the cameras, the judges, the strangers, the frighteners."

Hughes's attempt to move between the intimate particularities of his relationship with Plath and Plath's status as a nationalized subject recalls the previous chapter's argument about the irresolvable tension between individual acts of communication (i.e., contextually specific and embodied) and national representation (i.e., abstract and metonymic) in American readers and writers from Henry James to Mary McCarthy. Yet "Fulbright Scholars," which was written from Hughes's British point of view, shows us more clearly what reconciling these two modes of expression might look like in a non-American reader's response to Americanized acts of international communication. At first, Plath appears to the speaker of the poem through her publicity photograph as the quintessentially imposing American cultural diplomat of the 1950s, her toothy and metaphoric goodwill linked through her "long hair, loose waves," and "Veronica Lake bang" to the global distribution and propaganda networks of Hollywood films. Yet as the poem's speaker enhances the memory he is creating of her, Plath emerges as an embodied, emotionally available, and curiously unvoiced entity. Indeed, her physical presentation as an attractive and lovable silhouette is emphasized repeatedly throughout the poems in *Birthday Letters*. Hughes may swap out his Tinseltown references for the consumerist fads of Madison Avenue ("The Chipmunk") and the decaying upper crustiness of Boston architecture ("Caryatids"), but these only serve as backdrops against which to chronicle the nonverbal forms of intimacy that Plath's diplomatic presence inspires: all of the aching smiles, laughs, touches, and glances mediated by newspaper photographs ("Fulbright Scholars"), advertisements ("The Chipmunk"), and snapshots ("Caryatids"). Hughes's place-specific references thus interestingly invert Lytle Shaw's characterization of the transatlantic poet as an "on-location" ethnographer who responds with gestures, glances, and body language to subjects with whom he cannot speak.[4] Though at home in the United Kingdom, Hughes embeds the emotional dispatches of his silent American specimen—the feelings she incarnates and inspires—in her distinctly socionational milieu.

Hughes's confessional poetry thus entwines a feature of both international communication and reading that remained muted in the previous chapter's argument about speech and literary impersonation: the physicalized production, transmission, and reception of feeling. Unlike speech or style or the act of self-stylization, all of which seem to take place at the interactional surface of communication, the feelings evoked by human interaction are often theorized by sociolinguists as bodily, interior, precognitive, spontaneously generated, and subjective.[5] By these accounts, one does not learn how to feel stylishly or how to imitate the feelings of others as one does with speech or writing. Instead, we simply feel what we feel when we encounter another person—or in Hughes's case, when he projects a future encounter with a person by observing (or imagining that he has observed) a photograph of her face. On a very fundamental level, the same proposition holds true for how writers and literary scholars have discussed the feelings elicited by reading literature. "There are times when a feeling . . . comes to me, as if something is there, beneath the surface of my understanding, waiting for me to grasp it," wrote Plath in her journals, a long and oft-cited passage in which she struggles to describe her reaction to "the fine print, the swift, colored motion" of the best literary writing (15). Plath's metaphorical treatment of feeling as a deep and ungovernable wellspring echoes how distinct and otherwise incompatible groups of critics have talked about the first-person feelings evoked by reading literature, from the New Critics of the 1920s to the literary ethicists of today.[6] Even materialist scholars who have resisted treating feeling as a pure psychological state, choosing instead to approach it as a structured formation, remain less attentive than they might be to the specific spaces, expressions, and bodily practices through which literary "meanings and values" become "actively lived and felt."[7] Intriguingly, then, while methods of pairing affect with reading have varied wildly amid scholarly camps, the literary discourses of feeling—what we talk about when we talk about the feelings prompted by reading—remain polarized. An analysis of feeling is too often either the idealist pursuit of what blooms in each of us, separately and alone, or a symptom of structures so large and encompassing—capitalism or the state—that much social and situational particularity is lost.

Yet there is no compelling reason to assume that the depths of individual emotion remain immune to socially situated protocols of expression and interaction. As I will argue in this chapter, the midcentury boom in international communication reveals how a dense apparatus of institutions, literary and paraliterary texts, and human agents connected practices of reading American literature to norms governing how and what one learned to feel toward others—specifically, how one could learn to feel love by reading in overtly physicalized and even "shamefully concupiscent" ways, to recall Leslie Fiedler's hope for paraliterary reading that we encountered in the introduction. Only by explicating the textually and institutionally mediated contours of love's "feeling rules," as Arlie Hochschild refers to the internalized and imaginative protocols that regulate emotion, can we begin to properly historicize feeling while keeping individual actors in focus.[8] Or, more accurately, we can begin to unpack the messy and conflictual processes of learning to feel in collectively determined and discursive ways, bringing to light what sociolinguist James Wilce has called the "genres" of "emotional expression."[9] The discourses of what I identify as reading with feeling were defined through and against the midcentury's more dominant reading practice: the dispassionate and avowedly non-concupiscent teachings of the New Critics, whose prominent positions in national institutions of literary education eclipsed the alternative models of reading that were formulated in larger, less nationally enclosed spaces. It is no accident, then, that I locate practices of reading with feeling in institutions where reading American literature most thoroughly bisected internationalized protocols of communication: the Fulbright Program and its assorted parent institutions, from the American Studies Association (ASA) to the International Communication Agency (ICA) to the sprawling network of American studies departments abroad.

It is also in these institutional spaces that we can recover the textual evidence, both literary and paraliterary, necessary to lay claim to feeling as a carefully cultivated social practice. For both Hochschild and Wilce, the process of learning how to feel proceeds through, and is documented by, verbal assessments of one's own feelings and others' apparently emotional displays. We can discern a highly stylized version of the former in the one-sided monologue that Hughes stages in "Fulbright Scholars." As he scans the display in the Strand, the poem's speaker questions his reading of Plath's photograph— did he notice her or did he not? He concludes that whether he noticed her or not, the whole experience left him "feeling unlikely." By the end of the poem, this feeling of unlikeliness has become an object of criticism. As the speaker walks away from the photograph display and bites into a peach he has purchased, he finds himself suddenly judgmental, "dumbfounded afresh / by my ignorance of the simplest things." For Hughes's speaker, the encounter with Plath's photograph becomes intelligible as a discursive and educative occasion, an opportunity first to voice, and later to sanction, his perception of his own uncertainty. "Fulbright Scholars" thus presents its readers with one of the rarest of all emotionally reflexive displays: a man chiding himself for his lack of certainty.

For verbal judgments of others' emotional displays, we need look no further than Plath's cheerful testimony of her readerly romance with Hughes to the 1956 United States-United Kingdom Fulbright Commission. Although "Fulbright Scholars" was drafted nearly half a century after the couple's doomed relationship had come to an end, Plath's account suggests that the commission would have been thrilled to read the poem and doubly thrilled by Plath and Hughes's eventual marriage. "I went to London yesterday to make my announcement of marriage to the Fulbright [Commission]," Plath wrote to her mother on November 1, 1956, worried that the commission would strip her of her fellowship if she confessed her affair with Hughes, a poet she had met at Cambridge and whose work she had read and "much admired."[10] But as it turned out, the commission was far more sympathetic to her international liaison than Plath, a Smith alumna and product of the women's college system, had expected. "They raised no question of continuing my grant," she announced with apparent relief, and added, "I did not expect, however, the royal welcome I got! Congratulations from the handsome young American head who told me my work, both social and scholastic, in Cambridge was so fine they wished they could publicize it (!) . . . One of the main qualifications of the grant, I discovered, is that you take back your cultural experience to America, and they were enchanted at my suggestion that I was taking back double in the form of Ted." In Plath's account of her testimony before the commission, the "work" of the Fulbright scholar, described by the "handsome young American head" of the commission as equal parts "social" and "scholastic," reaches its triumphant apotheosis in the institution of marriage. Plath's plurality as an institutional subject—both a scholar and a wife—thus offers a model of international communication celebrated, and even publicized, by the commission for magnifying the exchange of "cultural experience." She was not only bringing her love of Hughes's poetry back to readers in the United States, but she was also "bringing back double in the form of Ted": Ted incarnate, a lover and a husband, as well as a reader of her work and a writer of poems about her, the Fulbright scholar. Given the national-institutional pressures that framed their relationship, one can better understand why Hughes's speaker may have chided himself for his lack of certainty. "Feeling unlikely," while fine for prolepsis and the poetry of recollection, was not a situationally appropriate response to the international circuit of feeling celebrated by the commission.

My emphasis on learning to feel through institutionalized practices of reading thus recasts feeling as a technique of self-governance and social expression rather than a disorderly and unconscious precursor to observable forms of individual action or behavior. Importantly, however, learning to feel does not always take place through explicit statements or voiced sanctions of emotional management, as Hochschild and Wilce claim and as we see in Plath's testimony. Learning to feel frequently depends on analyzing the expressive features of human interactions that are not exclusively or even primarily linguistic in nature. And learning to communicate what one feels just as often relies on similarly nonverbal cues. In contrast to the speech acts venerated by James and his readers as works of art, Hughes's reading response in "Fulbright Scholars" showcases the physical actions that his speaker sees Plath perform. The speaker subsequently entextualizes these actions and reciprocates in kind throughout the poems in *Birthday Letters*, with reported smiles, laughs, eye contact, and bodily posturing. Imaging one's reading of a publicity photograph in place of a text, then, functions less as a literal act of reading and more as an allegory for the kinds of expressive behaviors we may begin to read out of literary and paraliterary texts once discourse is no longer our primary criterion for what counts as meaningful communication.

We know from the previous chapter that broadening the category of communication to include nonverbal acts was crucial to the midcentury public sphere. As we will see throughout this chapter, the feeling rules articulated by the Fulbright Program, the ASA, ICA, and the international network of American studies departments relied on some rather unusual assumptions about the relationship between learning to feel and the ways in which readers' nonverbal responses to reading American literary texts communicated these feelings to others. This is not to claim that these readers' discursive responses, either in written or spoken form, were unimportant. Rather, it is to point to how nonverbal actions were imagined as compensating for— and amplifying—the affective impact of discursive acts that risked being distorted, muted, or otherwise lost in international transmission or translation. Unlike many literary critics of the time, the administrators, teachers, and scholars involved in designing the Fulbright Program tended to describe reader's physical manifestations of feeling not just as communicative acts, but as acts whose communicative efficacy transcended the efficacy of linguistic exchange in constructing and stabilizing international reading publics. For Hughes and Plath, F. O. Matthiessen, Robert Spiller, Alfred Kazin, John Ashbery, and other scholars who populate this chapter, the literary discourses that linked the act of reading American fiction to the emergence of nonverbal expressions of feeling formed the connective tissue of what Arkansas senator William J. Fulbright himself described in 1946 as the ultimate goal of all international communication: "To promote love between nations."[11]

WHAT WE TALK ABOUT WHEN
WE TALK ABOUT LOVE

To provide the historical context for institutional discourses of love, we only have to consider the second epigraph to this chapter, which comes to us by way of Robert Spiller, one-time ASA president and Fulbright Program administrator. "To discuss the effectiveness of a program of cultural exchange in developing good international relations is to raise at once the question of whether familiarity breeds love or contempt," Spiller wrote in 1967. Issued exactly twenty years after the whirlwind expansion of American studies departments across the Atlantic and Pacific began in earnest, Spiller's assessment of the program's historical "effectiveness" points back in time to its origins in the summer of 1947. This was the year when the first Fulbright administrators and American studies professors like Matthiessen, Spiller, Fiedler, and Alfred Kazin (who wrote Plath a letter of recommendation for her Fulbright application) began to theorize how international readers' emotional responses to American literary texts could "breed love." Importantly, what they imagined was a mass-mediated love—a love that, by transcending any individual instance of reading, made itself available to international publics as an active, reciprocal, and reproducible structure of feeling; a love that was thus capable of governing not only an individual's emotional responses but also an increasingly unruly geopolitical order at midcentury. Hence the commission's delight at how the program's "social" and "scholastic" dimensions had facilitated Plath's marriage to Hughes. No doubt marriage must have struck them as the institutional *ne plus ultra* of love, insofar as the legal order it imposed on Plath and Hughes's personal relationship microcosmically modeled the liberal political order Spiller and others imagined love could impose onto "international relations" through the reading of literature. No doubt, too, that the commission's feeling rules firmed up Plath's commitment to her autobiographical novel in progress, first titled *Hill of Leopards*, later changed to *Falcon Yard*, which would tell the tale of "an American girl finding her soul in a year (or rather, nine Fulbright months) at Cambridge." "Novel: *Falcon Yard*: central image: *love, a falcon*, striking once and for all," she noted in her diary (180, italics in original). "American versus British. Can I do it? Over a year maybe I can. Style is the thing. 'I love you' needs my own language" (185). Similar to Spiller's imagination of the link between reading for feeling and feeling as a geopolitical structure, Plath's confessional narrative was also shaped by the dialectic between national representation ("American versus British") and emotive genres of communication ("'I love you' needs my own language").

Ultimately, Plath's stylized language for "I love you" ended up differing greatly from the US government's anodyne proclamation of a mutually assured "love between nations," a point I will return to later in this chapter. For now, it is enough to observe that for the Fulbright Commission, the most appealing discursive aspect of love was how effectively its feeling rules inverted the material realities that made the international mobility of readers and teachers of reading possible in the first place. The 1946 brainchild of Senator Fulbright, his eponymous "exchange-of-persons" scholarship program was funded by the Office of Foreign Liquidation's sales of overseas properties abandoned after World War II; transactions conducted exclusively in depreciated foreign currencies now that the dollar reigned supreme as the Bretton Woods system's international monetary standard.[12] As Fulbright proposed in his amendment to the Surplus Property Act of 1944, the money from these property sales would help pay for equal numbers of American scholarship recipients to spend a year studying or teaching in an international university and for non-American scholarship recipients to spend a year doing the same in the United States. But despite the program's claims to international reciprocity, the equal "exchange of persons" proved deeply misleading. When one tallies the actual numbers of people exchanged in the 1950s through 1970s, American scholarship recipients far outnumbered their non-American counterparts. "Exchange of persons," then, offered a more fitting description for how the program's financial arrangements worked: by exchanging money for people. Foreign capital, bound up in discarded property and devalued currency, was exchanged for American dollars, only to be plugged back into international circulation in the human form of scholars, teachers, and writers from the United States, the vast majority of whom were literary critics and professors of American literature. This arrangement was, according to the State Department, a creative and benevolent extension of the United States' shift from a "debtor" to a "creditor nation" in the postwar era.[13] And everyone, it seems, wanted the chance to play the cultural creditor. As Plath wrote in a self-deprecating journal entry some months before submitting her application, "There is always the ambitious project of trying for a Fulbright to Europe (only a million people want them; no competition really)" (166).

Underlying these feeling rules was the commission's belief that teaching people how to love and how to communicate their love for one another could restore a sense of reciprocity to a materially imbalanced system of internationalized property relations. By the time Spiller sat down to assess the program's effectiveness in 1967, the program's administrators had already taken some obvious steps to inculcate into program participants and observers the expressive practices of love. From its inception through the late 1980s, the commission released a series of promotional books that rewrote scholars' post-fellowship debriefings and testimonials as sentimental nonfiction short stories. Taken together, these hundreds of stories reveal the staggering promiscuity of love in the language of returning Fulbright scholars across disciplines: scientists "fell in love with" their friendly hosts, who promptly fell in love with them in return; scholars conducted passionate "love affairs" with French, Sanskrit, Japanese, and Hindi, making these foreign tongues pliable to the expressive needs of one English speaker after another; teachers came back to the United States "madly in love" with the local merchants who showered them with free wares; moments of clear communication with students of another nationality were tenderly figured as "budding love." Even the most "jaded" of scholarship recipients, according to their preprogram self-assessments, quoted liberally from Walt Whitman and e. e. cummings on the power of love to transcend national difference.[14] Bound together in books with titles like *The Fulbright Difference* or *The Fulbright Experience*, and prefaced by Senator Fulbright's 1945 promotional materials for the program, these collected volumes of international love stories served as bibliographic vehicles for standardizing the program's feeling rules. More powerfully, however, these books also offered readers the opportunity to envision not just the affective lives of individual scholars but also the collective political aspirations of an entire nation. Through the nationalized organization of individual testimonies, the collected volumes reinforced the commission's notion that the authors' stories of love were constitutive of a broader geopolitics, whereby love could come to possess extraordinary powers of scale, transmuting individual experiences and expressions of love into love for social abstractions: peoples, languages, and nations. The production of these paraliterary texts and the stories contained therein thus made it not just possible but quite natural to speak of the love of "one nation for another," even though such an exchange of affection was, quite literally, impossible.

All of this sentimentality makes for a very pretty picture—much like the photo op that inspired Hughes's poem. But it also generates a peculiarly transactional conception of how love worked in the 1950s and 1960s international public sphere. When understood as a materially contingent set of regulations on self-expression and social interaction, the love felt and expressed by the Fulbright scholar asserted not only emotion's use value but also its exchange value: a market-based appraisal of feeling's efficacy that reflected the US-backed liberal capitalism that Fulbright also supported through the Surplus Property Act and the Marshall Plan. As Plath's letter to her mother makes clear, her marriage announcement was immediately reframed by commission members as a quantitative measurement of communicative utility. She was "taking back double" in the form of Ted, and thus amplifying the transactional value of her social and scholastic interactions on the flip side of the exchange. A more troubling vision of the program's affective economy, then, emerges in a subsequent letter she wrote to her mother, in which she described how her desire to write an international love story was guaranteed to "drive the Fulbright Commission wild with delight" (268). "I have the most blazing idea of all now," she declared. "Out of the many vital, funny, and profound experiences as an American girl in Cambridge, I am going to write a series of tight, packed, perfect short stories which I will make into a novel. . . . All the notes I've taken on socialized medicine, British men, characters, etc. will come in. Ted is with me all the way, and we are rather excited about this. It is 'my own corner' and his criticism as it is in progress, from the British slant, with his infallible eye, will be invaluable. What a product of the Fulbright!" The only downside to her "product," as she conceived of it, was the inevitable time lag between her production of the novel from her "notes" and her readers' consumption of it as literature. "The hardest thing for me now is not to share all this with a rich community of friends," she complained to her mother.

While her penchant for sharing "with a rich community" of readers may seem generous, such generosity was predicated on an extravagant fantasy of material possession and possessiveness. Not only did Plath cordon off her knowledge of "British men, characters, etc." as "my own corner," but she analogized her assemblage of amorous experiences to "having discovered the one only biggest diamond mine in the world and having to sit inside alone full of radiance and not tell anyone." Real enrichment, then, depended on letting these gems—notes turned into short stories, failed relationships turned into a successful marriage, lumps of coal turned into diamonds—loose on an international market; a market that would drive up their exchange value and help her reap the profits accordingly. Like the ominous diamond stickpin that Marco, the violent woman-hater in Plath's *The Bell Jar* (1963), will give to Plath's protagonist Esther Greenwood to claim her as his property, the radiance of the diamond mine Plath claims for herself as a product of love is saddled with a logic of market commodification that sits uncomfortably against the free flow of intimacy across people and nations; a violent extraction economy rooted in colonial relations that represents the flip side of the liberal internationalism the Fulbright claimed to represent.

Although the liberals of the period were—and continue to be—read as unabashed sentimentalists, we may see how an evaluative conception of love emerged from an institutional structure that relied on the exchange of cold, hard cash for feeling individuals.[15] It is striking how insistently the commission ascribes to love what Lauren Berlant has described as "an alter-power so far mainly given over to the money form."[16] The alter-power of money does not derive from its material capabilities—what money can and cannot purchase on the market. Rather, it originates from its ability to provide a "pervasive virtual infrastructure" that encourages and enables individuals to feel bound to one another, as well as to the imaginary totality of the world, inextricably and in perpetuity. In contrast to neo-Marxist thinkers who see love as radically opposed to the object relationships secured by market capitalism—propriety, possessive individualism, and narcissism—Berlant suggests that love cannot exist, either as a feeling or an ideology, without the "inconvenient appetites" that converge on such market-driving sentiments as self-interest or the narcissistic desire to encounter oneself in the people and things one loves. While we may want to sanction her dilution of love as unequivocally ugly or reprobate or pessimistic, the interlacing of feeling with capitalist desire invites us to delineate the historical conditions under which certain forms and expressions of intimacy became legible as "good love," while others were deemed "bad love"—that is, the institutional spaces where people with prices changed hands. To reframe Berlant's provocation in Plath's explicitly aesthetic terminology, we are invited to understand how different readers and writers developed different styles and genres of expressing "I love you," as well as why some of these styles and the forms of love they index were valued above others. The answer, I want to suggest, does not lie in the reified affective values of "good love" over "bad love" but in the material structures and literary discourses that underwrote the international mobility of teachers of reading and readers of American fiction.

Why have studies of international communication failed to appreciate the relationship between the material foundations of reading and feeling? By proudly touting their status as demystified readers of institutional discourse, many literary critics, historians, and in particular, scholars of American studies have eclipsed the ways in which their own critical discourses sanction certain readerly feelings while skewering others. In this sense, the last decade of scholarly production in American studies strikes me as an invaluable resource, for the feeling rules such work archives. Once the Cold War burned out and critiques of state power became de rigueur in American studies, love presented itself as one of the most powerful justifications for the discipline's abiding investment in the nation-state as its object of analysis and its organizing episteme. When considered from a more polemical angle, one could say that love is the only compelling reason for the discipline's continued existence at all. Take, for instance, Donald Pease and Winfried Fluck's confession of their melancholic attachment to the "lost love object" of exceptionalism, an emotional prelude to their assertion that the future of American studies must necessarily involve scholarly attempts to "bear witness" to this "injurious thing" called love.[17] Alongside their sweeping claims consider how quickly Dana D. Nelson invokes love to ward off her disciplinary anxieties, when she claims that she can only proceed with her work as an Americanist by "falling in love with [America], not idealistically, but with open eyes."[18] And from a more explicitly pedagogical stance, note how Dana Heller begins her fond recollections of teaching students in Moscow about the "transcendent dream" of American studies by appealing to Willy Loman's desire "to love and be loved" by the entire world.[19] No doubt there is something weird and intensely discomfiting about being implicated so explicitly in one's own object of critique, as these American studies scholars are by virtue of their disciplinary affiliations. But equally odd is the unwillingness to historicize the feeling rules that constitute and sustain this particular field as such—a field whose disproportionate importance in the American university and postwar public sphere cannot be overstated. Like a jilted lover who, in the same breath, announces his hatred for his former paramour and then dials her number from memory, American studies can't figure out how to quit the love of its past. Rather, the discipline has wholeheartedly enshrined love in its epistemological, pedagogical, and communicative practices. To understand why requires turning back in time to the internationalization of American studies and its institutionalization of reading for feeling.

AMERICAN STUDIES:
LOVABLE CANONS, PASSIONATE CRITICS

Despite the ease with which scholars of American studies from Spiller to Pease have moved from love to disciplinarity, the alliance of feeling with critical discourse has a complex institutional history. It begins not with the end of the Cold War, but with the Cold War's origins in the late 1940s, when the expansion of American studies departments to Eastern Europe emerged as the ASA, the State Department, and the Fulbright Commission's highest priority. If this geographically expansive institution-building mission provided federal bureaucracies with an early opportunity to test their theories of international communication and its political efficacy, it also lent ideological coherence to the fledgling discipline of American studies, both in the United States and outside of its borders. Although the early 1940s had witnessed the rise of American studies departments at Harvard, Yale, the University of Pennsylvania, and a dozen or so other institutions of higher education, the proto-discipline had yet to reach either a substantive consensus on "the nature of American experience" or a methodological consensus on "ways to study that experience," according to one anxious scholar.[20] From Gene Wise's historical analysis of American studies' discursive construction through the 1940s and 1950s, we know that this consensus ultimately came to rest on reflexive articulations of "the exceptionalist thesis": a sweeping assertion of American cultural distinction grounded in the belief that the "American mind" was "characteristically hopeful, innocent, individualistic, pragmatic, idealistic." What is less well known is how the discipline's constitution of its objects of study and its methods first postulated a link between reading a canon of American literary works and a reader's capacity to feel and communicate love.

The alliance between reading and feeling, I want to suggest, was what laid the groundwork for American studies' shift from a proto-discipline into a fully formed and internationalized disciplinary institution. The human agent at the center of it all was Spiller, whose résumé boasted a mind-boggling array of leadership positions at the nexus of literary study, university administration, and the federal government. He was, among other things, a founding member of the Fulbright board, president of the ASA and founder of its journal *American Quarterly*, chair of the University of Pennsylvania's American Studies department, editor of *The Literary History of the United States* (1948), and adviser to the American Council of Learned Societies' (ACLS's) new American Studies Abroad initiative. If, by 1940, Vernon Parrington had established himself as the discipline's intellectual progenitor with the publication of *Main Currents in American Thought* (1927), Spiller served as its institutional and international architect. He was a scholar who "knew more buttons to push in more bureaus than any other man in academic life," according to his admiring colleagues, as well as a savvy fund raiser whose "knowledge of the indirect and murky mazes of Washington and New York bureaucracy"[21] helped him raise substantial funds for the ASA. Spiller's camaraderie with the Carnegies and the Rockefellers, congressmen, and scholars made him the ideal plural actor to connect literary-intellectual labor to international communication. As he described his work in a dispatch on "American Studies and Foreign Policy" to the ASA, successful international communication required "a total and unified national character and culture which could be described, documented, and presented in a single package to our potential friends" around the world (13). And while the Norwegian poet and Fulbright administrator Sigmund Skard, Spiller's counterpart and frequent collaborator in Europe, noted that Spiller prided himself on his "complete lack of sentimentalism,"[22] his colleagues at the ASA and on the commission celebrated how powerfully Spiller's consolidation of American literary culture "made new claims on your heart."[23]

But why were such claims on the heart necessary in the first place? Spiller's desire to communicate a "total and unified" national culture emerged, in no small part, as a defensive response to what he perceived as haphazard approaches to reading American literature in the international public sphere. Since 1930, when publishers began to flood foreign book markets with cheap paperbacks of American novels and American translations en masse, the problem arose of distinguishing what Spiller called "our best writers" from "our worst ones." Amid the rapidly expanding international consumer demand for American literature, the project of bestowing distinction onto America's best writers seemed especially pressing to Spiller and his fellow literary taste makers, particularly given the tendency of international readers to confuse the former for the latter. In a 1946 *Life* article titled "U.S. Books Abroad," Spiller's friend and frequent correspondent Malcolm Cowley disdainfully anointed Margaret Mitchell's Reconstruction-era melodrama *Gone with the Wind* the "best example of a book that has received longer and more admiring reviews in the foreign countries than at home."[24] As evidence, Cowley cited the novel's stupefying international sales numbers and reach—1.6 million foreign copies sold in eighteen languages. But he also recounted a meeting with an esteemed German writer who had brought out a velvet-bound copy of *Gone with the Wind* from a secret vault in his house, cradled the book in his arms, and announced to Cowley that it was only after reading *Gone with the Wind* "not once, not twice, but three times, that I began to know what your country was like." From the German writer's declaration of his devoted rereadings of the novel to his material fetishization of the book as an object, we can deduce his quasi-spiritual attachment to American literature as a medium for social and political truth seeking—an aspiration that, as Cowley pointed out in his article, was hardly unique to this particular bad reader or even to the German public sphere. While such affections were not inherently unwanted, there was something specifically insidious about the truth communicated in the act of reading and rereading and re-rereading a novel like *Gone with the Wind*. Mitchell and other "specialists in colorful violence," as Cowley classified hard-boiled pulp novelists like Paul Cain and Damon Runyon, had proven popular with international audiences "less for their excellence" than for their "reportorial content": a combination of sensational plots and regional dialects that satisfied the curiosities of a readership "hungry for information about America." For Cowley and others, the problem was not that readers had turned to literary representation as a source of national "information" over and above aesthetic pleasure, literary appreciation, or as a model for individual self-stylization. Instead, the problem was that the information communicated by popular fiction appeared hopelessly "one-sided": not verifiable, not self-evident, and not particularly conducive to love in its presentation of American social and political life.

The informational value of literary discourse is a point that I will explore more fully in the final two chapters of this book, particularly as it frames questions about the incommensurability between the communicative labor of bureaucratic actors and the literary labor of writing. Here, however, I want to consider how Spiller and Cowley's concerns about which literary texts and genres would communicate truthful information about the nation to international reading publics reimagines the task of literary canon making in a way Pierre Bourdieu did not fully anticipate when he theorized cultural capital bestowed onto reading subjects by institutions of literacy education. For Bourdieu, and later for John Guillory, the historical intrigue of the modern literary canon resides in how its formation enabled the school and the school's gatekeepers to reproduce forms of cultural distinction and social inequality specific to the school's practices of reading. These distinctions cut across the exclusionary categories of race, gender, and class to create a specious unity of privileged, "canonical knowledge" enshrined in a privileged collection of texts: the properly "literary canon," which has remained strikingly consistent over the twentieth century.[25] But in 1947, Spiller and the ASA had the opposite problem. There existed no unified or transhistorical canon of American literature to offer to international readers and thus no corpus of texts that valued certain aesthetic forms or literacy practices over others in a nationalized hierarchy of knowledge production. Absent the pedagogical apparatuses of literary consecration and conformity produced by the school, such as classroom syllabi, reading lists or distribution requirements, international readers' default practice of reading was to read for information communicated about America—or so Spiller, Cowley, and other literary critics claimed. And reading for information, Spiller worried, was not compatible with reading to foster the deep and transformative feelings of love toward American literature that would lead to "the development of international good will" (1). Not only did international readers not know what to read, then, but they also did not know how to cultivate the specific techniques of reading that would result in "the softening of antagonism and the improvement of friendship" between imagined communities of nations (4). If, in the last chapter, we witnessed James's shift from the voices of American figures to voicing America, then Spiller's tripartite scale of emotional escalation pivoted from American forms to American figures to the figure of America.

The problem of American literature's cultural capital at midcentury did, however, result in a number of explicit and authoritative statements about the criteria one ought to use to assess the relative value of different forms of literary production. "We need not deliberately misrepresent, but we may select our evidence," Spiller announced to the ASA (4). His framing of canon formation with such politesse—what the ASA "may" do and what it "need not do" in singling out certain works of literature as nationally representative—foreshadows his discourse of aesthetic value as a function of the genteel social values thematized within literature. "If we are providing a list of books for translation into Hindi or Arabic," Spiller wrote, "we may select a history which stresses our gift of independence to Cuba rather than our intervention in the recent arms crisis. And if we are choosing only one recent novel, we may prefer the mature character analysis of Bellow's *Herzog* to the abnormal violence of Mailer's *An American Dream*" (4). The correlation between aesthetic value and political representation, while putatively based on formal qualities like "character analysis," actually makes Spiller's judgments of inclusion and exclusion a function of these novels' projected affective effects: the sensorially manic interiority of Mailer's murderous protagonist corresponds to an air of violent coercion, while Bellow's novel about an intellectual's struggle against ideology embraces romantic humanism. Of course, neither *Herzog* nor *An American Dream* fit neatly into the category of the middlebrow novel, which Christina Klein sees as central to Cold War literary sentimentality.[26] Yet Spiller, in his institutional position as a Fulbright administrator, nevertheless comes across as a far more literal minded reader of literature than he does in his scholarly work, so straightforward is the link he draws from literary themes to the political affects and effects of reading.[27] His politics of canon formation, when understood as contiguous with the politics of communicating information, assumes an affectively amplified relationship to practices of aesthetic evaluation—a sharp contrast to the discourses of rationality and detachment that scholars tend to associate with midcentury "information warfare."[28] We could even understand the intensified affective mediation of literary value, reading, and information transmission as the crux of what Richard T. Arndt, USIA attaché and president of the Fulbright Association, deemed the "American intellectual style": an emotionally heightened interrelation between national art and politics to the "foreigners who understand and love us."[29]

Not all administrators were as straightforward as Spiller in their discourses of literary value or in their theories of how aesthetic forms intersected with political representation. To teach international readers how to read American literature properly, Spiller tapped a number of prominent public intellectuals to serve as the inaugural recipients of Fulbright fellowships to Europe. His first generation of "warm-hearted communicators"—"intellectuals/adminis-trators/faithful bureaucrats" like F. O. Matthiessen, Alfred Kazin, and Les-lie Fiedler—bore the responsibility for organizing the first American studies departments, literary curricula, and even USIA libraries in international uni-versities (8). Today, the term *public intellectual* is often invoked nostalgically and retroactively as a catchall category, one that includes any midcentury scholar or critic with even the most tenuous nonacademic affiliations: to little and big magazines, political parties, and any other form of institutional orga-nizing that addressed itself to a larger public beyond the university. Conflat-ing good liberals with incendiary leftists, and atheistic socialists with Christian democrats, what the term actually registered was the partial convergence of aesthetic criticism with the Cold War politics of the American university, now propelled into the national consciousness by debates over academic freedom, progressive education, and the spread of communism on campus. Emerging from the American studies departments at Harvard and Yale, the politically inflected literacy practices of public intellectuals developed in opposition to two prevailing modes of reading: the seemingly unregulated consumption of American literature as information on the global market, which I have just discussed; and the notionally apolitical reading and writing practices of the New Critics, freshly consecrated as "literary" by English departments in institutions of higher education across the United States.

Turning from the canon's administrators to the canon's teachers takes us from the social imaginary of reading for feeling to its actual forms and techniques. Whereas Spiller, Cowley, and the ASA perceived of canon for-mation as itself a process of sui generis institutional formation—the im-position of some modicum of structure in the midst of anarchic literary consumption—the Fulbright intellectuals/administrators/bureaucrats posi-tioned their institution-building efforts as a dialogic response to the liter-ary methods of the New Critics. For Alfred Kazin, a 1951 Fulbright scholar to Cambridge and founder of the British Association for American Studies (BAAS), New Criticism's modish techniques of literary evaluation had im-properly emphasized the impersonal vocabularies of modernism, thereby deflecting from the real urgency of criticism today: the "passionate decla-ration of the true nature of man and what his proper destiny must be."[30] Eschewing T. S. Eliot's states of stylistic "fact" as an objective discourse of aesthetic form, Kazin drew inspiration from Ralph Waldo Emerson's "old Transcendentalist passion," as well as the "wholeness of passion" exalted by Walt Whitman's *Democratic Vistas*. Both represented unapologetically emotive models, Kazin argued, for how the patriotic American critic could use and teach the "passionate operation of his intelligence," and ultimately how he could produce a genre of criticism that Kazin called *histoire morale*: "the kind of criticism that ... sums up the spirit of the age in which we live and asks us to transcend it." What expressive forms this criticism would take remained an open question. Indeed, Kazin's invocation of passion as a descriptor for both the "passionate encounter between the writer [of criticism] and the book," as well as the "passionate journey of perception" that yielded a "constant sense of new *discovery*" for a reader, did not specify how passion would perform the critical work Kazin attributed to it. Or, put differently, Kazin left it to his readers and students to parse what it meant to produce passion through a specifically textual "operation" or "declaration," as well as what was at stake in such declarations.

The question of passion's communicative forms is worth examining more closely in light of the fact that passion is so often proffered as one of the feeling rules of love—a rule not about the content of feeling, but its intensity and, by extension, its temporality. Consider the particular temporality Kazin assigns to the passionate: nowness or newness. While the canonized aesthetic values of New Criticism appeared rule bound, timeless, and hemmed in by the "false sophistication" of its current practitioners—Cleanth Brooks and Robert Penn Warren, the "galley slaves" of T. S. Eliot—Kazin's discourse of passionate criticism took great pains to emphasize its coming-into-being as a product of the moment ("the spirit of the age in which we live"). The reflexive construction of passionate criticism's ongoingness—and thus its openness to change—aligned neatly with the commission's liberal discourses of international political openness, particularly when read alongside Kazin's insistence that passionate criticism could "create a future in keeping with man's imagination." To fully appreciate the performative texture of this demand, consider the emphasis on creating futurity in comparison to the previous chapter's theorization of speech and literary impersonation. Unlike the genre of the lecture, which made no timely or actionable demands on James's audience members (i.e., they did not feel compelled to parrot his speech at the exact moment in which he delivered it), the passionate declaration of the critic appeals to the reader's keen faculties of "perception" and, in doing so, commands a nearly instantaneous and transformative response. Indeed, the simultaneity of passion converts reading from an act of aesthetic appreciation or information gathering into an imagined interpersonal "encounter": a moment of shockingly "new discovery" of the relational potentiality among a writer, a reader, and a text.

Through passion's periodicity, we can see how Kazin's approach to reading lends some historical specificity to Stanley Cavell's theorization of the passionate utterance as a form of speech that "makes demands upon the singular body," betraying an urgency that literary impersonation forgoes.[31] As for Kazin, for Cavell, passionate utterance is characterized first by an emotive overture, followed by a moment of unforeseeable reaction, an anticipatory temporality that "puts the future of our relationship, as part of my sense of my identity, or of my existence, more radically at stake." More intriguing for my purposes, however, is that the demands of passion are not always asserted through speech or any other discursive form. Passion's performative effects, Cavell notes, "are readily, sometimes more effectively, achievable without saying anything," which "indicates that the urgency of passion is expressed before and after words." Perhaps because their trade is in words, neither Cavell nor Kazin follows this line of thought in any significant detail, even though it points to what has been, for theorists of affect, the more important facet of feeling: the bodily or physical. For the link between passionate criticism and nonverbal expressions of relationships, we will have to turn to the pedagogy of another public intellectual turned Fulbright teacher/administrator/bureaucrat, F. O. Matthiessen, who placed the body—fictional bodies, his body, and the bodies of his students—at the center of reading for feeling.

TALKING BODIES

The convergence of the lovable canon, passionate criticism, and bodily communication finds its fullest expressions in the social and scholarly work of F. O. Matthiessen, a New Critic turned passionate critic after his 1947 Fulbright year in Eastern Europe. More explicitly than Kazin, Matthiessen argued that the temporality of passion was essential to literary criticism in his 1949 essay "The Responsibilities of the Critic," which framed his break from New Critical orthodoxy. Nothing could be more devastating to a national literary tradition, Matthiessen lamented, than "intellectuals without love": an emotional sterility in the methods of Eliotian criticism that had produced a "self-enclosed knowledge" incapable of circulating outside of the national and scholarly institutions in which it had been generated (13).[32] By contrast, the spatial and intellectual openness of public intellectual love was a function of its futurist temporality; its refusal to accept as its telos "the unnatural point where textual analysis seems to be an end in itself" (284). The scholarly practice of "bringing everything in your life to what you read," as Matthiessen encouraged readers to do, imagined the loving critic as constantly punctuating reading with "ever fresh thought," borne out of "our need of being engaged in the public issues of our menaced time" (292).

Passionate declarations of love represented not inscrutable jumbles of un-spoken psychological affects but urgent act of "life-giving communication between art and society."

This is the critical issue that Matthiessen, an infinitely more discerning reader than Spiller, tackles in his unappreciated 1948 Fulbright memoir *From the Heart of Europe*. Appearing just six months after the publication of "The Responsibilities of the Critic," and a year before his tragic suicide, *From the Heart of Europe* opens on the plane to the first Salzburg Seminar, where Matthiessen would deliver the keynote address, and concludes with his return from his Fulbright year at Prague's Charles University. Kazin, who was also in attendance at the Salzburg Seminar, recorded in his note-books a brief psychological sketch of Matthiessen that explicitly—and troublingly—connected Matthiessen's public self-presentation as a teacher to the passionate expression of feeling. "Much of the drama at the semi-nar," Kazin observed, "is provided by F. O. Matthiessen who fascinates the European students, holds them in his grip, through an astonishing personal intensity, a positively violent caringness about everything he believes in and is concerned with that he cannot suppress in public. What drives the man and torments him so?"[33] Matthiessen's public excesses of feeling, at once awe inspiring and dangerous, appeared to Kazin as a way of "holding" the European students "in his grip," an idiom that registers the intense physi-cality with which he captivated his audience. Matthiessen's communicative intensity gives us some context for grasping the profuse and irrepressible textuality of *From the Heart of Europe*, which offers its readers not so much a coherent memoir or travelogue as a commonplace book of lecture tran-scripts, classroom notes, and diary entries logging Matthiessen's intellec-tual labors in the Eastern bloc. Indeed, the book's abundance of paraliterary genres and styles is, Matthiessen admits, largely compensatory: a frenzied attempt to communicate in material form what he could not in the "slightly ridiculous," "pulpy," and "sentimental passages" (in the words of reviewer Irving Howe) stitched together in *From the Heart of Europe*.[34]

As he announced at the outset of the book, Matthiessen's goal at the Salz-burg Seminar was to institute a universal American literary curriculum that would distinguish between "our best and our worst writers." Like Spiller and Cowley, Matthiessen also worried that American authors were "read indis-criminately," as they all seemed to offer "something new" to international readers. Yet unlike Spiller and Cowley, Matthiessen believed that the worst American writers were not those who depicted violent scenarios but those who betrayed "a lack of distinction in language" (25)—a judgment that did not merely equate a text's aesthetic value with its political themes. Thus he dismissed the "crude sensationalism" of much genre fiction and popular novels like *Gone with the Wind* not exclusively or primarily on the basis of their themes (as Spiller might have) but according to their aesthetic deficiencies—deficiencies on the level of style and genre that, Matthiessen claimed, also projected a kind of "imaginative violence" to international readers. Here Matthiessen's opposition of the imaginative to the informational rankled both his contemporaries and future critics, particularly the left liberals who viewed his admiration for the aesthetic as inherently apolitical, or even worse, politically conservative, in its apparent elitism.[35] And yet, for Matthiessen, it was precisely the aesthetic's partial insulation from the demands of political representation that made it capable of resisting the nationalist legacy of fascism and its absolute subjugation of the human spirit. The "masterfully exact style" of America's best writers offered a "critical luxury" with which to replenish the political and civic exsanguination of Western and Eastern Europe after World War II. The Fulbright scholar's mission, he suggested, was to show how "a new expression of that awareness [and] discrimination" in reading American literature could connect discourses of aesthetic value to a liberal institutional renaissance, thereby helping to "rebuild the civilization" of Europe anew.

In its attempt to shift between formal and political engagement, *From the Heart of Europe* presents a uniquely socializing discourse of aesthetic value that posits love as its end point. Indeed, Matthiessen begins by tracing the origins of an aesthetic of lovemaking back to two exemplary and complementary figures in American letters: Walt Whitman, "the poet as inspired seer," and Henry James, the writer as craftsman (149). While Whitman's vision of a maximally inclusive fraternity had already found a receptive audience among European Marxists from Ferdinand Freiligrath to Georg Lukács, and while the European Peace Council would soon use *Leaves of Grass* as the primary text in its international campaign against Stalinist imperialism, Matthiessen sought to renationalize the performative aesthetic of Whitman's poems. His seminar at Charles University, "The Age of Whitman and Melville," emphasized the socially enabling features of Whitman's stylization of "adhesive love" (112): his sensual rendering of bodies in readerly communion, enacted by Whitman's lyric address to an abstract and universal "you." It was this stylistic enactment of a readerly and national sociality that, Matthiessen claimed, made the institutional culture of American democracy distinct from other nation-states. If the performative poetics of adhesive love and its civic sociality staged a direct challenge to state-sanctioned totalitarianism, they also served as an antidote to the possessive and alienating logics of "finance capitalism"; an individualistic and alienating socioeconomic phenomenon that troubled Whitman in 1840 and Matthiessen in his newly assumed role as a spokesperson for a market-based institutional initiative like the Fulbright. Crucially, however, Matthiessen framed his teaching of Whitman's adhesive love as a challenge issued from within the very institutions that represented liberal capitalism's most ambitious manifestation. By reading Whitman's "you" as a group, he told his students across Eastern Europe, the reading public of the American studies classroom could begin to counteract the material and discursive underpinnings of market exchange, value, and utility that made Matthiessen's presence in the classroom as a Fulbright scholar possible in the first place. Of particular interest to Matthiessen, then, was the idea that Whitman's performative aesthetics could work from within liberal political spaces to reconfigure a democratic culture that had come to disproportionately promote individual liberty and equality over collective feeling. "Liberty and equality can remain intellectual abstractions if they are not permeated with the warmth of fraternity," he lectured to his students. "Whitman knew, through the heartiness of his temperament," he continued, "that the deepest freedom does not come from isolation. It comes instead through taking part in the common life, mingling in its hopes and failures" (90).

From his insider's diagnosis of American democracy's shortcomings, we may begin to theorize how Matthiessen's formally discriminating criticism, which draws his readers' attentions to the performative capabilities of Whitman's poetic address, locates its physical counterpart in the act of "mingling": a term Matthiessen invoked time and again in *American Renaissance* (1941) to describe the conjoining of "flesh and spirit" essential to a vibrant political culture.[36] Matthiessen's gradual overlay of the performative aesthetics of adhesive love with the physical embodiment of adhesive love—its literally adhesive quality, its ability to stick bodies to one another—begins with a relatively modest act of rereading Melville's *Moby-Dick*'s minor and marginalized characters as he was preparing his keynote address for Salzburg. "More than ever before," Matthiessen recalled, "I was moved by the scene where little Flask, the third mate, has mounted upon the shoulders of his harpooner, the massive Negro Daggoo, in order to see farther over the ocean's surface. Melville reflects how 'the bearer looked nobler than the rider.' Such reflection on the lack of any superiority owing to a race's whiteness is peculiarly moving today when the possibilities for any real democracy, both at home and in our relations abroad, depend upon the continual reaffirmation of that self evident truth" (36). Despite the personal quality of his account of *Moby-Dick*, Matthiessen's physical reading of the bodies in this scene—the "little Flask," the "massive Negro Daggoo"—amplifies a "peculiarly moving" vision of political institutionality. The system of governance that Matthiessen terms "real democracy," "both at home and in our relations abroad," emerges not from discourse, either textual or spoken, but through the easy touch of flesh to flesh.

The fullest realization of the pedagogical shift from poetic performativity to communicative physicality is not to be found in Matthiessen's reading of *Moby-Dick* but in *From the Heart of Europe*'s scenes of classroom reading, which stage the bodily features of passionate criticism (as Cavell suggests) with an extraordinary degree of pathos. "Whitman helped me begin to trust the body," Matthiessen confesses to his students at the start of his keynote address at the Salzburg Seminar (23). As we know from the previous chapter's analysis of the genre of the lecture and its heightened reflexivity, such a declaration cannot be issued without drawing attention to the "me"—Matthiessen—who presents his body to the audience, as well as "the body" as an abstraction that finds its generalized and particular incarnation in the many bodies of his listeners. (Not to mention, of course, the even more abstract metaphor of the body politic.) Matthiessen thus begins to proffer his body as a superior medium of communication for passionate criticism: more effective in its socializing work than either speech or writing alone. "We had no language in common," he observed after teaching a seminar in Bratislava, "and though only a fraction of a conversation can filter through an interpreter, you have the curious sense—since you have so much more time to study the other person's eyes and mouth and gestures—that you are establishing a close relationship after all" (151). The attentiveness to another "person's eyes and mouth and gestures," a disciplined "study" that originates in a close reading of *Leaves of Grass* or *Moby-Dick* and migrates seamlessly into the face-to-face interactions of the classroom communicates the intensity and immediacy of passion's social demands in the absence of a shared language. Importantly, such nonverbal features of communication emerge as an essential dimension of all acts of literary reception. When one of Matthiessen's students in Prague, upon reading *Leaves of Grass*, speaks with great conviction about the American doctrine of self-reliance, Matthiessen focuses not on his words but on a "light strong on his face"—as if the act of textual interpretation could illuminate not just his mind but his mien as well (111). Later, Matthiessen watches as his star pupil Jarka's "big, seemingly tireless body" and "sensitive friendly eyes" pore over *The Cambridge History of American Literature*, while another student offers a "broad mouthed generous smile" as he gazes at Matthiessen over a copy of *Moby-Dick* (114, 136,

159). Without saying anything, Matthiessen concludes, "you are establishing a close relationship after all."

All of these scenes of reading with feeling, however, pale before *From the Heart of Europe*'s climactic scene of mingling: a sing-along that interlaces the performative aesthetics of American literature with Matthiessen's and his students' physical bodies. On October 4, 1947, Saint Francis Day—Matthiessen's name day, he notes—his students serenade him with the abolitionist song "John Brown's Body": "Say, brothers, will you meet us / Say, brothers, will you meet us / Say, brothers, will you meet us / On Canaan's happy shores." The song, which is both an invitation to solidarity and a unified enactment of solidarity in the form of a choral performance, is followed by a strikingly unvoiced act of bodily adhesion. "Four of [the singers] grabbed my shoulders and feet, tossed me in the air, and bounced me, gently, on the floor," Matthiessen recalls. "After this all the men shook hands with me, I was kissed by the girls, and felt that I was really *in*" (98, italics in original). The students' performance of feeling, passionately yet quietly communicated by bouncing, kissing, shaking, and tossing, redounds on the song's performative overture ("Say, brothers, will you meet us?") and its political vision of democratic fraternity. Like John Brown at Harper's Ferry (or so he and his students imagine, setting aside the racial specificities of the Civil War), Matthiessen offers up his body—the adhesive body of the Fulbright scholar—as a totem of liberated institutional sociality to Eastern Europe's once occupied populations.

That Whitman's poetry of physical adhesion and its lyric address should inspire Matthiessen to transform his body into a site of intersubjective and physical mingling makes a great deal of sense; after all, that's precisely how Whitman once imagined that his vision of "adhesiveness or love" would "make the races comrades" and "fraternize all" in *Democratic Vistas* (1888).[37] What required some more creative critical maneuvering on Matthiessen's part was the attempt to make the novels of Henry James, which seemed at every turn to assert their autonomy from social, political, and even bodily materiality, amenable to the same reading practices. Although the assumption of autonomy was based on a rather small and selective sample of institutional readers, what is distinct about *From the Heart of Europe* is how subtly Matthiessen reframed scholarly discourses of aesthetic autonomy as a tenet of liberal humanism for precisely these "good" readers—a counterintuitive inversion of New Critical dogma that began with Matthiessen's lecture on *The Portrait of a Lady* at the Salzburg Seminar. James's "peculiar poignancy had never been more affecting than when reading *The Portrait of a Lady* in a Europe so distinct from the undistributed world of [James's] prime,"

Matthiessen noted. And yet the pastness of the novel, the frozen-in-time quality of its aesthetic, was what enabled "the release that James can give today." The temporal distance between James's "prime" and "today" was, for instance, what had "impelled several young American soldiers from Harvard to turn to [James] while they were in the army" (45). "They had felt a great need, during the unrelenting outwardness of those years," Matthiessen related, "for [James's] kind of inwardness, for his kind of order as a bulwark against disorder." Thus James's novels offered these soldiers "not an escape" into aesthetic autonomy, but "a renewed sense of the dignity of the human spirit" in the form of a well-wrought interiority (46).

If reading Henry James in the trenches paints an uncanny wartime image, its discordance offers an obvious counterpoint to Mitchell and her cohort of crude sensationalists from within a maximally violent situation. Formal refinement stood as a "bulwark" against spiritual devastation—a battlefield metaphor deployed here to indicate how literature could serve as the last line of defense against fascism by displacing a horrifyingly oversaturated political context with pure aesthetic decontextualization. In a conference presentation at Alpach titled "The Human Image in New American Literature," Matthiessen aligned this dialogic configuration of aesthetic and political value to "the agonizing nature of love" one could read out of texts ranging from James's *The Golden Bowl* to T. S. Eliot's *The Wasteland* and *Four Quartets*, the latter "written against the background of the air raids" (56). Think of the taut rhyme scheme of *Four Quartets*'s "Little Gidding," which ends with an invocation of love as the only redemption for the bombings of World War II: "The only hope, or else despair / Lies in the choice of pyre of pyre—/ To be redeemed from fire by fire. / Who then devised the torment? Love." If Whitman had given Matthiessen a theory of love as performativity and adhesive performance, James and Eliot had made love apparent in the "sense of life that comes from expert expression" (58).

Today, nothing seems more conventional than the canon Matthiessen stitched together on his Fulbright tour of Eastern Europe. Yet the criteria that Matthiessen used to restock USIS libraries with Whitman, Melville, James, and Eliot; to organize syllabi and seminars; and to supervise research were by no means apparent to his contemporaries—criteria derived from the institutionally specific convergence of learning to feel through reading a lovable canon, declarations of passionate criticism, and the physicality of communication. A perplexed Kazin tried but could not make sense of Matthiessen's syllabus and lectures. "I knew from Matty's book on Eliot and especially his grand work *American Renaissance* how much he saw writing in terms of the artist's 'craft'—a tradition linking James, Eliot, Hawthorne, really connected by the highly selective tradition rising out of *poetry* that Eliot had founded," Kazin mused, "and which certainly did not apply to loose novels like *Moby-Dick*."[38] Kazin is hardly alone in his diagnosis of Matthiessen's reading habits as purely idiosyncratic, subjective, and personal.[39] "A more appropriate title for this book of opinions and impressions of a visiting professor of American Literature would be 'From the Journal of F. O. Matthiessen'; for it is a highly personal record with little or no pretense to objectivity," sneered Frank J. Lewand to the American Academy of Political and Social Science.[40] The *New York Herald Tribune* mocked Matthiessen's "incontestably fine desire to 'bring man into communication with man.'"[41] Unlike these reviewers, we have the benefit of seeing how Matthiessen used the feeling rules of love to enfold the artist's craft into a discourse of corporeal literary reception within international American studies departments. In turning to Matthiessen's and Kazin's students, we will now witness how reading for feeling and its attendant forms of physical communication emerged as institutionalized condition of literary and paraliterary textual production for the next generation of Fulbright scholars.

SADOMASOCHISTIC PUBLICITY

In a journal entry dated May 15, 1952, Sylvia Plath, then a rising junior at Smith College, fantasized about her plans for life after graduation. "I will still whip myself onward and upward," she wrote. "Toward Fulbrights, prizes, Europe, publication, males. Tangible, yes, after a fashion, as all weave into my physical experience—going, seeing, doing, thinking, feeling, desiring. With the eyes, the brain, the intestines, the vagina" (102). More daring on the page than your typical Smith girl preparing for her experiences in international living, Plath's prophecy of self-flagellation aspires to "whip" literary production and prestige out of her "physical experience." We could even read her staccato listing of writerly accomplishments ("Fulbrights, prizes, Europe, publication"), actions ("going," "seeing," "doing," "thinking," "feeling," "desiring"), and body parts ("the eyes, the brain, the intestines, the vagina") as the discrete lashes of her figurative cat-o'-nine-tails, with each comma pausing to drive her artistic consciousness deeper and deeper into the private crevices of her body. By this reading, it would seem that Plath's insistently "personal style," described by Laura Frost and other feminist critics as alternatively "violent," "torturous," and "masochistic," had taken root well before she appeared to Hughes as an obediently grinning representative of Cold War American studies.[42]

And yet for Plath, the purpose of submitting her private physical experiences to the demands of writing was not primarily to secure her personal style as a writer but to establish a more "tangible" link between the interiorized pangs of personal feeling and the externalized pleasures of public communication. "From the inactive (collegiately), timid, introvertly-tended individual of last year, I have become altered," she continued in the same journal entry. "I have maintained my integrity by not being an office-seeker for the sake of publicity, yet I have directed my energies in channels which, although public, also perform the dual service of satisfying many of my creative aims and needs" (103). The "dual service" Plath refers to in her journal, a not-yet-fulfilled fantasy that weds "public" extroversion to "creative" individuality, would find its institutional apotheosis in her Fulbright scholarship to Cambridge, which she won in 1954 under the mentorship of Alfred Kazin, then a visiting professor at Smith College. And it was the program's feeling rules, I will argue, that first inspired her to elaborate, in literary form, a dialectical relationship between pleasure and pain—one that aligned textual practices of literary production with corporeal forms of international-institutional communication.

When considered alongside Matthiessen's passionate and programmatic desire to love and to be loved by his students, Plath's sadomasochistic bid for a public platform shows the troubles one could encounter in obeying Spiller's imperative to "breed love." Specifically, her violent eroticism reveals how thoroughly institutionalized feeling rules tend to normalize certain forms of emotional expression while sanctioning others as inappropriate, perverse, abject, or immoral. More painfully self-conscious than many of the Fulbright's readers and writers, Plath was, at every turn, concerned with fashioning and projecting a nationally representative image of herself and her body. And yet, as we will see, her preoccupation with the external constraints of feeling rules often ran counter to what she identified as her interior emotional states. In Plath's not-so-innocent approach to writing and reading sadomasochistically, we can see how an institutional subject might bend (but not break) the feeling rules she has been socialized into and how she may posit an oppositional (but no less disciplined) practice of literary production and social interaction. At the same time, Plath's writing and communicative efforts highlight sadomasochism's performative and public capacities, thereby rendering this quintessentially "inward pointing" form of literary expression ripe for addressing and forming new readerly communities.[43] Plath's navigation of sadomasochistic performativity thus offers a prelude to many of the paraliterary genre conventions that would come to characterize the confessional narrative from the 1950s to the present day, where it has emerged as a reflexively public and widely publicized form of writing about feeling.

Neither Plath's readers nor theorists of sexuality tend to think of her sado-masochistic idiom as performing a public "service," even if her poetry does occasionally allude to violent political themes and figures. And yet before *The Bell Jar* (1963), before *Ariel* (1965), even before Plath's casually girlish yet alarming proclamation in "Daddy" that "Every woman adores a fascist," Plath's stint as a Fulbright scholar in Cambridge gave her the first oppor-tunity to unite her self-disciplining tendencies with a national-institutional project of representation. As she described it in her journals, the fellowship represented "a kind of consecration from the powers that be," which in-spired her to start "fighting for a stoic and creative attitude" (202). Perhaps the most telling testament to her fighting spirit is a journal fragment from April 1, 1956 titled "Program: To Win Friends & Influence People." Inspired by Dale Carnegie's best-selling guide to public communication *How to Win Friends and Influence People* (1936), Plath's "Program" features a series of reso-lutions she had jotted down for her Fulbright year.

→ Don't drink too much—(remember misfortunes w. Iko after St. John's party, Hamish—2 dates, St. Botolph's party & London night); stay sober.[44]
→ Be chaste and don't throw self at people (cf. David Buck, Mallory, Iko, Hamish, ted, Tony Gray)—in spite of rumor & M. Boddy, let no one verify this term the flaws of last![45]
→ Be friendly & more subdued—if necessary, smog of "mystery woman"—quiet, nice, slightly bewildered at colored scandals. Refuse ease of Sally Bowles act.[46]
→ Work on inner life—to enrich—concentrate on work for Krook[47]—writing (stories; poems, articles for Monitor—Sketches)—French daily.
→ Don't blab too much—listen more; sympathize & "understand" people—Keep troubles to self (569).

Consider how the fine-tipped arrows, the underlines, and the list form of Plath's "Program" signal a typographical departure from the long lines of her daily journal entries, not to mention the first-person confessional prose style—the relentlessly feeling "I"—on display in *The Bell Jar*. The second-person, self-addressed feeling rules instituted by this loose sheet of paper, however, reveal the unappreciated degree to which Plath's aesthetic craft, and not just her "personal style" or the thematic content of her writing, embraced cer-tain sadomasochistic tendencies. While the "Program" ordered Plath again and again to discipline her excessive spoken communication of feeling—by not "blabbing," keeping her "troubles to self," avoiding "misquot[ation]," and being generally "subdued" and "stoic"—this outward stoicism was precisely what would enable her "to work on inner life": to appreciate how she had "felt deeply" by transforming her into an inward-looking subject. In turn, her interiorized dwelling in feeling, rather than its persistent and indiscriminate exterior transmission, would allow her finally to "WRITE." Compared to Matthiessen, Kazin, or the ASA's understanding of the relationship between reading and feeling, the link Plath draws in her how-to guide between communicative discipline, feeling, and literary production is interestingly inverted. Communication enables literary production not through the former's exuberant vocalization but through its notable repression, which the "Program" formalizes through the imperatives that Plath directs at herself over and over again. The "order, beauty, form" of written production—in short, its aesthetic pleasures—emerges from the institutionalization of a specifically discursive self-binding; what Plath described as "tighten[ing] up my program here" (208).

Equally important to note is how Plath's sense of her literarily productive capabilities depended on maintaining the dissonance between feeling deeply and communicating stoically. The aim here was not to acculturate herself in such a way that her exterior self-presentation would remake her interior world in kind, as it had for Henry James's young ladies, both real and imaginary. Indeed, James's masterful interweaving of the two—interior psychology and exterior communication—emerged for Plath as the explicit antithesis to her writing process. "Henry James, too elaborate, too calm & well-mannered," she reflected when struck with an especially acute case of writer's block. "He is too <u>fine</u> for me. . . . I am no Maggie Verver" (382). Conflating herself with James's character only to disavow any resemblance between the two, Plath's sadomasochistic craft carved out a very different path of aesthetic, subjective, and social production from her fellow Smith alumnae, on the one hand, and the ASA and Fulbright Program's passionate male critics, on the other. Her ambition was not to cultivate herself as a work of art. Nor was it to position herself as violently caring reader, whose pedagogical diffusion of feeling could interpellate a new and internationalized reading public. Rather, the postulation of a self-abstracted gap between feeling and communicating reveals that Plath was, after all, committed to the exoteric mechanics of national "publicity," albeit in a very different sense of the word than the unctuous self-promotion sniffed out by the figure of the "office-seeker" she decried in her journal.

Publicity is a term that is only ever used loosely and negatively in scholarly accounts of Cold War politics, but Plath's "Program" invites us to consider it as more than a matter of shallow advertising, propaganda, or image management.[48] If we consider publicity in its original sense, as "the condition or fact of being open to public observation or knowledge," we can better understand the seemingly paradoxical link between self-abstraction and communicative openness.[49] In order to do so, however, we must mobilize a very particular notion of openness: one that relies not on personal confession—what we might think of colloquially as one person "opening up" to another person or to a group of people—but on the disinterested anonymity of free-flowing discourse. As Cold War liberal Edward A. Shils described it to Plath's contemporaries in *The Torment of Secrecy* (1956), publicity "prohibits emotional intensity, especially emotional excitement continuing over long stretches of time or running on without any intermission."[50] The belief in the evacuation of feeling as a necessary precursor for openness, a belief that Plath and Shils arrive at from very different angles, thus makes Plath's sadomasochistic sense of publicity seem pure, even quaint, in its rational idealism.[51] While we think of her as the ultimate confessional subject, her aspirational model of publicity sits conceptually closer to contemporaneous discourses of "information warfare" than Spiller's dispatches from the ASA or Matthiessen's passionate pedagogy.

Yet spoken communication is, in a sense, always inimical to the abstractions of written discourse. The communicating subject's emotions can never be totally sundered from the communicative event, as Shils fantasizes they might be. The attempt to do so always involves a form of painful self-repression. After all, how can one invite others to react to one's speech with admiration, identification, possession, and love at the same time that one feels compelled to keep speech's emotional modalities under wraps? This is one reason, we could speculate, why discourses of publicity so often revert to the visual rhetoric of "image management" in the debates of the mid-1950s. Appearances or surfaces are easier to rinse of emotional subjectivity than speech. As it applies to Plath's desire to incarnate the "smog of [a] 'mystery woman,'" the dissonance between feeling deeply and communicating stoically required keeping the subject suspended in an ambiguous state of discursive repression, perpetually toggling between the pleasures of cultivating a stoic exterior and the pains of shutting down feeling's outward expressions. Plath's turn to the body, both in her self-presentation and her writing, registers precisely the sadomasochistic tensions of Cold War publicity.

And sadomasochistic publicity was, in fact, conducive to writing. The tension Plath sets up between literary-aesthetic dominance and communicative submission finds its fictional counterpart in her Fulbright short story "Stone Boy with Dolphin" (1956), the frankly autobiographical tale of the Cambridge party at which Plath and Hughes first met and the only remaining fragment from her novel in progress *Falcon Yard*.[52] Formally speaking, Plath routes the sadomasochistic imperatives of her "Program" through a series of curious ruptures in the short story's plot, when its third-person narrative voice is suddenly displaced by self-directed commands that order the characters to harm themselves and one another. Most important among the characters are Plath's protagonist Dody Ventura, an American Fulbright scholar to England, and Leonard, a British poet whose poems Dody has read and reread with unusual devotion: "Leonard. She didn't know him but she knew him by heart" (180). In the case of Leonard and Dody, to know is to know "by heart," albeit without any of the warmth or reciprocity that phrase generally entails. The story of their courtship begins chillily enough, with Dody trekking across "a snow-sheeted tennis court" in Cambridge, England, to prepare herself for a party later that night. The party is thrown by a group of British "literary boys" among whom she is desperate to make her mark, a mark first represented formally by the interruption of Plath's scenic description with an imperative intonation. "Let something happen. Let something happen," chants a new and as yet unidentified narrative presence. "Something terrible, something bloody. Something to end this endless flaking snowdrift of airmail letters, of blank pages turning in library books. . . . Let me leave my mark" (182). Registering Dody's desire to impress the literary boys as "something terrible, something bloody" blooming on the "blank pages" of unreadable "library books," the rift in narrative voice unites the anticipatory and ambiguous violence of sadomasochism with the pleasure of making one's mark in writing. Like the feeling rules of Plath's "Program," the imperative is repeated ("Let . . . Let . . . Let"), codified, and claimed by a looming narrative specter, which appears to issue from within Dody herself at the same time it orders her to do its bidding. The most telling feature of the sadomasochistic utterance, however, is how obviously it foreshadows Dody's ultimate proclamation of her love to Leonard, which comes not in the form of words but in the form of an intensely physical and affectively charged action. Soon Dody will gouge Leonard's cheek with her teeth to literally create the bloody, terrible mark the narrator prophesies. Over and above the verbal contracts of sadomasochism, then, is its purely physicalized and externalized communication in Dody's wounding of Leonard's face.

No doubt this was not the kind of face-to-face interaction that either Dale Carnegie or the United States–United Kingdom Fulbright Commission had in mind when they emphasized the need to win friends and influence people. And yet the narrative arc of "Stone Boy with Dolphin" suggests that, under the feeling rules of the "Program," disciplining one's speech and writing and inflicting bodily harm are, in fact, formally analogous activities. What it also indicates is that, for Plath, physical markings could be as important to national publicity as verbally repressed communications. The body, it seems, could speak too—or more accurately, the body's public presentation could mediate between the personal particularities of communicative acts and the impersonal abstractions of national representation. The convergence of physical marking and publicity is most strikingly apparent in the photo spread that Plath put together for Cambridge's *Varsity* magazine, in which she modeled and reviewed the latest trends in skirts, blouses, and swimsuits in writing. Adorned in a one-piece polka-dot bathing suit and white kitten heels, Plath bares the long lines of her shoulders and legs to the viewer while averting her gaze from the camera. The caption below the photograph reads: "Bought your May Week outfit yet? Sylvia Plath, American Fulbright Scholar at Newnham, reviews May Week fashions." Although she is identified by name, and although her indexical self appears in these photographs, the text of the caption nevertheless insists on Plath's status as a representative symbol: a curated advertisement for fashionable goods purchased by a nationalized scholar-subject. Intensely embodied yet spectacularly depersonalized, her body emerges as a public site to negotiate the consumption of commodity goods and national fantasies, rather than a private and self-identified entity. In other words, Plath presents herself an icon for whom the act of communication is purely exteriorized, unvoiced, and prosthetic, much as she appeared to Hughes when he examined her photograph in "Fulbright Scholars."

Painfully aware that her bodily self-presentation and personal behavior would be scrutinized in light of her coded status as a "representative of the stars and stripes," Plath worried that her "image" was "not worth the really good boys" (208). This ambitious cohort of English scholars—which included Hughes, E. Lucas Myers (Allen Tate's cousin), David Ross, and Nat LaMar (protégé of assistant secretary of state and librarian of Congress Archibald McLeish)—sat at the heart of the Fulbright-sponsored British Association for American Studies (BAAS) from 1955 to 1957. Beginning with Kazin's Fulbright lectureship at Cambridge in 1951, BAAS had grown out of the annual Fulbright exchanges between the United States and the United Kingdom as the institution charged with regulating "the bloc of human exports" that the United States government sent to supply "the most basic information about the United States" to British scholars.[53] The dissemination of information was nevertheless characterized by "élan, intimacy, and even jollity," according to

FIGURES 2.1 AND 2.2 *Above and opposite:* "Sylvia Plath Tours the Shows and Forecasts May Week Fashions." Photospread from *Varsity* (1956). Sylvia Plath Papers. Photograph: Courtesy Lilly Library, Indiana University, Bloomington, Indiana.

BAAS chairman and Oxford administrator Herbert Nicholas, who offered up the emotional pleasures of international communication as a check on "the atavistic attractions of nationalism."[54] If the feeling rules of nationalism were regressive, unruly, and dangerous, the feeling rules of international communication were progressive, tidy, and safe, as the latter were always mediated by departments, committees, programs, and bureaucrats, a spectrum of human agents and collective structures committed not to pure emotion but to emotion's institutional reconfiguration as rational public discourse. By 1956, the

FASHION NOTE

From front page of Varsity!
with love, from Betty Grable.

Bought your May Week
outfit yet? S y l v i a
Plath, American Ful-
bright S c h o l a r at
Newnham, reviews May
Week fashions on the
centre page.

perseverance of the BAAS's love for reading American literature depended
not on the performance and performativity of adhesive love, as Matthiessen
had once imagined, but on the "common possession of what we can only call
the liberal mind."[55] This insistence on reading as an entry point to the liberal
mind returns us to the notion of publicity as rational discourse, but from a
slightly different point of view. Not only did face-to-face communication have
to demonstrate the kind of rationality that publicity demanded, but literary
production had to live up to a similar burden. Just like people, literary texts
had to "represent the best intellectual tradition of the United States."

With this institutional context in mind, we may better understand why,
for Plath, the desire to repress her "true-confessional" tone seemed like such
a politically, as well as aesthetically, urgent imperative. "All interior 'she
felts' and appallingly awkward," she complained to her diary while drafting
"Stone Boy with Dolphin." "Again, I feel the gulf between my desire & ambition & naked abilities" (273). Her nakedness is literally covered up by the

iconicity of the Fulbright scholar's nationalized body, dressed in the most up-to-date May Week fashions and primed for publicity. But it also finds its fictional corollary in Dody's elaborate construction of her facial and physical appearance. Roaming the grounds of Cambridge with her "eyes lowered, obsequious, a false demure face on," Dody retreats to her room before the literary boys' party to refashion her face and dress (180). Like her practice of writing, her practice of playing dress-up is also disciplined by the interruptions of the sadomasochistic narrative voice: "This Friday night, Dody wore a black jersey and a black-and-white checked wool skirt, clipped to her waist by a wide red belt. I will bear pain, she testified to the air, painting her fingernails Applecart Red. A paper on the imagery in *Phedre*, half done, stuck up its seventh white sheet in her typewriter. Unwincing, in her mind's eye, she bared her flesh. Here. Strike home" (182). With obsessive attentiveness, Plath dresses Dody up, constructing her fashionable exterior with details reminiscent of the *Varsity* spread. Instead of puncturing her coolly made-up exterior with the true-confessional first-person, rendering her figuratively naked and emotionally exposed, Plath stages Dody's reflexive disciplinary utterances as a form of free indirect testimony. "I will bear pain, she testified to the air," all the while painting her fingernails the most American of colors, Applecart Red. This is a phantasmagorically unvoiced, public, and authoritative act of testimony, insofar as Dody does not speak to an audience who might respond to her—as Plath did in front of the Fulbright Commission—but to herself; a self who she nevertheless paints over as a nationalized source of discipline. And crucially, her testimony is immediately juxtaposed to the blank sheet of paper that sits in her typewriter, waiting for the "suffering and wisdom" with which she will mark its surfaces. Her imagined act of physical exposure ("in her mind's eye, she bared her flesh") and unvoiced command ("Here. Strike home") thus instantiate both the repression of spoken communication and the creation of the external marks of writing, which will register the interiorized pain caused by the repression of speech.

But if Dody serves as her own master and slave, occupying the role of the dominant and the submissive in her public imaginary, how does her sadomasochistic craft gain publicity in a more material and collective sense? How does she actually communicate in the kinds of impersonal and exteriorized ways Plath's "Program" imagines? To answer these questions, we need only turn to the climactic resolution of the story: Dody's maiming of Leonard at the literary boys' party. Although we know from the beginning that Dody knows Leonard's poetry "by heart," it is only at the party, where

Dody finds herself engulfed by small talk and idle chatter, that we learn why Leonard's poetry resonates so strongly with her. It is not because of his poetic aesthetic, about which we glean nothing, but because of the sadomasochistic effects Leonard's poetry has on Dody as a reader. "Only Leonard's words cut through the witty rot," Dody thinks. "She didn't know him, but she knew that, that shaped her sword. Let what come, come" (184).

What comes is a moment of violent coupling. In an attempt to cut through the endless babble of voices that surrounds her, Dody leaves her bloody mark on Leonard's cheek, biting him when he refuses to take stock of her made-up face and carefully clothed body. Explicitly cast as a moment of Christian communion, Dody's piercing of Leonard's skin is more subtly legible as a communicative act that inverts his piercing of her heart—not with words but with the body and, specifically, the face. "Leonard bent to his last supper. She waited. Waited, sighting the whiteness of his cheek with its verdigris stain, moving by her mouth. Teeth gouged. And held. Salt, warm salt, laving the taste buds of her tongue. Teeth dug to meet. An ache started far off at their bone root. Mark that, mark that" (192). On this occasion of face-to-face communication, the imperative "Mark that, mark that" does double duty. By commanding the physical mark that appears on Leonard's body, it also creates the literary mark that Dody wills herself to leave at the very beginning of the story. From Dody and Leonard's mirrored acts of readerly and writerly wounding, there emerges a communicative interaction that is simultaneously exteriorized and written down in a violent gesture of literary production but that is never spoken aloud—an antidote to the "witty rot" of verbal exchange that Dody disdains and that Plath had willed herself to repress throughout her "Program." Important here is that Dody—the feeling subject intent on repressing feeling by repressing speech—is not held responsible for the violence inflicted. The action itself is outsourced to an unclaimed set of "teeth" ("Teeth gouged. And held. Teeth dug to meet"), which betray no feeling until the very end, when an "ache started far off." Thus while Dody's act may appear sexually perverse, its masterful transfiguration of interiorized pain into a disinterested form of bodily communication and an act of literary production unexpectedly tracks the feeling rules prescribed by the BAAS's rational-liberal sensibilities.

Is there a qualitative difference between the communicative styles of the body and writing, on the one hand, and speech on the other? The sadomasochistic alliance between nonverbal communication and literary production, as I have theorized it here, depends on a shared discourse of self-abstraction, an emotional hollowing out of the communicative subject that must first posit perfectible techniques of repression to assert its impersonal, externalized, and publicity-seeking ideologies of expressivity. By contrast, spoken communication seems to invite markedly personal and indexical forms of aesthetic and political infelicities: speaking overlong, speaking out of turn, blabbing when drunk, letting something slip, misquoting, speaking too passionately, gossiping, and so forth. What the distinction between the two reveals, perhaps unsurprisingly, is that the disinterested and abstract quality of sadomasochistic publicity is most conducive to loving other impersonal and equally abstracted figures: strangers but also objects, commodities, and brands. To anticipate the next chapter's discussion of the relationship between reading and branding, let us turn to Plath's diary one last time to find an entry from February 1955, a recollection of a shopping trip that meditates on the limitations of love so conceived. "All stores closed, except Sayle's, where I bought an identical pair of red gloves to make up for the one I lost," Plath writes. "Can't be completely in mourning. Is it possible to love the neutral, objective world and be scared of people? Dangerous for long, but possible. I love people I don't know. I smiled at a woman coming back over the fen path, and she said, with ironic understanding, 'Wonderful weather.' I loved her. I didn't read madness or superficiality in the image that reflected in her eyes. For once. It is the strangers that are easiest to love" (204).

What is the appeal of loving the "neutral, objective world"? Here a pair of red gloves, identical to one that Plath has recently lost, occupies the same relationship to her as the anonymous, yet beloved, woman who crosses her path. "Strangers" are "easiest to love," Plath speculates, not because of the depth or sincerity of what they say (this stranger speaks of the weather with "ironic understanding"), but because the communicative relationships they offer are mediated solely by the exterior and physicalized features of the body—an "image" "reflected in her eyes" that is neither "superficial" nor probes the psychological and emotional depths of "madness." The necessarily externalized features of these interactions thus offer Plath the chance to "read" strangers as communicating subjects, just as Hughes once read Plath's picture and projected a future relationship of intimacy from her smile, and just as Matthiessen asked his students to read the performative aesthetics of a poem to inaugurate a new and reflexively embodied reading public. The question of whether one can relate to a commodity or a brand in equivalent ways—a pair of red gloves from Sayle's, bought to replace the same pair of gloves lost—is, for Plath, a more "dangerous" proposition. What kind of public intimacies can objects, brands, or commodities provide? Can such intimacies be forged through reading and writing? It is to this dangerous proposition that I will turn to in my discussion of the American Express Company in the next chapter.

INSTITUTIONAL COMEDY

Despite its violent depictions of Dody and Leonard's interactions, there is something slyly humorous, almost caricatured, about the denouement of "Stone Boy with Dolphin." This is not because of sadomasochism's gender positioning, which, as Eileen Gil*lo*oly has argued, often posits the submissive woman as the victim of a barbed sexual joke.[56] But Plath is far from the victim here. Rather, her riposte to the feeling rules of the Fulbright Program is so remarkably on the nose that it is the program and its institutions that take a metaphorical lashing. The totalizing practices of reading as feeling are punctured by her appropriation of the Fulbright's disciplining apparatuses to shocking ends. In fact, we could speculate that Plath is almost too dominant of an institutional subject or human actor; that is to say, she is hyper-attuned to her conditions of production such that my excavation of these conditions, as a critic, never quite seems to qualify as a full-on allegorical or symptomatic interpretation of her work. "Stone Boy with Dolphin" is, like much of Plath's work, more accurately read as a metanarrative about the interrelation between fact and fiction: the possibility of using her Fulbright "notes," her diary entries, her letters home, and her experiences to craft a fiction that bears an oblique or oppositional relationship to the structures of aesthetic value and literary craftsmanship championed back home. (We saw a version of this in the last chapter's discussion of "novels from life.") And while Plath's paraliterary strategy is interesting for feminist reasons, it is, for my purposes, even more interesting for socio-institutional ones. The wounds she delivers in her autobiographical writing bear a family resemblance to other humorous metanarratives about paraliterature that have issued from the Fulbright scholars who came after her.

Of course, Plath's sardonic humor does not betray her knowingness of her institutional position in the same way that, say, John Ashbery and James Schuyler's coauthored Fulbright novel *Nest of Ninnies* (1969) does, with its campy depictions of trips to the Salzburg Seminar, where French, American, and German scholars come together to pop bottles of champagne and produce erotic translations of Dashiell Hammett novels and other "racy" stories for European readers.[57] Written entirely through letters to one another, the authors' rebranding of the Fulbright fellowship as the "Ninny fellowship" would have appalled Ashbery's one-time teacher, F. O. Matthiessen, as would the authors' indulgences in "sexed-up" noir.[58] Nor does Plath ironize the Fulbright's feeling rules with the detached tones of a more recent Fulbright fellow, Ben Lerner, author of the avowedly autobiographical novel *Leaving the Atocha Station* (2011). (The novel's title comes from an Ashbery poem of the same name, but the novel itself is chock full of what it presents as mimetic chat transcripts, diary entries, letters, and other texts.) Lerner's scholar is an affectively flat protagonist named Adam Gordon, who must smoke weed every day in order to feel the internationalizing love that his fellowship demands. The final scene of the novel takes place at a Fulbright-sponsored poetry reading and plays up the feeling rules of love with exaggerated joy, the only moment in Lerner's peripatetic and largely plotless novel in which Adam's affect seems to soar. As Adam walks around the reading, embracing and kissing his fellowship administrators "warmly" and "without irony," he imagines what kinds of aesthetic and social transformations this reading will make possible. "Teresa [his translator] would read the originals and I would read the translations and the translations would become the originals as we read. Then I planned to live forever in a skylit room surrounded by my friends."[59] The performative work done by Adam's translator, Teresa, ("the translations would become the originals") inaugurates the same affectively marked reading public that Matthiessen once embraced. Adam's "friends" are uncounted, possibly endless, and all of them converge in a sentimental vision of eternity that's so idyllic it's absurd, laughable even. And indeed, this turns out to be a joke. The ending is another drug-induced fantasy: a punch line delivered by the novel's exaggeratedly sentimental scene of reading and its inflated sense of what literature can do in the world.

Who is on the butt end of the Fulbright scholar's jokes? Leapfrogging from Plath at midcentury to Lerner in the present day allows us to perceive how the international institutionalization of American studies, to return to the discipline with which I started this chapter, has now emerged as a target for gentle deflation. Even insiders can now jab at the "romance with American things," which refuses to end and which, more powerfully, insists on reading for feeling. But as I have shown, that romantic narrative and its attendant structures of feeling began to unravel the moment American studies started. Indeed, it might be more accurate to say that such a romance never really existed in the first place, at least not in the pure or uncomplicated form that critics have projected backward in time onto their own institutional pasts. From Matthiessen's passionate utterances to Plath's sadomasochistic craft to Ashbery's erotic camp to Lerner's drug-induced translation, we can see how fictional texts continually coexisted alongside institutional rules for how reading these texts ought to make their readers feel. To believe in a more abstract or psychological sense of literary love is to indulge in the same self-deluding high that Lerner's narrator ironizes: a vision of love that exists more powerfully, more perfectly, in another space and time, and thus avoids its material realities. It is a means of smuggling love back into the disciplinary epistemologies of the present—a way of nestling ever closer to the powers that be and never realizing whom, or what, we are still in love with.

CHAPTER THREE

Brand Reading

I see in every American Express
And in every army center in Europe
   I see the same face the same sound of voice
   The same clothes the same walk
I see mothers & fathers
   no difference among them
Replicas
They not only speak and walk and think alike
   they have the same face!
What did this monstrous thing?
What regiments a people so?

GREGORY CORSO, "The American Way" (1961)[1]

READING AND WRITING THE AMERICAN EXPRESS

The violent climax of F. Scott Fitzgerald's *Tender Is the Night* (1934) takes place at a jail cell in Rome, where Dr. Dick Diver, guilty of drunkenly assaulting a plainclothes police officer, waits for his sister-in-law Baby Warren to negotiate his release. Baby, an imperious busybody and consummate materialist, wanders the streets of the city center, incapable of soliciting clear directions to the American consulate. Deliverance appears when "emerging from one trail into the Piazzo d'Espagna [*sic*] she saw the American Express Company and her heart lifted at the word 'American' on the sign."[2] But on discovering that its offices are closed, Baby's patriotic reverie dissipates and is replaced with an inexplicable vitriol, a "clean-sweeping irrational temper" that cleanly sweeps her off the streets of Rome and out of Fitzgerald's novel by the end of the chapter (232). Dick Diver, on the other hand, remains in jail.

It seems an odd pairing of urban institutions. At the one end of the Piazza di Spagna are the alleys leading to the "impersonal" prison, where Dick's "humiliation" at the hands of the Italian penal system transforms him into a "different person," a "new self" that eclipses the "mature Aryan" he once was—Fitzgerald's moniker for the class of perennially tanned American tourists gallivanting around Europe in the 1920s (233). At the opposite end sits the American Express Company, whose prominent brand name affirms Baby's sense of national identity when she reads it closely—her "heart lifted at the word 'American'"—only to disappoint her with its impenetrable barriers to entry. Viewed in this light, Dick and Baby's identities as national subjects are equally, if oppositely, governed by the two most prominent institutions flanking Rome's Spanish Steps, a 1930s touristic mecca. And while Dick's prison seems more encompassing and more alienating than Baby's brand loyalty to American Express, several of Fitzgerald's short stories in *The Crack-Up* (1945) suggest that these two institutions both define experiences of the self away from home. Recounting a trip to an unidentified city sometime in the 1930s, he writes, "The city had been merely an unfamiliar rhythm persisting outside the window of an American Express hotel with days composed of such casual punctuation marks as going for the mail or taking auto rides that did not go back and forth but always in a circle."[3]

Here Fitzgerald's description of the tourist's circular routines—his inability to access the world, the auto rides to nowhere—unexpectedly and exaggeratedly aligns the American Express with the confining physical space of Dick Diver's jail cell. Both institutions appear as architectural configurations of what Erving Goffman would later describe as the "total institution," a social arrangement in which "all phases of the day's activities are tightly scheduled, with one activity leading at a prearranged time into the next."[4] Like the actions commanded by Plath's Fulbright "Program" in the previous chapter, the "whole circle of activities" limned by total institutions are imposed through "a system of explicit formal rulings": the metadiscursive protocols that govern all forms of speech, communication, and interaction in order to produce "disciplined, moralistic, and monochromatic" subjects.[5] The formal rulings of the total institution allow it to emerge as the unified agent and the unitary space of subjective, social, and representational determinism par excellence. When applied to the domain of leisure tourism, such rulings dramatically limit one's ability to experience the world outside. The "circle" of restricted space, Fitzgerald suggests, denies the "back and forth" essential not only to lived experiences of physical and discursive interaction but also the ability to narrate these experiences as literature.

But in an important sense, totality is always imaginative and asymptotic. No modern institution of literacy, be it the school, the prison, or the multinational corporation, can completely efface the points of discontinuity in its material and ideological operations. (We are far too Derridean for that.)

And for literary critics writing today, it isn't all that interesting to construct a perfectly isomorphic relationship between an institution and the subjects it creates, especially if one wants to produce a more sophisticated account of either subject creation or social production. Rather, institutional influence is more precisely and loosely constituted by what Michel Foucault, in his later works, has called the "apparatuses of domination": the diffuse strategies and technical instruments of power that regiment individuals through fairly unobtrusive, and thus less easily identifiable and contestable, structures of "lifestyle" management.[6] By Foucault's account, which echoes the anxieties of Fitzgerald's *Tender Is the Night* and *The Crack-Up*, it is neither the disciplinary institution of the prison cell nor the locked office space that functions as the most pervasive apparatus of institutional sociality. Rather, for the American Express, the largest provider of tourism services to US consumers from 1891 to 1977, it was the auto ride, the mail schedule, the organized tour, and, as I will argue in this chapter, the brand name that managed both literacy and lifestyle.

By initiating its brand-reading subjects into elaborately stylized representations of how Americans spent money on things, the company transformed paraliterary texts (like traveler's checks, travel guides, and customs declarations) and experiences (like tourism) into occasions for communicative action. In turn, brand reading made it possible for writers to signal not just how its brand was stylized or circulated but also how reading it came to symbolize a sanitized understanding of collective identity to consumers like Baby Warren who were devoted to the brand's nationally transcendent, even utopian, promises. Considered alongside the literary impersonation taught by women's colleges and the feeling rules modeled by the Fulbright Program, the aesthetic construct I identify as literary branding—a style of writing brands in fiction—reveals how patterns of consumption and the practices of reading they entailed became legible as powerful codes of both national representation and international communication.

Beyond whatever history we may uncover in investigating the American Express Company, which offers a wide-ranging and unexplored example of literary-corporate intimacy, literary branding offers an especially potent strategy for reorienting the relationship between literary fiction and the material realities of internationalism. In *Tender Is the Night* and *The Crack-Up*, Fitzgerald's invocation of the brand name allows him to anchor the novel to a world beyond the text in much the same way that Plath's caricaturing of proper names in "Stone Boy with Dolphin" allowed her to flag the story's attentiveness to its institutional conditions of production. Fitzgerald may describe the company's lifestyle management and the feelings of bourgeois alienation that result within the form of a novel, but his descriptions always seem to exceed the text's status as a literary fiction by willing us to read a discursive formulation—a proper name—that is derived from and circulates in a discursive sphere outside of literature. We can see a similar interdiscursive effect at play in Henry Miller's novel from the same year, *The Tropic of Cancer* (1934), in which Miller complains, "For five days I have not touched the typewriter nor looked at a book; nor have I had a single idea in my head but to go to the American Express."[7] This "single idea" invites the incessant repetition of the brand name in direct proportion to Miller's writer's block: the greater his inability to create literature, the more the brand name pops up on his walks through Paris.[8] We could read Fitzgerald's invocation of sloppy literary style in *The Crack-Up* in this same light—within the American Express, the city remains an "unfamiliar rhythm," while days are composed of "casual punctuation marks"—as we could Dick's recollection of his "foul" and "odiferous" "walk from the American Express" to "Keats's house," "where his spirit soared" once it was symbolically cleansed of capital (221). To read these novels is, in a sense, to read a kind of negative consumer report, one that uses the brand name to link literary representation—or, as in Miller, the inability to produce literary representations—to an overwhelming and pervasive experience of institutional reality.

More telling than both of these examples, however, is how literary branding is used to bring Goffman's conventional sense of the total institution into hysterical relief in the epigraph to this chapter, an excerpt from Beat poet Gregory Corso's poem "The American Way." Written nearly two decades after Fitzgerald's death and at the height of the Cold War, "The American Way" opens with a declaration of fear. "I'm afraid to go into the American Express," confesses Corso's speaker, who elides the apparatuses of lifestyle management that Fitzgerald identifies, and directly connects the institution's physical space to its totalizing production of fungible subjects: "I see the same face the same sound of voice / the same clothes the same walk / I see mothers & fathers / No difference among them."[9] The speaker's drone can barely restrain his horror. He is the only one, it seems, who can perceive the sameness of the families around him; the only one who can stand outside of the institution's hyperaggressive production of people to relate the dystopian shift from American figures to the American way of life. Thus he ends with an outburst of critical questions to which one suspects he already has the answer: "What did this monstrous thing? What regiments a people so?"

Yet we should be wary of how these questions interpellate us as well-trained critical readers, eager to interpret literature as a site of resistance to institutionalized power. The social and national determinism Corso attributes to the American Express Company reads as a pitch-perfect, even self-conscious, act of literary position taking, courtesy of a recognizably countercultural author. (The same could be said for Miller and, to a lesser extent, Fitzgerald.) It is striking how the strong distinction that the poem draws between the speaking "I" and the terrifying sameness of America's consumer-communicators—their "same sound of voice," their mindless donning of the "same clothes," their knee-jerk family values—formally reproduces the romance of resistance that has become so integral to the literary history of the 1950s and 1960s. By pitting Beat writers like Corso against the buttoned-up corporation man in the gray flannel suit, the story of the period that literary critics have put forth is always one of opposites who refuse not only to attract but who occupy completely separate domains of sociocultural production.[10] On the one hand, there is the defiantly bohemian world of literary actors and, on the other, the material institutions of economic capital. And if the former is committed to what Michael Clune has described as the "virtual spaces" of literature, the latter underwrites a vast global infrastructure of real-world objects, locations, and technologies: capital markets, telegrams, mail-forwarding services, office spaces, planes, trains, and automobiles.[11] Going against the grain of most literary histories of the counterculture, my central argument in this chapter is that the narrative of opposition is not simply registered or resisted by literary fiction's virtual spaces but partially produced by and circulated through literary branding. Nowhere is this more apparent than when literature is read in real economic spaces, like corporations, and alongside the paraliterary texts, like tourism guides and advertisements, to which its high cultural value is opposed and through which it is stabilized.

Indeed, even for a major market player like the American Express, whose services were billed as primarily financial in nature, reading materialized as a central technique for shaping the consumption of its touristic services. Take, for example, *Americans Abroad*, a pamphlet that the State Department and the American Express Company published and distributed widely in order to encourage consumers of tourism services to engage in "systematic activities" as "organized, sponsored travelers."[12] Such hardworking and behaviorally regulated travelers stood in stark contrast to the leisure time "character of the tourist," whose "purpose"—or so the pamphlet claimed—"is frequently novelty-seeking or just relaxation, and is least apt to want his fun curtailed by an admonition to be 'serious.'" While the tourist had reigned supreme as a popular archetype in early and midcentury literature, by the 1950s, he had become a much maligned character outside of literary fiction. "Tourists act like pigs," accused a 1954 headline in the *Saturday Evening Post*, an image that conjures up the "chattering, smoking, dirty-knickered American motorists" in Willa Cather's 1949 story "The Old Beauty."[13] The *Washington Post* called on the United Nations Educational, Scientific, and Cultural Organization (UNESCO) and the East and West Organization, chaired by Nobel Prize–winning novelist Pearl S. Buck, no great fan of tourists herself, to "promote instruction of responsible international behavior before the big ground swell of postwar travel gets under way."[14] Acting as a serious traveler also meant reading serious texts, which, more often than not, did not include literature. "For those who plan to take part in one of a series of vacation tours," *Americans Abroad* announced, the American Express Company had partnered with the Book-of-the-Month Club to send a "kit of carefully selected books about the countries and regions to be visited. These kits include not only guide books but also surveys of the history, customs and ways of life of the countries to be visited" (3). Reading across the right genres would help to steer consumers away from the characterological antics of the fictional tourist, thereby "prevent[ing] 'emancipation' from the sanctions that restrain [citizens'] conduct back home" while they were on vacation.

As I have observed in the previous two chapters of this book, regulating people's conduct through literary socialization was crucial to enacting international communications initiatives. Such initiatives were so deeply entwined with the American Express Company that CEO Ralph Reed, a frequent visitor to the Eisenhower White House in the 1950s, billed the company's touristic services as "the fifth point" in the "government's Point 4 [Program] for foreign aid" after World War II.[15] As Reed frequently boasted to his colleagues, American tourists existed in a state of almost total reliance on American Express's international products and services for the basic exigencies of travel—not just guide books and other reading material but access to written communications, financial liquidity, and freedom of movement. This complete consumer dependency was integral to what sociologist Dean MacCannell has described as the exploitative logic of postwar tourism.[16] As exemplified by services like organized tours or mail collection, tourism capitalized on the middle-class desire to gaze upon the cultural differences secured by labor: for instance, the desire to witness the tremendous amounts of work that went into building, staffing, and operating national treasuries, supreme courts, waste management facilities, and even American

Express offices in Paris, Rome, and other European capitals. In doing so, the tourist industry transformed the formerly elite notion of "leisure time" into an opportunity to experience the labor of others—an opportunity that, by 1950, approximately one million Americans per year could afford. But Reed also perceived with great canniness that the State Department and the White House were happy to piggyback on the precipitous increase in the consumption of tourism services as a means of promoting diligently supervised forms of international communication, and could thus encourage citizens to purchase tourism's structured activities at an even greater rate. In a symbiotic turn that MacCannell's theory of tourism did not fully anticipate, American tourists came to personify attractions in their own right, their self-regulating labors converging upon the labor on display at the monuments they visited in the quest for cultural difference. Well groomed, impeccably maintained, and made to shine, the travelers who read the federal-corporate complex's reading kits worked to rationalize the production of touristic behavior as a communicative medium: to convey to international audiences an "attitude of respectful admiration" that could "extend beyond immediate social relationships to the structure and organization of the total society."[17]

That, at least, was Reed's and the State Department's fantasy of how they could scale up from the figure of the American to the figure of America abroad, and, like all the fantasies we have encountered so far in this book, the ways this federal-corporate project actually played out were imperfect and discontinuous. But not everyone represented it as such. Recall the exaggerated fear of the company expressed in Corso's poem. If, for Corso, the company regimented people, then the poem "The American Way" similarly regimented the company's representative strategies, aligning the institution of the American Express with Corso's dystopian vision of what social totality looked and sounded like. The poem's representation of the world thus helped sustain the narrative of countercultural struggle that has become all but normalized by postwar literary history. As expressed by Mr. Small, a professor of sociology attempting to track the "migrations" of the counterculture in McCarthy's *Birds of America*, one does not "go to the American Express to find the Beats" (290–91). "You should not find them banding together, like heterosexual similars, to charter an airplane or bus," he declares to McCarthy's protagonist Peter (293). As we will see throughout this chapter, Mr. Small's sociological assessment is simply not accurate, even if it accurately represents how the federal government, college educators, corporate admen, and the Beats themselves talked about the internationally oppositional role of the counterculture. "Bearded, penniless Beatniks hitching their way around Europe have worn out their welcome," announced the *Christian Science Monitor,* a sentiment echoed by the *New York Herald Tribune* ("a beard even in Europe nearly always qualifies its wearer as a Beatnik"), the *Globe and Mail* ("France has been sprucing up its buildings and monuments so it can look its best for visitors, but the Beatniks ... put a crimp in the newly scrubbed look"), and in an odd little couplet appearing in the *Baltimore Sun* ("The Beatniks have appeared on the scene. / Why so frowzy, unkempt, and unclean?").[18]

Yet once one sees the romance of resistance for what it is—a literary-social fiction that self-consciously constructs institutional totality in the extreme only to make the act of defying it that much more meaningful—a new approach for relating counterculture literature to brand reading presents itself. By insisting on its oppositional position in the field of cultural production, the counterculture paradoxically ends up nestling even closer to the economic institutions of mass culture and their apparatuses of power. This is true not only thematically, insofar as corporations like the American Express invite literary representation, but formally as well. Corso's anti-institutional "I" attempts to transform a literary representation of an institution into a seemingly structural truth about its workings. As McCarthy's novel reveals, these apparent truths can give rise to literary-sociological discourses that have tremendous cultural endurance. Against the subversive energies of much postwar literary criticism, then, "The American Way" suggests that the discursive realities one attributes to an institution may be a product of rebellious literary forms doing disciplinary work, just as the nationalized subjects that speak, walk, and think alike appear as a product of an institution's formal rulings. In other words, both the poem and the institution present readers with strategies for normalizing far more complicated histories of the relationship between literary and economic institutions at midcentury.

Read in this light, a poem like "The American Way" is neither for nor against the institution. Rather, the poem stages a strategy for instituting sociological discourse—how we talk about the socializing rules of institutions—through literary form. Literary branding functions as a formal strategy for writers to construct their own institutional fictions on which their claims of national identity are based. The strategy is especially effective when the institution's aspirations to totalization seem to discourage individual subjects from carving out any existential distance between themselves and their conditions of cultural production, as both *Americans Abroad* and Corso's poem imagine the American Express does for its brand-reading subjects. To exist in the American Express office is to exist only as a "mother & father" and just one of many humanoid "replicas"—unless, of course, one is the speaker of the poem, who has somehow escaped this fate from inside the institution and whose very ability to speak thus calls into question the causal movement from the institution to its production of a totalized institutional subject.

The account of brand reading and literary branding I develop in this chapter thus helps us perceive patterns of reading, subject formation, and sociality that are neither totalizing nor subversive but remain ambiguously entwined with institutional conditions that subjects do not wish to fully inhabit. "I am not American Express," Corso's friend and fellow Beat writer William S. Burroughs claims in the "atrophied preface" to his 1959 novel *Naked Lunch*: "If one of my people is seen in New York walking around in citizen clothes and next sentence Timbuktu putting down lad talk on a gazelle-eyed youth, we may assume that he (the party non-resident of Timbuktu) transported himself there by the usual methods of communication. . . ."[19] Burroughs's declaration of nonidentity ("I am not American Express") is both an obvious statement of fact—after all, people are not corporations any more than corporations are people—as well as a denial of communicative responsibility. As a writer, he refuses to take credit for the narrative space-time it would take to move a character from New York to Timbuktu. Instead, he outsources this act of "communication" to the American Express's "usual methods," which he begrudgingly accepts but juxtaposes to his specifically literary mode of communication: the metalinguistic interjection "next sentence" that teleports "one of my people" from New York to Timbuktu. Once the "party non-resident of Timbuktu" has arrived, he may spend the time he has saved in transit "putting down lad talk on a gazelle-eyed youth." The nonresident's erotic chatter, which stages an emphatically queer form of communication, thus provides a striking contrast to the disembodied and infinitely replicating "mothers & fathers" that "speak" "alike" in Corso's depiction of the American Express office.

Who constitutes the shadowy network of "my people" that Burroughs juxtaposes to the brand-reading subjects of the American Express? His possessive claim is a shorthand for all those consumers whose ways of being and belonging run counter to the institutions that organize the social order. But more specifically, it provides an apt description of the Beats' coterie culture, as well as a way for us to theorize its social formation through its double movements toward and away from national, consumer, and sexual identity claims. The novels that I take up in this chapter, from *Naked Lunch* to James Baldwin's *Giovanni's Room* (1957) to Corso's long-ignored novel *The American Express* (1960) to Erica Jong's second-wave feminist best seller *Fear of Flying* (1973), thus advocate neither the utopian overthrow of market institutions nor a total retreat from the socioeconomic powers that be. Rather, these novels wholeheartedly embrace literary branding—and thus, brand reading—as a creative strategy through which economic institutions might be made to support individual subjects and social relationships outside of their normal and normalizing functions. At its most ambitious, then, brand reading reveals how we might begin to dismantle the wall between representation and reality that nearly all historical and contextual criticism takes as its precondition for reading—and for producing readings of—literature.

WRITING CHECKS, READING IDENTITY

If asked to pinpoint the dawn of the modern tourism industry, we might reasonably propose July 7, 1891: the day when American Express general manager Marcellus F. Berry was granted four copyrights for the world's first international traveler's check. As Berry envisioned it, the check would replace the traditional letters of credit that nineteenth-century travelers were required to carry on their person at all times—the only way for them to prove that they were who they claimed to be when attempting to access funds at international banks. Berry believed that corroborating one's identity need not involve so much "irksome formality."[20] Nor did travelers have to run the risk of penury should they happen to misplace their letters of credit or fall victim to a thief or pickpocket. "There's one thing every person does in a distinctive way," Berry postulated. "That is writing his signature. Therefore, the foolproof device for taking money to strange places must carry the signature of the bearer. It must declare that it will be cashed only when a second, and matching, signature is added before witnesses."[21] The "foolproof device" of the traveler's check thus ushered in a new global economy of inscription: a system of capital distribution premised on millions of performative acts of writing, rewriting, and reading, each of which constructed and authenticated the identity of every "distinctive" person presenting the traveler's check to strangers in "strange" lands. Importantly, as financial reporter Roger Warner observed in a 1919 issue of the *Bankers Magazine*, the extension of "universal recognition" to the act of signing a check required "the expenditure of thousands of dollars" to prepare the institutional spaces in which the written enactment of identity could be witnessed, read, and sanctioned.[22] "Banks had to be circularized to introduce to them the travelers check," Warner explained. "Hotels, restaurants and shops, tourist bureaus, ticket offices and steamship lines had to be told of

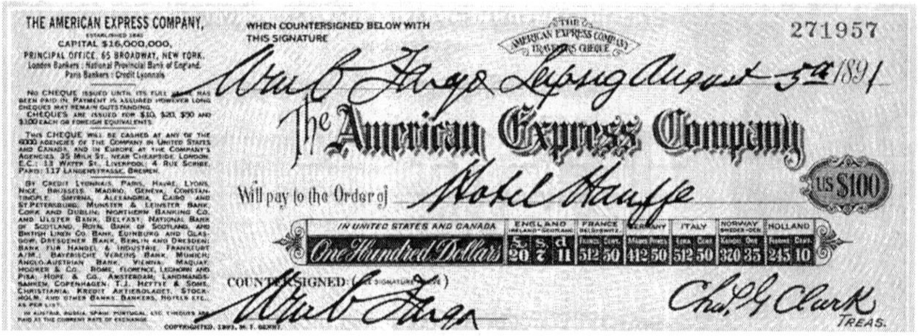

FIGURE 3.1 American Express Traveler's Check (1891).

its strong points and of the responsibility of the great business organization back[ing] it." It was the traveler's check that ultimately gave rise to the
sprawling network of American Express offices whose global reach would
fascinate everyone from midcentury families on tour to Fitzgerald, Miller,
MacCannell, and the Beats in their frenetic movements from Peru to Paris,
Mexico City to Calcutta.

Just a quick glance at the design of the traveler's check is enough to reveal
how the inscription of personal identity required an appeal to consumerist-
national power to guarantee its performative success. As exemplified by its
prominent display of the brand name of "the great business organization"
backing it, as well as the overlay of the "United States Dollar" and the head
of a Roman gladiator, the check aligned the United States' currency and
the American Express with the historical omnipresence of empire. (In later
iterations of the check, the Roman gladiator would find himself flanked
by marketing slogans that called the check "the sky-blue passport" and "a
Super-man.") Although Berry had invented the instrument as a "unit of
universal currency," the check's visual design came courtesy of American
Express advertising director S. Douglas Malcolm, who embraced the language and imagery of international transcendence with an adman's eye to
maximizing sales. "In planning advertising such as this company carries on,
petty vision has no place,"[23] Malcolm proclaimed. He touted the traveler's
check as "a financial talisman" that could "be spent the world over": a magi-
cal object whose perfect dollar-based fungibility would allow the American
traveler not only to consume internationally but also to "see the world
as a unit." The check's circulation of American branded capital, Malcolm
suggested, could reproduce the address of the company's headquarters of

"65 Broadway, New York" in "the mud village in Central America, in the disorganized towns of Soviet Russia, in the circle of the best London clubs." By allowing nationally and corporately branded capital to transcend the structural inadequacies of other nations' financial institutions or currencies—a risky proposition for travelers who worried about swindlers and counterfeiters who ran amok in "disorganized towns" and "mud villages"—the check could guarantee the safety of a consumer's money and the integrity of his identity across national borders. And, as we can see in Malcolm's illustration "Anywhere—Everywhere, The Round World 'Round," the check could also guarantee the consumer's freedom to go where he wanted and do what he wished, emblematized by Lady Liberty circling the globe as a representative of the company. We need look no further for a positive customer testimonial than Burroughs, who describes in a letter to Allen Ginsberg how the male prostitutes he frequented in Peru would steal traveler's checks from him but not know how to forge his signature to access his funds. "Rolled for $200 in traveller's [sic] checks. No loss really as American Express refunds," he wrote after one wild night, with relief and a touch of glee.[24]

By midcentury, the company's textual ability to institute and stabilize their customers' individual and collective identities had so thoroughly penetrated the tourism industry that CEO Ralph Reed dubbed the American Express, over and above the US armed forces, the "benevolent protector of Americans everywhere."[25] Indeed, the story that Reed felt "best typified" the company's identity politics was that of an elderly woman he had spoken to while on vacation in Madrid, an encounter he narrated to the influential business interest group, the Newcomen Society of America, at their 1952 holiday banquet. "Day after day," Reed relayed, "this woman dropped into our office and sat in one of the armchairs. Finally, one of our travel men asked her if she would not like to do some local sightseeing. 'No,' she replied. . . . 'If you don't mind, I'll just sit here for an hour or two each day. You see, this is the only place in Madrid that makes me feel that I am back in America.'" Interestingly, Reed's chosen tale was not about this tourist's consumption of cultural difference but her desire for cultural similitude. Unlike Fitzgerald's narrator in *The Crack-Up*, who chafes against the insistent and repetitive sameness of the office, Reed's little old lady relishes the connection she draws between a geographically international space and the affirmation of her nationalist-consumerist identity. Her story would forever be enshrined in the pamphlet the Newcomen Society printed shortly after the banquet, "American Express, its origin and growth," and distributed to its seventeen thousand members, as well as corporations and libraries

**Anywhere — Everywhere
The Round World 'Round**

On the sands of Sahara, or at a Ritz Hotel—in all lands, at home or abroad, or sailing the Seven Seas

American Express Travelers Cheques

DOLLARS — STERLING — FRANCS

are always good as good American gold

Acceptable everywhere. The insured money of all nations. Guard your travel funds against theft or loss.

Convenient, simple, safe, these "sky blue" financial passports command the service and attention of the thousands of representatives of a great International, Financial and Travel organization.

For sale at Express Offices or Banks

For all journeys secure your steamship tickets, hotel reservations and itineraries, or plan your cruise or tour through the American Express Travel Department.

American Express Company

65 Broadway, New York

International Banking—Shipping—Travel and Foreign Trade

Emphasizing the fact that they are
universally accepted as money

MORE than acceptable everywhere. Better than good American gold the world over. Proof against loss or theft.

**American Express
Travelers Cheques**

DOLLARS — STERLING — FRANCS

The Insured Money of All Nations

For sale at Express Offices or Banks

For all journeys secure your steamship tickets, hotel reservations and itineraries; or plan your cruise or tour through the American Express Travel Department.

American Express Company

65 Broadway, New York

International Banking   —   Shipping   —   Travel and Foreign Trade

A national campaign introduced the
checks to the public

FIGURE 3.2 American Express, "Anywhere—Everywhere The Round World 'Round." Ad from *Bankers Magazine* (1921).

FIGURE 3.3 American Express, "The Insured Money of All Nations." Ad from *Bankers Magazine* (1921).

across the United States and Europe. Hers was just one of the many social fictions that Reed and his admen would offer their customers over the next two decades to model how everyday acts of writing and reading in the American Express could become occasions for constructing and circulating one's identity.

If the rapidly expanding economy of inscription was designed to make the world over in American Express's image, by the 1950s, these inscriptions were intimately linked to the economic and cultural rise of the new American leisure class: the middle-class families targeted by the tour programs the company had designed in close collaboration with the State Department after World War II. By now, it is common knowledge that the middle-class family—or "nuclear" family in its weaponized form—served as a representative touchstone for the federal government's Cold War *Kulturkampf*.[26] The "Family Circle," as one critic notes, traced a metaphoric "fortress" of intimacy that protected white, suburban consumers from "urban blight, teenage crime, and racial Others," as well as the non-normative ideologies of free love and sexual revolution embraced by hippies, Beatniks, queers, Socialists, and Communists.[27] As tourism became increasingly important to the federal government's communications efforts, the nuclear family and "family men" would emerge as leading players in the regulated consumption of leisure time. Drawing on a large and already captive consumer base, the American Express Company began promoting a series of family-friendly tour programs and advertisements, which included government-sponsored travel for military families who wanted to see Europe, the first postwar ocean cruise (an extension of the "family automobile trip"), and Ralph Reed's highly publicized "Family Tour" to the Pacific with his wife and daughter. Reed even grew fond of telling stories at board meetings about how the company had helped to construct families. His favorite romantic tale, which he also had reprinted in "American Express, its origin and growth," involved a North Carolinian GI and a French piano player. The two had met when the pianist had played the US national anthem for the GI after the Liberation of Paris on August 19, 1944, and when they had fallen out of touch, the American Express had played "matchmaker" by reuniting them.[28] In Reed's whimsical fiction, international communication appeared as a romantic communion that triangulated national, consumer, and sexual identities, which in turn aligned the company's production of the "serious" traveler with the representative mission of the "ambassador." This American Express ambassador, like the Fulbright scholar, came bearing the affective gift of "goodwill" in the institution of marriage and the family.

Reed's preferred character types (the domestic woman), genres (the romance), and textual objects (the business pamphlet) shored up for his business elite readers precisely those aspects of the dominant culture that so many self-proclaimed countercultural writers had gone abroad to escape. Indeed, what Michael Warner and Lauren Berlant have referred to as the "nostalgic family values covenant" of the American public sphere—the effort to locate discourses of national belonging in the privatization of sexual and reproductive intimacies—doubled as the organizing principle of the company's marketing strategy and its representation of national identity.[29] To walk into an American Express office in 1957 was not just to enter a space overrun by the American family but to perceive the American family as instituting a particular spatial and temporal organization of touristic experience—specifically, the reproductive temporality that Jack Halberstam sees as organizing both the Family Circle's "normative scheduling of daily life" and its "generational time."[30] Halberstam's claim extends in a rather

FIGURE 3.4 American Express, "Time to Travel!" Ad from pamphlet (1949).

straightforward way to the idea of "family vacation," the very modifier "family" domesticating and normalizing the leisure time of "vacation." Beyond the semantics of tourism, however, its structuring of leisure time was inevitably wedded to the gendered and sexualized spaces of consumption. For the company's vacation organizers, feminized public spaces like luxury boutiques, perfumeries, and hotel sitting rooms were cordoned off for mothers and daughters; hotel bars, government monuments, auto rides, and nightlife were the domain of fathers and sons.[31] The "systematic activities" that "organized, sponsored travelers" participated in thus mapped out a markedly heteronormative timetable, one that replicated the dominant discourses of national identity as family identity. To read the brand name of the American Express was not only to encounter the company's myriad narratives of family formation but also to be socialized into these narratives' temporal and spatial forms, whether from the position of the tourist or the local observer of American tourism in action.

Given this historical context, the scenes of literary branding that Corso's "The American Way" and Burroughs's *Naked Lunch* stage are notable for how they invoke the brand name to negotiate their ambiguity toward the company: the tension between necessity—the company's support of their basic communicative needs—and the company's apparatuses of representation, which deem certain kinds of subjects and social interactions normal and others not. Both authors thus gravitate to the company's construction of sexual identity not to repudiate it outright but to queer it at its most powerful site of public expression: family and family time. Corso's and Burroughs's representational claims against the company's identity strategies—its scheduled family tours, its intragenerational family values—disrupt, pervert, or otherwise destabilize the company's social fictions of what (and who) counts as normal and what (and who) constitutes the national. Appropriately, their claims against family time are registered, first and foremost, by the queering of progressive narrative temporality. Recall the speeding up of narrative time in Burroughs's outsourcing of communication to the American Express and his metadiscursive enactment of literary teleportation ("next sentence"), all for the sake of "putting down lad talk on a gazelle-eyed youth" halfway across the world. Recall also the slowing down of poetic time achieved by Corso's speaker's repeated "I see," which freezes "mothers & fathers" in the timeless present of the American Express office. We may thus understand the queering of literary space-time that takes place in the American Express as intimately tied to the queering of the periodic and progressive time of the family, the main pillar of the company's sexual identity claims. In the next section, we will see just how such queer forms engage the company's vision of consumerist-national totality by latching on to its discursive apparatus— its brand name—to create the romance of resistance.

For now, however, we can see the social position taking performed by literary branding at play in the writing of another figure allied with both queer aesthetics and, to a less obvious degree than the Beats, the 1950s and 1960s counterculture: James Baldwin. In *Giovanni's Room* (1956), Baldwin's narrator David makes daily visits to the American Express office in Paris's Ninth Arrondissement to cash his traveler's checks, pick up his mail, and pick up money that his father wires him. This daily pilgrimage is one that David's lover Giovanni insists on, for it is crucial to their survival: "Giovanni tried to keep panic out of his voice when he asked me every morning, 'Are you going to American Express today?'"[32] A daily financial habit that Baldwin himself had cultivated during his years in Paris, going to the American Express every day helps David perceive how national identity is stabilized and communicated by consumption, heterosexuality, and institutional regimentation. Ironically, this perception comes by way of David's avowed inability to perceive the individual identities of the people in the office space. "Walking into the American Express Office," he writes, "I was forced to admit that this active, disquietingly cheerful horde struck the eye, at once as a unit. At home, I could have distinguished patterns, habits, accents of speech—with no effort whatever: now everybody sounded, unless I listened hard, as though they had just arrived from Nebraska. At home I could have seen the clothes they were wearing, but here I only saw bags, cameras, belts, and hats, all clearly from the same department store" (89). Here, as in Corso's poem, David's identity as a narrator is set apart from the identity of the American Express's "disquietingly cheerful horde" by his insistence that he cannot distinguish between individuals. He speculates about the work he "could" or "would" have performed if he had observed the communicative behavior of these individuals at home, from classifying singular "patterns, habits, accents of speech" to perceiving the shapes and colors of "clothes." Yet the failure of individual description forces him to default to depicting the social "unit" instead. And in making the scalar leap from the individual to the unit, a new material reality is born. "Bags, cameras, belts, and hats, all clearly from the same department store" instantiate a network of consumption that conspiratorially links this unnamed clothing retailer to the American Express office. Both institutions seem to have collaborated to produce the spectacle of national-consumerist identity that transpires within the office space, one that entirely occludes the figure of the American to promote the corporatized figure of America.

Even more important for the company's sexual identity claims, however, is how David's spectacle of sartorial reality culminates in the radical dematerialization of the human bodies that sport these bags, cameras, belts, and hats. "At home," he continues, "I would have had some sense of the individual womanhood of the woman I faced: here the most ferociously accomplished seemed to be involved in some ice-cold or sun-dried travesty of sex, and even the grandmother seemed to have no traffic with the flesh. And what distinguished the men was that they seemed incapable of age; they smelled of soap, which seemed indeed to be their preservative against the dangers and exigencies of any more intimate odor. The boy he had been shone, somehow unsoiled, untouched, unchanged through the eyes of a man of sixty, booking passage, with his smiling wife, to Rome. His wife might have been his mother, forcing more oatmeal down his throat, and Rome might haven the movie she had promised to allow him to see" (90). In the social unit that David describes, heterosexuality is stripped of any erotic appeal and replaced by a practice of incestuous time travel that resists the progressive movement of reproductive time. The man of sixty reverts to a boy bereft of his "intimate odor," a boy "unsoiled, untouched, unchanged," whose excitement is the childish joy of seeing a movie. His wife morphs into his "mother, forcing more oatmeal down his throat." The forced sterility of the Family Circle—a circle that now encloses generational time as well as national space—reproduces the family as a figural unit (man, woman, and child) without reproducing the family sexually. This is the real "ice-cold or sun-dried travesty of sex" that Baldwin observes in the American Express—a desireless disruption of "family time" whose recursive doubling back from present to past mirrors David's own seesawing narrative temporality throughout the novel.

What is distinctly queer about the identity claims of *Giovanni's Room*, then, is not the fact of David's sexuality or his outsider self-positioning vis-à-vis the normalized national-consumer subjects he sees in the American Express. Rather, David's construction of his national identity operates by queering the normal: by making the normal family unit perverse, incestuous, and hermetic so that he may subsequently identify with it. This strategy resists the claims to unitary identity made not only by the American Express but by Giovanni's labeling of David as a *"vrai* American"—a "true American." "I resented . . . being called an American (and resented resenting it)," David reflects, "because it seemed to make me nothing more than that, whatever that was; and I resented being called *not* an American because it seemed to make me nothing" (88). For Baldwin, literary branding reconstitutes as non-normal the institutional spaces of the dominant culture so that his protagonist may sustain his attachment to his contradictory individual, national, and sexual identities. Thus whereas Corso's poem ends with the insistent demand for corporate accountability ("What did this monstrous thing? / What regiments a people so?"), David ends by acknowledging that "what I was seeing was but a part of the truth and perhaps not even the most important part; beneath these faces, these clothes, accents, rudeness, was power and sorrow, both unadmitted, unrealized, the power of inventors, the sorrow of the disconnected" (90). Reflexively, he acknowledges that his temporally perverse and hypostatizing description of the American Express and its family units is one of many partial and imperfect correspondences between the perceptive language of fiction and institutional reality.

Of course, the literary branding of *Giovanni's Room* is not as effective as "The American Way" or *Naked Lunch* at securing the novel's (or the authorial figure's) countercultural status by constructing an oppositional fiction of institutional totality. Just as banks had to be "circularized" to introduce them to the traveler's check, so too did novels require reading publics that were primed to interpret the sociological work of literary branding as a structural reality. And Baldwin, whose critics have tended to read his fiction as relatively apolitical in nature, was not obviously plugged into the same networks of literary and lifestyle experimentation as the 1960s counterculture or its readers.[33] He despised what he perceived of as the Beats' shallow attempts at collective meaning making. He mocked Allen Ginsberg and Gary Snyder's Buddhist writing retreats as the play-acting of "the Suzuki rhythm boys"; he "put Bill [Burroughs] down" after reading a draft of *Naked Lunch*; and he refused to let Jack Kerouac sleep on his floor when he was in Paris.[34] For the transition from literary branding to the construction of new institutional realities, we must now turn to Corso's *The American Express*: a text less well known today than *Giovanni's Room* but one intimately studied by both the company that Corso kept—the Beats and Beatnik readers—as well as the company whose brand name Corso brandished in the title of his first and only novel.

WAITING FOR THE DOUGH

En route from Mexico City to Paterson, New Jersey, in December 1956, Allen Ginsberg sent an uncharacteristically terse letter to his publisher Lawrence Ferlinghetti at City Light Books in San Francisco. The letter was to inform Ferlinghetti that Ginsberg; Ginsberg's lover, Peter Orlovsky; Orlovsky's brother Lafcadio; and Jack Kerouac had been forced to abandon a broke Gregory Corso in Mexico. "We left Gregory waiting for money order to arrive in Mexico City; it was sent the worst and slowest way possible, mail money order; several weeks ago, he was still waiting. December 3. Money order from his girl so he could fly home fast."[35] Corso had spent most of that week shuffling from the dilapidated local post office, where his girl had postmarked his money order, to the American Express, where he received and sent letters. Deeply wounded by the irony of a money order impeding rather than hastening his return to New York, he addressed a series of furious correspondences to Randall Jarrell expressing as much. On November 29, 1956, with vitriol: "How impatient I am! Money order was sent to me on the 20th, it still hasn't arrived. I hate banks. I hate post offices. I hate waiting.... Allen and group have left already. I am alone waiting for stupid international money transaction."[36] On December 3, with despair: "I am miserable. God knows how long I have to wait. How funny when I first hit Mexico I felt a sense of doom, can this then be my doom? Waiting day after day for a money order that never comes?"[37] And the following day, conceding defeat: "After fifteen days of expectancy and futility, I am finally resigned to come what may."[38]

Nothing chafes at the social organization of time quite like waiting, especially waiting alone in Mexico City's American Express office. It is tempting to laugh at the Kafkaesque absurdity of Corso's predicament or to dismiss as hyperbolic his abjection at the idea of never reuniting with "Allen and group," the literary coterie that Corso—a lifelong ward of the New York City foster care system—had naturalized as his "blood" and "heritage."[39] But we should pause to reflect on the sense of doom one feels when capital networks and institutions fail, and how their failure may take coextensive structures of social organization down with them. The failure of institutionalized forms of communication, which I will return to in the final two chapters of this book, is presaged here by how the breakdown of a market institution yields the breakdown of a literary coterie. Not only does the uneasy proximity between the failure of capital and the failure of the counterculture illuminate a new angle from which to read Corso's *The American Express*, the novel that resulted from his experience of abandonment, but it also encourages us to theorize how the social unit of the literary coterie might be organized by more than just the interpersonal dynamics of small-group kinship, friendship, literary lineage, or exclusionary aesthetic practice.[40] Corso's panicked letters suggest that the coterie might, in fact, rely on larger and seemingly oppositional institutions to sustain both its literary experimentation and experiments in international living.

But first, let us detour into *The American Express*'s publishing and reception history to see how literary branding became central to the coterie's organization. Released by Maurice Giordias's Olympia Press in 1961, Corso's novel was packaged and promoted as part of the New Traveler's Companion (NTC) series. NTC was not a series of guidebooks, as one might quite reasonably expect. Rather, it was a thoughtfully curated collection of now-famous avant-garde fiction (*The Tropic of Cancer*, *Naked Lunch*, and *Lolita*) interspersed with sadomasochistic gay erotica, including such titles as *Lust*, *Rape*, *Roman Orgy*, *Mistress-Slave Contest*, *From Slut to Slave*, and *120 Days of Sodom*. While Doubleday was the first press to approach Corso about publishing his book, Corso was determined to go with Olympia precisely because "they did all those porno books."[41] If the novel's inclusion in NTC's offerings seemed like an obvious affront to the institutions of mainstream publishing, it also made American Express's most prominent apparatus of power—its brand name—vulnerable to an unexpected form of discursive appropriation. What Loren Glass has detailed as the incorporation of the avant-garde into postwar publishing economics is playfully inverted in the case of *The American Express*: here the company's brand is co-opted by an

FIGURE 3.5 Cover of Gregory Corso's *The American Express* (1961).

avant-garde publisher of "porno books," and thus inserted into a new and notably queer context for literary reception and the production of brand-reading subjects.[42] (Think what it would mean for Baby Warren's heart to lift at *this* American Express.) Corso's appropriative strategy thus relies on contaminating the representational and economic capital of the brand with the cultural capital of Olympia. And the cover of the first edition announces as much, by placing Corso's image just to the right of an "American Express" office's double-storied signage.

Yet despite the naughty company it keeps, *The American Express* depicts nothing even remotely prurient taking place in the company's offices—a fact that Corso would draw attention to when questioned by one of the company's public relations executives after the book's publication. A Cold War bildungsroman of sorts, *The American Express* tells the story of an anonymous boy, born and abandoned in the basement of an American Express, who constructs an avant-garde artistic lair underneath the office space. Like the twice-abandoned Corso, the novel's protagonist is eternally alone, waiting for a biological family that will return to claim him and, in doing so, bestow value onto his artistic work. And like Baldwin's sexlessly reproducing family unit in *Giovanni's Room*, the novel's prologue, in which the protagonist is conceived and born in the

American Express, turns on the total absence of bodily interaction or affect from heterosexual reproduction. Even the layout of the prologue helps us see how the replication of the family as a social unit relies on an aesthetic of touristic communication that is replicative, rather than reproductive.

'He's beautiful—' said the young lady of the only man in the American Express.
'Why don't you go speak to him,' nudged her lady friend.
'But will he speak to me?'
'What man wouldn't?'
'He is beautiful—'
'Go. Go and say something nice to him—'
The young lady approached the man.
He smiled.
'Sir, will you present me with a baby?'
The man looked at her with sequined eyes—then his eyes widened and his face became aglow.
'My hotel is a street away,' said the man.
'Have you ever presented a woman with a baby before?'
'I don't remember,' gleamed the man.
'Have you ever had sex?'
'Yes—'
'What happened?'
'What happened? What do you mean what happened?'
'Something must have happened—'
'Nothing happened.'[43]

Like Baldwin's transformation of individuals into family units, Corso imagines how familial autogeneration might take place through a distinctly abstracted form of communication between tourists. The spoken exchange between the woman and her lady friend that opens the prologue is almost entirely metacommunicative—a conversation about speaking that has nothing to do with the specific content of speech and everything to do with whether speech will take place. The subsequent exchange between the woman and the "beautiful" man begins with a request for a baby, then devolves into mirrored acts of compulsive repetition and replication that fixate on the word *happened*: "What happened? What do you mean what happened? Something must have happened—Nothing happened." Within the socio-institutional protocols of the American Express office, it seems that "nothing" meaningful or even memorable "happens" during sex if the man does not ultimately "present the woman with a baby"; a logic that is simultaneously puritanical in its sexual sanctimony and queer in its nonreproductiveness.

And while Corso implies that the man and the woman retreat to her hotel room, the narrative elides the time between courtship and birth: there is no foreplay, no sex, no gestational period, no follow-up meeting between the man and the woman. There is simply a Burroughs-esque flash-forward to "nine months later" when the woman delivers her baby in the basement of the same American Express office, surrounded by a group of tellers who do double duty as vicious midwives: "They yanked the child from her, they punched it into life, they threw it out on the street, it lay there until dawn" (4). Violently propelled into the world and into the center of the novel, the unnamed protagonist crawls back into the American Express office. For the next eighteen years, he will star in a panoptic fable of institutionalized subject creation that is even more extreme—architecturally, physically, affectively, and aesthetically—than Goffman's total institution.

Like the incongruous domains of economic and literary production that Corso brings together in his branded title, the plot of *The American Express* is propelled by the tension between institutional totality and the social possibilities of literature—how literary form can discursively transform the American Express into an institution capable of sustaining a social unit other than the consumerist nuclear family. On the child's eighteenth birthday, the American Express finds itself at the mercy of two feuding ideologues battling for control of the company's financial networks and the fate of its protagonist's basement artwork. There is Hinderov, a peddler of nuclear weapons, who believes that only the leveling force of the atomic bomb can "break the universal deadlock" of the Cold War's bipolar power struggle (31). And there is his opponent, Mr. D., a literary aesthete who wants to "find a good language for the new consciousness" of the counterculture—a "word-man" who Corso would later claim was inspired by Burroughs and his work with the cut-up method.[44] Like Burroughs's techniques of cutting and collaging poems, Mr. D. is in the business of purchasing individual words from the entities that own the rights to them: the neologisms of the Royal Shakespeare Company; the hieroglyphs of the Egyptian government; and Old English derivatives like "button, basket, brake, cart, crook, gown, grid, kilm, mattock, mop, rasher, whip, and wicket" from the nation of Albion's Cynings ("Kings" in Old English) (30). And like Burroughs's belief that cutting up words is not only art but *something to do* with art, Mr. D. believes that the radical decontextualization of language and its insertion into new discursive contexts will allow readers to alter the world's material realities.[45]

Standing in opposition to Hinderov's nationalist and militaristic exercise of power, Mr. D. zips from nation to nation attempting to create a literary economy in which the words that make up literature are valued like brands

FIGURE 3.6 "Birth in the American Express" from Corso's *The American Express* (1961).

FIGURE 3.7 "American Express Scene" from Corso's *The American Express* (1961).

and where their prices index their relative supply and demand in a rapidly internationalizing market for language. Yet while Mr. D. labors to make literariness a function of capitalist forces, he also imagines that his new language will have the ability to remake the institutions of capitalism. This is especially true when it comes to the American Express, the nexus of all human connectivity. Indeed, Mr. D. dreams that his painstakingly constructed language will articulate a new consciousness not just for people but also for institutions, enabling a revolutionary form of transnational and transhistorical identity, one that distends the space-time continuum and supersedes the company's national-consumerist identities. For Mr. D., a brand reader and writer par excellence, all institutions can be remade by reading literature.

In contrast to Mr. D., Hinderov wants to co-opt the American Express's communications networks to distribute his nuclear bombs. Paradoxically, he imagines that order is needed to create disorder—that the world and its conditions of production can be wrecked in systematic and totalizing ways. We can see this most clearly in a speech he delivers after taking the manager of the American Express hostage. "Yes, in unimaginable transactions I will partake!" he exclaims. "Not with materialists, overfed and misshapen, no, not with families who want to be happy and so go on tours, no, but with parliaments! banks! nations! All networks will be operated from here by me!" (121). Forsaking those whom the company has historically encompassed as part of its representative identities ("materialists," "families"), Hinderov instead embraces a world of utter meaninglessness; a world inaugurated by a meta-institutional totality in which "parliaments! banks! nations!" bow to him from his position as the head of the American Express. There he reigns as the supreme dictator of a disordered world. "The American Express will serve my purposes," he continues, for "it is a simple, admirably functional organization, extremely orderly, efficient, and to an extent, benevolent—indeed it is just such a system that can appreciate whatever I deem to channel through it" (121). Disorder thus requires that one infinitely mutable individual rule over everything, and that he do so with maximum efficiency and instantaneity; the exact opposite of the longue durée of literary creation embraced by Mr. D.'s new language. "Disorder demands immediacy!" Hinderov crows just before rebranding the American Express "The Hinderov Express."

The desire for ordered disorder also extends to the family unit, where Hinderov's hostile takeover involves ridding the world of woman: a misogynistic fantasy of homosociality that recalls many critical indictments of the Beats' antifeminist tendencies. "She's your mother your sister your wife your child your master your entire womankind!" Hinderov preaches from his pulpit in the American Express. "I say womankind is surmounting the mankind plain! I say *down with human milk*!" (68). The syntactical collapse of female roles (mother, sister, wife, child) into the figure of the "master" suggests the complete overhaul of the world as the domain of "womankind." Hinderov's world is not overrun by the family, as is Baldwin's or Corso's, but by an all-male utopia; here a literal "mankind" overthrows the biological family by rejecting the power of "human milk" and the reproductive need for women. If Hinderov's campaign evokes the image of the gay counterculture frequently foisted onto the Beats by their critics, it does so only to mock the critical tendency to normalize sociobiological structures of sociality with the same intensity as family-values advertising does.[46] In fact, Hinderov's homotopia parodies the romance of resistance, insofar as there exists no salient structural difference between the "nuclear family" and Hinderov's atomically secured "mankind plain."

If neither a world of men without women nor the biological family unit, what model of social connectivity does *The American Express* imagine? We can find the answer in the unnamed protagonist's site-specific art installation in the basement of the American Express office: a phantasmagoric labyrinth whose interior is decorated by murals that offer counterfactual and imaginative glimpses into the past, present, and future of the company. A literal underground art scene, the boy's creation only acquires value in the presence of an interpretive language that can give meaning to his images and an interpretive community that can share in the practice of meaning making. Although he initially seeks such a community out in his own biological family, the man and woman of the prologue have long since returned to their homes. As the American Express janitor tells Mr. D. when he stumbles on the boy crying, "It was easy enough to see that something was wrong—he started calling me his father—well, I didn't mind that because I was old enough to be his father, but when he started crying for his mother, it got to be too much" (123). The artwork only acquires meaning in the presence of Mr. D. and his fellow word-men, whose language for a new consciousness proffers the possibility for a shared discourse of aesthetic appreciation and affective communion, and ultimately, a new family for the boy. As *The American Express* would have it, the coterie structure of artistic production and reception demands neither the total destruction (or failure) of socio-institutional systems nor total domination by them. Rather, it requires transforming their linguistic apparatuses of power through readerly strategies of reference, intertextuality, and circulation. Only then can the powers that be embrace the cultural differences inherent in national identity, rather than assert its cultural similitude.

In the Beats' vast archive of letters, one can find more and less dramatic stories of how this strategy paid off in the form of the coterie's international communicative strategies: Ginsberg and Orlovsky's flirtatious correspondences, in which they arranged romantic meet-ups in American Express offices in Athens, Tangier, Istanbul, and Haifa; or Burroughs's tendency to put down lad talk on men who lurked outside of American Express offices in South America, even though they continued to roll him for his checks.[47] But perhaps the best example of how this strategy exceeded the coterie comes from Olympia Press's launch party for *The American Express*, which included among the guests an unidentified representative from American Express headquarters in New York. In a short article titled "So This Is Literature?" partygoer and humorist Art Buchwald noted that the man from American Express had attended because "he thought that Mr. Corso's book had something to do with the company. It was only when he realized that Mr. Corso's publishers put out most of the English erotic books in Paris that he became a little frightened."[48] When Buchwald later asked Corso to recount what he

FIGURE 3.8 "Underneath the American Express" from Corso's *The American Express* (1961).

and the company man had talked about, Corso relayed a stilted exchange over two brand readers' competing perceptions of representation and institutional reality:

> "What is the book about?" the man from the American Express asked.
>
> "It's a tribute to your benevolent firm," the author said. "You must admit things are going on there."
>
> "What kind of things?" the man asked nervously.
>
> "You ought to take a look at some of that mail that comes in."
>
> "Is there any sex in the book?" the man asked.
>
> "No sex at all," Mr. Corso said. "Just one kiss, and that doesn't even take place at the American Express."
>
> He showed the man some illustrations from the book which he himself had done. One showed . . . a man called Hinderov who is trying to take over the American Express so he can give free bombs to everyone. . . .
>
> The American Express man thought the scene wasn't representative of the American Express, but Corso assured him the scene was taken from the book and you had to read the book before you made any flash judgments.

One suspects from the company man's questions that he is there to report back to his superiors on the possibility of brand destruction: the tarnishing of the company's representational value through negative association with

unsavory characters. And yet the way that Corso deflects the man's questions is both a brilliant and hilarious extension of the pragmatic work that
literary branding does in the novel. In insisting that the confused American
Express man "admit that things are going on there" and that he "ought to
take a look at some of that mail that comes in," Corso claims for his literary work a more accurate knowledge of the company's operations than its
own employees. Even more telling is that the company man does not resist
or question Corso's knowingness. "'What kinds of things?'" the man asks
"nervously." His nervousness suggests that he is unable to read Corso's tone.
Is Corso sincere? Or is he playing an elaborate joke? (We could imagine the
American Express man as the source of the question posed by the title of
Buchwald's article: "So This Is Literature?") It does not appear at all clear to
the company man that "this"—*The American Express*—is a work of art firmly
enclosed in the domain of literary production. Rather, it seemed possible
that "this" is real. As such, it bears the burden of being "representative of
the American Express" and its brand name. And Corso's response to the
American Express man's complaint is not a denial of his literary representation's correspondence with reality but an insistence on it. He invites the
company man "to read the book," so that he too may understand how a
representation of a man giving away free bombs in the American Express
might emerge as a representative identity of national-consumerist culture.
To answer Buchwald's question—"So This Is Literature?"—we might say
that, for the man from American Express, *The American Express* is not literature but paraliterature in its most threatening incarnation.

The epilogue to the reception of *The American Express* is, in a sense,
deeply anticlimactic, as the story ends with the corporation's co-optation
of the counterculture to increase its brand equity. This was by no means
an unusual phenomenon: think of Allen Ginsberg and Jack Kerouac's posthumous ads for the clothing retailer The Gap or Burroughs's cameo in a
Nike commercial.[49] By 1967, the American Express had set up sidewalk cafés and cigarette bars outside of their offices in Athens, where Corso was
living as "the crown prince of the local Beats," according to local newspapers. Once there, they began a campaign to rename the Beatnik travelers
who gathered at these cafés the "American Expressnik," a fitting rejoinder to
Corso's incorporation of the company's brand name into the literary novel.[50]
Corso, for his part, seems to have realized even earlier that his act of literary branding may have backfired. On January 20, 1962, he reported waking
up in tears after dreaming about the Beat Hotel at 9 Rue Git-le-Coeur in
Paris, one of the sites where Ginsberg, Kerouac, and Orlovsky had helped

Burroughs assemble the manuscript of *Naked Lunch*. He penned a rueful letter to Ginsberg: "I woke after my dream with awful feeling that I missed out when I wrote *American Express*, that I should have written about 9 rue Git-le-Coeur."[51] One can't help but wonder if Corso's remorse stems from his desire for a purer space of shared aesthetic labor, one in which artisanal economics rather than multinational capital flows underwrite the coterie's cultural productions.

We will see how the seemingly total co-optation of literary production and national identity by brands poses an interpretive problem for readers in the case of Erica Jong's novel *Fear of Flying*. But before turning to Jong, I want to return to Corso's book launch to consider a more optimistic angle on literary branding. Before the American Express man left the party, he asked Corso to sign a copy of his novel. Here is Corso's recollection of their exchange: "I said, 'Who should I autograph it to?' He said: 'Just autograph it to the American Express.' So I did, but I added, 'With love.'" The unexpected intrusion of "love" into the autograph is not only a sentimental parting gift but also a markedly demanding one—a rhetorical overture to the company man and, by extension, the company that he represents, to treat his literary production and the company's literary reception as singular acts of love. Unlike the performative act of signing a traveler's check, Corso's signature transforms the book from a fungible commodity, a piece of company swag, into a medium for securing his identity through one-on-one intimacy. His signature is thus the final act of inscription—a different kind of literary branding—that implicates the American Express in the Beats' coterie culture, marking his ambiguous, if affectionate, relationship to the institution that he hails "With love." It is with an abiding sense of this affection that he then turns to his rowdy party guests and shouts, "In case of trouble we'll go to the American Express. Let the squares go to the Embassy."

BRANDING THE LITERARY

What happens when a countercultural work of fiction is read too widely across the dominant public sphere? Put differently, what happens when a literary work once considered genuinely oppositional or experimental becomes branded as "mainstream," "popular," or "too familiar" to encode a culturally subversive mode of discourse? This is the charge that feminist scholars have often leveled against Erica Jong's 1973 novel *Fear of Flying* after it emerged as a key text for second-wave feminism, one of the top ten best-selling books of the decade—more than twelve million copies sold—and, in Jong's words, "a declaration of independence" for women everywhere.[52] The declaration issues from Jong's first-person narrator Isadora Wing, a Columbia graduate school dropout, budding writer, and neglected wife of psychoanalyst Bennett Wing, whom Isadora abandons at the Congress of Psychoanalysts in Vienna to traipse around Europe in hot pursuit of her erotic fantasies. Equal parts female picaresque and *Künstlerroman*, *Fear of Flying* initially garnered lukewarm reviews in the *New York Times* and other American newspapers of note as "trendy feminist literature."[53] Reviews in UK papers were notably harsher. Travel writer Paul Theroux deemed Isadora a "mammoth pudenda" before declaring that *Fear of Flying*'s vulgarization of feminist discourse represented "everything that is to be loathed in American fiction today."[54] That the novel was "written with a grant (gratefully acknowledged on page 5) from the National Endowment for the Arts should surprise no one already familiar with the ways American money is used, though ample justification for any of us refusing to pay his taxes this year," Theroux concluded. Although there is a puritanical undertone to Theroux's insistence on no taxation without upstanding sexual representation, he was hardly the only reader to suspect that the "American money" responsible for the novel's production was partially responsible for how the novel had popularized—and, by many accounts, cheapened—feminism in the Western world. Even the novel's loudest champion, John Updike, who wrote a glowing review of *Fear of Flying* in the *New Yorker*, began by noting how American branded capital had made Isadora's touristic consumption of sexual experience possible in the first place: "Childless, with an American Express card as escort on her pilgrimage, and with a professional forgiver as a husband, Isadora Wing, for all her terrors, is the heroine of a comedy."[55]

Unlike Theroux's complaint about "American money," which takes aim at the novel's economies of production, Updike's observation appears entirely diegetic in nature, insofar as it registers Isadora's rapturous account of how she accesses money as a tourist. In Updike's brief plot summary, Isadora's ubiquitous credit card takes the place of her flesh-and-blood "escort on her pilgrimage," Adrian Goodlove, the Laingian analyst with whom Isadora flees Vienna. Adrian is "the true, ultimate zipless A-1 fuck" whose penchant for swinging and group sex Isadora believes will replace her domestic dissatisfactions with ecstatic, anonymous, and guiltless pleasure (11). That Adrian's promise of good love should be so readily displaced by a piece of plastic, a "passport" to a world of hedonistic pleasure, is both apt and troubling: apt because Adrian turns out to be mostly impotent, and thus less useful—less plastic—than Isadora's credit card; and troubling as it conflates

Isadora's vagrant desire to "live without worrying about possessions or possessiveness" with her unlimited purchasing power and easy access to global credit markets. Indeed, the vaguely Marxist feminist bent of Isadora's aspirations sits awkwardly alongside the patterns of consumption that the credit card makes possible within *Fear of Flying*'s narrative: from the purchase of Isadora and Adrian's rattling rental car and meager pension accommodations to the expensive Swiss chocolates, stuffed goose livers, and gourmet beer they consume on their road trip from Vienna to London.

Looking beyond the details of Isadora's touristic consumption, we may be surprised by how completely *Fear of Flying*'s plotting of Isadora's sexual repression and sexual liberation is subtended by its secondary plot of Isadora gaining, losing, and regaining access to American money. Here is Isadora trying to decide whether to leave Bennett for Adrian, a pivotal moment that appears halfway through the novel: "I agonized in the American Express office where, at 2 PM, we stood trying to decide whether to get two tickets for New York or two for London or one or none. It was all so dismal. Then I thought of Adrian's smile and the possibility of never seeing him again and the sunny afternoons we'd spent swimming and the jokes and the dreamy drunken rides through Vienna and I raced out of American Express like a mad woman (leaving Bennett standing there) and ran through the streets" (171). Bennett's reaction to her departure similarly reroutes Isadora's claim to sexual liberation through her access to credit. "Bennett wanted to know if I had travelers checks and my American Express card. Was I alright? He was trying to say 'Stay, I love you.' this was his way of saying it, but I was so bewitched that I read it to mean 'Go!'" (173). And when Isadora later leaves Adrian to return to Bennett, it is actually her quest for American branded capital that leads her back to her husband: "Suddenly I remember that everything which stands between me and destitution is in my handbag: passport, American Express card, travelers checks—and I hobble back" (294). At odds with the liberatory sexual ethos of the 1970s, Isadora's credit card seems like a brand-name object better suited to the bad boys of 1980s finance capitalism: Patrick Bateman, who whips out his platinum and gold American Express cards no less than fifteen times throughout *American Psycho* (1991) to pay for his compulsive consumption of brand-name clothing, haute cuisine, and high-end escort services; or the narrator of Jay McInerney's *Bright Lights, Big City* (1984), who uses his platinum American Express card to cut lines of cocaine for the models who crowd around him at New York nightclubs. What, if anything, to make of literary branding in *Fear of Flying*, a novel premised on a woman's simultaneous refusal of sexual propriety and property, yet whose production seems so intimately bound up with the capitalist communication technologies of international tourism? Can brands overrun literary fiction? Can they institute their own conditions of literary reception and their own practices of reading?

Perhaps the best place to begin to answer these questions is with the unfavorable reception of the novel by feminist critics in the 1980s, whose writings I want to treat as primary sources. (My aim here is not to quibble with their interpretations of the novel but to understand a particular mode of reader response that issues from culturally elevated readers.) So successful was *Fear of Flying* as a declaration of women's independence one imagines it would be difficult to avoid in a study of 1970s feminist fiction, yet that is precisely what Rita Felski sets out to do in the introduction to her book *Beyond Feminist Aesthetics* (1989). "The novels of Erica Jong," Felski announces, "which have been marketed as examples of feminist writing do not seem to me to reveal any serious questioning of the existing basis of male-female relations or any sustained refusal of the values of a male-dominated society. It can be noted in this context that some feminist ideas which might have once been considered radical (such as the critique of the sexual double standard) have filtered down the extent that they are now relatively familiar."[56] For Felski, Jong's ideas had "gradually become incorporated into a great deal of material," and as such, her novels could no longer be "constructed as consciously feminist or oppositional in any meaningful sense." We may note in Felski's principled refusal to discuss Jong's novels (although her refusal does, in fact, constitute its own form of discussion) the murkiness of the passive tense. What constitutes a "serious questioning" of male-female relations? Which readers "once considered" ideas like Jong's "radical" but now cannot construct them "as consciously feminist or oppositional in any meaningful sense?" And why must a feminist reader engage only the most radical of works in order to say something about feminist ideas? Underlying these questions is an implicit accusation about false advertising in the literary marketplace: a basic incommensurability between how Jong's novels "have been marketed" (by whom?) and what Felski considers "serious" or meaningful feminist art. Intriguingly, the reason that Felski offers for excluding Jong from her studies is not aesthetic (that Jong's writing is tedious or vulgar, say) or even rigorously theoretical (that her ideas are unsophisticated). Rather, the problem for Felski is one of overconsumption, overcitation, overcirculation, and overcommunication—in short, a problem of excessive reading. Jong's novels are excluded because of how many people, and specifically how many women, have read them only to recite, reuse, or rehearse their now "filtered down" ideas in "a great deal of material."

If this seems like an unusual rationale for refusing to discuss a female writer, it is also a useful entry point for considering the relationship between literary branding and reading novels—or rather, not reading them, something scholars do all the time but rarely talk about in mixed company. Beginning with the unanticipated success of *Fear of Flying*, Jong's novels have addressed an expansive reading public whose practices of reading Felski and others have aligned not only with how novels are marketed but also with market forces that allegedly diminish the oppositional force of feminist critique. Like Felski, Lauren Berlant notes how "in the early days, Erica Jong virtually meant 'feminist art,' art full of female rage and *ressentiment*, sexual fantasy, and experimentation."[57] By the late 1980s, however, Jong's affiliation with feminist art had loosened. Now, Berlant observed, "Jong's power as a professional feminist derives from her high visibility as an early spokesperson for sexual liberation and mainstream feminism." It is no accident that Berlant deploys the language of brand promotion to describe Jong's cultural demotion: she is a "professional" feminist, a first-to-market "spokesperson." While Felski refuses to engage with Jong's work, Berlant devalues it by asserting Jong's biographical status as a symbol, an icon, and a proper brand name circulating widely in the public sphere— "Erica Jong virtually meant 'feminist art.'" The problem with Jong, then, is not her popularity per se but with how her popularity has been produced, commoditized, and circulated.

Yet as various defenders of the novel have pointed out, *Fear of Flying* is deeply sympathetic to its readers' *ressentiment* of the relationship between feminist power and capitalism's marketing schemes. More important for my purposes is how the novel's literary branding functioned (and continues to function) as a crucial interdiscursive feature of the text—one that not only made it possible for the novel to enjoy the kind of mass-market visibility that it did but that, I will argue, made "Erica Jong" a literary brand name in the first place. Such nuance gets lost when one understands brand reading as a capitalist force that acts on the novel's persuadable readerly publics or glamorizes its author figure but exists outside the diegetic world of narrative fiction as mere historical context. In particular, the brand name of the American Express occupies a curiously discursive position with the novel. It is not presented primarily as a brand that mediates and oppresses female subjects, but as a communications technology favored by Henry Miller, the Beats, and others members of a masculinized literary counterculture—a history of which Jong, a savvy brand reader herself, is keenly aware. When Miller would roam the streets of Paris "looking for literary echoes, his final destination was always the America Express office at 11 rue Scribe, and always there was the desperate hope of news and money," Jong writes in her biography of Miller.[58] Paradoxically, *Fear of Flying* uses this particular brand name to write itself into the countercultural legacy of literary production and touristic communication, while simultaneously critiquing the distinctively "American" apparatuses of branding in the postindustrial economy of the 1970s: a system of exchange in which targeted advertising and marketing media conspire to corral many different categories of identity—male, female, gay, straight, queer—under the all-encompassing sign of national-consumerist identity.

Here it is worth noting how awkwardly the company's persistent presence sits alongside the novel's notionally feminist critique of brands and advertising slogans. "Growing up female in America. What a liability!" Isadora complains, "What litanies the advertisers of the good life chanted at you! What curious catechisms! 'Be kind to your behind.' 'Blush like you mean it!' 'Love your hair.' 'Want a better body? We'll rearrange the one you've got.' 'That shine on your face should come from him, not from your skin.' . . . 'How I solved my intimate odor problem.' 'Lady be cool.' 'Every woman alive loves Chanel No. 5.' 'What makes a shy girl get intimate?' '*Femme*, we named it after you'" (9). Her breathless recitation of these decontextualized, yet ultimately recognizable and real, slogans parodies the mass media's construction of femininity as a form of consumption. The effect of these performative utterances is an adult woman with "a mind full of all the soupy longings that every high school girl was awash in"—a woman waiting "to be filled up by a giant prick spouting sperm, soapsuds, silks, and satin, and of course money" (10). Yet by chanting these "curious catechisms" back to its readers, the novel begins to concretize a specific kind of authorial figure: one who invites the reading "you" hailed by the slogans ("*Femme*, we named it after you") to identify not only with Isadora but also with Jong, who, we believe, must have had these real slogans chanted at her in order to reproduce them in the novel for her readers. The literary branding of the novel thus constructs its author as a publicly mediated figure and one limned primarily through her body: her behind, hair, odor, blush, and so forth. Here the double move to abstraction (through the generality of the "you" being addressed by the brands) and particularity (in the figure of Jong the author, who both receives and redirects these addresses to her readers) indexes the communicative contradiction at the heart of literary branding; a self-abstraction similar to the previous chapter's discussion of Plath's Fulbright fashion shoot. In *Fear of Flying*, the consequences of branding's contradictions are the violent and desirous oppression of women's bodies through consumption, on the one hand, and women's erotic liberation through consumption, on the other.

While Jong's parodic pile-up of slogans does a fine and funny job indicting branding's mass-mediated subject, we encounter brand marketing's first negative consequence—the violent and desirous oppression of women—in the form of domestic violence: both domestic violence as violent abuse by a spouse and the existential violence inflicted upon women in their construction as national subjects. As Isadora flees Vienna with Adrian, she recounts to him how her first husband, Brian, descended into madness after he dropped out of graduate school and began to work long hours at a market research firm. There, he "sweated over the computers, anxiously awaiting their answers to such earthshaking questions as whether or not women who have had two years of college will buy more detergent than women who have graduated from college" (193). As his foray into market research escalates from a part-time job to a full-time passion to a psychotic break with reality, Brian clings to a newfound spiritual belief in the totalizing power of capitalist consumption: an infinitely networked system of valuation and purchasing patterns that he imagines only he can control. "What if (Brian asked) Christ came back to earth as an obscure market research executive?" Isadora recounts (198). "What if He blessed the computers and instead of spewing out printed sheets about which housewives buy the most detergent, they suddenly started spewing out loaves and fish? What if the world really was controlled by a gigantic computer and nobody knew it except Brian?" And perhaps the most frightening of all questions: "What if we were all controlled by complex machines which were controlled by complex machines which were controlled by other complex machines? What if we had no freedom at all?"

Brian's obsession with women's detergent consumption patterns conjures up the soapsuds emitted from the oppressive and oppressively large penis in *Fear of Flying*'s opening pages: the "giant prick" spouting soapsuds and slogans that washes over both the hypereducated Columbia graduate and the dopey high school student alike. But the giant prick has more than just a passing association with the spewings of the computer and the spewings of "loaves and bread" that analogize the pressure to consume to the pressure to conform to religious dogma. Delusional though they may be, Brian's technospiritual "catechisms" register the same mass-mediated structures of oppressive marketing as the "curious catechisms" that "advertisers of the good life" chant at their female customers. What if a woman's only path to subjective self-affirmation and socialization is the one laid down by an "obscure market research executive" who determines how a woman's detergent purchases help to construct her identity? What if she has no freedom at all outside of an infinitely recursive marketing system whereby a woman's value is a product of flexible capital inputs? To take these catechisms as a starting point for thinking about femininity and consumption is to make the female body nothing more than the brands that are written upon it. Brian's extreme complicity with brand reading, then, is not just tragically psychotic but horrifically misogynistic. On the night of his hospitalization, Isadora recalls how "Brian fucked like a machine" before attempting to choke her to death (201). "I begged him to stop," she recounts, "but he wouldn't. He kept banging away at me like an ax-murderer." That Isadora should route Brian's violently desirous impulses toward her body through the simile of the "machine" is no coincidence, but rather the consequence of his computational yearning to transform women's bodies into fully branded subjects. And if Brian had his way, neither the Columbia graduate nor the dopey high school student would be exempt from getting fucked by the system.

Yet as was the case for Baldwin and the Beats, consumption can also underwrite a countercultural economy of literary production that uses the communicative apparatuses of the corporation to construct alternative identities. In the case of *Fear of Flying*, the climactic moment of appropriation comes not during Isadora's flight from Bennett but in an earlier touristic experience: a summer abroad in Italy with her best friend Pia, during which each woman seeks to escape an unfaithful lover back home. As their ultimate "act of expiation," the women decide to mail their diaphragms to their former lovers "to try to make *them* feel guilty instead" (228). And so "we troop off to the American Express (where we have slept with half the leering Florentine clerks)," Isadora relays, and "are told to make out a customs declaration." But the textual conventions of the American Express's customs declaration form seem ill suited to mailing a diaphragm. "What to *put* on the customs declaration?" Isadora wonders as she rehearses and discards various options: "'One diaphragm, used?' 'One diaphragm, much abused?' 'Used clothing,' perhaps? Can a diaphragm be considered an article of clothing? Pia and I debate this. 'You *do* wear it,' she says. I maintain that she ought to send it to Boston as an antique and thus avoid all import duty. What if her erring boyfriend had to pay duty on her old diaphragm? Would that be adding expense to injury, insult to guilt?" The real question underlying Isadora and Pia's debate over what to write on the customs declaration is one of value: how much are a woman's past sexual experiences worth on a marketplace that constructs the body ("Used?" "Much abused?") as a medium of communication? And if the customs declaration raises the question of value as mediated by textual performativity—whatever value is written down is the value of the object—then Pia responds in kind. "'Fuck *him*!' Pia said. '*Let* him pay import duty on it and be as embarrassed as possible.' And with that she labels the package: 'I Florentine leather bag—valuation $100.'"

Although the diaphragm may strike Isadora as "a holy object" or a "fetish," and thus a priceless device for controlling her reproductive future, it is not worth $100. But Pia's audacious misrepresentation of the diaphragm as a "Florentine leather bag" offers a technique for artificially inflating not just the diaphragm's value but also the value of the bodily experiences that the diaphragm indexes. The textuality of American Express's customs declaration offers a delightful parody of the misogynistic economics of brand marketing: the diaphragm, a repository for all the sudsy sperm of the past, is sold back to men like Brian—men who tried to sell Isadora and Pia the fantasy of fidelity and sexual satisfaction in the first place. Indeed, the customs declaration offers a written technology for valuing a woman's intentionally nonreproductive bodily labors—all those "leering Florentine clerks" of the American Express they have slept with not-so-long ago. Of course, the declaration does not secure the transcendent vision of feminist liberation that defenders of the novel have claimed for it—a conclusion drawn by reading Isadora's international flight from her husband as homologous to Isadora's "total withdrawal from systems of capital," according to one of the novel's readers.[59] But nor does it confirm the "non-threatening (but readily marketable)" variety of American feminism that other readers have ascribed to the novel by virtue of its (and its narrator's) productive reliance on "American money."[60]

How does the novel's literary branding secure the authorial figure of Erica Jong and her own "brand name," a term she has frequently invoked to refer to her status as a public subject?[61] We cannot equate Jong's "brand name" to the distinction secured by cultural capital (she is no "Joyce" or "Eliot" or "Woolf"), but we also cannot reduce it to the commercial success conferred by the mass market (she is not "Grisham" or "Patterson" or "Robertson"). Instead, her brand formation—the production of her popularity as what Jennifer Wicke has called a "celebrity feminist"[62]—mimics the double move to particularity and abstraction we see in Isadora's recitation of slogans in the novel's opening pages: the paradoxical collision of the author as a solitary and privileged observer of capitalist systems and the author as a figure inevitably formed by capitalism's marketing strategies. Perhaps given the company's experience with Corso, it is not too surprising that their advertising team was aware not only of Jong's brand name but also of how its communicative valences were suspended in between the feminist counterculture and the domestic market.[63] Nancy Novogrod, editor-in-chief of American Express's *Travel and Leisure* magazine, boasted that she had recruited Erica Jong as "a writer who wasn't typically a travel writer" but who could boost American sales based on her name recognition among readers.[64] (Jong would go on to write a travelogue of "banal musings" called "My Italy" for the magazine, a foray that did not pay off for either *Travel and Leisure* or Jong.)[65] And when the company sponsored a meeting of the Association of Women Business Owners at Barnes & Noble, they held the meetings alongside the aisles that shelved Jong's books, as if to draw inspiration through osmosis—the mere presence of her name on the cover emitting an aura of feminist-consumerist success.[66] For Jong, the contradictions of literary branding emerged as a source of self-referential humor in her later novels. "The amazing thing about being a well-known writer is that your name is well known, but your face, reinterpreted through so many distorting book-jacket photos is not," quips an older Isadora Wing in the sequel to *Fear of Flying, Parachutes and Kisses* (1984). "In Italy the publicity photos make you look Italian; in Japan, vaguely Japanese; in France, French; in Germany, German; *und so weiter*. But when people see the name—exactly like in those American Express ads, they gasp. 'You? The writer? I read your book.'"[67] That the gap between a reader's recognition of Isadora's internationalized "name" and her nationally customized "face" should invoke a reader response "exactly like those American Express ads" is no coincidence. It is precisely the condition of reception that *Fear of Flying*'s strategy of literary branding has instituted for its author figure.

THE "REAL PERMISSIVENESS" OF INSTITUTIONS

We may see now how reading brands in Jong's fiction becomes inseparable from branding Jong the author, as well as how her novels claim the aesthetic of literary branding that emerge from Cold War patterns of touristic consumption as a specifically feminist form. And yet to equate reading brands with branding people in any simple or deterministic fashion is to miss how consumerism can inaugurate a version of queer or feminist freedom that denies the regimenting totality of economic markets and institutions without eschewing them entirely. Indeed, the relationship between institutions and countercultures that I have theorized in this chapter offers us one way to reframe the social relationship between expressive subjects and the discursive protocols of the institutions in which they exist. For Baldwin, the Beats, and Jong, the relationship emerges as one of constrained freedom: a self-reflexively limited exercise of autonomy whose very limitations give fodder to experimental reading, writing, and communicative practices. Nowhere is this more apparent than at the very end of *Fear of Flying*. On her train from Paris to London, Isadora chances upon a chemistry professor who is teaching on a Fulbright at Toulouse and who is a firm and puritanical advocate for the disciplinary functions of institutions: "'Discipline!' he said. We need more of it in America—didn't I agree?" (302). Isadora doesn't agree. In fact, she believes the chemist's desire to enhance institutionalized discipline is fundamentally misguided: "'I think we have too little *genuine* permissiveness,' I said, 'and too much bureaucratic disorganization masquerading as permissiveness. Real permissiveness, constructive permissiveness is another story altogether.'"

One could hardly ask for a better phrase than "constructive permissiveness" to describe how the literary branding performed by and through the American Express underwrote the coterie formation of the 1960s counterculture. It makes a good deal of sense that the idea of constructive permissiveness would emerge from an institution that appeared to make fewer demands on its subjects; this in contrast to the spatially, temporally, linguistically, and emotionally immersive "experience of international living" demanded by both the women's college and the Fulbright Commission. Yet as I suggested at the beginning of this chapter, and as I will argue more forcefully in the chapters to follow, an institution's concentration or dispersion of discursive authority does not necessarily correspond in a one-to-one fashion with the expressive demands it makes on its reading subjects. This seems especially true when an institution's mission is one of literacy socialization, which can proceed either through physically bounded scenes of reading instruction (as we have seen in the ladies' culture clubs and international classrooms of chapters 1 and 2, respectively) or more diffuse techniques and technologies of readerly initiation (as we have observed in this chapter's brand reading). The latter is no less demanding or less enduring than the former.

We have seen the "constructive permissiveness" of brand reading play out in the real and fictive brand readers we have encountered throughout this chapter—Reed's little old lady and the millions of check-cashing tourists like her, Fitzgerald, Corso, the American Express public relations representative, Baby Warren, Mr. D., Isadora Wing—but it gains a particularly penetrating edge in Graham Greene's introduction to *The Collected Stories of*

Patricia Highsmith (2001). The internationally itinerant Highsmith, who always received her letters and money "care of Mrs. Somebody" while "standing in line at American Express offices from Opera to Haymarket, Naples to Munich," bestowed on her characters—most famously, the queer sociopath Tom Ripley—a similar tendency to use the American Express to swap identities, cash checks, and flee European cities in the 1950s.[68] Her acts of literary branding are not lost on Greene, for whom the brand name of the American Express transcends the fictional discourse of Highsmith's novels to make unpleasant phenomenological demands on him as a reader nearly a half century later. "Going out into the familiar street" after reading Highsmith's work, Greene writes, "we pass with a shiver of apprehension the offices of the American Express, the center for so many of Miss Highsmith's dubious men, of their rootless European experience, where letters are to be picked up (though the name on the envelope is probably false) and travelers' checks are to be cashed (with a forged signature)."[69] That the brand name should cause not just Greene but "we" readers to "shiver," and that our shivers should originate from such seemingly minute acts of inscription as a falsified name or a forged signature, stands as a testament to how powerfully the institution's discursive technologies of lifestyle management can co-opt the minds and bodies of readers.

If the first three chapters firmly situated bad readers in the brick-and-mortar institutions in which they were forged—women's colleges, American studies departments, American Express offices—the last three chapters of this book consider how the circulation of paraliterary texts can institute routine and repetitive practices of reading and writing literature among people who exist at great distances from one another. Yet it would be incorrect to think that the practices of these reading publics were mediated solely by the circulation of texts. Or rather, to focus on circulation alone would be to miss the complex processes by which the institutions that produced these texts, which range from magazines to bureaucratic documents, carefully engineered their styles, genres, and material forms to illicit certain predictable responses in their readers, a social phenomenology akin to Greene's shivers. Indeed, once the physical space of the institution is no longer a constraint on readers, we can begin to map an even larger expanse of human actors, textual objects, and reading methods than we have so far. In the following chapter, we turn from the American Express to one of its closest advertising partners, the *National Geographic* magazine, in order to address a new challenge in triangulating literary and paraliterary texts with readers and reading practices, on the one hand, and institutions of communication, on the other.

CHAPTER FOUR

Sight Reading

"You see the magazine, of course?"

"Absolutely."

"Have you seen the number with the colored plates of the North American fauna?"

"Yes. I have it in Paris."

"And the number containing the panorama of the volcanoes of Alaska?"

"That was a wonder."

ERNEST HEMINGWAY, "Homage to Switzerland" (1933)[1]

DO YOU SEE THE *GEOGRAPHIC*?

In a letter to her friend Betty Hester dated June 28, 1956, novelist and self-proclaimed homebody Flannery O'Connor posed a question that may have struck Hester as a little bit nutty. "Oh, I want to ask you," O'Connor wrote, "do you read the *National Geographic* or do you smell it?"[2] Perhaps anticipating Hester's bemusement that reading the magazine and smelling it were the only two options available to her, O'Connor took the liberty of answering her own question. "I smell it," she continued. "A cousin gave me a subscription when I was a child as she noted I always made for it at her house, but it wasn't a literary or even a geographic interest. It has a distinct unforgettable transcendent apotheotic (?) and very grave odor. Like no mere magazine. If *Time* smelled like the *Nat'l. Geo.* there would be some excuse for its being printed." What is striking about O'Connor's letter to Hester is not her confession that she smells the *Geographic* but her choice of smell as the sensual corollary to the "literary" act of reading. If smell is often prefigured, in the words of one critic, as an "inveterately low, corporeal, animalistic, primitive, and therefore degraded" sense, O'Connor's gravitation to it seems willfully designed to jettison the more elevated sense of sight and the act of looking at the color photographs for which the *Geographic* was internationally renowned.[3] When discussing a magazine famous for printing the first "rich," "stunning," and "lush" images of bare-breasted women and naked men, the question one naturally expects O'Connor to ask is the same question one might have asked of *Playboy*'s subscribers: "Do you read the articles or look at the pictures?" But O'Connor ignores the photographs all together. Or more precisely, she registers as smell the chemical-saturated, rotogravure printing process that magazine editors have used to brighten and sharpen photographs since the 1940s, but she does so without attending to the magazine's visual aesthetic. All this avoidance raises another question: what's the harm in just looking?

One way to begin to address the competing sensory dimensions of reading is to note that O'Connor's description of smelling the *Geographic*—"transcendent," "apotheotic," "very grave"—echoes the adjectives that critics have used to characterize reading O'Connor's own novels and short stories. If smell enables the transposition of the photograph's technologies of production into a distinct bodily experience, then O'Connor presents this bodily experience as an invitation to aesthetic, almost synesthetic, appreciation: the act of discriminating, dwelling on, and describing the magazine's smell just as her readers have dwelled on and described her literary works. While it may seem unusual to understand smell as having aesthetic qualities akin to literature, the two are more alike than one may initially think. As Frank Sibley has observed in his consideration of smell and taste as aesthetic objects, the appreciation of smell evokes questions of value that are "not separable from justifying the application of descriptive adjectives" in expressing to others the specific qualities of a smell.[4] More so than sight or sound, smell depends on the externalization of imaginative language and, in particular, the deployment of metaphor to communicate its aesthetic value—in this case, metaphors of the divine. To read O'Connor's letter in this light is to recognize that the godliness she ascribes to the *Geographic*'s smell places it atop not just the aesthetic hierarchy of the senses but the cultural hierarchy of reading material as well. Indeed, it is the presence of the divine that distinguishes the *Geographic* from a lesser photographic publication like *Time*, elevating the former to a position of distinction "like no mere magazine." In this sense, smelling the *Geographic* approaches a "literary" "interest" more closely than O'Connor would have Hester believe.

Crucially, however, O'Connor's exaltation of the *Geographic*'s aesthetic and cultural value requires turning a blind eye to the magazine's photographs and their attendant essays, captions, credits, and advertisements. This is true not just by her logic, or by the logic of many of the magazine's contemporary subscribers and collectors but as a general phenomenological principle.[5] (Try smelling this book head-on. As you bring it closer to your nose, your eyes will cross and your vision will blur, until eventually you are enshrouded in complete darkness.) Beyond her childhood idiosyncrasies, then, O'Connor's habitual blindness to the magazine's most celebrated feature suggests that her insistence on smelling the *Geographic* exists in relation to a broader cultural dialectic between reading and seeing—and more specifically, between reading and the highly ritualized practice of looking at photographs. Her letter to Hester thus offers us a fascinatingly wry introduction to what this chapter identifies as sight reading: a discourse of literacy sustained by the assumption that the visual field presented viewers with a symbolic system that could be read like a text.

As demonstrated by the popularization of pedagogical terms like *visual literacy* and *visual reading* from the 1940s onward, the rampant spread of sight reading counted as "the greatest single factor in the growth of demand for pictures," according to *Library Journal*'s survey of the field of photography in 1949.[6] But I am less interested in a historical account of the photograph's saturation of American culture than I am in the simultaneously emergent idea of how one might learn to read or write literature as a well-trained sight reader. "The relation of visual instruction to reading literature is fundamental," declared the inaugural newsletter of the Society for Visual Education.[7] "Carefully selected situations, photographed by the best picture experts, and edited by those who know what these pictures should contribute as a part of the regular instructional work of the school, furnish not only an opportunity, but supply an important demand in modern education." The "leader in supply" was "the National Geographic Society," which was "now offering their materials for educational uses" and had expressed their desire "to incorporate these materials into an organic relation with the curriculum" of primary and secondary school literature classrooms. Whereas the newsletter and others like it remained vague about the precise details of the "organic relation" between the visual and textual field, this chapter elucidates the imaginative logics whereby learning to look at photographs could alter how one read and wrote literature and, in turn, the communicative actions motivated by reading and writing.

As we may glean from O'Connor's implied juxtaposition of the literariness of smelling the *Geographic* to the vulgarities of looking at *Time*, not everyone wholeheartedly embraced sight reading as a beneficial enhancement of one's readerly capabilities. "We have lost book literacy while acquiring visual literacy," fretted a Columbia Teachers College newsletter titled "Communication and the Communication Arts" in 1955.[8] For the *Princeton University Library Chronicle*, it was similarly "the decay of our verbal literacy" that had "made room in our minds for visual literacy such as has been never known."[9] From the brow-furrowing perspective of teachers of English and university librarians, their concern that the mediation of texts by images might prove detrimental to linguistic communication was not unfounded. As we will see, sight reading turned on an ideology of visual apperception that discouraged the use of rational discrimination or discernment when encountering a photograph. While these faculties were undoubtedly integral to practices of close and critical reading at midcentury, such interpretive skills were denigrated as superfluous at best and dangerous at worst when compared to the surface aesthetics of visual objects. "A display does not have to be a work of art; if it were, it might obscure the message," warned John Ball and Frances Bynes in their 1960 primer on *Practices in Visual Communication*.[10] "It should be simple, pleasing, and communicative." In contrast to the cognitive labors one performed when reading a work of literature, midcentury sight readers were trained to regard photographs as objects keyed to the indexical, evidentiary, and objective transmission of ethnographic realities—a trickling down of pseudoscientific discourse from the realm of geography, anthropology, and cartography to a mass reading public. Sight reading's claim to the relatively unmediated transmission and reception of knowledge thus offers us an ideology of communication in its most aggressively naturalized form: a discourse of photographic production and reception that high theorists of photography, ranging from Roland Barthes to Susan Sontag, have to varying degrees essentialized as a feature of the medium's "innocence."[11] To revisit these theorists' assertions about medium specificity is to perceive how even the seemingly innocuous idea of "reading" photographs—not staging them, not editing them, not framing them, but simply believing that one can read them—was the product of a cultural-institutional literacy project with pointed aesthetic, communicative, and social stakes.

To begin to elaborate these stakes, it may help to return to how O'Connor's habit of smell registers her high-cultural antipathy toward photographs, photographers, and the reading conventions of photojournalism: one of the fastest growing paraliterary genres of mass cultural production after World War II and, at least where literary critics are concerned, a field whose production and consumption practices have been analyzed almost exclusively through the prism of domestic documentary photography.[12] Although magazines dedicated to photojournalism sold exceptionally well from the 1940s through the 1970s, not all readers and writers greeted the rise of photography with unqualified enthusiasm. "I find you are peculiarly helpless about pictures," O'Connor complained to Hester in a subsequent letter she wrote detailing her dislike of *Time* versus her enthusiasm for the *Geographic*.[13] When Hester misread the "you" of O'Connor's letter to mean her specifically, O'Connor clarified. "For 'You are peculiarly helpless about pictures' read 'one is peculiarly helpless about pictures,'" she instructed Hester. "I wasn't meaning you. I was meaning me, and I ought to learn to use the 'one is' formular [sic] but I just ain't a 'one is' type. What I mean to say is any jerk can take a picture of you and do with it what he will. I am sure there are now in existence hundreds of horrible pictures of me that I have no control over. Your face ought to be sacred but it is not."[14] For O'Connor, the horribleness of photographic reproduction did not derive from any individual subject's aesthetic or any individual photographer's artistry. Rather, she was galled by photography's status as a rapidly democratizing medium and its subsequent erosion of the visual arts' social distinctions. The ubiquity of camera technologies made it possible for "any jerk" to violate the "sacred" status of one's face and to label this violation as an act of artistic production—a debased claim to aesthetic value that carried with it an aggressive act of ethical transgression. The photographer's assertion of his omnipotence over his subjects without their consent—his godlike ability not only "to take a picture of you" but to also "do with it what he will"—could not be undone by anything, not even the passage of time. What scholars of photography have traditionally valorized as the photograph's enduring physical connection to its subject was, for O'Connor, precisely the source of its anti-artistry.[15] "Photographers are the lowest breed of men," O'Connor concluded to Hester, articulating a critique that was simultaneously aesthetic, social, and ethical in its principled distaste.

We can thus locate in O'Connor's *Geographic* letters an irritated foreshadowing of postwar sociology's rationale for classing photography as a quintessentially "middle-brow art," a designation that Pierre Bourdieu first derived from analyzing the communicative functions of photographs. For Bourdieu, the "mechanical transcriptions" of the photograph's production allowed it to "present itself with all the appearances of a symbolic communication without syntax."[16] A photograph encoded a "natural language," one that prompted its viewers to "resort to certain systems of reading" that foregrounded the "faithful reproduction of the real" over and above the aesthetic and critical practices called for by more elevated art forms like literature. More skeptical of claims to medium specificity than the high theorists of his time, Bourdieu's sociological schematic may prompt us to reframe O'Connor's opposition between reading the magazine and smelling it as her objection to the photograph's inferior "systems of reading" and their subsequent distortion of aesthetic value. Yet even this reframing takes us only so far, for the simple reason that a photograph does not "present itself" to be read any more than do the literary and paraliterary texts—novels but also lectures, memoirs, diaries, conduct guides, and financial instruments—we have encountered in the past three chapters. What this chapter takes as its entry point to sight reading are the institutions of reading that worked to naturalize the claim that a photograph is, in fact, an object that can be read, and that reading a photograph can, in fact, function as a form of communication. The institutional systems of reading I will consider are not merely analogic to literary reading, as critics from W. J. T. Mitchell to Michael North have suggested.[17] Rather, they are meticulously calibrated practices of visual and somatic training derived from—and often in opposition to—literary discourses of perceiving people through written techniques of visualization.

It would be a fool's errand to try to track every instantiation of the dialogic relationship between photographic and literary discourses of reading. But O'Connor's invocation of the *Geographic* as the most widely circulated periodical in the world and one whose production and reception was largely subsidized by the United States' military intelligence bureaucracies, offers us a particularly rich example of how sight reading, photographic aesthetics, and the international imaginary of face-to-face communication converged at midcentury. Sight reading reached its apotheosis within a nationalized scientific community preoccupied with gaining knowledge of other peoples through visual technologies and enframing that knowledge through the reproduction and circulation of mass-mediated visual forms. The particular genre of photographs that O'Connor pointedly ignores in her letters to Hester—the geographic, cartographic, and ethnographic images encased within what Elizabeth Bishop once described rapturously as "the cover; the yellow margins, the date" of the *Geographic*—is emblematic of how practices of photographic consumption overlay the production of international communication in its most explicitly virtual form: the idea that simply looking at the image of a person could count as an act of face-to-face communication.[18] Underlying this imagined act of exchange was a logic of physical perception similar to the gestural, bodily, and affective cues we saw in the theorization of reading as feeling in chapter 2. (Recall Hughes's "reading" of Plath's publicity photograph.) But even more explicitly than the talking bodies of Fulbright scholars, the magazine's exoticized and often eroticized photographs yoked the act of perception to the experiential consumption of cultural difference that underwrote the tourism industry's model of reading as branding in chapter 3. Taken together, the perception and consumption of cultural difference through visual cues stabilized the imaginary acts of international communication that millions of subscribers participated in as part of their monthly reading habits.

In detailed accounts of reading from Ernest Hemingway (with whom I opened this chapter), Marianne Moore, Elizabeth Bishop, Beverley Bowie, Walter Abish, and O'Connor (to whom I will return at the chapter's end), we will see a compelling discursive continuity between how internationalized reading subjects learned to consume magazines and how they learned to experience cultural differences between people, a project that endures to this very day. Yet we will also see how the continuity between sight reading and perception influenced the way that magazine readers imagined writing as a technical apparatus for learning how to categorize and communicate cultural difference in turn. As we will soon discover, the relation of visual literacy to writing grew increasingly intimate over the decades, thanks to the professionalization of photography and the technologies of production developed to fuse visual codes with textual syntax across a number of different domains: anthropology, ethnography, military scientific writing, and, perhaps most surprising of all, literature. Thus while the history of sight reading may coalesce around the *Geographic* and its devoted subscribers, this chapter shows how the practice ultimately became the defining feature of literary discourse about the visual field, at home and in the world at large.

SIGHT READING AT HOME

Before I begin to reconstruct the historical discourse of reading photographs, it is worth pausing to consider the institution of the magazine and how, precisely, its genres and forms are thought to communicate. As I suggested at the end of chapter 3, the magazine differs from the other institutions this book has considered—schools, academic departments, corporations, federal bureaucracies—which exist as discursive constellations of norms as well as more easily locatable brick-and-mortar structures. While magazines may issue from institutions of publishing, critics rarely perceive the textual object of the magazine as instituting anything among its readers. Magazine readers appear too diffuse, too different from one another, to prove good human agents for literary-sociological inquiry. In fact, the higher the number of readers, the lower our ability to draw any conclusions without cherry-picking our evidence[19]—a methodological constraint which may explain why literary historians have chosen to focus on the coterie cultures of "little magazines" instead of what Donal Harris has called the "big magazines" of twentieth-century mass culture.[20] Moreover, while the other institutions in this book have expressed explicit interest in staging face-to-face scenes of communication, a magazine only simulates such encounters. Even the most whimsical reader knows that looking at a photograph of a person's face is not the same thing as interacting with that person. As such, the inclusion of the magazine in this book invariably recalls a question that will prove especially important for this chapter and the two that follow. What salient differences exist between the kinds of reading practices that are instituted through the expansive circulation of texts and the kinds of reading practices naturalized by the centralized literacy teachings that take place in a bounded physical space?

The differences are matters of degree rather than kind. Big magazines, particularly those published with a high degree of punctuality and stylistic standardization, cultivate repetitive practices of reading that resemble the habitual activities of the institutionally socialized literary impersonators, passionate critics, and brand readers we have encountered so far throughout this book. Consider how O'Connor "always made for" the *Geographic* at her cousin's house, or how poet Marianne Moore ritualistically "kept [the *Geographic*] home from the library about a month copying things out of it."[21] Consider also how avid reader and writer Elizabeth Bishop reflects on her quasi-instinctive desire to go to the library to read the magazine's back issues while drafting her poem "In the Waiting Room," which depicts a scene of reading the *Geographic* in a dentist's office inspired by Bishop's childhood memories. "It was funny—queer," she wrote in a letter to Robert Lowell. "I actually went to the Library & got out that no. of the *NG*—and that title, 'The Valley of 10,000 Smokes'—was *right*, and has been haunting me all my life, apparently."[22] Bishop's haunted state directs us to the magazine's powerful social phenomenology: the demands it once made for a specific and embodied habit of readerly attendance stirring again after a long period of dormancy. Drawing equally from the formal properties of a textual genre and the sociomaterial routines of a concrete institution, the big magazine offers us this book's first compelling example of how a paraliterary genre might emerge as an institution in its own right.

So how did photojournalism's editors, writers, photographers, and publishers habituate millions of subscribers to approaching photographs as both readable and communicative objects? We can see their instruction beginning as early as 1915 with the issue of a pamphlet titled *The Story of the Geographic*, which was distributed to subscribers, donors, museums, and professional scientific organizations two decades after the magazine was first founded in 1888. Written by the magazine's assistant editor and vice-president of the National Geographic Society, John Oliver LaGorce, the pamphlet announced the society's desire to retool its practices of literacy education. Whereas the *Geographic* had begun its life as a dry professional journal publishing the technical details of the society's archaeological expeditions, LaGorce claimed that the magazine was now ready to introduce a new medium of global communication to a more expansive reading public. "The *National Geographic Magazine*," LaGorce boasted, "has found a new universal language which requires no deep study—a language which takes precedence over Esperanto and one that is understood as well by the jungaleer as by the courtier; by the Eskimo as by the wild man from Borneo; by the child in the playroom as by the professor in college; and by the woman of the household as well as by the hurried business man—in short, the Language of the Photograph!"[23] In 1915, the "Language of the Photograph" would have offered readers of the pamphlet a truly original claim about what counted as language, and so LaGorce provided an elaborate psychotechnological explanation for why the photograph's "universal" communications "require[d] no deep study." The *Geographic*'s photographs were more than just "illustrations," he explained. They were "Talking Pictures." Intensely vivid in their form and dazzlingly exotic in their content, these "Talking Pictures" proved so "absorbing" that knowledge could be "planted" in the reader's mind "without the reasoning process being unduly taxed by subsequent disturbances of the mental digestive track [*sic*] in the assimilation of new facts."

Like the first sound films—those other "Talking Pictures" with which readers would have had at least a passing familiarity—the photograph proffered a fantasy of immersive, unmediated communication that evoked the primacy of orality only to immediately transcend it. Unlike "illustrations," whose scriptural craftsmanship always betrayed the presence of a mediating figure of production between the magazine and its reader, LaGorce suggested that photographs transmitted their content directly into the reader's mind. And unlike the literally spoken international language of Esperanto, photographs required no language-based interpretive activity that might tax the reasoning process, disturb the "mental digestive track," or otherwise preclude the reader's "assimilation of new facts" as the magazine presented them. By eliminating syntactic and grammatical reasoning of any kind, LaGorce's sight reading practice effectively eliminated the need for language altogether as the foundation of a globalized reading public.

The radical attenuation of language as a socializing feature of magazine reading receives amusingly satirical treatment in Ernest Hemingway's minimalist epigraph to this chapter, drawn from his short story "Homage to Switzerland." In a brief dialogue between two *National Geographic* readers who encounter each other in a train station in Switzerland, each stranger

---

DR. SIGISMUND WYER, PH.D.

MEMBER OF THE NATIONAL
GEOGRAPHIC SOCIETY,
WASHINGTON, D. C., U. S. A.

FIGURE 4.1 "National Geographic Card" from Ernest Hemingway's "Homage to Switzerland" (1933).

can only confirm to the other that his reading practice involves "seeing" various "panoramas" and "colored plates" in the magazine. ("'You see the magazine, of course?' 'Absolutely.' 'Have you seen the number with the colored plates of the North American fauna?' 'Yes. I have it in Paris.'") Appropriately enough, the conversation about what they see, and the narrative of "Homage to Switzerland" itself, are brought to an end by the sudden appearance of a National Geographic Society business card, which one of the men—a longtime member—presents to the other. Set apart from the rest of the text, Hemingway crafts the card with careful attention to its typography, lines, and pagination. Designed to suggest a real artifact rather than a fictive object of exchange, the card functions as a promissory token between the two strangers, intimating a future relationship mediated not by learned "scientific conversation," the presenter explains, but by the shared "artistic value" of what the two men both "see" in each issue of the magazine to come. Like Hemingway's visual promise of international intimacy through sight reading, LaGorce's "Language of the Photograph" quiets the preexisting communicative habits of everyone around the world, from the preliterate "jungaleer" to the highly literate "courtier," from the babbling "child in the playroom" to the silver-tongued "professor in college." All forms of linguistic difference and distinction yield to the visual dimensions of the photograph and its project of global literacy training. LaGorce's instruction to readers in *The Story of the Geographic* thus best exemplifies the tongue-in-cheek question that Walter Ong poses at the outset of *Orality and Literacy* (1982): "We have all heard it said that one picture is worth a thousand words. Yet, if this statement is true, why does it have to be a saying?"[24]

While the pseudoscientific ideologies of sight reading worked to obscure the photograph's densely mediated existence as a communicative technology, they also encouraged readers to cultivate an understanding of the photograph as a proto-virtual reality experience. What LaGorce referred to in the pamphlet as "armchair travel"—the kinetic simulation of geographic displacement across space—similarly relied on the erasure of language. In its place, LaGorce substituted a quasi-hallucinatory promise of literal space-time travel, underwritten by the photograph's ability to give its viewer access to the exact moment and the state of reality in which the photograph was taken, a romantic possibility akin to what later theorists would describe as the photograph's indexicality. Despite its mystic and decidedly unscientific nature, the discourse of armchair travel proved immensely popular among magazine readers. "*National Geographic* takes me to all parts of the world, many of which I have visited without having to leave my chair," testified one subscriber in a 1924 letter to the editor. "Should one happen to visit strange lands," wrote another in 1921, "I think it would seem more like revisiting after reading the wonderful descriptions in *National Geographic* and looking at the pictures."[25] When "my life seems dull, walled in by monotonous repetition," one self-identified housewife observed, "I go traveling by reading the *Geographic*."[26] The gap between these readers' stubborn adherence to their physical sites of reading—the "monotonous repetition" of the home, one's comfortable "chair"—and the "strange lands" they seek had the paradoxical effect of situating the readerly imaginative consumption of cultural difference in scenes of cultural similitude. (This is not unlike Ralph Reed's story in the previous chapter about the old woman who frequented the American Express office in Spain in order to "feel at home," which envisioned a similarly exorbitant form of playing at mobility.) In the discourses of armchair travel, however, the actual spaces that readers inhabited—regional, institutional, architectural—could differ wildly from one another, so long as they had access to the same reading material.

Enabled by a boundlessly mobile and virtual gaze, sight reading thus posited for its readers a virtual subjectivity that transcended all material, bodily, and national limitations. The reader was free to go where he or she wished, to inhabit whatever lands he or she desired, and to return to the comforts of home consequence free. Somewhat ironically, the conjoined notions of a globalized reading public and the public's virtual subjectivity found its most extravagant expression not in a photograph but in an illustration that LaGorce tucked into *The Story of the Geographic*: a rendering of four naked figures linking hands to embrace the world. (Compare this image to S. Douglas Malcolm's roughly contemporaneous illustration of Lady Liberty circling

THE GEOGRAPHIC BRINGS THE WORLD TO YOU.

FIGURE 4.2 "The Geographic Brings the World to You" from *The Story of the Geographic* (1915). Photograph: Courtesy of National Geographic Archives, Washington, DC.

the globe on behalf of American Express from the previous chapter, which stages a similarly appropriative sense of international connectivity.) LaGorce, however, promised his viewers not the connectivity of capital but a knowledge of the world that was aggressively natural and naturalized. In a literal puff of smoke, everything his winged seraphs observed from their god's-eye view was instantaneously transmitted to the reader, from the insurmountable slopes of mountain peaks to the glassy lake to the trees that arced to the heavens. Even if the reader chose not to leave the comforts of home, he or she could still receive dispatches from the world beyond through the *Geographic*'s "Talking Pictures." This was the gist of LaGorce's promise to subscribers at the bottom of the page: "The *Geographic* Brings the World to You," a promise that, by World War II, at least 5.5 million households had bought into as part of their monthly consumption habits.

The iconographic resonances between the *Geographic* and the American Express advertisements from the previous chapter are no mere coincidence. Like the tourism industry, which transformed the consumption of cultural difference into an opportunity for institutionally regulated communication, geographic and scientific education had deep ties to internationalizing projects undertaken during the postwar period. The *Geographic* was an especially active nexus for such alliances, given that it did not establish a true in-house staff until World War II and thus relied on military personnel, diplomats, and explorers as its content producers. Many readers from World War I onward would have known about the composition of the society's board of directors, which included high-ranking officials from the State Department, the US Treasury, the Bureau of Ethnography, the US Geological Survey, and the armed forces, all of whom also ranked as frequent *Geographic* writers. A particular point of pride for the society was the role it had played in designing the White House's Map Room, which the *Geographic*'s editors had outfitted with a full set of exquisitely detailed and resplendently colored *National Geographic* maps just days before President Franklin Delano Roosevelt announced that the United States would enter World War II. "A map is the greatest of all epic poems," proclaimed the *Geographic*'s inaugural editor Gilbert Grosvenor to Roosevelt.[27] It was an appropriately heroic and nationalized literary analogy to offer one's president as the country geared up to do battle, with Roosevelt acting as a "global leader" and Grosvenor as the world's self-proclaimed "circulation leader."[28] According to the society's historian Robert Poole, Roosevelt would "use a *National Geographic* map showing which parts of Germany would be the American sector, which would be the British sector, which would be the Soviet sector."[29]

Carving up the epic poem that was the map into its component national zones would not have seemed unusual to sight readers, for whom reading the magazine was also an exercise in claiming knowledge of international territories and peoples as their own. The representative work of sight reading was less about representing the nation to others and more about representing the nation's emboldened geographic prowess to its own people by "bringing the world" to them. But sight reading offered more than just an analogy to institutional projects of international expansion. As we will now see, it laid the technical foundations for how these projects were conducted by the military, corporations, and federal bureaucracies of communication.

SIGHT WRITING IN THE MILITARY

We can mark an influential origin point for the myth of photography's medium specificity—its apparently indexical relationship to reality—in the pseudopsychological model of sight reading elaborated by *The Story of the Geographic*. This fantasy of unmediated communication would find itself echoed in other contemporaneous collections about magazine reading, from the connoisseur's guide *Collecting National Geographic Magazines* to the more tourist-friendly *Pan-American Flights: Compiled Articles from the National Geographic*. Yet while these guides had much to offer by way of fanciful cognitive science, they had far less to say about the pragmatic instructions one might follow in order to become a well-trained sight reader. What were the practices of looking by which pictures could "talk"? When the pictures spoke, what did they have to say? How could one ensure that the pictures said the same things to different readers? Surely skimming, flipping the pages, or only reading the articles would not suffice.

To answer these questions requires a turn from magazine consumption to magazine production, as the producers of the magazine—chiefly its editors and writers—invested a tremendous amount of time and energy aligning the magazine's aesthetic forms with the kinds of effects they intended for the magazine to produce on its readers. At the heart of their investment was the desire to standardize the communicative immediacy that LaGorce championed: the idea that when photographs spoke, they deployed an objective, predictable, and straightforward evidentiary code that would assist in the "planting" of "knowledge." Forged at the crossroads of geography, photography, and military-scientific expansion, the magazine's discourse of objective knowledge processing would come to define the superficiality of communicative practices in the postwar period.

The 1930s and 1940s would witness the codification of its loose, preexisting set of sight reading and writing practices into a distinctive magazine style that set the terms for nearly all of photographic production in the years to follow. Some of this work would take place through explicit editorial dictates issued from the top of the masthead down. Gilbert Grosvenor was fond of reminding his writers that each article was to be "an accurate, eyewitness, firsthand account" that "contained simple, straightforward writing—writing that sought to make pictures in the reader's mind" by deploying only vocabulary and syntax "so simple that a child of ten can understand it."[30] Yet until World War II, the *Geographic* had almost exclusively solicited contributors from the military men who inhabited the upper ranks of the society and from the occasional amateur photographer: a wealthy businessman or his wife, who was only too glad to sell her leisure-time photographs to the magazine at a low price or even donate them in exchange for a byline. Indeed, in the late 1930s, there were only two writers and one cameraman officially on staff at the *Geographic*, driving both labor costs and overhead down to levels that other magazines of mass culture had not enjoyed since well before World War I.

Many of the lectoral techniques for sight reading, then, were developed in the adjacent institutions that the magazine's editors, writers, and photographers inhabited in their roles as geographers, explorers, and military personnel and smuggled back into the magazine's headquarters. During World War II, many of the writers and photographers who worked on the magazine led double lives as military operatives, working to educate others as to how sight reading could not only entertain mass readers, but also help the massive number of US troops that Roosevelt had deployed to Europe. While decorated members of the US military, navy, and air force all held positions on the *Geographic*'s editorial board and frequently wrote for the magazine, the society's personnel enjoyed the closest ties to the Office for Strategic Services (OSS), the precursor to the Central Intelligence Agency (CIA). For Edward Lansdale, chief of the OSS's Intelligence Division, spying was less the glamorous business that so much of postwar fiction and film would make it out to be and more like "being a walking and talking version of *National Geographic*."[31] In an interview conducted some years after he had left his post at the OSS, Lansdale would sharpen the analogy by describing his work as "almost like being an editor of the *National Geographic* magazine in that we collected photographs of not only airstrips and beaches for landings but also roads and bridges and more pedestrian types of geographic information. We also went into details on people who lived in places, their potentials for helping our troops."[32] The technical practice of collecting and detailing photographs like "an editor of the *National Geographic*" was crucial to the institutionalization of intelligence work, specifically, to articulating the role that the visual played vis-à-vis the lingual in the production of strategic knowledge. While the OSS and the *Geographic* shared an interest in how images might be made to communicate, for the editors, writers, and photographers who ping-ponged from intelligence bureaucracies to the magazine and back, the more pressing questions were questions of what counted as knowledge, how that knowledge could be accessed, and how that knowledge could be expressed to maximize its usefulness to the war effort. And for military intelligence agencies, what it meant to know the "details on people who lived in places" and to gauge "their potentials for helping our troops" was intimately linked to how one read and wrote about those people or places based on photographs of them.

Few activities proved more important to the Research and Analysis (R&A) Bureau of the OSS than reading and writing. As the single largest employer of geographers and *Geographic* writers from 1941 to 1947, the R&A counted in its ranks "fieldmen" like Beverley Bowie (assistant editor), Charles Mc-Carry (senior editor), Ilia Tolstoy (writer and grandson of Leo Tolstoy), and Brooke Dolan (photographer), as well as Frankfurt school émigrés Franz Neumann, Herbert Marcuse, and Otto Kirchheimer, who headed up the Central European Section.[33] The fieldman's training, according to an R&A memo, required that he "prepare himself to select representations of typical photographs which best bring out the characteristic combinations" that indicated a "militarily significant landscape."[34] Operating under the guidance of Richard Hartshorne, author of the field-defining textbook *The Nature of Geography* (1939) and president of the Association of American Geographers, fieldmen were instructed to "cultivate what might be called a clinical attitude": an empirical, positivist, and dispassionate manner of attending to and describing the "representations of typical photographs" selected for inclusion in intelligence reports. Hartshorne's frequent scolding of his fieldmen, particularly the historical materialists, for not producing "mature and objective scholarship" demonstrated precisely what the stylistic markers of such a clinical attitude were and were not.[35] In a memorandum to his R&A teams, he noted that while "the rules for objective writing are presumably familiar to all the research workers on our staff, experience suggests that it is necessary to remind ourselves of them. The most obvious and yet most common crime against objectivity is the use of hortatory and value words and phrases. Generally speaking, 'should' and 'ought'—not to mention 'must' are taboo. Value adjectives and nouns are to be avoided no matter how much they appear to add literary quality. Intelligence reports find their merit in terseness and clarity rather than expressive description. Proust, Joyce, or Gertrude Stein would all be equally out of place in R&A."[36] Equally important to Hartshorne was that his fieldmen avoid having an overly "critical" attitude toward their objects of study, by which he meant that fieldmen were not to question the logic of the descriptive relationship between photographs and knowledge that was central to the R&A. (Here Hartshorne singled out Herbert Marcuse, whose principled stance against positivist science as the "mere duplication of the real in thought," did not align well with his reading and writing instructions.)[37] Taken together, objectivity and uncritical thinking were key to populating the archives of the three-by-five index cards that served as the agency's privileged medium of communication.

That Hartshorne should cite the decadent interiority of Proust or the dazzling language games of Joyce and Stein as examples of how not to write as an OSS agent, all the while directing his fieldmen's attentions to the "typical" features of geographic landscapes, points to the discursive linkage between spying as an act of textual production and spying as a corporeal practice of looking at and "reading" a photograph. Like LaGorce's insistence that the language of the photograph required no "deep study" or Grosvenor's direction to his writers to tailor the magazine's prose style to a ten-year-old child's vocabulary and syntax, Hartshorne's "clinical attitude" prioritized exoteric and visual details over either the "expressive description" of literature or the "critical" attitude required to interpret it. Far more important than "value adjectives" or "nouns," which we might consider the bread and butter of literary prose, are absolute adjectives (e.g., distances, colors, materials, shapes) and verbs of action. The morphological and visual qualities of R&A writing— that is, the fact that the fieldmen's descriptions were not value laden and thus seemed to denote objective features of a noun—worked to transcribe the places, people, and actions visually observed by the fieldmen into the typological content of an intelligence report—one that focused not on specific individuals or landscapes but on "typical" "representation" of individuals and landscapes as its strategic knowledge. Such regimented practices of sight reading made it possible for intelligence officers to write with the "terseness and clarity" necessary to fit on the compact index cards that President Roosevelt and the Joint Chiefs of Staff called "the most powerful weapon in the OSS arsenal."[38]

Unsurprisingly, the staff members who came from the *Geographic*, many of whose reports were published by the magazine once the war had ended, proved more adept at adjusting themselves to the material and ideological constraints of sight writing than the critical theorists. A prime example comes from OSS agent and *Geographic* writer Lieutenant Colonel Ilia Tolstoy's account of smuggling a "letter of goodwill" from President Franklin Delano Roosevelt to the Dalai Lama in a 1944 article titled "Across Tibet from India to China."[39] (The letter was really a public diplomatic alibi for scouting out supply routes to China.) While the reader may expect a declassified OSS intelligence report to feature breathtaking mise-en-scène, death-defying action sequences, and whispered conversations with covert informants, Tolstoy's style, unlike that of his grandfather's sweeping novels, spares the reader every adjectival detail. True to Hartshorne's writing guidelines, the story is gerund heavy, every sentence a short account of Tolstoy "going" and "coming" from place to place. The report's lack of emotional or psychological expressivity is starkest when its account is the most harrowing. "At 14,000 feet we sometimes felt the effect of the altitude and thin air and would wake up in the night gasping for breath," writes Tolstoy with studied detachment on his climactic ascent of the Himalayas. "We found that propping ourselves in a semi-sitting position was best for sleeping. In the daytime it was difficult to walk any distance uphill without frequent stops and rests, and we soon got used to doing everything if in slow motion." "Slow motion" doubles as an apt aesthetic description for how the diachronic structure of Tolstoy's field report reads, with every sentence slogging through the perpetually present tense actions taken at night and at day, and the next night and the next day, and so forth. The "clinical attitude" encouraged by the OSS—and, by extension, the *Geographic*—thus manifests itself in the slow, steady, and objective prose of the adept spy on a mission.

Both the quality of the spy's prose style and its epistemological consequences receive a cutting send-up in *Operation Bughouse*, a 1947 satirical novel written by *Geographic* editor and OSS agent Beverley Bowie just after he returned from a covert OSS intelligence operation in Bucharest, Romania. World War II and its immediate aftermath offers a rich setting for wartime satires, from Joseph Heller's *Catch-22* (1961) to Kurt Vonnegut's *Slaughterhouse-Five* (1969), all of which are preoccupied not with the dangers of war but, as Heller once noted, "people in danger" from "their own superiors from within the organizations of which they are a part."[40] To wit, these novels each begin by introducing a character whose literary aspirations seem comically, perhaps disastrously, out of sync with the institutional protocols of their military regiments, from the textual "games" Yossarian plays with censored letters to "reach a higher plane of creativity" to *Slaughterhouse-Five*'s narrator's metafictional disavowal of his novel as a "lousy little book."[41] In *Operation Bughouse*, the literary character in question is Group Captain Boneridge, a writer of spy novels tapped to serve as the senior intelligence officer of a sprawling, uncontrollably self-duplicating institution of military photography referred to only by the acronym HQ. A prolifically successful novelist, Boneridge turns out to be an abysmal spy; this despite the fact that he is "thoroughly identified in his own mind and in that of his public with his indestructible hero," a posh British schoolboy and top-notch espionage operative named Alan Douglas.[42] "Literature had, as it were embalmed him," observes Bowie's omniscient narrator of Boneridge's epistemological inflexibility: his unwillingness to participate in the objective observation and information gathering that is the work of spies. This attitude finds its aesthetic counterpart in Boneridge's romantic and decidedly nonscientific rendering of landscape details (2). He conceives of strategic waterways as "streams sprung from the brow of Jove" and the enemy officers standing guard over them as "pensive gods and marble nymphs" (1). More alarming than the purple prose of Boneridge's reports, however, is his utter incompetence as an administrator, a job for which he is far too flexible. Incapable of appreciating the spans and layers of military bureaucracy—the spies of literary fiction are, after all, admirably self-reliant—he begins firing the institute's longtime staff willy-nilly. Yet the one person he cannot fire is Colonel Caesar Augustus Holliday, a ridiculously named recent graduate of the "Photo Interpreters School, to which the Army sent him for reasons never too clear" (12). Now at HQ, Holliday is part of a group of cloistered, rule-abiding, and well-behaved readers and writers, "a rather scholarly outfit which performed its allotted tasks in a pedantic, open-and-above-board manner" (87).

As a parody of both Hartshorne's R&A unit and the *Geographic*'s "Photo Interpreters School" of visual production, *Operation Bughouse* transforms the "clinical attitude" of the fieldman, responsible for producing "typical" prose, into a character type of its own. Compared to Boneridge's mock-aesthete disregard for institutional history and protocols, Holliday seems like the ideal intelligence man: one whose "quality of detachment" flattens him psychologically while simultaneously permitting him to excel at his job; a man who has "one lobe of his brain in this world and the other tuned to some quite different existence" (12). As such, he has cultivated a gift for "character-reading" "the faces that confront him" in reconnaissance photographs of densely populated landscapes (26). If character reading attends to the morphological qualities of faces, it does so by treating facial features not as natural facts but as signs that point to strategic national affiliations. The affiliations between faces and military strategy are ripe for US political and economic exploitation as suggested by the layered construction of Colonel Caesar Augustus Holliday's name: the empire-building ambitions of "Caesar" and "Augustus" married to the leisure-time connotations of "Holliday." While en route to the country of Carpathia—a thinly veiled representation of Romania—for a covert operation, Holliday compares his professional habitus as a character reader favorably to his fellow spies, many of whom are not well-trained photo interpreters like himself but failed literary writers. "It was my avocation to edit the unperformed plays of Henry James," one corporal confesses to Holliday, who admits that he "had never had much to do with writers, and rather distrusted them," taking them to be "simply unfortunate people who suffered periodically from hot flushes of words to the head" (40).

Operation Bughouse's visual aesthetic is specifically photographic—one that rejects the "hot flushes of words to the head" in favor of the mechanistic transcriptions of reality. Instead of the comic picaresque of Heller's *Catch-22* or *Slaughterhouse-Five*'s grotesque descriptions of untamed European landscapes, the shared "clinical attitude" cultivated by *Operation Bughouse*'s writer (Bowie) and its protagonist (Holliday) materializes through the pile-up of morphological details that Holliday must pick his way through once he is separated from his unit in Carpathia. Consider Holliday's early encounter with a group of peasants riding atop a fruit cart, who, for the sake of his survival, he must immediately assess as a friend or foe to the United States. The cart, Holliday notes, was "piled high with melons, squash, and cabbage; on top of the vegetables was a layer of straw, and on top of the straw a layer of peasants. Between the shafts, which lifted it almost off the ground, so that its hooves seemed always to be pawing for contact with the earth, trotted a scabrous stunted little horse which was able to keep the cart in motion but not much more. The women wore black shawls covering their hair and bulbous cheeks; on their stumpy straight legs they had white socks and black boots" (53). Note the verticality of how the description proceeds: the upward layering of produce, straw, and people; the upward movement of the horse, who is visualized as a combination of texture ("scabrous") and size ("stunted little"). Note also the downward movement of Holliday's observation of the women, from their shawls to their hair, their cheeks, their legs, their white socks, and their black boots. Paralleling the up-and-down motion of the seeing eye gazing on a photograph, Holliday's diligently exteriorized description models how sight reading may yield character reading as a heuristic practice. What harm, after all, can come to an intelligence operative from the type of woman possessed of such "bulbous cheeks" and "stumpy straight" legs? Such authoritative interpretive leaps from character to type in the service of producing politically useful knowledge are hardly a unique occurrence in *Operation Bughouse*, which, as one reviewer noted in the *New York Herald*, "is unsparing in [its] depiction of both the methods and characters of the participants in this opera bouffe"—characters that Holliday's photo interpretive eye (and Bowie's satirical prose) fixes as pictorially constructed and physiognomically oversignified representations of human beings.[43]

The descriptions that characterize *Operation Bughouse*'s photographic aesthetic thus register the novel's institutional conditions of production—that is, the knowledge work undertaken by the international spy—while revealing the ideologies of reading required to sustain these working conditions. Appropriately enough, then, Holliday's superiorly objective sight reading turns out to be his downfall. Once in Carpathia, Holliday embarks on a wild goose chase to retrieve a stolen laundry ticket onto which he has written the coordinates of the Romanian air force's biggest jet engine and jet engine assembly plant. He falls in love with a cool blonde Romanian double agent named Melanie—an angelic-looking femme fatale who defies Holliday's exteriorized and typological character reading of her by double-crossing him, stealing the plant's coordinates, and delivering them to Soviet spies. In the car chase scene that concludes the novel, Holliday is carried past Melanie's fleeing automobile, whose progress he attempts to freeze in time and space. Yet the car passes "at a scant two or three yards distance, but so rapidly that it seemed to him he had been, like a photographic plate, exposed to the tableau for only a fraction of a second" (230). In an unexpected reversal of technological subject and technological object, the photograph reader becomes the photographic plate. But a fraction of a second is too short for adequate mechanical reproduction, and Holliday emerges as a failed photograph, streaked and overexposed and incapable of speaking the "Language of the Photograph" he has relied on for his professional success as a spy. "Holliday had opened his mouth to cry out," the narrator relays, "yet when the sound actually came, the car and its occupants had vanished" (230). Stripped of his communicative functions, Holliday can only internalize the image he has seen: "He retained for long rocking miles thereafter an exact imprint of the scene, which, though he closed his eyes and covered them with his hands, remained always visible" (231). By the novel's end, which finds Holliday nursing his broken heart and broken career in the office of HQ's in-house psychoanalysis, the failed sight reader has resorted to the language games of Joyce and Stein. Possessed by his excessive sense of interior imagery, he can only express his subjective vision of the failed photograph in fragments, lyrics, and rhymes. From a sight reader and writing, he has degraded into a modernist poet.

Although Bowie continued his work with the *Geographic* until his death in 1958, just one year after incoming editor-in-chief Melville Bell Grosvenor jump-started the magazine's "golden age," he remained skeptical about the value of spy work as a form of international knowledge production. "This is heresy," he complained of Pulitzer Prize–winning journalist Edgar Ansel Mowrer's call for the US government to "create the biggest and best information service in the world."[44] "Nobody has yet demonstrated convincingly that a soldier will fight better or hold out longer just because he is better informed," Bowie argued. As evidence, he marshaled the hundreds of "discussion guides, radio talks, film documentaries, clipsheets, posters and news maps" produced by the R&A and Office of War Information (OWI) on a weekly basis for domestic and international readers. "You can't change attitudes just by dispensing better information," Bowie complained of R&A's ceaseless textual production. Read in this historical light, *Operation Bughouse* is less valuable as a satire of war than as a satire of the dialectic between two competing modes of reading and writing that lay claim to knowledge about the world and a satire of what that knowledge can do: the OSS/*Geographic*'s sight reading and informational writing on the one hand, and the commitment to cultivating a literary aesthetic of expressive depth as represented by modernists like Proust, Joyce, and Woolf. The interplay between communicative surfaces and expressive depths thus illuminates the magazine's claims to a distinct form of textual and visual production that underpin the distinct techniques of reception we observed amid its sight readers and armchair travelers.

EXPERIENCING LIFE IN ROTOGRAVURE

So far, I have argued that the military-geographic institutions of World War II drew on the discourses of sight reading to formulate the necessary techniques for sight writing, which, in turn, helped to institutionalize the aesthetic cues for sight reading. The military-scientific developments of the postwar period had the effect of aligning the imagined communication of sight reading with the experiential consumption of cultural difference that we examined in the previous chapter. By returning now to the years in which O'Connor was ardently sniffing her *Geographic*, I want to suggest how the material conditions of middlebrow magazine publication paradoxically doubled down on the shallowness of photojournalistic aesthetics to create a transportative and communicative experience for subscribers. Whereas LaGorce had simply asserted the communicative capabilities of its "Talking Pictures," and Bowie had worked to standardize that communication, now writers and editors worked to amplify the photograph's visual chatter through a constellation of technological innovations, both aesthetic and militaristic, that aimed to maximize the photograph's virtual reality effects. Understanding this history will in turn suggest how consuming a secondhand experience—looking at a photograph that someone else took—became as "real" an occasion for communication as an actual, embodied act of discursive exchange.

The interpenetration of magazine reading protocols, color printing, and midcentury tourism begins with the National Geographic Society's "golden age": the years after World War II when the *Geographic* committed itself to enhancing its house style using technologies of color production.[45] Bookended by the decade-long editorship of Melville Bell Grosvenor, Gilbert Grosvenor's son and the magazine's second editor-in-chief, the golden age of the *Geographic* began in 1957 with a total overhaul of the magazine's offices. A graduate of the United States Naval Academy and, by many accounts, a gruff and commanding leader, Melville Grosvenor's editorship capitalized on the staggering rise of international tourism in the 1940s and 1950s to expand and professionalize the *Geographic*'s staff. By the 1950s, the increase in touristic consumption drove an increase in subscriber demand for more articles per issue and more geographic variety among the articles; even the experience of cultural difference, it seems, needed additional differentiation to keep up with the postwar economy. Accordingly, the *Geographic* needed more contributors who could produce work on company time and under company policies rather than the wealthy travelers and military men who took photographs during their leisure hours. Hiring aggressively from the Missouri Photo Workshop, which Clifton C. Edom of the Missouri School of Journalism had founded in 1949 to encourage documentary photography with an ethnographic flair, Grosvenor transformed a three-person operation into a well-oiled, hundred-person machine that worked tirelessly to overturn what Edom described as the "shallow flash-on-camera, stand 'em up and sit 'em down technique then in vogue."[46] Once the institution had undergone its dramatic overhaul, Grosvenor wasted no time in announcing the creation of "a dynamic new National Geographic Society" that would "burst out of its shell," propelled into the public eye by a magazine that was "faster, better, brighter."[47]

"Faster, better, brighter" most directly referred to a series of technological innovations in photography first popularized by the *Geographic* for the purposes of making its "Talking Pictures" more vividly communicative, but these technologies would soon become the cornerstone of a new scientific visual paradigm that emerged in the postwar period. For Grosvenor and his staff, the most important change was the magazine's regular use of what he described as the "unnaturally bright" and iridescent 35 mm Kodachrome film.[48] Although Kodachrome had been discovered by *Geographic* photographer Luis Marden as early as 1936, it had proven too expensive and technically unwieldy to incorporate into the printing process, despite the immense promise it held for photojournalistic creativity. Whereas the graininess and pockmarked surfaces of grayscale photography had prevented photojournalists from photographing their subjects in motion, Kodachrome enabled photographers on the move to capture subjects that were similarly mobile. By liberating photographers from their heavy cameras and tripods and the requirement of static positionality, color photography had the potential to singlehandedly rescue photojournalism from the "stand 'em up and sit 'em down" technique that Edom had decried. But it took the invention of rotogravure printing by the Beck Engraving Company, the printing firm responsible for producing the magazine's images, to make Kodachrome an affordable option for all of the articles the magazine published.

Once color saturation emerged as a standard practice of production, editors and photographers gravitated to adjacent technologies of visual enhancement to create rotogravure photographs that were, in the words of one editor, "realer than real": cropped portraits, a narrow depth of field, low-lit blurring of background, the extravagant coloring of maps, and the dressing up of subjects in colorful dress and fashion accessories for the camera, all of which emerged as aesthetic staples of the "Red Shirt School of Photography."[49] The amped-up, crystalline color that saturated pictures of subjects in motion only augmented the preoccupation with the photograph's ability to communicate knowledge to its readers about places and people they had not experienced firsthand. As one editor boasted, the introduction of color profoundly intensified the "haptic *availability* of what was displayed" to the magazine's readers.[50] In a phenomenological extension of the virtual mobility of the reading subject, readers were encouraged to stroke and touch the photographs—and, by imaginative extension, the photographed subjects—as part of their reading experience.

The institutional and technological reforms of the "golden age" not only insisted on color as crucial to the *Geographic*'s visual culture but also urged the appropriation of the magazine's specific visual aesthetic in the work of archaeologists, ethnographers, geographic explorers, and even advertisers. Such appropriation was welcomed by other fields, as the *Geographic*'s visual aesthetic stood in distinct opposition to the documentary photograph that characterized the 1930s and 1940s New Deal image making of the Farm Service Agency (FSA), the Federal Writers' Project, and *Life* magazine's gritty and grim social exposés. Yet this aesthetic came with its own political baggage. As chronicled extensively by anthropologists Jane Collins and Catherine Lutz in their decade-long survey of the magazine's readers, the *Geographic*'s manner of coloring and editing photographs and maps played a major role in actualizing an ethos of conservative humanism in social scientific study: a celebration of cultural difference similar to touristic consumption but one that proceeded by relegating non-Anglicized peoples to earlier stages of progress. A more politically pernicious instantiation of time travel in the experience of virtual mobility—traveling in space as traveling in time to a different epoch of development—by altering the color palette of the world, the *Geographic* changed how that world could be consumed by its American readers.

The ideological underpinnings and material effects of the magazine's "golden age" color technologies are dramatized vividly in *Geographic* reader and experimental writer Walter Abish's novel *Alphabetical Africa* (1974), which explicitly links the *Geographic*'s visual representations to both tourism and the conservative humanism that Collins and Lutz detail. *Alphabetical Africa* is a pseudo-alliterative text whose first chapter contains only words that begin with the letter "A," the second chapter words that begin with "A" and "B," and so forth until chapter 26. For a novel so determined to subsume narration, plot, and character to the demands of language, it seems telling that Abish's narrator, a tourist named Alfred, perceives the entire continent of Africa as subordinate to its coloring in the maps of the *Geographic*. "Life in Tanzania is predicated on the colored maps of Africa that hang in the palace, courtesy of *National Geographic*," he observes in chapter 20.[51] "On the maps Tanzania is colored a bright orange. Neighboring Malawi is light blue." When the queen of Tanzania takes Alfred on a helicopter tour, he is astonished to observe that, from a bird's-eye view, the colors of Africa's contingent states correspond perfectly to the *Geographic*'s flattened rendering of these territories in bright colors and striking contrasts. This is no mere trick of the light. "Each day one hundred thousand Tanzanians carrying ladders, buckets of orange paint and brushes, are driven and also flown to different sections of the country," she explains to Alfred. "They paint everything in sight. Since I manufacture acrylic paints, everything needs a frequent going over. It takes about six months to paint this country by hand." The queen's color scheme represents an extravagantly laborious and time-consuming act of *Geographic* mimesis, one in which the constant application and reapplication of color multiplies the number of domestic jobs available for Tanzanians. "At present half a million men are building roads for the painters, the Queen had told me," Alfred relays. "It'll enable the painters to do their job in half the time." Yet the development of Tanzania does not reduce the number of times the country must be repainted with the queen's acrylic paints.

Important to note, then, is how the queen's aesthetic intensification of geographic difference serves economic rather than artistic ends, artificially inflating Tanzania's labor, manufacturing, and infrastructural sectors, while enhancing her own personal wealth. "The maps are the key to our future prosperity," the queen confesses to Alfred. The communicative artifice of color thus proxies the artifice of Tanzania's development economics: the creation of jobs, the investment in roads, the increase in trade with its neighbors, as well as the corruption of the postcolonial state and its Cold War alignments. "The Queen also proudly explains that Malawi has also decided to conform to international mapping standards," Alfred notes, "and since Tanzania had a technological head start, she could export a light blue paint to Malawi. Angola is another matter entirely. Angola is green on the map, and that may account for their huge relief rolls." In maps furnished "courtesy of the *Geographic*" and made real in resource-intensive ways by the queen, color acts as the initial flush of capital that stratifies relations between economies modeled on and by the developed world, like Tanzania, and economics that refuse to progress toward self-sufficiency. Angola, for instance, continues to rely on "relief rolls" not because the nation is impoverished or in the midst of revolution, but by virtue of the fact that it is "green on the map"—an imposition on the part of the United States via the *Geographic*. By parodying how the aesthetics of mass culture communicate, and thus dictate, the material realities of international production and consumption, *Alphabetical Africa* brilliantly suggests how a hyperstylized visual field could reify readers' sense experiences in abiding economic and social structures—structures that exceeded any individual readers' experiences and spilled over into the distinctly institutionalized context of international politics.

And yet Alfred's eyeballing of the generalized patchworks of color on display in *Alphabetical Africa* shows only one facet of how the stylistic overhaul of the magazine's production process trained its readers in even more elaborate practices of looking. Despite LaGorce's insistence that the "Language of the Photograph" could initiate and sustain communicative action on its own (and despite the fact that 53 percent of readers claimed to only look at the photographs), the staff of the golden age *Geographic* was keenly attuned to how crossing the threshold that separated text from image could reassert the power of sight reading. To supplement the editorial investment in color technology, the most touted strategy of textual and visual fusion was reading by synecdoche: in the article or captions that accompanied photographs, writers described to readers how to simulate the experience of virtual mobility through small and precise movements of the reader's eye. By shifting the eye up and down a photograph or by scanning from left to right across a panorama, the reader could not help but to "extend his horizon, to reach out into the unknown, and to identify himself a little more closely with the world of which he is a part," wrote *Geographic* staff photographer Maynard Owen Williams.[52] While retaining LaGorce's commitment to the communicative primacy of the visual, textual synecdoche demonstrated how the performance of sight reading might train those readers who did, in fact, read the articles instead of looking at the pictures. Even then, writers were instructed to continue to conform to Grosvenor's mandate that the text remain simple enough for a ten-year-old to understand it. As reading by synecdoche suggests, the effect of Grosvenor's stylistic instruction was to continue to enforce sight writing's moratorium on the use of figurative and imaginative language in favor of a positivist and descriptive aesthetics that complemented the discourses of photographic communication.

Here the *Geographic* turned back to its old ally, the military, to help dole out the meticulously calibrated physical training required for sight reading through an action-based prose style. Consider the complex crafting of synecdoche in "Artists Roam the World of the U.S. Air Force," an article written by Curtis E. LeMay, chief of staff of the United States Air Force, running mate of presidential candidate George Wallace, and regular contributor to the magazine during the 1950s and 1960s. The article does not begin by describing LeMay's or other pilot's flights of adventure but by describing a series of brightly colored murals depicting Air Force missions; murals which were painted by American artists and which now decorate the walls of the Pentagon. As LeMay narrates his long walks through the Pentagon while on furlough, he carefully attends to the images on the wall, which the editors reproduce in the article as photographs. The nesting of medium into medium here—a photograph of a painting of a military expedition—has the double effect of asserting the paintings' reality claims through the photograph, while distracting the reader from any political questions she may have about LeMay's bombing missions by relegating them to the status of an artistic representation. And for LeMay, there appears to be no difference between paintings and photographs, at least not when it comes to the production of virtual reality effects for his readers at home. "One day my eye may fall upon the lonely grandeur of an Alaskan peak," LeMay writes of his observations of the Pentagon's murals. "The next I am transported to the everlasting sun that burns North Africa. Succeeding days bring scenes of Roman times, an Ecuadorian jungle, a Thailand bucket brigade. Even though I have piloted our mightiest jets to the far reaches of the globe, still, like other members of the National Geographic Society, I find armchair travel stimulating." As LeMay narrates the apparently spontaneous movements of his eye ("One day my eye may fall upon . . .") from the sublimity of the Alaskan mountains to the earth-scorched deserts of Africa, his text moves from left to right across the bottom third of a full page spread, the top of which is filled by photographs of the murals he describes to his readers. Given how both text and image are spread along the horizontal axis of the magazine, the reading subject must also move her eye anaphorically across the photographs of the white peak of a mountain, the yellow sands of a desert, and the lush greens of a tropical jungle as she reads LeMay's descriptions. While feigning a certain degree of informality in his narration, the alignment of LeMay's narrative eye with the reader's eye, and the alignment of the text with photograph, creates a methodical symmetry between LeMay's "armchair travel" and the reading subject's phenomenology of virtual displacement.

Beginning with LaGorce's entreaty to read the "Language of Photograph," we have so far traversed a visual tradition that encompasses the typologically descriptions of Bowie, Hartshorne, and Tolstoy, the color technologies of Grosvenor and Abish, and the synecdochal reading of Williams and LeMay. What we have seen throughout is the construction of sight reading as a technologically, textually, and institutionally mediated practice of literacy— an extensive apparatus of reading keyed to the assumption that midcentury photographs could communicate expressively without language to taint the process of mimetic and objective transmission. The discourses of photographic communication have emerged both in the form of the photograph itself and in its transposition into descriptive language through sight writing. Returning now to the work of Flannery O'Connor, I will show how the discursive contours of photojournalism structured the interpretive discourses of literary reading and literary writing.

ANTI-PHOTOGRAPHIC POINTS OF VIEW

Given what we know of her noted history of illness and domestic seclusion, we do not tend to think of Flannery O'Connor as a travel writer or a writer interested in questions of travel like Hemingway, Bishop, Moore, or Abish. Yet O'Connor's status as a homebody was in part a deliberate choice, geared to producing the working conditions she believed were most amenable to literary writing. In 1958, O'Connor took her first and only disastrous trip to Lourdes, which was organized by her cousin Kate in conjunction with a major travel agency, an institution that O'Connor would grotesquely personify as the "Travel Ogre."[53] Prior to her journey, Kate gifted O'Connor two "leather-bound travel books" which she instructed O'Connor and her mother to "fill up about our experiences abroad and let her read when we got back."[54] Kate's good-natured, but ultimately burdensome, insistence on reading O'Connor's account of her experiences abroad prompted O'Connor to question "experience"—a key category of perception and action for the tourists of the previous chapter, as well as many of O'Connor's contemporary novelists and poets—as a useful impetus to the production of fiction. "Miraculous and marvelous ill health prevented me from filling mine," O'Connor wrote to her friend Margaret Lee of her blank travel book, "but I have just finished typing up my mother's so that when we go to Savannah Saturday we can present it. The charity is a good deal stronger than the prose in it. Maybe some day I will write mine, when the reality has faded. Experience is the greatest deterrent to fiction." In articulating her desire for a faded version of reality to spur her to fiction writing, O'Connor rejects what she understands as the mechanical transcription of life into art, deploying the same logic she used to reject the easy and democratizing aesthetics of the photograph to reject the experience of travel; the travel book's "charity is a good deal stronger than the prose in it." Taken together, the rejection of photographs and the rejection of experience as a source of literary inspiration point to a double rejection of reading about—and looking at—other peoples' experiences of the world as communicating some kind of virtual knowledge. As we will see, O'Connor's vexed status as a nonreader (but ardent smeller) of the *Geographic* and an unwilling producer of literary photo-essays put her in a unique position to craft an aesthetics of visual communication inhospitable to practices of sight reading and its attendant discourses of virtual experience and knowledge production.

Many critics have noted Flannery O'Connor's thematic preoccupation with sight and seeing, but none have connected this to her lifelong disdain for photography. Theirs is a surprising oversight, not simply because she announces her disdain for photographs and photographers so frankly in her letters, but because the photographs she features in her fiction assume a ghastly and heavy-handed symbolism otherwise absent from her writing.

Consider the photographs of self-anointed, backwoods prophet Mason Tarwater, which are printed in a "schoolteacher magazine" in *The Violent Bear It Away* (1960).[55] The photographs, taken by Tarwater's great-nephew and ward, are intended to showcase "a type that's almost extinct" to the magazine's middlebrow readers.[56] On the back of the schoolteacher magazine, Tarwater has written, "THE PROPHET I RAISE OUT OF THIS BOY WILL BURN YOUR EYES CLEAN"—an ironic prophecy given that the great-nephew will eventually be raped and blinded in his quest to fulfill his great-uncle's prophecy. Consider also the two snapshots of a young girl in a concentration camp that Polish émigré Mr. Guizac gives to a black field hand in O'Connor's short story "The Displaced Person." The photographs serve as IOUs from Guizac to the field hand, securing the girl's hand in marriage in exchange for a portion of the field hand's wages; this despite the fact that the girl has almost certainly died in the camps. Less obviously loaded, but no less important, are the color tints of French bakers that aspiring fiction writer Mrs. Willerton contemplates as a source of inspiration in "The Crop"; the weekly magazines that litter the interior of the car in which Bailey and his family will die in "A Good Man Is Hard to Find"; and the "pitcher" an old Confederate general cherishes of his youth in "A Late Encounter with the Enemy." Most notable from the standpoint of photojournalism and its institutions of production, however, are the real photographs taken by *Pathé News* of one of O'Connor's pet chickens in 1930, when O'Connor was only five years old, right about the time she started smelling the *Geographic*.

The chicken, a "buff Conchin Bantam" capable of "walking both forwards and backwards" predates O'Connor's famous pet peacocks and emerges as the initial subject of O'Connor's celebrated 1961 photojournalistic essay "Living with a Peacock."[57] "Living with a Peacock" is a first-person account of raising peafowl, which O'Connor unhappily wrote for the September 1961 issue of *Holiday* magazine, then the *Geographic*'s stiffest competition when it came to shaping the American imagination of international mobility. According to the marketing journal *Tide*, while magazines like "*National Geographic*, for example, had tackled some phase of the travel business," no publication had "devoted itself as fully to the subject as *Holiday*," and certainly none that expressed its devotion as a specifically highbrow literary preoccupation.[58] This was most apparent in the magazine's aggressive recruitment and generous compensation of celebrated fiction writers as the magazine's featured contributors, a list that included Graham Greene, Truman Capote, Jack Kerouac, Paul Bowles, and Mary McCarthy. O'Connor, however, was not moved by the magazine or its aspirations to literary distinction. "I'm amused by the letter from *Holiday*," she wrote to her agent Elizabeth McKee of her correspondences with editor Ted Patrick, a former advertising executive at the Compton Advertising Agency and head of the graphics section of OWI during World War II.[59] "The fellow obviously thinks it's a great accomplishment to write for them," she scoffed. "I have never seen *Holiday* in my life," she continued, "and don't aim to put any money back into the firm except the price of one issue, that being the correct one." The article, for which she earned $750, doubled her next highest payment for a magazine piece, but still she remained unimpressed by the magazine. "Crime pays," O'Connor wrote to Betty Hester in October 1960 when she submitted her draft of "Living with a Peacock," and six months later, on February 15, 1961, she informed Cecil Dawkins that she and her mother were dreading the arrival of the photographer from *Holiday*.[60] "We are expecting the photographer from *Holiday* to come tomorrow to take the peafowls' pictures," she wrote. "I am sure that the scoundrels will sulk or spread only in front of the garbage can or go all off in the woods until he leaves, and as my mother points out, there is nowhere on this place that you can take a picture without having some ramshackle out-building get in it. In addition I fully expect it to rain."[61]

Considering O'Connor's pessimistic attitude toward the photographer's arrival, perhaps it is not surprising that "Living with a Peacock" opens with a flashback to the arrival of the *Pathé News* photographer. "When I was five, I had an experience that marked me for life," she recalls. "*Pathé News* sent a photographer from New York to Savannah to take a picture of a chicken of mine. This chicken . . . had the distinction of being able to walk either forward or backward. Her fame had spread through the press and by the time she reached the attention of *Pathé News*, I suppose there was nowhere left for her to go—forward or back. Shortly after that, she died, as now seems fitting." The account is both hyperbolic and understated: hyperbolic because of its precocious insistence that the act of photographing the chicken "marked [her] for life" and understated in that *Pathé News* did much more than take a single photograph of the chicken. (In fact, they filmed it for a newsreel feature called "Do You Reverse?" on animals that walked backward.) The irony of the introduction inheres in how a simple technological encounter could spur her chicken's untimely death, its rate of decline proceeding in direct proportion to the amount of mass publicity the chicken experienced. It is, at the same time, an astute commentary on O'Connor's own increasing mass publicity, the result of which was her being paid more than ever before to write for a photojournalistic outlet like *Holiday*. What begins as ironic comedy in the beginning of the essay thus returns in lethally allegorical form by its end, when O'Connor recalls her childhood experience not in a flashback but as a dream. "Lately I have had a recurrent dream," she writes. "I am five years old and a peacock. A photographer has been sent from New York and a long table is laid in celebration. The meal is to be an exceptional one: myself. I scream 'Help! Help!' and awaken" (20). For a writer who detested easy allegory as much as O'Connor did, why end a photo-essay with a dream vision that begs for a Freudian interpretation of mass cultural cannibalism? Why was her macabre hallucination featured in *Holiday*, a literary magazine that Patrick positioned as the *Geographic*'s leading competitor in "spurring the leisure-time interests of a sizable number of moderately well-heeled Americans"?[62]

"Living with a Peacock" suggests that O'Connor's writing, which is so frequently read alongside its regional context of production, may actually illuminate how readers treat images of the unknown and the exotic as communicating objective knowledge. Like many of the writers we have encountered throughout this chapter, the dark humor of O'Connor's dream suggests that she is wryly clued into literary discourse's preoccupation with psychological depth, on the one hand, and photographic discourse's positivist rejection of depth, on the other hand. Indeed, "Living with a Peacock" positions O'Connor's unconscious quest to revisit her scene of childhood trauma against her study of "the picture in Robert Ripley's *Believe It or Not*, of a rooster that had survived for thirty days without his head"—a photograph she "ponders" to better understand her own heady predicament but abandons when she realizes she lacks a sufficiently "scientific temperament" (5). No doubt the joke here is that one would never read Ripley's *Believe It or Not* scientifically in the first place, as its pseudoscientific ethnography of strange and foreign natural phenomena makes no claim to objectivity. But by classing all photographs, no matter how sensational or blatantly unscientific their content, as a type of empirical representation, O'Connor glibly suggests that the medium demands of her a reading temperament she cannot bear to cultivate. "Instinct, not knowledge, sent me to them," O'Connor writes of her peacocks (6). "A sensualist am I," she attests to Hester while drafting the account of her chicken's death by photograph for *Holiday*. "This is in the same category as smelling the *Nat'l Geo*."[63]

While the valorization of smell over sight offers one readerly strategy for disavowing the photograph's claim to knowledge, O'Connor's prose style in "Living with a Peacock" more seriously engages sight reading's simplistic equation of language with visualization as a problem of point of view. O'Connor presents point of view, which has different implications for the study of photography and the study of literature, as the formal category that relates prose to photography as a competing media forms. Whereas the essay begins with the arrival of the *Pathé* photographer—the man who, by formally immobilizing O'Connor's chicken through the static positioning of his camera, seals her fate—it immediately juxtaposes the camera's compositional limitations with O'Connor's method of looking at the peahens she has purchased to the place of her dead chicken. "As soon as the birds were out of the crate, I sat down on it and began to look at them," she observes (7). "I have been looking at them ever since, from one station or another, and always with the same awe as on that first occasion; though I have always, I feel, been able to keep a balanced and impartial attitude." The kinetic dynamism of her point of view, shifting as it does from "one station or another," sustains her sense of "awe" by rejecting the synecdochal reading practice that Grosvenor perfected for the *Geographic*'s readers/lookers. But O'Connor's method of looking, we are led to believe, also bestows unto the peahens a kind of sensual livelihood that neither the *Pathé* photographer nor Ripley's *Believe It or Not* nor any other photograph in O'Connor's short stories allow its represented subjects to enjoy. While those subjects were all, as you will recall, dead or about to die, the peacocks—that O'Connor intends "to let multiply" under her gaze—live on, for "in the end, the last word will be theirs" (20).

Importantly, then, seeing in a way that the photograph does not permit us to see also allows O'Connor to tap into the "unforgettable transcendent apotheotic" of sensory language that the discourses of sight reading foreclose. Like O'Connor's practiced repositioning of her visual point of view, the essay also insistently repositions its narrative point of view from first person to second person to third person, creating a multiperspectival community of lookers to gaze upon the peacocks. We can witness the restless shifting of narrative point of view in the essay's depiction of how the peafowl spreads his feathers—a scene that follows on O'Connor's color-saturated descriptions of the peacock's initially unimpressive aesthetic. "Not every part of the peacock is striking to look at," she writes. "His upper wing feathers are a striated black and white and might have been borrowed from a Barred Rock Fryer; his end wing feathers are the color of clay; his legs are long, thin and iron-colored; his feet are big; and he appears to be wearing the short pants now so much in favor with playboys in the summer. These extend downward, buff-colored and sleek, from what might be a blue-black waistcoat. One would not be disturbed to find a watch chain hanging from this, but none does" (8). Should O'Connor's third-person emphasis on color ("black

and white," "color of clay," "iron-colored," "buff-colored," "blue-black") recall the coloring of magazine photographs, so too does her half-joking description of the peacock's sartorial style ("short pants," "waistcoat," "watch
chain") fix him as a distinctly human type: a "playboy," a fop, or dandy who
gravitates to the worldly pleasures of money and women. Yet to fix him in
the style of a color photograph is to miss precisely what is awe inspiring
about the peacock. "When the peacock has presented his back, the spectator
will usually begin to walk around him to get a front view; but the peacock
will continue to turn so that no front view is possible," O'Connor continues
(10). "The thing to do then is to stand still and wait until it pleases him to
turn. When it suits him, the peacock will face you. Then you will see in a
green-bronze arch around him a galaxy of gazing haloed suns. This is the
moment most people are silent. 'Amen! Amen!' an old Negro woman once
cried when this happened and I have heard many similar remarks at this
moment that show the inadequacy of human speech." Shifting from the
third-person point of view of the "spectator," who attempts to "get a front
view," to the second-person "you," who simply lets the peacock do what
"suits him," to the old woman's spiritual proclamation of "Amen! Amen!"
back to the first person, O'Connor demonstrates the "inadequacy of human
speech" to capture the peacock's visual aesthetic. She creates, on the level
of form, a virtual community of spiritually humbled onlookers who congregate
around the peacock's "galaxy of gazing haloed suns." Compared to the uni-
versality ascribed to "Language of the Photograph," the visual field created
by O'Connor's use of language transcends the world, rising straight up to
the heavens. It is brought back down to earth by her reminder that there
exist those who remain utterly unmoved by the peacock's beauty and performance, again undercutting any claim to a universal language of viewing.

What begins as an act of readerly position taking—smelling a magazine
instead of looking at it—emerges as an intermedial technique for crafting
point of view in the genre of the photo-essay. Although the commentary it
offers most directly implicates its own genre, O'Connor's anti-photographic
point of view also invites us to reread the scenes of photography in O'Connor's
short stories. The story that profits the most from this medial contextualization is "The Displaced Person," which appeared in O'Connor's 1955 collection *A Good Man Is Hard to Find and Other Stories* and was originally titled
"King of the Birds"—the title O'Connor would subsequently use to retitle
"Living with a Peacock" when it was reprinted in her essay collection *Mystery and Manners: Occasional Prose* (1969). As the fictional counterpart to the
photo-essay for *Holiday*, "The Displaced Person" is one of O'Connor's only

stories explicitly concerned with international communication, albeit a kind of virtual or imagined communication that takes place on a Southern dairy farm populated by sight readers. The farm belongs to Mrs. McIntyre, who has decided to take in a "displaced person"—Mr. Guizac, a Polish escapee from the concentration camps—along with his family. Mrs. McIntyre's decision does not sit well with Mrs. Shortley, whose husband also works for Mrs. McIntyre as a handyman and illegally distills liquor on the property. As Mrs. Shortley awaits the Guizac family's arrival, she positions herself on top of the hill that overlooks the farm with no one but a peacock for company. "She stood with the grand self-confidence of a mountain and, and, rose, up narrowing bulges of granite, to two icy blue points of light that pierced forward, surveying everything," O'Connor writes.[64] The peacock astride her looks, too, as if "his attention were fixed in the distance on something no one else could see" (194). As they prepare to look down on the scene as third-person observers, however, O'Connor's prose shifts into free indirect speech as a way of entering Mrs. Shortley's insecure psyche. "These people who were coming were only hired help," Mrs. Shortley thinks, "yet here was the owner of the place out to welcome them. Here she was, wearing her best clothes and string of beads and now bounding forward with her mouth stretched" (194). The two concentrated "icy blue points of light," that, we are led to believe, issue from Mrs. Shortley's eyes, serve as the metaphorical aperture of a camera lens when Mr. Guizac arrives, prompting O'Connor to shift back to the objective third person: "Mrs. Shortley's vision narrowed on him and then widened to include the woman and two children in a group picture" (195). The oscillation from third person to free indirect discourse back to third person tracks the human eye as camera—one prepared to do a great deal of damage to its subjects.

By acting as a virtual photographer who narrows and widens her perspective to create first an individual and then a "group picture," Mrs. Shortley fixes the Guizac family in a series of portraits that are remarkable to her for their very unremarkable nature. "The first thing that struck her as very peculiar," O'Connor writes, "was that they looked like other people. Every time she had seen them in her imagination, the image she had got was of the three bears, walking single file, with wooden shoes on like Dutchmen and sailor hats and bright coats with lots of buttons" (195). The association of the Guizac family with bears, Dutchmen, and sailors anticipates a horizon of cultural difference, which is, for Mrs. Shortley, radically biologized (i.e., the Guizacs are bears; she is human) and iconized (i.e., they wear distinctive hats, coats, and shoes; she wears nothing of note) into discernible types. (It may be worth pointing out that the issue of the *Geographic* O'Connor was sniffing while writing this story had a photo spread dedicated to Dutch villages and their merrily dressed inhabitants.) Failing to locate the experience of cultural difference she seeks in her capacity as a virtual photographer, Mrs. Shortley thinks instead of another photograph in "a newsreel she had seen once of a small room piled high with bodies of dead naked people all in a heap." Yet before "you could realize that it was real and take it into your head, the picture changed and a hollow-sounding voice was saying, 'Time marches on!' This was the kind of thing that was happening every day in Europe where they had not advanced as in this country, and watching from her vantage point, Mrs. Shortley suddenly had the intuition that the Gobblehooks"—her xenophobic renaming of the family—"like rats with typhoid fleas, could have carried all those murderous ways over the water with them directly to this place" (196). From her typological "vantage point," Mrs. Shortley cannot recognize that the Guizacs are the victims of the Holocaust rather than its perpetrators. She thus substitutes in the photographs from the newsreel to transform her cutesy dehumanization of the Guizacs into the specter of international and political danger.

Yet as Mrs. Shortley imagines it, the greatest danger she sees in both the Guizacs and the newsreel photographs is not physical but communicative. Indeed, her greatest fear is a linguistic battle between her family and the Polish family: "She began to imagine a war of words, to see the Polish words and the English words coming at each other, stalking forward, not sentences, just words, gabble gabble gabble, flung out high and shrill and stalking forward and then grappling with each other. She saw the Polish words, dirty and all-knowing and unreformed, flinging mud on the clean English words until everything was equally dirty. She saw them all piled up in a room, all the dead dirty words, theirs and hers too, piled up like the naked bodies in the newsreel" (209). Like the "Language of the Photograph," the "war of words" Mrs. Shortley imagines is not syntactical ("not sentences") but symbolic and visual: a "gabble gabble gabble" of words that she "saw" as "dirty." The radical attenuation of language through the prism of photographic visualization leads not to a universalizing vision of life but to a universalizing image of death.

Beginning with Mrs. Shortley, the medium of photography is repeatedly linked to the dangers of international communication and communion in "The Displaced Person." The vantage point of Mrs. Shortley, who eventually flees the internationalizing farm "to contemplate for the first time the tremendous frontiers of her true country" (214), yields to the vantage point of

Mrs. McIntyre, who soon discovers that Mr. Guizac is using photographs of his twelve-year-old niece to extract wages from her field hand Sulk. Incapable of appreciating the complex human transaction that is taking place— Mr. Guizac wants his niece to escape from the Nazis by marrying an American; Sulk wants to escape from his status as a field hand by marrying a white woman—Mrs. McIntyre thus begins her transformation into a photographic aperture. This time, it is not the lens of a camera but the sight of a gun. She "narrows her gaze" around Mr. Guizac "until it closed entirely around his diminishing figure on the tractor as if she were watching him through gunsight" (224). The tractor will indeed emerge as the scene of Mr. Guizac's demise, although not at the end of a gun. Mr. Shortley will back over him with the tractor and kill him instantaneously. Mrs. McIntyre, who watches the death scene unfold, has trouble processing what she sees. "She felt she was in some foreign country where the people bent over the body were natives, and she watched like a stranger" (235), O'Connor writes. Indeed, the internationalization of the farm's communications and transactions has transformed Mrs. McIntyre into a stranger on her own land. "The Displaced Person" thus ends with her shutting down the farm, losing her eyesight, and keeping only the peacock as company. "You can't have a peacock anywhere without having a map of the universe,"[65] O'Connor wrote to a friend when asked why the figure of the peacock had migrated from the *Holiday* essay to "The Displaced Person." Unlike "The King of the Birds," however, the "map of the universe" that Mrs. McIntyre's peacock presents is not the celestial map of haloed suns encoded in his tail but a linguistic-geographic map of internationalized suffering, one that presents no hope for redemption through communication.

Of course, we should remember that, for O'Connor, the interplay between language and photography was never a political issue but a technical one: a way of crafting a story from multiple perspectives while maintaining its unity. "Point of view runs me nuts," she wrote to a young fan who had asked her for advice on short story writing. "If you violate the point of view, you destroy the sense of reality and louse yourself up generally."[66] In the same letter, which she wrote while confined to her mother's farm in Andalusia, she noted that "the two colored people in 'The Displaced Person' are on the place now. The old man is 84 but vertical or more or less so. He doesn't see too good and the other day he fertilized some of my mother's bulbs with worm medicine for the calves. I can only see them from the outside. I wouldn't have the courage of Miss Shirley Ann Grau to go inside their heads." O'Connor's reference here is to Shirley Ann Grau, a National Book Award nominee and

Pulitzer Prize–winning short story writer, whose 1955 collection *The Black Prince* shifted its point of view across stories from black to white narrators. Unlike Grau, O'Connor's timid refusal to "go inside" the "heads" of black characters manifests itself in her deft attention to the exteriorized presentation of the real human beings who worked for her and her mother. Like Mrs. Shortley's attendance to the Guizacs, O'Connor "can only see them from the outside." As a result, the two real people in O'Connor's employ become legible as her characters: "the two colored people in 'The Displaced Person.'" A more aggressive version of this characterological transmutation holds true for the European refugees whom O'Connor's mother hired to work on the farm, and whom O'Connor identified in her letters as "D.P.'s" after the title of her short story. "Our D. P. has gone and we are fixed up with some PWT [Poor White Trash] and it is a big relief,"[67] O'Connor wrote to her friends and fellow authors Brainard and Frances Cheney in March 1957 on the departure of her Polish émigré, Mr. Matisiack, and his family from Andalusia. "English is flowing freely for the first time in three years." The acronymic ease with which O'Connor moves from a particular character to a type of individual—a "D.P.," a "PWT"—is, if not explicitly linked to photography, nevertheless a troubling example of how seeing someone "from the outside" communicates their characterological qualities via language. The "free flow of English" is only possible after the stop gap of the D.P. is removed, and, once he is replaced with "PWT," neither the dirty gabble, gabble, gabble of language nor the temptation to see difference poses a threat to O'Connor's homegrown sensibilities.

"I begin to feel like a displaced person myself, writing papers and not fiction,"[68] O'Connor observed in a letter to Granville Hicks, the director of Yaddo artists' colony, after she had accepted one too many invitations to lecture to college students around the country. Whether in the form of a lecture delivered far from home or as a photograph staged in a remote corner of the world, O'Connor's anxieties about her displacement from literary fiction articulate the competing logics of sight/sensuality, communication/language, and literary/paraliterary production that this chapter has posited as an integral part of postwar photojournalism and its institutions of production and reception. This then marks one end point in the circuit of international communication that this book has traced so far: from the literary imaginations of the displaced students, teachers, diplomats, tourists, spies, and writers to the imagination of displacement communicated by photographs to American readers and writers. As I have mapped it, it is a remarkably successful circuit of communication, not only in the sense of the literary productivity but also in the sense of institutional longevity. Each chapter covers nearly a century's worth of institutionally grounded practices, habits, rituals, and techniques, and, while we have observed change over time, we have not seen the kind of upheavals or meltdowns that were often experienced within institutions around the world.

All this constancy thus raises an interesting series of methodological questions. What might the literary history I have sketched so far look like if success were not the operative metric for institutional selection but failure? As many social and political theorists have argued, the postwar era is better known for its institutional failings than for its successes. What might the communicative schemas and literary discourses of failed institutions have to teach us about the intersection of literature and liberal politics at mid-century? Conversely, how might their discourses of literacy reveal why these institutions failed in the first place? To answer these questions, the final two chapters of this book probe the analytic benefits of failure in two implicitly opposed institutions of international communication: the People-to-People Program, chaired by William Faulkner, and the Franco-American Fellowship, headed by Richard Wright.

CHAPTER FIVE

Reading like a Bureaucrat

The people to people is what will save the world.

DWIGHT D. EISENHOWER, "Remarks in New Delhi" (1956)[1]

The only way two people can communicate is to meet one another in quiet. I don't think they can do it over any artificial means of communication like radio or telephone. They've got to meet face-to-face because only a very small part of communication is from speech, and how a man in Detroit and an Algerian shepherd can meet I don't know, but all they need to do to communicate is to meet in solitude and peace.... But the pressure is against that, people mustn't do that. They must function through committees with slogans and catch phrases, polysyllabic abstractions that really mean nothing.

WILLIAM FAULKNER, "Freshman Writing Class" (1958)[2]

THE FAILURE OF PEOPLE-TO-PEOPLE

Before September 15, 1956, media-shy novelist William Faulkner had never sent a letter of solicitation to his literary friends, let alone one written at the behest of Republican president Dwight D. Eisenhower. But that Saturday morning in Oxford, Mississippi, Faulkner set aside work on his novel *The Town* (1957) to draft the invitation letter for Eisenhower's new People-to-People Initiative (PTPI): an independent, private organization of Americans who would travel around the Soviet bloc to promote "friendly contact" and "person-to-person communication"—this according to a White House press release issued months before Eisenhower's 1956 reelection campaign against Adlai Stevenson.[3] Eisenhower had asked Faulkner to chair the literary committee of PTPI in May, and Faulkner, despite his reservations about organizing artists under a government-sponsored institution, could not bring himself to turn down his president. "When your President asks you to do something, you do it," he explained.[4] Working alongside Random House publicity director Jean Ennis—"our beautiful slave girl,"[5] as Faulkner called her— and Harvey Breit, a reviewer for the *New York Times Book Review*, Faulkner mailed a letter of invitation and a White House–issued PTPI program description to a guest list that now reads like a *Who's Who* of twentieth-century

American literature: Saul Bellow, John Berryman, Elizabeth Bishop, John Dos Passos, Donald Hall, Robert Lowell, Marianne Moore, Katherine Anne Porter, John Steinbeck, Allen Tate, Lionel Trilling, Robert Penn Warren, E. B. White, and William Carlos Williams, to name just a few of the writers on the list. "Dear _____," he wrote, "The President has asked me to organize American writers to see what we can do to give a true picture of our country to other people. Will you join such an organization?"[6]

But Faulkner's attempt to organize American writers did not succeed, at least not as he had initially imagined. After a flurry of correspondences with the courted writers, a preliminary steering committee meeting, and the presentation of the writers' suggested policies to the PTPI board, Faulkner's branch of PTPI quietly receded into the bureaucratic shadows of the White House and died a forgettable death. By February 1957, all that remained of his organizational labors was an archive of astoundingly eloquent letters, meeting minutes, and questionnaires from the twentieth century's most prominent American writers, many of whom had questioned PTPI's right to exist in the first place. "I'm not sure I want to join an organization," mused E. B. White in his response to Faulkner's circular letter.[7] "I feel healthier and friendlier when in a non-organized, or disorganized condition—which is essentially the proper condition of writers in America." Conrad Aiken echoed White's hankering for disorganization when he proclaimed, "The whole notion of getting writers together, in any sort of organization—and for such a purpose—seems to me unpromising, and probably unworkable."[8] And Faulkner's biggest fan and otherwise shameless sycophant, Southern novelist Shelby Foote, explicitly linked the writer's nonorganized condition to literature's ability to communicate a true picture of America. "If as you say a 'true picture' is what is wanted, I think the best thing we writers can do is stay at home, unorganized, and work," Foote wrote.[9] "Whatever few truths I have discovered, I have discovered them alone, and whatever few truths I have managed to communicate, these too have been accomplished in solitude, without the elbow-jogging distractions of help or hindrance." Thus he concluded, "In any contest such as the present one between us and the Communists, truth is on the side which has the largest claim to right, and I think the right's chances of winning are in direct ratio to its ability to tell the truth. Clarity itself is enough when the cause is just—to show is to explain, and to show clearly is to convince. But clarity can only be approximated (by artists I mean) alone. (If we were on the wrong side, or I thought we were, then I would be for organizing, since distortion is best accomplished in a body.)"

Foote's letter raises two separate, yet interrelated, questions about the re-lationship among institutional organization, international communication, and what the "work" of a writer entails. First, what are the differences be-tween joining "an organization," existing in "an organized condition," and simply "organizing"? Interestingly, Foote's letter does not indict the end goal of Faulkner and Eisenhower's PTPI efforts, which was to build an enduring civic institution: a set of rules and regulations that would govern how writ-ers should communicate in the presence of quasi-governmental oversight. Unlike so many of the other institutions this book has examined, Faulkner's letter makes no mention of any prescriptive programs, protocols, or tech-niques that may cause Foote to balk at the invitation to join PTPI. Rather, Foote, like Aiken and White, seems to question the very process of "orga-nizing" in the first place: a process composed of hundreds of individual events of writing, reading, and face-to-face interaction. We could even think of "organizing" as beginning with Faulkner's circular letter and extend-ing to all of the spoken and written acts undertaken from that moment forward: the letters, questionnaires, interviews, agendas, membership lists, speeches, testimonies, and votes, all of which make visible the painstaking procedural labor it takes to create an institution from nothing at all. Even in PTPI's nascency, the circulation of written texts and the entextualization of its members' organizing discourses—the transformation of spoken (and sometimes shouted) exchanges into textual artifacts, like meeting minutes or vote counts—make PTPI legible as something distinct from the "solitary" working conditions of writers in America, even if that something's exact contours have yet to be determined. Far, then, from foreclosing any critical consideration of its status as an institution, a failed institution like the PTPI writer's committee allows us to probe some of the most controversial his-torical, sociological, and literary dimensions of how midcentury programs of international communication were instituted in the first place.

If the methodological significance of failure stands as one of this chapter's guiding interests, its second similarly arises from a question raised by Foote's letter: what is the relationship between the procedural and bureaucratic work of institutional organizing and the apparently "literary" work of writ-ing and reading? For Foote, organizing is anathema to literary productiv-ity: the ability to write without the "elbow-jogging distractions of help or hindrance" from others. But even more important from a communicative perspective, organizing seems to taint the propositional value of the litera-ture produced: its ability to "discover" and "communicate" a "true picture" of social reality to audiences. The truth value of literary communication is first determined by its ethical "claim to right" which, in turn, determines a literary work's aesthetic quality or "clarity." Here Foote's nested alignment of politics, ethics, and aesthetics articulates a monolithic notion of truth telling—or "truthiness," if you will—that would come to characterize much discourse about Cold War communications, from Senator Joseph McCarthy's "$64 question" ("Are you now or have you ever been a member of the Communist Party?") to the Armed Service Committee's insistence in their military education programs that the "American people are instinctively ready to hear the truth, even though it may not be so pleasant."[10] Yet professions of absolute truth telling must always posit other forms of communication as their discursive antithesis in order to buttress their singular claims to clarity, righteousness, and beauty. Here the bureaucratic communiqués of PTPI, which Foote codes as distracting, wrongheaded, and aesthetically distorting, appear as the alternative to literary communication. "I think it is the condition of the tournament," Foote concludes gamely about his schematic division of a writer's life into right and wrong conditions of existence—a statement that attempts to naturalize literature and literary labor's autonomy from bureaucratic structures of reading and writing. Against Foote and his fellow naysayers, this chapter will show how American writers thrived under the pressures of organizing even when that organizing failed. The scene of "people to people" exchange, I will argue, enabled writers to test out their boldest theories about how practices of literary reading and writing could standardize lived practices of person-to-person communication.

Despite its long-term failings, PTPI is no exception to what we have seen throughout the chapters of this book: that the notion of the literary and the paraliterary, with all of their attendant forms and practices of reading and writing, only emerge within a competing field of communicative forms. In this chapter, however, the opposition is even starker than in previous ones, given how many avowedly incompatible approaches to communication besieged PTPI and its administrators in its initial stages of formation and during its eventual decline. My argument is thus, by necessity, a bit more diffuse in the connections it draws between international communication and literary discourse. This chapter boasts no literary impersonators, literary lovers, literary branders, or literary seers for the simple reason that the historical longevity of the other institutions I have examined in this book does not exist for PTPI. And yet as Jonathan H. Turner points out in *The Institutional Order* (1997), the textual archives of failed institutions are chock full of arguments over the pragmatics of communication: how bureaucratic administrators speak, whom they speak for and against, and the ways in which these speakers imagine and address their multifaceted constituencies.[11] Indeed, the procedural labor of transforming many different and competing forms of expression into a publicly authorized way of communicating sits at the heart of "representation" in two different, yet intimately related, senses of the word: political representation, on the one hand, as a spokesperson or delegate's ability to speak and act on behalf of his constituency; and symbolic representation, on the other, as the stylistic features that attend to any individual spokesperson or delegate's use of language. When these two understandings of representation come into conflict with each other—that is, when the group attempts to withdraw the authority it has bestowed onto the speaker or when they dispute how he has stylized his acts of communication—we can see most clearly the fictitious underpinnings of the idea that there may exist a single person who, by virtue of his style, can speak on behalf of a group or even an entire nation. Failure thus gives us an especially rich opportunity to measure the gap between American figures and the figure of America. This is a fiction that plays out not only within the paraliterary genres of PTPI's bureaucracy but also in the production and reception of the fictional texts written by those who were involved with PTPI from 1956 to 1957: Faulkner's *The Town*, the European performances of Thornton Wilder's *Our Town* (1938), and Saul Bellow's *Henderson the Rain King* (1959), which serve as the literary touchstones of this chapter.

One way to reframe the representative tensions at play in Faulkner's organizing work is on sociologist Max Weber's terms, as the tension between charismatic authority and bureaucratic structure concentrated in a single figure asked to play two very different roles.[12] From one angle, the specter of charismatic authority helps explain the honorific, voluntary, and literarily prestigious reasons why Faulkner was chosen to serve as Eisenhower's spokesperson. Interestingly, charisma both helped and hurt him in his attempt to get writers to join PTPI. "I shall not make this occasion for a fan letter," Katherine Anne Porter wrote with anger upon receiving Faulkner's invitation letter.[13] "I believe you should not have lent your great name and prestige to this purely expedient political device of a Presidential election campaign." A slightly less vitriolic, but also bemused, response came from Lionel Trilling, who confessed to Breit, "If it were anyone other than Faulkner, I'd simply side-step the whole thing as politely as I could. . . . But, as I say, since it is Faulkner who puts the question, I'm willing to go along."[14] Contrast the charismatic authority registered by Porter and Trilling's responses to the regimented and stratified nature of the organizing work Faulkner performed: a specialized administrative function (i.e., to design an institution

of communication) was allocated by a superior (i.e., the president) to a func-
tionary with specialized training (i.e., Nobel Laureate William Faulkner),
who in turn allocated various tasks to secretaries (i.e., "beautiful slave girl"
Jean Ennis), publicity managers (i.e., Harvey Breit), and other writers. From
this angle, then, we may begin to understand the reading and writing practices that attended Faulkner's representative work as distinctly bureaucratic
in nature: hierarchical, routinized, and impersonal engagements with the
paraliterary forms and genres that governed the creation and legitimation
of representative authority. As we shall see, the strategies Faulkner and his
fellow writers devised for asserting their individual aesthetic styles within
bureaucratic texts emerged as the hinge linking literary discourses about
the work of reading and writing to the paraliterary genres of institutional
organizing.

There was good reason for many of the participants to think that PTPI
would manage to sidestep the problems of nationalized representation by
enlisting large quantities of literary writers as its communicative agents instead of students, diplomats, ambassadors, tourists, scientific explorers, ethnographers, and spies. "I think that most of us are too dumb and too serious,"
wrote Robert Lowell to Faulkner on the benefits of populating PTPI with
writers.[15] "Life is too short; we are deeply saturated with our country. If
we can only meet writers from other countries, naturally, humorously, with
curiosity and humility, then they might see that we are human." Striking a
less sentimental note than Lowell, Donald Hall eagerly recommended to
Faulkner that PTPI "ship five hundred intelligent Americans to Italy for two
years, and exchange five hundred Italians, and we will all be better off."[16]
And John Dos Passos applauded the ability of Faulkner and other writers to
work outside the "official stamp" of governmental approval.[17] While the belief in the "deeply saturated" writer's ability to stand at a remove from structures of power may strike us as painfully naïve today, the fantasy of bringing
a specifically literary sensibility to international communication articulated
by Lowell, Hall, and Dos Passos suggests that the writer's boldest claim to autonomy comes not from disavowing social or political institutions (as Foote
argues) but from transforming these institutions into guardians of literary
value from the inside. As Allen Tate insisted to Faulkner, PTPI should include
"only good writers—or artists or composers, etc.—and not people who seem
to 'represent' something," as there was "never anything to be accomplished
for good will by lowering critical standards."[18] Although Tate does not go on
to offer a more detailed theory of aesthetic value, the scare quotes he places
around "represent" reveal how the duality of representation—social/sym-

bolic, bureaucratic/charismatic, literary/paraliterary—might be thought of as a distinctly aesthetic problem, one familiar to us from F. O. Matthiessen's preoccupation with teaching an American literary canon in chapter 2: that the nation would be best represented not just by writers who had written on certain kinds of themes or who had certain types of political allegiances, but by writers who had produced literary works with an attentiveness to aesthetic distinction.

If Foote's totalizing philosophy of truthiness gives us an anti-institutional take on the entanglement of politics and aesthetics, Tate's complication of "representation" offers a productive antithesis for understanding how so many writers convinced themselves to stumble toward a shared sense of institutional collectivity by positing the autonomy of literary-aesthetic value as the antidote to the dangers of bureaucratic and symbolic representation. These discourses of literary-aesthetic value had to be located within processes of institutional formation so as to check the bureaucratic impulse to promote bad literature under the banner of good political ideology. The nesting of discourses of literary value within allegedly unliterary discourses of reading and communication (like reading for propaganda or reading like a bureaucrat) is what inaugurates PTPI as a uniquely hybridized example of bad reading, even if its bad reading practices had the good intention of "saving the world" (to quote Eisenhower's epigraph to this chapter).

To recall the argument that I have made throughout this book about expanding the scale of sociological analysis by expanding the numbers and types of human agents involved in the production of discursive activity, we may appreciate how this chapter, as well as the one to follow, expands the human scale of analysis while dramatically contradicting its historical range. In a sense, each of the formal and sociological arguments I have advanced across this book are both micro- and macrosociological: micro insofar as they concern real or imagined situations of face-to-face interaction; and macro given that these interactions constitute and are constituted by larger units of organization, whether these units are groups, coteries, classrooms, schools, bureaucracies, or magazines. In the case of failure, the messiness of scaling up from the microsociological level of analysis to the macrosociological becomes abundantly clear, as we can sense from the second epigraph to this chapter: an excerpt from Faulkner's 1958 lecture about his participation in PTPI, delivered to an undergraduate writing class he visited while serving as a writer in residence at the University of Virginia. "Mr. Faulkner, how does a man who works in a chewing gum factory in Detroit communicate with a man who shepherds sheep in Algeria?" asked an unidentified classroom participant after Faulkner had finished.[19] Interestingly, Faulkner does not dispute the idea that two people must "meet face-to-face" in order to communicate, given that "only a very small part of communication is from speech." He does, however, question the institutionalization of communication, which, as he sees it, takes place through "committees with slogans and catch phrases, polysyllabic abstractions that really mean nothing." If the tension between specifically stylized acts of communication and generalized protocols rings familiar from previous chapters, here PTPI's lack of any generalized protocols, "slogans," and "catch phrases" forces us to default from a longitudinal history to a snapshot of the irreconcilable discursive activities of dozens of actors—an appropriate shift from meaningless and decontextualized "polysyllabic abstraction" to linguistic particularity. Given this rare behind-the-scenes glimpse at institutional organizing, we may also see what—and who—gets left out of narratives of literary sociology: the debates, disputes, resolutions, and irresolutions among writers who occupy vastly different political, social, and aesthetic positions. (Faulkner's invitation list, for example, includes virtually no black or politically radical writers, who, according to Richard Wright, were often considered "counterpropaganda abroad" by the federal government—an act of exclusion that I will return to in the next chapter.) The somewhat overcrowded quality of this chapter's analysis of PTPI, which corrals more than twenty different literary figures under the umbrella of one failed institution, thus offers an alternative model for exploring how people read from different institutional positions: as writers compelled to do double duty as bureaucrats.

BUREAUCRATIC LITERACY

What might it mean to write and read like a bureaucrat? The blank line that opens Faulkner's circular letter of invitation ("Dear _____") offers a natural starting point to consider these twinned questions, as it is the first document to instantiate the written process of institutional organizing. A blank is both wholly impersonal and imminently personalizable: anyone's name may be written into it. Yet the drama of filling in the blank, as Lisa Gitelman has astutely argued, is not primarily one of identification, like the travelers checks from chapter 3, but of institutional solicitation: a drama in which the soliciting agents—Faulkner, Ennis, and Breit, backed by the seal of the Eisenhower White House—are "endowed with agency according to the bureaucratic processes of knowing that they don't have the information they need."[20] In September 1956, the information Faulkner and his cochairs needed was, first and foremost, knowledge of each writer's enthusiastic commitment to joining the organization, followed by "a sentence, a paragraph, or a page, or as many more as you like" detailing "your private idea of what might further this project." Underneath the blank line and the request for writing, Faulkner enclosed his ideas as a sample of the kind of ideas the writers could submit:

1. Anesthetize, for one year, American vocal cords.
2. Abolish, for one year, American passports.
3. Commandeer every American automobile. Secrete Johnson grass seed in the cushions and every other available place. Fill the tanks with gasoline. Leave the switch key in the switch and push cars across the iron curtain.
4. Ask the Government to establish a fund. Choose 10,000 people between 18 and 30, preferably Communists. Bring them to this country and let them see America as it is. Let them buy an automobile on the installment plan, if that's what they want. Find them jobs in labor as we run our labor unions. Let them enjoy the right to say whatever they wish about anyone they wish, to go to the corner drugstore for ice cream and all the other privileges of this country which we take for granted. At the end of the year they must go home. Any installment plan automobiles or gadgets which they have undertaken would be impounded. They can have them again if and when they return or their equity in them will go as a down payment on a new model. This is to be done each year at the rate of 10,000 new people.[21]

The circular letter, with its jumbled typographical conventions and linguistic registers exemplifies how the conflict between literary-charismatic authority and bureaucratic duty emerges as an aesthetic problem: a problem of both tone and genre. Consider how Faulkner's typically sardonic style is at variance with the more officious form of the numbered list, in which each bullet point iterates an act of forcible, even tyrannical, seizure of corporeal assets ("vocal cords"), material possessions ("automobiles"), and nationalizing documents ("passports") from his fellow Americans. Intriguingly, Faulkner derides his fellow Americans not for possessing these assets in the first place but for using them to communicate with others in an unruly manner—akin to the unchecked growth of "Johnson grass seed," a virtually unstoppable domestic weed. Here the problem with American speech and its mobility is not a problem of poorly stylized metonymy, as it was for James and his squawking, squealing, and barking young ladies, but a problem of poor contextualization.

Face-to-face communication, Faulkner suggests, cannot succeed when faces and voices are detached from their contexts of origin; hence his subsequent critique in a PTPI meeting of the "fiasco that came from the Voice of America program (VOA)" and its reliance on radio's "artificial means of communication" as a medium of circulation.[22] Implicit in Faulkner's letter is an argument about the context of communication that becomes clear by the fourth and final idea that Faulkner offers. Point number four—that the government establish a fund to bring 10,000 Communists to live in the United States— is less an imperative than a relatively thick description of how and where nationalized subjects speak, interact, and consume: freely, in workplaces, labor unions, corner drugstores, and automobile dealerships. Indeed, it is the local specificity of these activities, and their lack of regulation, which makes apparent "all the privileges of this country which we take for granted." What begins as Faulkner's curt parody of large-scale programs of international communication thus modulates into an almost ironic admiration for the small-scale institutions of American domestic discourse.

This point will become important in a moment, when I turn from PTPI's organizing texts to *The Town*, the novel Faulkner was working on as he was organizing PTPI. For now, however, I want to pivot from the paraliterary forms and genres of bureaucracy to its reading practices. How does one read like a bureaucrat? Faulkner's follow-up to his letter—a five-page fill-in-the-blank questionnaire that aggregated the ideas he had read in every single one of the responses he had received, even the hesitant or angry ones—reveals his comic, even mocking, penchant for intertextual play and citation.

Consider, for instance, one busy page of Marianne Moore's questionnaire, which shows how Faulkner curated the writers' resistant and puzzlingly irrelevant responses across eight vertically arranged items per page: "Shocked by your letter; will come to meeting out of curiosity; writers shouldn't be organized—must be free."[23] "Writers should stay at home, unorganized, and work." "FREE EZRA POUND!!" Neither Foote nor his fellow dissenters could have anticipated how Faulkner would read, dissect, and reinscribe their letters in the questionnaire to implicate them in his process of organizing, even if the purposes of their missives was to deliver a simple and resounding "no" to Faulkner's PTPI invitation. In turn, Faulkner, who instructed his respondents to rank each suggestion on a scale of one to four—"1) Excellent, 2) Good, 3) Poor, 4) No"—could not have predicted how bad writers would be at reading and following his directions, perhaps deliberately so. The ranking system he had instructed writers to follow did not offer a sufficiently compelling constraint on their creative activity. Blanks were ignored, list items crossed out, and long sentences substituted for numerical designations. Marianne Moore, for instance, simply struck a line through Foote's suggestion that "Writers should stay at home, unorganized, and work" and wrote underneath it that "Writers should sally out as well"; John Berryman responded with, "Not shocked; will try to come; agree freedom shd [*sic*] not be interfered with."[24] "I have tried to fill out the form you sent but in almost all cases my reaction to the statement is useless,"[25] confessed Donald Hall, who simply wrote Faulkner a letter instead. If these were acts of minor resistance on the parts of these writers, their bad bureaucratic reading nevertheless played right into Faulkner's hands, modeling consensus building in its most parodic and inefficient form.

More interesting, however, were the debates about bureaucratic reading and writing that took place on the margins of the questionnaires: responses to the questionnaire that indicted not only the substance of the ideas proposed by other writers but also the reading and writing practices of the writers from whom these suggestions issued. "There seems to be a general recalcitrance against joint action, some of which sounds vain, megalomaniac (imagine thinking that this committee would help Eisenhower be elected!) and exhibitionist to me," wrote Hall after he had given up on the questionnaire. "The man who says, 'writers shouldn't be organized—must be free' is not reading your letter." In response to the idea that writers should "have our works properly translated and distributed abroad, without special frills or official commentary," Moore responded, "Yes—but pretty complex. I wouldn't want any poltroonery translated, of which a few of these answers are part." Hall's and Moore's imagined projection that the questionnaire items themselves might be translated and distributed abroad, and that the questionnaires might out as cowards, megalomaniacs, exhibitionists, and narcissists those writers who had refused to participate in PTPI's project of liberal institution building, reveals their exquisite attunement to the recursivity of reading and filling out a questionnaire. Like any national-sociological text, whether literary or bureaucratic in form, the questionnaire could not help but communicate something about America to those who might read it. And unlike Faulkner's ironic-idyllic vision of small-scale and nonabstracted communication, the questionnaire and PTPI's other consensus-building documents indexed precisely the kind of representative abstraction he detested. Through various reading and writing strategies designed to decontextualize communication—editing, citing, cutting and pasting the writers' responses into larger items—the questionnaire enacted the shift from particular and identifiable desires to a collective program for PTPI: a program organized under the aegis of

Suggestions	1	2	3	No

NO
Contemptible
Suggests program be dropped; thinks it's
unworkable. As you say, "anesthetize,
for one year, American vocal chords."
— *Craven suggestion*

NO
very poor
Afraid of left-wing past; writers can't
work through institutions; won't be
associated with anything sponsored by
Republican Party.
— *If it time to stop...on Parties / It is American not Party. In DDE / We have a man we can really work with*

Poor
Futile. We are barbarians anyway.
— *Not*

Excellent
Free and untampered exchange of books.
— *Yes*

?
Suggests working through PEN Club.
— *Is it not to such a dynamic... although Mitchell... is an expert (and as conscientious as John Bunyan)*

Poor
possible
Program should be free of government;
suggests letter-writing between
authors of the world; interchange via
National Institute, American Academy
and PEN Club.
— *Not letters between authors I would say National Institute, I think. (Filling Office & Manual...get things done)*

Yes
Good
Person-to-person communication through
lectures, travel, writing; postpone
first meeting until after election
because of differing political views
among authors.

POOR
Shocked by your letter; will come to
meeting out of curiosity; writers
shouldn't be organized- must be free.
— *(Curiosity!) Pathetic. trivial - and Writers proud of effrontery, are no help*

Poor
Suggests examining discrepancy between
what President says he wants and State
Department's refusal to grant passports for cultural missions to such
places as China.
— *Wasteful. We haven't vitality for everything*

Poor
Exchange intelligent men; reform
America first. *cliché, vague* *how?*

Counteract dark picture of America
given by books now available to
foreigners by distributing translations of books that show a happier
side of American life.
— *Yes*

Understand ourselves first. *No*

Be honest about ourselves with other
peoples. *Certainly*
— *Casuistry*

Good
poor
Exchange scholarships, professorships;
quiet meetings without oratory;
personal friendships between authors
of various nationalities.
— *Yes / No meetings; no. friendships*

adroit
good
Suggests some of our corporations
invite groups of young foreigners to
visit American manufacturing plants.
— *Yes*

Such an organization would be auto-
matically suspect as being government-
sponsored. *What of it?*
— *Depends on how it's done*

taken
for
granted
Believes in example rather than
preachment. Deeds are enduring
propaganda. American ideology must
be defined. Films should be considered to further understanding.
— *Preaching our theories? No; except if they unmistakably stand out in pronouncements like General Eisenhower Philadelphia Speech*

Films: good

FIGURES 5.1 and 5.2 *Above and opposite:* Marianne Moore's Questionnaire, People-to-People Initiative (1957). Photograph: Courtesy of The William Faulkner Collection, Albert and Shirley Small Special Collections, University of Virginia, Charlottesville, Virginia.

Suggestions	1	2	3	No

Poor — Expedient political device. Besides, she's a Democrat.

Insincere *Ignore him* — *POOR* Doesn't understand intention of program. Wants to know if it's to help re-elect Eisenhower. He's for Stevenson!

Very impatient of egotism like this

Wants articulate form for cultural exchange.

Poor — Abolish literary agents; satirize America in our writings; send articles on American authors abroad for publication; establish worthy literary prizes; exempt authors from income tax; etc. etc.

Undergrown phase of paranoia

Poor — If first meeting is held after election he will join, since then Eisenhower will perhaps have four years to follow through with it.

bad logic

Good — Convey ourselves to others through our writing.

Certainly

Poor — Stop all propaganda. *very weak attitude*

good — FREE EZRA POUND!! *Y E S*

Self-evident — Authors' works are best propaganda. *Certainly but why stop there?*

Writers should stay at home, unorganized, and work. *and Sally out as well*

Good — Have our works properly translated and distributed abroad, without special frills or official commentary. *Yes — but pretty complex. I wouldn't say Montgomery translated, but ½ of these answers are part.*

Good — Circulate books and magazines more widely in other countries; soften up the rigid political barriers that are the real reason why people have very little "friendly contact;" plug European federation along the lines suggested by Dr. Adenauer; and elect Stevenson.

Character matters — A man who quotes another only out of context to sink him, is no mouthpiece for me. A shabby American in the White House would not help international reciprocity.

Suggests a series of small conferences of Europeans, Asiatics, etc., to be held in Washington, over a period of about two years.

It isn't practical. Big-wig-&-beguine can hardly be achieved

Marianne Moore
Nov. 1st 1956

the questionnaire's constructor and administrator, William Faulkner. In serving as a "mouthpiece" (to borrow Moore's term), he had to maintain his status as a charismatically distinct entity—a fictional "character" himself—while nevertheless speaking for everyone.

Taken together, then, the metadiscourses about PTPI's organizing processes bear a striking resemblance to the novel *The Town*, the Yoknapatawpha novel that Faulkner slowed his work on in September 1956 to assume his PTPI duties, and thus another text in which we can see Faulkner formally navigating the duality of his existence as both a literary figure and a bureaucratic one. The second book in the Snopes trilogy and one of Faulkner's least discussed late novels, *The Town* takes as its subject matter the evolution of the country town—"one of the greatest American institutions; perhaps the greatest," according to economist Thorstein Veblen.[26] More explicitly a novel of small-scale bureaucracy and its pitfalls than the other two books in the Snopes trilogy, *The Hamlet* (1940) and *The Mansion* (1959), *The Town* painstakingly details how the Snopes family establishes their dominion over Jefferson, Mississippi, beginning not from scratch but from total nonexistence. ("Scratch? Scratch was euphemism indeed for where he started from," Faulkner writes of the first Snopes to step foot into Jefferson.)[27] The novel's fictional discourse is a direct violation of the Snopeses' prohibition on narrating their history, a half-century-long narrative of fraud, chicanery, and institutional conquest that they "have sworn never to tell anybody": how "they had all federated unanimously to remove being a Snopes from just a zoological category into a condition composed of success" (113). Their federated "condition" is instituted by and through Jefferson's tight-knit and expansive network of banks, schools, power plants, restaurants, general stores, canteens, labor unions, corner drugstores, and automobile dealerships. While critics have described the Snopeses as running the gamut from unsavory to pure evil, Faulkner nevertheless depicts the family's petty politics with a begrudging admiration.[28] For Faulkner, the town encapsulates "the most solvent and economical" and "self-perpetuating" kind of institution, one in which consensus building is as natural as banding together members of an animal species (122). When compared to the bureaucratic incompetence of Faulkner's PTPI administration, the Snopeses' processes of organizing offer both the ideal model for scaling representation from the individual to the social and a vision of the gothically terrifying consequences that may result.

Whereas the Snopeses' history offers a dark mirror to hold up to Faulkner's PTPI efforts, the narrative organization of the novel better approximates the tension between literary-charismatic authority and the bureaucratic duties of organizing. The novel is relayed in the first person by a rotating cast of three characters—the young Charles Mallison, his Harvard-educated uncle Gavin Stevens, and traveling salesman V. K. Ratliff—whose accounts of the town's evolution all take place in the shadow of the US government and its international communications bureaucracies. Charles, who opens the novel, is not yet born at *The Town*'s inception; everything he recounts in the opening chapter comes secondhand from his second cousin Gowan Stevens, who has been sent to live with the Mallison family after "the State Department sent his father to China or India or some far place, to be gone for two years" (3). Similarly, large sections of Gavin Stevens's narration are dispatches from Europe, where he has been appointed by the State Department to "some kind of board or committee or bureau for war rehabilitation" that is responsible for setting up institutions like the American-style canteen in France and Germany. And Ratliff's status as a Russian émigré, revealed for the first time in *The Town*—his full name, we learn, is Vladimir Kyrilytch Ratliff—marks him as an aspiring American—one still in the process of national acculturation through his interactions with the Snopeses and their institutional networks.

Yet what elevates *The Town*'s bureaucratic resonances with PTPI into more than just thematic overlap is the formally isomorphic relationship the novel reveals between telling a fictional story about institutional formation and actually creating an institution. *The Town* is not as concerned with the specific policies or politics of the Snopeses' institutions as it is with tracing the fraught and messy processes by which they come to exist in the first place. For the Snopeses, these processes are overwhelmingly discursive in nature. They do not establish their federation through violence, like the barn burnings or murders of *The Hamlet*, but through carefully crafted repertoires of double speak, false promising, insinuation, and, most important of all, textual inscription. Consider the novel's dense documentary economy of employment records, ordinances, bank ledgers, sales tags, letters, wills, titles, and notes—written genres produced, edited, and circulated around Jefferson by Snopeses who work as "clerks and book-keepers in the stores and gins and offices" with such nationalist-consumerist names as Wallstreet Panic, Watkins Products, and I. O. ("Interest Owed") Snopes (14). Given their bureaucratic dispositions, it is no surprise that the way Faulkner depicts the Snopeses' processes of writing is intensely routinized and impersonal in nature. To watch a Snopes at work, Uncle Gavin reports, is to see a Snopes "bow over a book-keeper's desk in an attitude not really of prayer, obeisance; not really of humility before the shine, the blind glare of blind money; but rather of a sort of respectful

humble insistence, a deferent invincible curiosity and inquiry into the mechanics of its recordings" (45). Gavin's deferral of positive description tries
on, and then rejects, more legible models of institutional subjectivity: first,
the piety of the religious scribe, then the humility of the mesmerized materialist. Yet after wading through what kinds of people the Snopeses are not,
the descriptions Faulkner does give us ("respectful humble insistence," "deferent invincible curiosity") are not particularly concise or coherent. The ac-
cretion of adjectives, and contradictory ones at that, is, at best, only "sort of"
able to relay how the Snopeses orient themselves to the bookkeeper's desk
and the mechanics of its recordings. But the abstracted quality of Faulkner's
description is precisely the point: this is how the bureaucrat writes, with
vigor for a distant and impersonal institutional approval.

Yet communicating a systematic story of institutional formation requires
a corresponding act of reading the bureaucratic texts that the Snopeses have
written. For the three narrators, fantasized representatives of a local civic
elite, the act of telling the story of the Snopeses emerges through reading
the bureaucratic texts the Snopeses have written and producing detailed
commentaries about these texts for the reader. In contrast to the omniscient
narration of its predecessor *The Hamlet* or its sequel *The Mansion*, *The Town*'s
narrators take turns testifying to, describing, and citing one another's descriptions of the Snopeses' activities. "This is what Ratliff said happened
up to where Uncle Gavin could see it," begins Charles Mallison in chapter 16, which narrates I.O.'s attempt to cheat an illiterate widow through
a mule trade, asking her to sign documents she cannot read (241). "No, no,
no, no, no. He was wrong," Ratliff counters at the start of chapter 18, which
contests Gavin Stevens's account in chapter 17 of the Snopeses' attempts to
alter a will to disinherit a noncooperating member of the family/federation
(309). The narratological insistence on bureaucratic literacy as a mode of civic
storytelling shows how institutional organizing is not anathema to literary
production or literary representation, as Foote had once suggested, but central
to the novelist's ability to communicate a "true picture" of small-scale social
interaction. In *The Town*, the narrators' nested attempts to read the Snopeses'
bureaucratic genres of texts smooth over the rough procedural seams by
which the town's institutions—and, by extension, the Snopeses' federation—
are stitched together as a single, sui generis social entity. The novel thus
comes to serve as the unifying and representative mouthpiece for the un-
speaking Snopeses and the gently squabbling narrators alike. Unlike PTPI's
texts, the novel's form derives from its highly stylized consensus building by
the town's true leaders.

On the level of the novel's fictional discourse, then, we can appreciate the writing and reading practices through which institutional formation is narrated. Turning back to PTPI, however, we can begin to see how the fictional conventions for representing institutional formation could trouble the actual communicative work of bureaucratic organization, which can rarely tolerate the stylized procedural murkiness that has made *The Town* so interpretively unwieldy for literary critics. On November 29, 1956, after compiling the responses to all the questionnaires he had received, Faulkner hosted a cocktail hour meeting in New York to draft a "Distillate"—a document that summarized the committee's recommendations—to send to the White House. Neither the meeting nor the resulting document was a success; this despite the fact that the writers in attendance included Donald Hall, Saul Bellow, Edna Ferber, William Carlos Williams, John Steinbeck, and ten other literary luminaries. At the center of the meeting's drama was Faulkner, who Hall described that night as "a small, tidy, delicate, aloof, stern, rigid, stony, figure . . . sitting in his chair rather away from the rest of the people" issuing a series of "absurd proposals."[29] As detailed in the "Distillate"—which Faulkner, Steinbeck, and Hall drafted and sent to Eisenhower—Faulkner's proposals to "achieve better communication" included the following: "(1) To reduce visa requirements to a minimum and abrogate red tape for the Hungarian people and any other people who may or will suffer the same crisis. (2) To try to bring people from all over the world who do not agree with us to this country for a duration of at least two years to lead a normal American life, to see and experience what we have here that makes us like it. This will necessarily require a revision of the McCarran Act. (3) To disseminate books, plays, and moving pictures through our Government, at least to match what the Russians are doing."[30]

Despite Faulkner's insistence to Eisenhower that American writers were "loyal citizens and cognizant by our craft of world conditions," the tone deafness of the "Distillate" suggested otherwise. For many committee members, the notion that a writers' committee could persuade the government to reduce visa requirements or repeal the McCarran Act—the piece of legislation from which McCarthyism derived its ability to detain or deport suspected Communists—revealed the mismatch between the political limitations of bureaucratic labor and the imaginative possibilities of literary craftsmanship. "Perhaps it is just as well that writers do not have political power," wrote Steinbeck after receiving the first draft of the "Distillate" from Faulkner.[31] "They might well tear up an already disordered world but with the best of intentions. Perhaps a writer's first duty is to get himself crucified if he can, but failing that, simply to stay out of jail." Thornton Wilder's editorial comments—"I don't think it's very well expressed, or organized"—paled alongside Saul Bellow's embarrassment at Faulkner's desire to contextualize American communication as if he were elaborating the mise-en-scène for one of his novels.[32] When one writer asked, "Mr. Faulkner. Don't you think people behind the Iron Curtain already know the difference between their country and this one?" Bellow recalled cringing at Faulkner's reply: "Suh! Knowin' is one thing, experiencin' is another!"[33] The distinction between "experiencin'" and "knowin'"—a tension Flannery O'Connor's writing touched on chapter 4—was one Faulkner reasserted when Steinbeck suggested that the writers could "describe America to another country by a Sears & Roebuck catalog—how we live and how we pay for it."[34] The descriptive work of the catalog, Faulkner suggested, was too vulnerable to misappropriation if it was simply received abroad, rather than lived at home. His sentiment would soon be mirrored by Gavin Stevens's account in *The Town* of how the Snopeses corrupted the American canteens exported to Europe by the State Department: they sneaked onto the government's committee for war relief and transformed the canteens into brothels, thus showcasing the worst aspects of how Americans lived—pruriently, lasciviously—and how they paid for it.

By reading the committee's debates about bureaucratic versus literary work, we may begin to see where the novel's representation of institutional formation and PTPI's actual formation diverge: whereas the novel can succeed in operating as a metadiscursive "mouthpiece" that organizes its characters' bureaucratic communications, Faulkner was increasingly unable to create the same fiction of unity as PTPI's spokesperson. In fact, the schism between the two may help us understand a puzzling formal shift that takes place toward the end of *The Town*, particularly in the chapters written during the last three months of Faulkner's bureaucratic duties. Upon his return from a State Department stint in Europe, Gavin, who has harbored a longstanding and obsessive love for Eula Snopes, is desperate to save her daughter, Linda, from the Snopes federation. When Eula insists that Gavin marry Linda, so that he may disrupt the Snopeses from within their own federation, Gavin decides instead to "develop her mind" by tutoring her in poetry and classic literature at the corner drugstore. (Gavin, as Faulkner observed in "Requiem for a Nun," "looks more like a poet than a lawyer.")[35] In a rare glimpse into the mind of one of the Snopeses—Flem Snopes, Linda's father and patriarch of the family—via free indirect discourse, we learn that literature presents an even greater threat to the Snopeses than marriage. Flem, who is "already destined to own at least a Ford agency if not an entire labor union" fears that Gavin is meeting Linda "not just to entice and corrupt her female body but far worse: corrupting her mind, inserting into her mind and her imagination not just the impractical and dreamy folly in poetry books but the fatal poison of dissatisfaction's hopes and dreams" (285). If the literary's dominion over Linda's "hopes and dreams" stand in stark opposition to the Snopeses' material and institutional realities, then the literary is also the key to destroying these realities. Gavin's literary-charismatic pull as an instructor, his penchant for nonbureaucratic reading, must sow the seeds of "dissatisfaction" within the institutional status quo to wrench control of the town away from the Snopeses.

On the level of form, the novel's closing chapters also wrench control away from its three narrators and their metadiscourses of institutional formation. Instead of their densely citational and interdiscursive mode of description, *The Town* abruptly shifts to a different pragmatic register: Gavin's repeated professions of truth telling as a self-appointed and institutionally autonomous literary authority figure, which pit the truth communicated by literature against the coherence of the Snopeses' institutionalized power. The Snopeses, Gavin thinks, "aren't interested in poets' dreams. They are interested in facts. It doesn't even matter whether the facts are true or not, as long as they match the other facts without leaving a rough seam" (330). This emerges as a mantra of sorts, a series of phrases that Gavin repeats with slight variation and increasing insistence until the end of the novel: the Snopeses "are interested in the reality of facts, they don't care what facts, let alone whether they are truth or not if they just dovetail with all the other facts without leaving a saw-tooth edge" (338); and even Linda was "not interested in truth or romance but only in facts whether they are true or not, just so they fit all the other facts" (358). As we have seen in Foote's letter to Faulkner, all professions of truth telling must proceed by assuming that the audience one addresses has already been hailed by a competing representation of the world. Here, too, the incessant opposition that Faulkner sets up between literary representation, which lays claim to both absolute "truth" and "romance," and "the reality of facts," which need not be true but must "dovetail with all the other facts," throws into relief *The Town*'s competing forms of narration: Gavin's literary truth telling positions itself against the texts the narrators have sutured together to create the socially constructed fiction of the town as an institution. Sadly, the truth that Gavin speaks is not enough to save Eula, who will take her own life. Linda, however, will leave Jefferson and the United States to fight in the Spanish Civil War as a convert to communism. She will eventually return to the town in *The Mansion* and will team up with Gavin to destroy the Snopeses' federation by preaching tolerance, plurality, equality, and individualism—the ultimate act of liberal-artistic triumph.

Gavin's staging of poetic authority not only reconfigures the aesthetic of the novel, shifting it from an institutional fiction to a romantic assertion of literary autonomy, but it also remarkably—and tellingly—foreshadowed Faulkner's pronouncements in the final PTPI meeting he would attend. In preparing for the fictiveness of his role as a representational character, Faulkner finished *The Town* just one week before he returned to New York from Oxford, Mississippi, to present the writers' committee's findings to the PTPI board on February 4, 1957—a week in which he did very little but send the final chapter of *The Town* to the *Saturday Evening Post* and drink to excess.[36] He and Breit had prepared a short speech outlining their policy proposals that they were to present to State Department liaisons and other subcommittee chairs, who would then pick the best proposals to forward to Eisenhower. But when Faulkner arrived at the 8:30 a.m. meeting at the Algonquin Hotel, hung over and surly from drinking an entire bottle of Jack Daniel's Black Label the night before, he refused to present the writers' proposals. Instead, he took a page from his own book. "Here's what we should do," he told Breit.[37] "We should get two stamps, one 'True' and the other 'Not True.' And we take every book that goes out of the country and we stamp it 'True' or 'Not True.'" When Breit resisted and pointed out that the committee had approved the proposals already, Faulkner replied, "That don't make no difference. We stamp it 'True' or 'Not True.'" While it may be too much of a stretch to claim that Faulkner deliberately took Gavin's professions of truth telling as his characterological model of testimony, the rhetorical and performative resonances between the two are undeniable. Even the timing is suspicious. And while we may read Faulkner's performance ironically, the PTPI board did not extend to him the same generosity in evaluating his proposal for exporting truth in the form of literature. Faulkner's testimony effectively ended his and the rest of the writers' participation in the program, undoing the past year of bureaucratic work just as the final chapter of *The Town* attempted to undo the Snopeses' and the narrators' institution-building efforts.

Other than revealing the full extent of Faulkner's debilitating alcoholism, what does the failure of PTPI communicate? In other words, how might we engage Marianne Moore's projective fantasy that these bureaucratic documents would one day be read—by me, by you—and that the controversies they encapsulated would reflect the political dynamics of a particular historical moment and a distinctly internationalized space? In a counterintuitive sense, we could see institutional nonexistence as PTPI's end goal all along, albeit in a more complex way than Foote or Aiken or White had imagined in their initial letters. The fictional discourse of poetic truth telling in *The Town*, once incarnated in Faulkner's PTPI testimony, emerged as an institutionally oppositional act of literary position taking, one geared to dismantling its context of utterance. This, Faulkner believed, would serve a broader political purpose by confirming the singularity of the writer's representative work: not as a spokesperson or mouthpiece for the organization, but as an advocate for the individual—the most quintessentially American truth teller one could imagine. We could thus read the stylistic dimensions of Faulkner's truth telling as performing his commitment to individuality: an exaggerated and institutionally unproductive (or destructive) version of the "American ideology of freedom" that the White House imagined PTPI would communicate to audiences behind the Iron Curtain. When pressed about the dissolution of PTPI one year later, while lecturing to undergraduates at the University of Virginia in April 1958, he explained that his proposal to stamp books as "True" and "Not True" was intended to undermine "the mythology that one single individual is nothing, and can have weight and substance only when organized into the anonymity of a group."[38] To read the failure of PTPI is to understand how Faulkner's specifically American notion of literary truth telling helped him throw his weight around as a bureaucratic reader, writer, and destroyer; a critical overlay between his representations of institution building and his communicative acts as a representative that made PTPI cohere, and then dissolve, if only for a brief moment in history.

PRESIDENTIAL READERS, READING HIERARCHIES

In my reading of Faulkner's role as PTPI spokesperson, I have argued that the failure of PTPI helps us understand how discourses of institution building and practices of bureaucratic literacy might double as literary forms. Yet there exists a deep and instructive irony in what Faulkner failed to do—to create an institution by building consensus among writers—that complicates any optimistic interpretation of his individualistic truth telling at the Algonquin Hotel. Faulkner failed to reconcile the writers' competing discourses about communication: which social contexts, genres, and media forms were, in fact, most amenable to successful international communication? More important, for my purposes, was that his impromptu and unilateral performance of truth telling occluded the conflictual history that links the first circular letter to the agreed-upon proposals that were supposed to be presented to the board. (Without reading through the PTPI archive, all one could glean from the biographies of individuals involved is that Faulkner behaved like a fool and PTPI dissolved because of his foolishness.) In an early exchange of letters with Robert Penn Warren, Faulkner had agreed with Warren that PTPI should wear its commitment to American democratic pluralism on its sleeve. "There ought to some way to dramatize, personally, the pluralism of America, the divergence of opinion and conviction, on all points, historical and contemporary, and to indicate the fact that despite this pluralism and intense debate, we somehow keep on managing to do business," Warren suggested.[39] There was little doubt, however, that the writers' committee was closed for business precisely because Faulkner could not "personally" "dramatize" pluralism and its consensus-building protocols as a bureaucratic actor.

But our perspective changes if we expand our focus from Faulkner's individual and representative performance of bureaucratic incompetence to the writers' committee as a whole. The failed pluralism of the PTPI writers' committee allows us to excavate competing claims about international communication made by other writers—claims that bear an intimate relationship to how these writers represented communication in their literary works. The bickering between Faulkner and the other writers, registered in great detail by PTPI's bureaucratic texts, invites us to shift our focus from Faulkner's burdens of representation/representative action to the politico-aesthetic positions staked out by his fellow writers. How might the communicative repertoires of a participant, who is merely one of many human actors in PTPI's institution-building dramas, diverge from the formal and stylistic preoccupations of its spokesperson? What kinds of small, unregistered, and auxiliary literary and bureaucratic labors might such debates make visible?

Take, for instance, Faulkner's argument with Thornton Wilder over the manner in which Faulkner constructed his "Distillate" to the White House. You will recall that Wilder had already criticized Faulkner for the document's aesthetic and formal sloppiness. "I don't think it's very well expressed, or organized," he had noted. Yet Wilder went on from this general criticism to perform a virtuosic close reading of the text's inappropriate mode of address, beginning with its opening lines to the president:

Dear Mr. President:
We in America tend to overestimate our enemies. For example, we have believed that the Soviet state has been able to condition their people so that they

are impervious to the outside world. In recent months this has been proved completely untrue in Hungary and Poland. The human animal is not conditionable to the extent that we've been led to believe. Therefore, we are convinced that free and honest communication will not fall on deaf ears. The first step of a dictator is to cut off communication of ideas, of people, or arts, to close borders and to stop the interchange of messages. This being so, it is to our advantage to enter into communication upon any or all levels.[40]

Wilder—who circled Faulkner's repeated use of the first-person plural pronoun "We"—wrote, "One does not address the President as though he were a stupid man, or a public meeting, or a high school student."[41] Because it was not immediately apparent that one would use identical manners of address when speaking to a stupid man, a public meeting, or a high school student, or even what stylistic markers might characterize this form of address, Wilder attempted to clarify his point by mimicking the tone of Faulkner's "Distillate" in a parenthetical aside: "(Mr. Eisenhower—where have you been?—we think you ought to be told that the first step of a dictator is to cut off communication.)" If Wilder's act of textual ventriloquism seems exaggerated, it is pointedly so. When one addresses the president of the United States as a reader, one does not tell him what he "ought to be told." This prescriptive act of communication fails to respect the power of authority that the president holds over his people in all contexts, a power with which they have endowed him. For Wilder, Faulkner's act of telling "Mr. Eisenhower" what he "ought to be told" relegated the president to the communicative footing of a stupid man, a child, or a member of an undifferentiated public—all readers over whom Faulkner could less objectionably assert his intellectual and cultural power as a writer. Thus Wilder ended his letter by issuing an ironclad rule for Faulkner's future correspondences with the White House. "No rhetorical objurgations. No periods for the gallery," he ordered Faulkner. That is to say, no more scolding your presidential reader.

That this act of scolding may double as a performance for "the gallery"—as if PTPI's organizing were not only a bureaucratic but a theatrical endeavor—suggests a connection between the performativity of communication and the genre of performance. As the only playwright asked to participate in PTPI's international efforts, Wilder's attunement to the audience effects of address invites us to consider what forms of national-social institutions and face-to-face relationships scolding underwrites—especially when compared to, say, *The Town*'s vision of the Snopeses. Anyone familiar with Wilder's theatrical work would have instantly connected Wilder's mimicry of Faulkner's "rhetorical objurgations" to the performances of scolding that open so many of Wilder's plays. Most notable among them is *Our Town*, which played a unique role in American international communications as the most popular play translated and staged outside of the United States. First produced in 1938, *Our Town* received its warmest reception not in New York or Boston but in West Germany and Austria in the mid-1950s, at precisely the same time Wilder was working with Faulkner on PTPI. From 1954 to 1957, *Unsere kleine Stadt* was produced in Berlin, Frankfurt, Hamburg, Bochum, Düsseldorf, Kiel, and Munich, where, as Wilder noted, "matinees were given for superior selected students of high-school age" and "a prize was offered for the best essay by a student of the play, and the thirty best essays were sent to me."[42] For German theater critic Horst Frenz, who documented Wilder's striking popularity among German audiences after World War II, *Our Town* nourished the identificatory "desire in the German spectators to view these lovable people in the hope to find a new order in themselves."[43] As the first American awarded the German Bookseller's Peace Prize in September 1957, Wilder visited West Germany later that year to receive the order *Pour le Mérite* from the president. His visit to Germany overlapped not only with his PTPI work but also with his adaptation of *Our Town* for the British Broadcasting Corporation's (BBC) *Sunday Night Theatre*, which BBC had planned to air across its worldwide radio services in Africa, the Middle East, and the Indian subcontinent. And according to Frenz, in the parts of Europe most proximate to the Soviet bloc the play was the thing to ignite public debate over how "the sociological and spiritual situation" of the newly divided continent could be reconstituted through "literary revolution."[44] As Wilder stated in an interview with Bob McCoy, the confluence of theatrical performance and political reform hinged on the performative work done by "ordinary daily conversation between ordinary people" who lived in the fictional New England town of Grover's Corners.[45]

The performative and performable magic attributed to *Our Town*—its perceived ability to dramatically reshape the social institutions of Eastern Europe along liberal democratic lines—presents us with an especially compelling reason to read the play alongside Wilder's participation in PTPI, which concerned itself with precisely the question of ordinary daily conversation between ordinary people. Populated by stupid men, public meetings, and high school students, *Our Town*'s dialogic form is best described as a series of rhetorical objurgations. The play opens with fathers scolding sons (Dr. Gibbs to George: "Didn't you hear your mother calling you?")[46] and continues with mothers scolding chickens (Mrs. Gibbs to her chickens: "What's the matter with you?" [19]); Mr. Webb scolding his daughter Emily ("Who do you think you are today?" [29]); Howie Newsome, the milkman, counterscolding his cow Bessie by claiming that she "keeps scolding me" (13); and members of the "audience" (themselves actors) breaking the fourth wall to scold the actors (The Belligerent Man to Mr. Webb about lax moral standards in the town: "Why don't you do something about it?" [27]). In each case, the errant actor (or animal) is put into his or her place by a superior through a performative/performed act of patrolling speech and behavior. "You know the rule's well as I do," Mrs. Webb says to her children at one point—an acknowledgment of the shared social order that everyone in the play is being pulled toward (15). (The Wooster Group would later register the play's "reactionary conservatism" as an issue of tone. "The tone is pedantic and condescending, and it is clearly directed to a high school audience," wrote Donald Haberman, inadvertently echoing Wilder's criticism of the "Distillate.")[47] And yet this imposition of a benevolent and vigilant hierarchy by family members, neighbors, and fellow theatergoers suggests why, after the fascist destruction of German civil society after World War II, German audiences eagerly received the play as a model for a "new order" founded by the "lovable people" of Grover's Corners. When one considers that Wilder's 1942 play *The Skin of Our Teeth*, the second most popular play in Germany, was translated into German as "We Got Out Alive," the benign, small-scale, and protective intrusions of *The Town* do not seem so bad after all.

Yet how new is this order really? Unlike *The Town*, which, according to Wilder, abounded with "Faulkner's relish for skulduggery" in all matters institutional, the social conservatism of *Our Town* emerges from the play's embrace of a quintessentially liberal hierarchy. The institutions of the town—from the family to the church where George Gibbs and Emily Webb get married to the theater in which the play takes place—create and enact order from the top down.[48] And while the local hierarchies of *Our Town* are not exactly militaristic in form, one can hardly miss the parallels between an earlier and metaphorical "European Theater of Operations," presided over by Eisenhower in his role as a self-proclaimed "Theater Commander," and Wilder's literal theatricalization of an orderly all-American hierarchy.[49] The parallels between the GI occupation of Germany's Theater of Operations and *Our Town*'s occupation of the German theater stage just one decade later suggests how the latter (representation) displaced the former (military power) as the mediating agent between the United States and Germany, while nevertheless maintaining some of its key structural features. Thus we may also understand why both the play's form and its reception chafed at Marxist critics in East Berlin, where Wilder faced frequent condemnation in the press as "a typical apologist" for "an unsatisfactory social order."[50] In Communist media outlets like *Der Morgan* and *Die Welt*, reviewers accused *Our Town* of parochially insisting that "Europe and American" should "be fused into one"—an act of artistic internationalism that sought to "replace progressive ideas" of socialism with the bourgeois mystification of small town American liberal hierarchy.[51]

In articulating the complex interrelationship between "ordinary daily conversation," theatrical performance, and social institutions, *Our Town*'s acts of scolding track nicely onto Wilder's command that Faulkner not scold the president for the gallery in the "Distillate" and the bureaucratic-editorial work this command subsequently entailed. As Wilder explained it at the end of his reading of Faulkner's "Distillate," PTPI's primary purpose was not to do serious revolutionary or intellectual work but to issue well-written statements of presidential support. "I gathered that what the President wants is mostly two things," Wilder wrote. "An expression of support from as many writers as possible—to strengthen his hand when he comes before Congress to ask for the money. An 'activity' on the writers' part that will alert the U.S.A. to the importance of such an expenditure."[52] And interestingly, Wilder's proposed edits to the "Distillate" all proceeded by counterscolding Faulkner for his hierarchically inappropriate address while simultaneously staging a defense of a scolded Eisenhower—a shadow reader who Wilder projects as an unfairly embattled authority figure governing from the lonesome top. In response to the first suggestion—that PTPI help reduce visa requirements for Hungarians—Wilder wrote, "The President has opened the doors as far as he is able and farther than one could have predicted. This recommendation now clutters and lames the force of what follows." Or consider his somewhat more sarcastic response to Faulkner's suggestion about broadening international exchange programs among intellectuals: "It sounds as though the idea has just dawned on the Committee."[53] In each instance of Wilder's scolding of Faulkner, the expectation was that Faulkner, much like the characters in *The Town* or even the inhabitants of East Berlin, would fall in line with existing models of address that respected social and political hierarchies rather than attempting to stake out a new institutional order. In this sense, too, we can see Faulkner's failure as a more powerful assertion of the writer's individual capabilities than the comparative conservatism of liberal institutional success—or what he described to the undergraduate writing class at the University of Virginia as running "full tilt into what might be called almost a universal will to regimentation."[54]

Of course, the point of analyzing such conflicts is not to line writers up on relatively limited spectrum of liberal to conservative impulses. Rather, it is to show how different textual forms may lend themselves to different discursive logics of institutional creation, each one attractive to different audiences based on their particular political demands. The popularity of *Our Town* in Germany shows how the performative instantiation of institutional hierarchies were a drama that needed to be perpetually rehearsed on stages around the country. Such occasions for iteration and perfectibility were unavailable—and, one could speculate, unpalatable—to the performers in PTPI, whom Robert Penn Warren had called on to "dramatize" American social life. In turning now to our final member of the writers' committee, Saul Bellow, we will see how his writing, both literary and bureaucratic, presented the repetition of institutional performativity/performance as a serious threat to the novelist's imaginative sensibilities.

BUREAUCRATIC IDEOLOGY, NOVELISTIC MISOLOGY

How might the writers' committee have fared if it had not been a committee populated by writers? This question, while ultimately impossible to evaluate as a historical counterfactual, was nonetheless central to Faulkner's thinking after he walked away from PTPI in February 1957. "What doomed it in my opinion was symptomized by the phraseology of the President's own concept," he explained to students at the University of Virginia in his 1958 lecture on PTPI.[55] "Laborer to laborer, artist to artist, banker to banker, tycoon to tycoon. What doomed it in my opinion was an evil inherent in our culture itself; an evil inherent in (and perhaps necessary though I for one do not believe this) in the culture of any country capable of enduring and surviving through this period in history. This is the mystical belief, almost a religion, that individual man cannot speak to individual man because individual man can no longer exist." If Faulkner's statement seems naïve in its wholesale dismissal of the regional, racial, gendered, and class distinctions between individuals, it nevertheless raises the question of what the limitations on communication between individuals may be. How might communicative practices and the way we talk about them change if what we were interested in were mixing and matching interactions between laborers and bankers, tycoons and artists, bureaucrats and novelists? Or to recall the question one student had asked Faulkner during this classroom visit, how could a man who works in a chewing gum factory in Detroit communicate with an Algerian shepherd?

Whereas Wilder and Faulkner's performative talk of the town finds its expression in relatively circumscribed disputes over PTPI's foundational documents, Saul Bellow's novel *Henderson the Rain King* (1959) amplifies the question of bureaucratic literacy in a more expansive scene of international communication: the face-to-face interactions of a middle-aged Jewish millionaire, Eugene Henderson, and the leader of an African tribe, King Dahfu of the Wariri. Importantly, the novel allows us to approach the question of international communication from the perspective of literary production rather than bureaucratic production (as was the case for Faulkner) or literary reception (as was the case for Wilder). In continuing to foreground the productive failures of PTPI in analyzing the differences between bureaucratic and literary work, the history of *Henderson* is the closest that we can get to a natural experiment: a before-and-after examination of how an institutional perturbation or conflict qualitatively shaped the forms of literary representation. While Bellow was no strong champion of either PTPI or Eisenhower, he did participate in Faulkner's organizing processes from the circular letter to the "Distillate" to its editing process—a chain of bureaucratic tasks he juxtaposed not entirely favorably to his "Russian lack of organization" when he wrote from home in Tivoli, New York.[56] Institutional work offered both a respite from and a new angle from which to approach *Henderson*: the story of a millionaire pig farmer who travels to Africa to conquer his midlife existential anxieties. If the committee's meetings were indeed a kind of theatrical gallery as Wilder suggested, the performance space gave Bellow an opportunity to stage the characterological dimensions of Henderson through his expressed annoyance toward liberal consensus building. "When I was working on *Henderson the Rain King*, I imitated Henderson," Bellow explained to reporter Nina Steers in a 1964 interview that, in detailing his bad behavior, was aptly titled "Successor to Faulkner?"[57] "I went roaring at people, making scenes. It was one of my more trying periods." On the receiving end of these scenes was Faulkner, who, as Donald Hall recalled, emerged as a contemptible bureaucratic figurehead for Bellow. "Saul got really mad," Hall recounted.[58] "Faulkner suggested we should bring ordinary folks over here, give them a used car and a job, and show them how America really worked. Bellow pointed out that these ordinary folks would be put in jail or executed when they got back home." As the meeting "degenerated into a free-for-all," Bellow grew angry, shouted at Faulkner, and stormed off. What delighted Hall was not the drama per se, but what he described as the "phraseology" of the exchange: the rhetorical contrast between the laconic organizer Faulkner, grasping for some key words and slogans to slot into the

"Distillate," and the blustering Bellow, who refused to recognize the validity of the exercise. After the writers' committee dissolved, Bellow wrote to John Berryman to inform him that the experience had motivated him to scrap his first draft of *Henderson*. He had "started de nouveau."[59] The resulting novel, which was rewritten at breakneck speed in the six months after Bellow had played an intense and controversial role in PTPI's bureaucratic failure, thus registers the fraught conditions of bureaucratic work and person-to-person communication in both its forms and themes.

Here a little more historical context may help us better understand why his PTPI experience endured in Bellow's literary imagination. When Faulkner initially wrote to him in September 1956, Bellow had only just begun to articulate his liberal humanist distaste for the federal government's love affair with technomodernism. His hostility toward the State Department's sponsorship of business enterprise and science research would reach Pulitzer Prize-winning proportions with the 1975 publication of *Humboldt's Gift*, but Faulkner's PTPI questionnaire provided him with an initial opportunity to air his grievances about literature's comparatively diminished standing in the public sphere. "The attitude of our President & his government toward literature and other branches of culture cannot be concealed," he wrote on the bottom of the questionnaire's last page and in response to no question in particular.[60] "Business and war are at the top of the heap. Science in the middle. We are at the bottom. Shall we celebrate this condition before the world? No ideology. No bunk." Unlike Wilder, who was perfectly happy to lend his unconditional support to the president and his missions, Bellow's anger about—and assertion of—the erosion of literature's cultural distinction could not assume the form of an ideological statement or a questionnaire ranking. To do so would have been to "celebrate this condition" (i.e., the diminishment of literary writing by the form of the bureaucratic document) "before the world." We can see this most clearly some years later in *Herzog* (1964), in a painful, if humorous, letter that disaffected novelist Moses Herzog would draft to Eisenhower about a committee on international communication called the "Industrial Statesmen."[61] In regard to this obvious PTPI stand-in, Herzog would write, *"I wonder if the people you appointed to it were the best for the job—corporation lawyers, big executives. . . . Intelligent people without influence feel a certain self-contempt, reflecting the contempt of those who hold real political or social power, or think they do.* Can you make it all clear, in few words? It's well known he hates long, complicated documents. *A collection of loyal, helpful statements to inspire us in the struggle against the Communist enemy is not what we needed"* (176, italics in original). The meandering and pensive quality of Herzog's letter to Eisenhower makes Bellow's point about the anti-ideological quality of writing and reading literature on the level of both its theme and form. Note its self-reflexivity about Eisenhower's reading practices ("Can you make it all clear, in a few words? It's well known he hates long, complicated documents"), as well as its italicized starts, stops, and rewrites, against the comparatively "few words" and terse sentences Bellow is limited to by the questionnaire. In *Herzog*, the drama of cultural distinction between writers and "Industrial Statesmen" plays out as the drama of bureaucratic reading embedded in, and struggling against, the form of the novel. The opposite is true for PTPI, in which individual participants fluent in the forms of the novel struggled against the ideological performativity required by "a collection of loyal, helpful statements" to communicate with others.

While Bellow's sense of literary writing's expressive superiority to the communicative work of "corporation lawyers" and "big executives" in PTPI received its most explicit treatment in *Herzog*, the inverse relationship between bureaucratic ideology and literariness was an idea that he had first begun to develop in *Henderson*. "I think positions *emerge* in a work of art, and you seem to think they're imposed," he debated in a 1957 letter to Leslie Fiedler after PTPI had disbanded.[62] "Ideology is of no use to us in refurbishing the house." Indeed, when it came to anti-communist activity, liberalism at home and abroad was best served not by the dramatic performances of truthiness that encoded government ideology but by literary comedy, which struck Bellow as "the most subversive of all" genres. "*Henderson* is not Reichian confusion, but comedy," he concluded to Fiedler. "I shun doctrine. I am willing if I must to be a destroyer, but not on a doctrinaire basis." This is not the first time that we have seen the subversive work of comedy at play in this book. (Recall Ashbery's campy coauthorship of *A Nest of Ninnies* in chapter 2 and the Beats' literary branding of *The American Express* in chapter 3.) Yet *Henderson* lays claim to a different discourse of comedy—comedy not as an inside joke designed to subtend an avant-garde or countercultural coterie's adjacent relationship to institutional life, but comedy as a historical and national genre. Packing as much potential as Robert Oppenheimer's atomic bomb, to which Bellow alludes when he expresses his willingness to serve as a "destroyer," the comedy of *Henderson* is a comedy of what Fiedler called "misology": a hatred of rationalized argument and reason, and in particular, the avenues through which argument and reason become yoked to techniques of bureaucratic-national management.

To be sure, Bellow's sense of himself as a destroyer on par with Oppenheimer is a hyperbolic claim but one fitting to the hyperbolism of *Henderson*'s newfound novelistic form. *Henderson* before PTPI was quite different from

Henderson after Bellow's tussles with Faulkner and his immersion in bureau-cratic and communicative work. Before, Henderson had served as but a thinly veiled caricature of Bellow's neighbor in Tivoli, New York; a kooky pig farmer named Chandler Chapman who in real life, as in the novel, had traveled to Af-rica where he was tapped to serve as an adviser to an African village after sparking up a close friendship with its leader. But after months spent answer-ing Faulkner's letters, filling out questionnaires, and attending meetings in New York, Bellow's subsequent revision of *Henderson* increased the "formal assistance" he claimed to have given to his protagonist.[63] To his friend Mar-garet Shafer, Bellow noted that the revised Henderson had come to display "new forms of hysteria, cunning, and aggression" that Chapman had lacked; to writer Josephine Herbst, he explained that the novel's aggressively comedic tone derived from the fact that he had "got literature mixed up with lots of other matters."[64] We can see from the novel's opening, in which Henderson scrutinizes his own position in the cultural-institutional hierarchy of America, what these other matters may entail. "People might say, 'Do you see that great big fellow with the enormous nose and mustache? Well, his great-grandfather was Secretary of State; his great-uncles were ambassadors to England and France, and his father was the famous scholar Willard Henderson who wrote that book on the Albigensians, a friend of William James and Henry Adams.' Didn't they say this? You bet they did."[65] Henderson's mocking ventriloquiza-tion here of what "people might say" situates him squarely at the nexus of *Herzog*'s "Industrial Statesmen" that stretches as far back as the two great American dynasties of the Adamses and the Jameses. Henderson's incredulity stems precisely from this historical understanding of who he is: an institu-tionally overdetermined and flat character—the spitting image, and an ugly one at that, of his forefathers. The repetition of his history, both discursively in what people say about him and in his position as heir to his family for-tune, is the background against which another form of "terrible repetition" emerges: what Henderson describes as a "disturbance in my heart, a voice that spoke there and said, *I want, I want, I want*" (24, 43, italics in original). Like Bellow before him, and Herzog after him, what Henderson wants is a mode of self-differentiation that is singular, meaningful, and narrative; a sweeping edit to "the same old story" told by his predecessors' acutely nationalized legacies.

And so Henderson goes to Africa. Or rather, he tags along with a taciturn *National Geographic* photographer named Charlie, "trying to interest [him-self] in his photographic problems" until he realizes that "photography is not one of [his] interests" and sets off on his own (41). Against the photographer's closemouthedness (as we know from chapter 4, the photographs should speak for themselves), Henderson's main interest is talk and talking. Talk is an activity featured on nearly every page of *Henderson*—by my count there are fifty separate uses of the word itself—but it gains a specifically comedic centrality to the story Henderson narrates when he meets King Dahfu, who, Henderson notes, was the first African who "wanted to talk to me in my own language" (143). The interest of Henderson's relationship with Dahfu lies in how Bellow counterposes their face-to-face talk—unmediated, idealistic, an ability to get "clean away from everything"—to the terribly repetitious institution speak and existential disturbances that preoccupy Henderson (46). "Some voices once heard will never stop resounding in your head, and such a voice I recognized in his from the first words," Henderson thinks when he first hears Dahfu speak (154). Dahfu, in turn, views Henderson's visit as "a chance for conversation in English" (156). Preserving this focus on the quality of their voices, the near incessant dialogue throughout the novel's long middle section gives Bellow a pretext for voicing anti-bureaucratic misology through Dahfu in a "soft, personal tone peculiar to him," and thus incapable of repetition (260). At one of the climactic moments in their communication, Dahfu lectures Henderson on the relationship between imaginative production and the production of personal meaning, beginning by disavowing what he calls "bookkeeping"—the bureaucratic management of the decisions one makes—in favor of the irreducible particularity of the kind of human interaction he and Henderson have pursued (271). "So many factors are mediating," Dahfu explains solemnly. "Fomenting. Promulgating. Everyone is different. A billion small things unperceived by the object of their intelligence. True, pure intelligence does the best it can, but who can judge. Negative and positive elements strive." His quasi-mystical speech concludes with an exhortation to embrace the creative imagination of man as the antidote to the bureaucrat's bookkeeping. "Imagination is a force of nature," Dahfu proclaims. "Is this not enough to make a person full of ecstasy? Imagination, imagination, imagination. It converts to actual. It sustains, it alters, it redeems!" Faulkner's hypothetical scenario of the man from Detroit and the Algerian shepherd talking face-to-face without any "artificial means of communication" finds its purest, most transcendental incarnation in Henderson and Dahfu's talk—so pure, in fact, that it should give us pause.

While readers from Toni Morrison onward have characterized Bellow's Africa—and the novel's earnest projection of the king's voice—as a colonial fantasy, the novel's attunement to its own earnestness nevertheless makes it, in part, a subversive comedy.[66] The talk in *Henderson* is always exaggerated, overdone in its length, its affective intensity, its verbal profundity, and the influence it exerts on its listener; Henderson admits that the king "could convince me of almost anything" (297), including such ludicrously dangerous feats as learning how to "imitate or dramatize the behavior of lions" (263) by living in close proximity to them. Yet despite its comedic dimensions, Henderson and Dahfu's talk is revolutionary to Henderson's mind, insofar as it crowds out all other forms of ideologically charged and institutionally sanctioned communication. When Dahfu dies trying to capture a lion for Henderson to imitate, Henderson leaves the Wariri's village and takes the lion's cub home with him to the United States. Passing through Khartoum, he must stop at the US consulate, where, stripped of his money, clothing, and otherwise American identifiers, he encounters once again the forms of bureaucratic speak he had mimicked so derisively at the beginning of the novel. "They tried to pump me about my trip, and asked how I had lost all my stuff," he writes of the consulate's staff (331). " 'It's none of your lousy business,' I said. 'My passport is okay, isn't it? And I've got dough. My great-grandfather was head of your crummy outfit, and he was no cold-storage, Ivy League, button-down, broken-hipped civilian like you. All you fellows are just the same. You think U.S. citizens are dummies and morons. Listen, all I want for you is to expedite—Yes, I saw a few things into the interior. Yes, I did. I have had a look into some of the fundamentals, but don't expect me to tickle your idle curiosity. I wouldn't talk even to the ambassador, if he asked me.' " Henderson's indignation at the fact that all the members of the foreign service "are just the same" (i.e., Ivy league WASPs) and his refusal to "talk even to the ambassador" finds its stylistic corollary in his censorship of the consulate's side of a bureaucratic routinized conversation. We may venture a guess at their side of the story from the interrupted moments in Henderson's blustering speech ("—Yes, I saw a few things in the interior. Yes, I did. I have had a look into some of the fundamentals"), but Henderson's anticommunicative stubbornness functions as the novelist's riposte to the bureaucrat's blank: to represent the consulate's dialogue would be to make institutionalized speech available for literary reading, reception, and repetition. The one-sided form of the conversation is the aesthetic apotheosis of both *Henderson*'s misology and Bellow's belief, as expressed to Faulkner, that writers should "write our books and leave ideology to the advertising people"—a stark contrast to the bureaucrats who believe that "U.S. citizens are dummies and morons" and thus ought not to talk except through official channels.

READING BETWEEN INSTITUTIONS

If we look beyond the immediate institutional context of PTPI and even the Eisenhower presidency, there exists a great deal of irony in the commonly accepted belief that *Henderson* inspired John F. Kennedy to establish the

Peace Corps in 1960: a volunteer program whose aim was to bring "technical advice and assistance to the underprivileged and backward Middle East."[67] According to the Washington, DC, rumor mill, the president was encouraged by reviews he had read of *Henderson* in liberal and anti-communist magazines, like Harvey Swados's write-up in the *New Leader* or Frances Kelly's in the *Monthly Review*, where she explained to readers that "Mr. Saul Bellow invented a Peace Corps in *Henderson the Rain King*, which carried dynamics caps to Africa and brought back spiritual enlightenment."[68] (Of course, the review was published after Kennedy was killed, so he couldn't have been encouraged by it.) *Henderson* was one of the texts featured in the "book lockers" that the Peace Corps book committee designed and distributed to each of its volunteers, alongside Eugene Burdick and William Lederer's *The Ugly American* (1951), Malcolm Lowry's *Under the Volcano* (1947), and Graham Greene's *The Heart of the Matter* (1948). As Peace Corps director Robert Shriver explained to the US Senate's Committee on Appropriations in 1963, "In assignments where there are few other means of intellectual simulation, the book lockers are the primary source of reading material for most volunteers. Volunteers also use the books for teaching, for informal English classes, and for lending to friends and associates in their communities."[69] *Henderson*, however, seemed like an unintuitive choice to many volunteers, who "had been warned about adopting a Noble Savage stereotype of 'host country nationals,' or of trying to 'go native,'" according to Peace Corps literary educator Dennis Carlson.[70] "Yet here was a book that did just that," Carlson puzzled over its selection for the book locker: "Perhaps, I thought, the novel was included in our library precisely because it was supposed to serve as an example of 'going native.'" Regardless of the motivation for selecting the book, Carlson noted how, after reading Bellow's novel, both he and his students "identified with Henderson," insofar as he (and they) "wanted out of the madness of America and the deepening despair that gripped my country and my life." While the Peace Corps educators' intentions were anti-ideological in one sense—they wanted to guard against damning stereotypes of colonial relations—the novel's reception context chafed against the very critique of institutionalizing literary communication that Bellow had voiced through Henderson and Dahfu's talk. Thus while the book locker was eliminated in 1969, *Henderson*'s brief history as an identificatory teaching text reveals how Bellow, like Foote, was roped into an institutional process of which he was critical: an act of institutional training on the part of the Peace Corps book committee that encouraged readerly identification, all the while occluding the novel's critical edge.

Although it pushes this chapter's analysis outside the orbit of PTPI, the link between *Henderson* and the Peace Corps exemplifies just how challenging it is to keep all scales of sociohistorical analysis constant even when an institution's failure is the premise from which we begin. If we recall my argument in the first chapter about the unappreciated importance of human actors, here we can see another angle from which to broaden our sense of scale while keeping constant the limited times and spaces of institutional existence: the interconnections between institutions which can be traversed by following the actions of paraliterary readers. The connectivity forged by reading, writing, and circulating literary fiction within nascent institutions offers a valuable perspective on recuperation, insofar as it lets us excavate the work of organizations that have been lost to scholarly modes of inquiry until now. From a theoretical point of view, the work of historical recuperation also allows us to rectify (somewhat belatedly) Robert Penn Warren's concern that bureaucratically sanctified texts and representative actors will white-wash their pluralist origins and contentious processes of formation, thereby rendering it impossible for anyone to understand how, despite divergences in individual opinions, writers continued to play a massively important role in shaping the forms and genres of international communication. Yet the example of PTPI, while rich and complicated and intellectually productive in its own right, does not go far enough. Consider, for instance, that Faulkner's list of invited writers already encoded a set of exclusionary strategies for who was authorized to weigh in on problems of liberal democratic representation: no black writers and no political radicals made the final cut. To see a distinctly radical counternarrative of institutional constitution through discourse, we must now turn to another productive case of failure: Richard Wright, James Baldwin, John A. Williams, and other Afro-modernist writers and artists who banded together, only to fall apart, in opposition to Faulkner and Eisenhower's institution-building project.

CHAPTER SIX

Reading like a Revolutionary

There are some things that require no speech whatsoever.

JOHN A. WILLIAMS (1966)[1]

In a world where no one need be delusional to find evidence of systemic oppression, to theorize out of anything *but* a paranoid critical stance has come to seem naïve, pious, or complaisant.

EVE SEDGWICK, "Paranoid Reading and Reparative Reading" (1997)[2]

WHITE INSTITUTIONS OF POLITICS

In the penultimate chapter of John A. Williams's 1967 novel *The Man Who Cried I Am,* the protagonist, a black American journalist named Max Reddick, unearths a government conspiracy to exterminate the black population of the United States. The conspiracy is referred to simply and quaintly as "KING ALFRED," after King Alfred the Great, the first king of the Anglo-Saxon line.[3] Rifling through a suitcase filled with papers that his friend and fellow writer Harry Ames has left behind after his mysterious death in Parisian exile, Max reads through a carefully curated collection of dossiers that detail the bureaucratic organization and logistical execution of the King Alfred plan: memos, lists, committee reports, maps, operation plans, time-tables, and personnel files, created by the NSA, CIA, FBI, and the Departments of Justice, Defense, and the Interior, all acting at the behest of a sinister institution of liberal internationalism called the Alliance Blanc. Williams presents the dossiers as photostat replicas of documents that exist outside the fictional world of the novel, and they bear both the rudimentary typography of bureaucratic composition and the flatness of tone unique to committee writing: the impersonal plurality, yet implied authority, of the shadowy "We" who has authored the documents; the reliance on hierarchical commands; the dispassionate rhetoric of legal proceduralism. Indeed, the documents bear a strong similarity to Faulkner's People-to-People Initiative (PTPI) writings from the previous chapter—except for the fact that, in *The Man,* the multi-institutional apparatus that has produced these documents

has a horrifying task at hand: the elimination of an entire race of human beings. Why? In order for the United States, as a newly inaugurated kingdom
of Anglo-Saxons and leading member of the Alliance Blanc, to wage a more
homogeneous Cold War against the Soviet Union.

As he reads through the King Alfred Plan (and as we read over his shoul-
der), Max's lifelong suspicion—that the institutionalized racism of the US
government is designed to "keep black men niggers"—finds a distinct "form
and face and projection" in the dossiers (386). "Before," Williams's narrator explains, "all was nebulous; there were few names and places and the
form was so all-pervading that it seemed formless. But now the truth had
literally been placed in Max's lap." The truth, the narrator suggests, is instantiated through and verified by the distinctly bureaucratic aesthetic of the dossiers. The dossiers impose "form" onto a once "formless" feeling, rendering
systemic oppression readable with the syntactical precision needed to cor-
roborate and to actualize Max's paranoid imagination. Once he reads the
documents and attempts to reread them over the telephone to Minister Q—a
Malcolm X-style leader of the new nationalism movement in Harlem—Max
is gunned down by two struggling black American writers working as agents
of the Alliance Blanc. A little bit of knowledge is quite literally a dangerous
thing—even, and especially, if that knowledge only serves to confirm what
one already knew all along.

Crucial for my purposes is that the textual "form and face and projection"
that the paranoid reader's truth assumes in *The Man* convincingly mimics for
its nonparanoid readers the paraliterary genres produced and circulated by
real institutions of liberal internationalism like PTPI, institutions to which
Afro-modernist writers like Williams were routinely denied access. No one
was more aware of the exclusionary politics of liberalism and its texts than
Williams, except for maybe his close friend and fellow novelist Richard
Wright. Wright, who served as the inspiration for Harry Ames's character in
The Man, was, like Ames, a self-proclaimed exile in Paris. From 1947 until
his death in 1960, he devoted himself to organizing black Americans and
French nationals into institutions of cultural diplomacy explicitly opposed
to the racially and politically homogeneous bureaucracies that the US government had established. "The American government finds Negros abroad
'counter-propaganda' in face of the ideals of democracy which it preaches,"
Wright announced at the initial meeting of the Franco-American Fellowship (FAF), a short-lived PTPI-style counter-institution that he founded in
1949 and that boasted Jean-Paul Sartre, Simone de Beauvoir, Louis Fischer,
William Rutherford, Gordon Parks, and James Baldwin as members.[4] As

had been involved with black men, Enzkwu's photostats disclosed a clear and unrelenting danger. Recorded in cold black type were lists of statesmen and diplomats, the records of their deeds, what they planned to do, when, where, why and to whom. The list of people dead, Max knew, and therefore murdered, if their names appeared in Enzkwu's papers, included the residents of four continents. African airfields equipped for the handling of jets and props, along with radio and power stations, the number of men in the army of each country, plus a military critique of those armies, were set down here.

Now Max's hand held another numbered packet, but above the number were the words: THE UNITED STATES OF AMERICA — KING ALFRED. Slowly, he pulled out the sheaf of photostats. So, this is King Alfred, Alfred the Great. He mused, Why is it called King Alfred? Then he saw the answer footnoted at the bottom of the first page.

KING ALFRED*

In the event of widespread and continuing and coordinated racial disturbances in the United States, KING ALFRED, at the discretion of the President, is to be put into action immediately.

PARTICIPATING FEDERAL AGENCIES

National Security Council	Department of Justice
Central Intelligence Agency	Department of Defense
Federal Bureau of Investigation	Department of Interior

PARTICIPATING STATE AGENCIES
(Under Federal Jurisdiction)

National Guard Units	State Police

PARTICIPATING LOCAL AGENCIES
(Under Federal Jurisdiction)

City Police	County Police

* 849-899 (?) King of England; directed translation from the Latin of the *Anglo-Saxon Chronicle.*

371

FIGURE 6.1 Pages from "The King Alfred Plan," from John A. Williams's *The Man Who Cried I Am.* Copyright © 1967 John A. Williams. Published in 2004 by The Overlook Press, www .overlookpress.com. All rights reserved.

Memo: National Security Council

Even before 1954, when the Supreme Court of the United States of America declared unconstitutional separate educational and recreational facilities, racial unrest and discord had become very nearly a part of the American way of life. But that way of life was repugnant to most Americans. Since 1954, however, that unrest and discord have broken out into widespread violence which increasingly have placed the peace and stability of the nation in dire jeopardy. This violence has resulted in loss of life, limb and property, and has cost the taxpayers of this nation billions of dollars. And the end is not yet in sight. This same violence has raised the tremendously grave question as to whether the races can ever live in peace with each other. Each passing month has brought new intelligence that, despite new laws passed to alleviate the condition of the Minority, the Minority still is not satisfied. Demonstrations and rioting have become a part of the familiar scene. Troops have been called out in city after city across the land, and our image as a world leader severely damaged. Our enemies press closer, seeking the advantage, possibly at a time during one of these outbreaks of violence. The Minority has adopted an almost military posture to gain its objectives, which are not clear to most Americans. It is expected, therefore, that, when those objectives are denied the Minority, racial war must be considered inevitable. When that Emergency comes, we must expect the total involvement of all 22 million members of the Minority, men, women and children, for once this project is launched, its goal is to terminate, once and for all, the Minority threat to the whole of the American society, and, indeed, the Free World.

Chairman, National Security Council

Preliminary Memo: Department of Interior
Under KING ALFRED, the nation has been divided into 10 Regions (See accompanying map).
In case of Emergency, Minority members will be evacuated from the cities by federalized national guard units, local and state police and, if necessary, by units of the Regular Armed Forces, using public and military transportation, and detained in nearby military installations until a further course of action has been decided.

372

FIGURE 6.1 (continued)

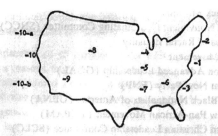

1 — Capital region
2 — Northeast region
3 — Southeast region
4 — Great Lakes Region
5 — South central region
6 — Deep South region
7 — Deep South region II
8 — Great Plains, Rocky Mountain region
9 — Southwest region
10 — a, b — West Coast region

No attempt will be made to seal off the Canadian and Mexican borders.

Secretary, Department of Interior

Combined Memo: Department of Justice
Federal Bureau of Investigation
Central Intelligence Agency

There are 12 major Minority organizations and all are familiar to the 22 million. Dossiers have been compiled on the leaders of the organizations, and can be studied in Washington. The material contained in many of the dossiers, and our threat to reveal that material, has considerably held in check the activities of some of the leaders. Leaders who do not have such usable material in their dossiers have been approached to take Government posts, mostly as ambassadors and primarily in African countries. The promise of these positions also has materially contributed to a temporary slow-down of Minority activities. However, we do not expect these slow-downs to be of long duration, because there are always new and dissident elements joining these organizations, with the potential power to replace the old leaders. All organizations and their leaders are under constant, 24-hour surveillance. The organizations are:

373

FIGURE 6.1 (continued)

1 — The Black Muslims
2 — Student Nonviolent Coordinating Committee (SNCC)
3 — Congress of Racial Equality
4 — Uhuru Movement
5 — Group on Advanced Leadership (GOAL)
6 — Freedom Now Party (FNP)
7 — United Black Nationalists of America (UBNA)
8 — The New Pan-African Movement (TNPAM)
9 — Southern Christian Leadership Conference (SCLC)
10 — The National Urban League (NUL)
11 — The National Association for the Advancement of Colored People (NAACP)
12 — Committee on Racial and Religious Progress (CORARP)

NOTE: At the appropriate time, to be designated by the President, the leaders of some of these organizations are to be detained ONLY WHEN IT IS CLEAR THAT THEY CANNOT PREVENT THE EMERGENCY, working with local public officials during the first critical hours. All other leaders are to be detained at once. Compiled lists of Minority leaders have been readied at the National Data Computer Center. It is necessary to use the Minority leaders designated by the President in much the same manner in which we use Minority members who are agents with CENTRAL and FEDERAL, and we cannot, until there is no alternative, reveal KING ALFRED in all its aspects. Minority members of Congress will be unseated at once. This move is not without precedent in American history.

Attorney General

Preliminary Memo. Department of Defense
This memo is being submitted in lieu of a full report from the Joint Chiefs of Staff. That report is now in preparation. There will be many cities where the Minority will be able to put into the street a superior number of people with a desperate and dangerous will. He will be a formidable enemy, for he is bound to the Continent by heritage and knows that political asylum will not be available to him in other countries. The greatest concentration of the Minority is in the Deep South, the Eastern seaboard, the Great Lakes region and the West Coast.

374

FIGURE 6.1 (continued)

While the national population exceeds that of the Minority by more than ten times, we must realistically take into account the following:

1 — An estimated 40-50 percent of the white population will not, for various reasons, engage the Minority during an Emergency.
2 — American Armed Forces are spread around the world. A breakout of war abroad means fewer troops at home to handle the Emergency.
3 — Local law enforcement officials must contain the Emergency until help arrives, though it may mean fighting a superior force. New York City, for example, has a 25,000-man police force, but there are about one million Minority members in the city.

We are confident that the Minority could hold any city it took for only a few hours. The lack of weapons, facilities, logistics — all put the Minority at a final disadvantage.

Since the Korean War, this Department has shifted Minority members of the Armed Forces to areas where combat is most likely to occur, with the aim of eliminating, through combat, as many combat-trained Minority servicemen as possible. Today the ratio of Minority member combat deaths in Vietnam, where they are serving as "advisers," is twice as high as the Minority population ratio to the rest of America.

Below is the timetable for KING ALFRED as tentatively suggested by the JCS who recommend that the operation be made over a period of eight hours:

1. Local police and Minority leaders in action to head off the Emergency.
2. Countdown to eight hours begins at the moment the President determines the Emergency to be:

    A. National
    B. Coordinated
    C. Of Long Duration   8th Hour

3. County police join local police.   7th
4. State police join county and local forces.   6th
5. Federal marshals join state, county and local forces.   5th
6. National Guards federalized, held in readiness.   4th
7. Regular Armed Forces alerted, take up positions;

FIGURE 6.1 (continued)

Minority troops divided and detained, along with all
white sympathizers, under guard.   3rd
8. All Minority leaders, national and local, detained.   2nd
9. President addresses Minority on radio-television,
gives it one hour to end the Emergency.   1st
10. All units under regional commands into the Emergency. o

'O' Committee Report:
Survey shows that, during a six-year period, Production created 9,000,-
000 objects, or 1,500,000 each year. Production could not dispose of
the containers, which proved a bottleneck. However, that was almost
20 years ago. We suggest that vaporization techniques be employed to
overcome the Production problems inherent in KING ALFRED.

Secretary of Defense

Max smoked and read, read and smoked until his mouth began
to taste like wool and when he finally pushed King Alfred from
him, he felt exhausted, as if he had been running beneath a gigantic, unblinking eye that had watched his every move and determined just when movement should stop.

Yeah. Jaja had done his work well. He could have embarrassed
and startled a lot of people, blacks and whites, but you have to
weed a garden for the flowers to grow. Those dossiers, he knew
pretty much what was in them. Well, he had known it; there are
always dues to pay. A smoldering anger coursed through Max's
stomach. Yes, those leaders clearly had left themselves vulnerable,
vulnerable for the hunters who, for a generation and more, sought
Communists with such vehemence that they skillfully obscured the
growth and power of fascism. How black skins stirred fascists! Perhaps because it was the most identifiable kind of skin; you didn't
have to wait until you got up close to see whether a nose was
hooked or not; a black skin you could see for a block away. And
in the face of the revelations in Jaja's papers, Harry and Jaja both,
made giddy by the presence of that massive, killing evil, had dared
to toy with it; had dared to set their pitiable little egos down before

376

FIGURE 6.1 (continued)

anecdotal evidence, Wright pointed to the fact that he had "directed many persons to government agencies in the past few years to apply for work" in Europe, and that while "many of the whites had been hired," "none of the Negroes" had found employment. For Wright, the obvious solution to institutionalized racism was the formation of a separate, but similarly structured, civic institution for black Americans, although he was quick to disavow FAF as fundamentally political in nature. "I'm not selling any political medicine," he proclaimed flatly to Allan Temko, in a 1951 interview with the *San Francisco Chronicle*. Temko's sarcastic response—that Wright appeared to be "selling plenty of nonpolitical medicine"—registered the impossibility of excising the problems of national representation from the desire for international cultural solidarity.

Indeed, few issues were more contentious for black American "counter-propagandists" than the question of how to respond to liberalism's representational dramas and historic injustices. Williams put the matter more bluntly than Wright in an essay he wrote for *Nugget* nearly a decade later, after Wright had died and precious little had changed in the way of racial discrimination at home or abroad. "Now, of all white institutions I detest politics the most," he declared.[5] Unlike Wright, Williams's hatred for political institutions derived not from the overt and symbolic racism of their propagandist representations, but from the illiberal procedures that subtended their day-to-day operations: their debates, deliberations, votes, and corresponding textual productions that took place without any black American representatives at hand. "There are too many men who, with too little equipment, have come to this place of power simply because millions of people—black people—have had no voice in the matter," Williams inveighed. Given that all institutions, whether political or nonpolitical in nature, established themselves through some procedures of exclusion—some fundamental division between belonging and not belonging—this inherently limited approached to sociality did not strike Williams as the proper way to give black people "a voice" in the public sphere. In *The Most Native of Sons* (1970), a short biography of Wright that Williams wrote after his friend's death, Williams was predictably dismissive about Wright's FAF work, which he portrayed as a form of affective and immaterial labor: an organization founded to "help ease the distress of the black Americans who came to Paris and encountered discrimination" but not to protest or subvert the material operations of racial injustice at home and in the world at large.[6]

Taken together, Wright's enthusiasm for political organizing and Williams's antipathy toward it raise the two key questions that frame this book's final chapter. What alternatives were there to the "white institutions" of politics through which black American writers could communicate? And how did racialized practices of reading shape these communicative acts? Wright's formation of a minoritarian institution like FAF offered one answer to the problem of exclusion, but, as we will see, FAF was not immune to the representational problems that besieged the dominant political institutions after which it was modeled. Yet another approach was for black American writers to try to assimilate themselves to white political institutions by appealing to a utopian vision of liberal pluralism. Such appeals, however, served only to reinforce the liberal establishment's always already exclusionary dynamic, thereby amplifying the sense of political futility that Williams expressed in *Nugget*. As one can see from Williams's essay, liberal politics was not just a fruitless enterprise; it was a distinctly self-alienating one, forcing him "outside myself, watching myself move, listening to myself speak, sensing myself think." If the self-reflexive publicness of political communication had provided Faulkner, Wilder, and Bellow with a tempting opportunity to try to square bureaucratic labor with their literary works, for Williams, the only thing politics offered was "a difficult and painful lesson to learn" about how white people in positions of institutional authority judged his speech, movement, and thought, and how they found him lacking as a normative political subject.

In contrast to both minoritarian politics and political assimilation, this chapter argues that paranoid literary aesthetics and discourses of paranoid reading, as modeled by *The Man* and its reading publics, emerged as a surprising entry point to international social activism for black American writers and readers. The turn to paranoia is surprising because in literary critical accounts of the period, paranoid aesthetics are persistently treated as immune to readers' "post paranoid utopian projects," to quote Patrick O'Donnell.[7] All the more unexpected, then, to try to reconcile a literary discourse of paranoia with a concrete history of social organizing, which would seem to resist paranoia's fuzzy systematicity at every turn. And yet, as we will see in the work of Wright, Williams, James Baldwin, Gil Scott Heron, and thousands of black American readers in the 1960s and 1970s, it was precisely the diffuseness of paranoid reading that enabled its emergence as a potentially revolutionary strategy for shaping how subjects denied access to political institutions could transform their linguistic performances into the discursive equipment of social protest. And while some readers, like the editorial board of the historically black American newspaper, the *Bay Street Banner*, conceived of paranoid reading as a "misleading," "inflammatory," and "unsoulful" tactic for linking literacy to activism, a far greater number embraced paranoid reading as the only method for reading like a revolutionary social actor.[8]

MAKING PARANOIA REAL

Across the spectrum of reading practices that this book has taken as its examples of bad reading, paranoid reading stands out for its affiliation with a formerly valorized (i.e., "good") but now "obsessive-fatalistic style of interpretation" that literary critics have attempted to disavow in recent years.[9] Once the methodological darling of Foucauldian historicism, queer theory, and Marxist critique, paranoid reading's governing assumption—that modern systems like the state, late capitalism, and global technology exert total power and control over their subjects—has "cast a pathological shadow over styles of reading," according to Rita Felski. For Felski and other literary theorists who seek to dislodge paranoia from its position of epistemological dominance, the pathological nature of paranoid literacy derives from its inability to do anything but "discern" the "hidden truths" encoded in literary form. The relentless interpretive scrutiny of what lies beneath aesthetic forms not only fails to motivate meaningful political change but also relegates the paranoid reader to the ethical position of a "privileged," but lonesome, observer of social systems. By self-reflexively distancing herself from the "dubious or disingenuous motives" of everyone who surrounds her, the paranoid reader emerges as an asocial, obsessive, and even "monomaniacal" subject. Some half century after paranoia's colonization of Cold War politics and the literature classroom, the paranoid reader is no longer an unequivocally good reader. She is a self-aggrandizing killjoy, a downer, a pariah, and worst of all, a total bore.

But what if, under certain local and contingent conditions of reading, paranoia could do more than what Felski and others ascribe to it? What if instead of dismissing paranoid reading as universally alienating, diagnostic, and impotent, we pursued a different idea of paranoid reading, one that emphasized its performative ability to convert suspicious aesthetic discernment into social action? To do so might necessitate stepping away from those we take to be paranoid reading's best and most privileged practitioners—literary critics—to ask how readers more aggressively interpellated by the coercive mechanisms of the state imagined that paranoid reading could exceed individual feelings of suspicion, skepticism, and superiority to a shared material reality. By this account, paranoid reading and paranoid aesthetics could offer us a literary discourse allied with solidarity among the state's most marginalized subjects rather than the singularity that encloses its most culturally elite.

To split the difference between these two camps of readers, we might turn to John Williams's firsthand experience with the American Academy in Rome, which offers us an especially self-conscious example of how paranoid reading might actualize the material realities of racial oppression. First awarded the Prix de Rome in 1962, a fellowship which tasked him with traveling to Italy to represent American writers, Williams was subsequently stripped of the award and his responsibilities as a literary ambassador after an interview with Richard A. Kimball, the academy's director and former deputy director of the War Production Board (WPB) during World War II. Williams recounted the interview in his 1962 essay "We Regret to Inform You That . . . ," the essay's title an early example of how Williams would mimic the textual genres of the authority—in this case, the rejection letter—to expose racial injustice. According to Williams, the academy's reasons for rescinding the award were either political (he had once organized a Socialist rally for the National Committee for a Sane Nuclear Policy), racial (he was about to marry a white woman, Lorraine Isaac), or some combination of the two. Although he had no evidence to support any one of these claims, the academy's refusal to supply an explanation served, for Williams, as its own act of verification. "The vast silence—the awful, condoning silence which has surrounded this affair fits a groove well worn," he wrote after the *New York Times* nixed an investigative piece on the Prix de Rome scandal. Not a single member of the academy's jury—not John Hersey, not Dudley Fitts, not Louise Bogan, not Phyllis McGinley, not S. J. Perelman, not Robert Coates, not John Cheever—came forward to issue a statement.[10] Stonewalled by the academy, Williams reasoned, "The rejection confirms suspicions not ever really dead, confirms an inherent distrust and makes my 'paranoia' real and therefore not paranoia at all. That is the sad thing, for I always work to lose it. It is costly and sometimes crippling to have about. But I would be an ass, wouldn't I, to toss my armor into the moat while the enemy continues his charge?" The converging metaphors of economic disenfranchisement (paranoia as "costly"), bodily harm ("sometimes crippling"), and military denuding ("toss my armor") suggest that the transposition of paranoia from a feeling of "inherent distrust" into an externalized structure—something that hurts, that damages, that kills—is mediated by bureaucratic discourse. Paradoxically, it is the conspicuous lack of commentary in the "awful, condoning silence" of the newspapers, the committee, and Kimball, the institution's representative mouthpiece, that produces Williams's pronouncement of paranoia's reality factor.

For Williams, the absence of official institutional commentary called for a specifically literary discursive response to counter the academy's preemptive silencing of him as a literary communicator and a representative American. Considering Williams's and his protagonist Max's shared logic of how paranoia becomes "real," we should not be surprised that the Prix de Rome incident would make its way into an early chapter of *The Man*. Harry, the world-renowned social protest novelist, finds himself stripped of a fellowship to the American Lyceum in Athens. The fellowship is subsequently awarded to a white poet in an elaborate presentation ceremony that Harry refuses to attend. Presiding over the ceremony is none other than Burke McGalpin, "the Master of Southern Literature" (139), who the government has "dredged out of the Okefenokee Swamp and urged to set his bourbon aside" to official Harry's exclusion from the white institutions of politics. ("Burke McGalpin. William Faulkner? Probably O.K.," noted the legal team that Williams's publisher Little, Brown and Company had hired to vet *The Man* for potential libel claims.)[11] To Harry, the message conveyed by the presence of this Faulknerian spokesperson, a Southern apologist for slavery plunked deep into the federalized territory of fellowships, prizes, and cultural diplomacy, is all too clear: "It was almost as if the Northern Literary Masters were saying to him: 'This is how we handle our niggers'" (140).

If Faulkner's PTPI grandstanding in the 1950s modeled the individual affordances of liberalism, Williams's agonized disgust with Faulkner and the "Northern literary masters" in the 1960s reveals the growing distrust in liberalism's always already corrupt political processes. But it also makes visible an entirely new style of literary discourse about institutions. In the previous chapter, writerly discomfort with bureaucratic projects of literary socialization materialized in relatively self-contained acts of blustering or drunken proclamations of truth telling, but large-scale social protests against such institutions required a more forceful expressive form—what Williams, in an interview with his friend Chester Himes, called "a style of [one's] own."[12] This style was a radically experimental mash-up of literary realism (Williams reproduced the exact text and monetary terms of his fellowship offer letter in *The Man*) and the paranoid aesthetics of the King Alfred Plan. Although the novel's formal hybridity has long puzzled its critics, the problem clarifies once we recognize that the realism of the Lyceum episode is not separable from the paranoia that attends to Max's reading of the King Alfred documents at the end of the novel, even if the two do seem to occupy very different formal domains. Whatever we may perceive as their obvious representational differences, for Williams, the two exist on a spectrum of systemic oppression and paranoid suspicion whose effects gradually amplify over the course of *The Man*: from the individually excluded character of Harry Ames to the elimination of the entire black population; from a single quasi-governmental institution to every major branch of the US federal bureaucracy and its international allies. The scaled-up connection between realism and paranoia seems quite clear to Max, even though the former relies on a lack of evidence presented through the replication of a real text (the letter), while the latter relies on a superabundance of evidence presented through a fictive literary text (the King Alfred Plan).

More conceptually interesting, then, is how all three literary episodes—Max's diegetic experience of reading the King Alfred Plan, the formal shift of the novel *The Man* from literary realism to paranoid aesthetics, and Williams's biographical struggle against white institutions—point to the strange slippage by which, to quote Williams, one's "paranoia" becomes "real" and "therefore not paranoia at all." Whether in the form of an actual bureaucratic document or as a fictionalized set of dossiers, the possibility that one's paranoia may actually become real, and thus become a form of truth telling, raises the question not only of paranoia's aesthetics or its reading practices but also its social efficacy. Among the first readers of *The Man* to draw the connection between paranoid aesthetics, truth telling, and social action was Chester Himes. "*The Man Who Cried I Am* is *the* book, and it can never be cast aside," Himes prophesied in a letter he wrote to Williams shortly after the novel's publication. "Each year it will take on greater stature, because it is the story of our time, as much, if not more, than the space program, the nuclear bomb, the missiles. Because it is so devastatingly true. And in time, all people will realize this truth."[13] For Himes, the crucial political question about the book's reception was whether paranoia's newly anointed epistemological status as "truth" could elevate the problem of institutionalized racism to the same level of social consciousness as "the space program, the nuclear bomb, the missiles." Paranoia, by Himes's account, did not lead to "analysis paralysis": the reflexive uncertainty we witness in literary paranoiacs like *The Crying of Lot 49*'s Oedipa Maas or *The Names*'s James Axton, who, as Emily Apter has argued, keep coming back to the idea that "everything is connected" but cannot verify their suspicions.[14] Rather, paranoia offered a way of knowing systemic injustice and circulating knowledge of it through more efficacious forms of communication than literary realism or social protest fiction's engagement with race-based politics—more powerful, as we will see, than the politics of counter-institutional formation that Williams's friend and mentor, Richard Wright, had embraced nearly a decade earlier.

It may seem difficult to square Williams's and Himes's hypertrophic notion of paranoia-as-truth with the model of paranoid reading with which literary critics are most familiar and which frequently serves as their normative horizon of good reading: paranoia as a suspicious and demystifying critical position, but one that is not ultimately capable of—or interested in—making truth claims.[15] Yet we can see a stronger and more productive adjacency between Williams's insistence on paranoia-as-truth and a theorist of critical reading like Eve Sedgwick, for whom the default paranoid position of literary criticism relies on an unshakeable faith in the goodness of exposure: the assumption that "the one thing lacking for global revolution, explosion of gender roles, or whatever" is that the painful effects of oppression are "sufficiently exacerbated to make the pain conscious" and "intolerable."[16] One of the more flagrantly misread theorists of reading, Sedgwick is less interested in the content of the knowledge that paranoia produces—for her, as for Williams, paranoia's exposure only confirms what we already know—than she is what that knowledge does: how that knowledge's performativity allows people to "move among its causes and effects." In this sense, she helps us reframe Williams's elision of paranoia and truth telling as a problem not primarily of knowing but of doing—of taking action. For Sedgwick, the crucial question is: what can a person, or a group of people, do with the truth once they come to possess it in some incontrovertible form? Sometimes the answer is nothing, particularly for the kinds of readers to whom Sedgwick addresses her essay: literary scholars. But for readers who are not scholars and who are not interested in producing scholarly discourse, paranoid performativity may have something more to offer than mere impotence.

Williams's model of paranoid reading as a form of doing, rather than a fact of exposure, thus opens onto a more capacious institutional history of literacy socialization than the relatively circumscribed debate over paranoid reading may initially suggest. At its broadest point, it invites us to tease apart the alliance between literary realism's specific "names and places" (in contrast to paranoia's projected social imaginary) and the social protest championed by black internationalists like Wright. While the literary critical tendency remains to align literary realism with social protest, this alignment has proven both historically inaccurate and intellectually staid. As Kenneth Warren has pointed out time and again, the unfulfilled promise of African American literary realism as an inspiration for radical politics stems from realism's inability to transcend existing socio-institutional discourses, whereby "all doors leading beyond the influence of social institutions are to be closed."[17] No doubt this is a problem for literary fiction from the nineteenth century onward. (Think, for instance, of *Uncle Tom's Cabin*, whose representation of the civilizing effects of slavery effectively undercut the antislavery passions galvanized by its sentimentalism.) Yet the tenuous connection between realism and social protest becomes especially charged at the precise historical moment when American literature and internationalism converge to transform the issue of black politics into a supranational concern.

This is a moment bookended by the later life and death of Richard Wright, or Harry Ames, who similarly attempted to reconcile paranoid aesthetics with realism, but through a different series of institutional texts than Williams. Wright's FAF efforts against the white institutions of politics represented by William Faulkner, or Burke McGalpin, may have ended up intimately aligned with the exclusionary operations of liberal institutions, but they began as an attempt to transform a literary illusion into a series of actionable antiracist policies. Various representations of the infighting at FAF offer us a methodologically productive example of failure that illuminates the limitations of bureaucratic literacy from a very different angle than the failure of the PTPI writer's committee. In the next section, we will see the specter of the paranoid bureaucrat not as a threat to the charismatic and individual truth teller but as a hindrance to the solidarity of black social activism.

HALF TRUTHS, PARANOID DELUSIONS

"All other racial and national and minority groups in France have their organizations," announces a black intellectual named Ned Harrison to a roomful of black American expatriates in Paris about midway through Richard Wright's unpublished novel *Island of Hallucination* (1957).[18] Ned continues his pitch: "The French government permits it. Only we American blacks are unorganized. The white Americans have their organizations but they exclude us. . . . Let's build a little American island here and keep a sense of ourselves alive." The "island" to which Ned refers is not, however, synonymous with the *Island* in the novel's title. If the former represents an "organization" with clearly delineated "racial and national and minority" criteria for inclusion and exclusion, the latter stands in for a dream vision of black anticolonial transnationalism: the island in the Seine on which, according to William Maxwell, the novel's "progressive de-Americanization" proceeds through a hallucinatory mingling of black Americans—GIs, spies, Marxist intellectuals, paranoid writers—with "Africans, Chinese, Indonesians."[19] Yet we might pause to consider how Ned's insistence on the markedly American

nature of his organized island suggests some initial resistance to black transnationalism, now commonly fetishized by literary critics as the unfettered
mingling of all blacks, of all different nationalities, from the midcentury onward.[20] In 1950, when Wright teamed up with former United Nations Educational, Scientific, and Cultural Organization (UNESCO) staff writer and
future management consultant William Rutherford to found FAF, the desire
to limit communication—what Ned calls "mutual aid"—to black Americans
and Europeans still ran strong.[21] The failure of FAF some two years later,
then, marked the waning days of a specifically and exclusively black American strand of internationalist discourse, at the same time that it heralded a
key beginning in the critical narrative of black transnationalism that would
dominate discussions of midcentury arts and letters for many years to come.
But how did Wright and other Afro-modernists come to trade the discourses
of one minority "island" for a more inclusive and institutionally unbounded
Island? And what role did paranoid reading play in their institutional labors?

One approach to answering these questions is to compare the literary
discourse of the paranoid novel to its alleged institutional counterpart:
Wright's real-life "little American island" for black Americans in France that
he attempted to establish a decade before the suggestion of it appeared in
Island of Hallucination. Before *Savage Holiday* (1954), before *The Long Dream*
(1958), and roughly contemporaneous with "F. B. Eye Blues" (1949), Wright's
aspirations for black internationalism made their first appearance in FAF's
Constitution and Statement of Aims, which Wright, who had declared himself FAF's interim president, was singlehandedly responsible for writing.
"Rough notes on the broad aim of the group: an exposure of the baleful
affects [*sic*] of an irresponsible nationalism upon the personalities, cultures, and mind of man," he wrote in his first draft of the Constitution.[22]
This draft, however, did not pass muster with the FAF executive committee: Ligon Buford, former director of the World Refugee Office, journalist
Ollie Stewart, GI turned Negritude poet Samuel Allan, and GI turned soul
food restaurant owner Leroy Haynes. "Exposure," they argued, was not a
persuasive or concrete enough directive to attract members or raise money.
Because FAF had no material support from either the US or French governments, it relied entirely on the persuasiveness of its foundational texts
to fund its operations. "About the other people of FAF no news from anybody," wrote Colette Lacroix, Wright's self-proclaimed "poor, nervous, tired
and broke secretary" in her early efforts to mobilize members.[23] "I have
not seen yet Leroy or Edward [Myers]," she continued. "Only Clifford who
gave 10,000 and [Jean] Maho who promises [*sic*] some money for the end

of the month." Genevieve Huezé, a writer for the United States Information Service–sponsored organization France-États-Unis, seemed equally
distressed by FAF's lack of direction. "So many things had to be considered
and so many people had to be consulted," she wrote to Wright after an unproductive meeting at the Maison de la Mutualité.[24] "Should we organize a
meeting? Should we print a pamphlet? Practically, we did and do nothing,
looking for better circumstances."

Because exposure had proven an ineffective goal for securing the "better
circumstances" that Huezé and others desired, Wright drafted a Provisional
Organizational Program, complete with a bullet-pointed list to clarify what
"the programmatic energies of this organization" would be "devoted to":

1. Resistance to the extension abroad of American racial practices in the
   employment field.
2. The exposure of American racist influence abroad.
3. Orientation towards and appreciation of the values of French culture
   and civilization.
4. The convening of public forums for the discussion and clarification of
   pertinent public issues.
5. To encourage the appreciation and recognition of worthy artistic talent
   handicapped and stifled by discriminatory practices.[25]

Without entirely excising the call for "exposure of American racist influence
abroad," Wright nestled it within a more distinct articulation of the affects/
effects of nationalism run amok. "American racial practices in the employment field," he claimed, had extended across the ocean from Washington,
DC, to Paris, accompanied by certain "discriminatory practices" that "handicapped and stifled" "worthy artistic talent." The solutions that Wright proposed to the expanding geographies of institutionalized racism, however,
merely reverted to the exhortatory language of international-institutional publicity, with its mutual "appreciation" of other nations' "values," "civilization,"
and "culture." Sitting awkwardly alongside one another, Wright's charges of
racial injustices and his solutions to those problems differed not just in tone
but also in their basic imagination of how FAF would take action and where
such action would be located. Was the point of such a counter-institution
to "resist" one nation's historical wrongs? Was it to harness the reparative
energies of an as-yet undefined, but presumably racially unmarked, international public sphere? Similarly, the rhetorical vacillation of Wright's bullet
points from exposure to appreciation, inclusion to exclusion, raised some

urgent questions about the role a nationalized discourse of race would play in enacting exposure, resistance, discussion, and recognition among the constitution's readers. Did the performativity of exposure require that those doing the exposing present a homogeneous racial and political front? Did the same hold true for appreciation and discussion?

Undergirding these specific concerns was the basic problem of how FAF imagined its counter-institutionalism in relation to structures of liberal pluralism, whose dynamics of inclusion and exclusion it was supposed to resist in the first place. The recorded minutes of FAF's first meeting reveal that the organization's jumbled political desires presented a bigger problem than Wright anticipated when he pitched FAF as a long overdue minoritarian rejoinder to the government's classing of black Americans as "counterpropaganda abroad." Take, for instance, Lacroix's transcript of Wright's opening remarks: "In the United States at present democracy is necessarily being more dramatically demonstrated than ever in the battle of ideologies between our country and others which claim to be more completely democratic. In contrast, Americans abroad are behaving in a manner which is more reactionary than ever. If the French government and people know that Negroes themselves are fighting against the spread of race hatred by Americans, they will offer support in the battle."[26] Here the attempt to link FAF's uniform racial composition—it was made up of "Negroes themselves"—to a politics of anti-Americanism elided the central problems of liberal institutionality: whose beliefs, needs, desires, and voices within the black expatriate community are represented and how? By treating racial identity as a de facto politically unifying force for FAF's constituency, Wright's statement only rigidified the "the battle of ideologies" whose faux democratic demonstrations he had initially critiqued. Having shored up these battle lines, he proceeded to link FAF's racially and politically unified front to an international front against United States liberal capitalism, thereby aligning the economic interests of "the French government and people" with FAF's desire to expose the geographic extension of American racial practices. "It is possible some Americans will react immediately to the existence of an organization of Negro Americans in Paris by labeling it 'Communist,'" Lacroix's transcript continues. "We should make it clear that the group is not against the ideals of the Marshall Plan but against the 'Americanization of Europe.' Thus we would be combating the same evils which the Europeans themselves fear."

Neither the assertion of FAF's racial homogeneity nor Wright's vision of a transatlantic, left-leaning politico-economic unity were unequivocally accepted by the meeting's attendees, whose vocal objections register the problem of projecting political ideology from racial identity. "Several people raised the question of the dangers which might arise out of a deliberate setting apart of themselves by American Negroes in a foreign committee," Lacroix recorded. One noted meeting "disrupter," Stanley Patrick, indicted the "serious distortion" of representation's plurality endemic to Wright's "professional 'anti-Americanism,' even when it was expressed in the 'neutralist' and dulcet tones" that Wright had deployed at the meeting.[27] According to Lacroix's notes, Wright dismissed offhand potential members' concerns about FAF's corruption of political representation. "Mr. Wright," she wrote, "pointed out that membership must of necessity be entirely voluntary, individuals being free to leave when they felt the group contributed nothing to their welfare and that they had nothing to contribute to such a group."[28] Wright's defensive insistence on the voluntarism of FAF recast the organization's exclusionary logics as a matter of individual contributions and free association—a false choice, insofar as it obscured the imposed ideologies, both racial and political, that limited the forms that the "group" assumed and the practices it adopted. To institutionalize Wright's particular vision of separatism, then, was to disable representational politics by reinforcing the very procedures of discrimination FAF intended to expose in the first place

Of course, these theoretical concerns were largely overshadowed by the practical necessities of building an institution from scratch. As Rutherford pointed out to Wright after the first meeting, one of the worst things any new organization could do was to artificially suppress its membership numbers before it got off the ground. Accordingly, Wright modulated his stance on group affiliation and collective identity as members registered their wariness of institutionalizing separatism under the aegis of representational diversity. "It seems to me that it would show a certain largeness of spirit if no racial lines were drawn," wrote Russell Porter, a black expatriate who Wright had asked to help edit FAF's documents. With his letter, Porter enclosed a mimeograph copy of the constitution of the Caledonian Society, a Catholic institutions of international communication, as an example of how to revise FAF's constitution toward a more charitable model of inclusiveness. By the second meeting, the issue of the organization's name had emerged as a proxy for its debates over the racial identities of its constituency. "There was some discussion on the question of a name which would include Negro or Afro-American in itself," recorded Lacroix.[29] But "it was pointed out by Mr. Wright that this might not be wise, inasmuch as later it might be found desirable to invite non-Negroes into the membership."

But the disagreements over FAF's constituency prompted a discernible crisis in Wright's commitment to organizing, as we can see from Lacroix's notes on the executive committee meeting that followed. "Difficulty in formulating unanimous statement of aims (too far left—not far enough left)," she wrote. "Program must follow directly from aims; and in terms of actions not wishes. Do we continue or not?"[30]

Before we continue, however, it is instructive to consider how these ordinary institutional quagmires become distorted in a quasi-fictionalized account of how Wright's racial politics—and his paranoia, specifically—led to FAF's eventual failure: the narration of the first FAF meeting that James Baldwin undertakes in his essay "Alas, Poor Richard." Written one year after Wright had died, "Alas, Poor Richard" betrays Baldwin's urge not just to kill his "spiritual father" (as he claimed in the essay), but also to eviscerate his literary and political reputation after Wright had dismissed Baldwin's prose in *Giovanni's Room* as "a kind of shameful weeping."[31] "Alas, Poor Richard" thus opens by comparing the "untimely" death of the author to the unexpected failure of an "institution" and welcoming the sense of liberation that attends his/its collapse (604). The disappearance of the author is an "unadmitted relief," Baldwin confesses, "for the baffling creator no longer stands between us and his work," shading his readers' experiences of his novels with "his personal fortunes and misfortunes, his personality, and the social facts and attitudes of his time" (605). Wright's death allows Baldwin finally to entertain the suspicion "that Richard Wright was never, really, the social and polemical writer he took himself to be." "I was always exasperated by his notions of society, politics, and history, for they seemed utterly fanciful," Baldwin explains. "I never believed he had any real sense of how a society is put together . . . his major interests as well as his power lay elsewhere" (606). That "elsewhere" lies in Wright's "association with the French intellectuals, Sartre, de Beauvoir, and company"—white French intellectuals who could not sense, as Baldwin claimed he could, that "in Richard Wright [was] a Mississippi pickaninny, mischievous, cunning, and tough" (606). The stunningly racialized nature of this compliment—if one can truly call it that— offers us our first glimpse of Baldwin's "Poor Richard" as a man deceived by his imaginary notions of social and political systems—a man whose mind has turned him against himself, against his national origins, and, most damning of all, against his race. He is the quintessential paranoiac.

The most dramatic and unwitting performance of his paranoia appears on "one bright, sunny afternoon, on the terrace of the Royal St. Germain," when Wright approached Baldwin with the idea for an "Alliance." "He wanted to do something to protect the rights of American Negroes in Paris," Baldwin writes, "to form, in effect, a kind of pressure group which would force American businesses in Paris, and American government officials, to hire Negroes on a proportional basis." With Baldwin going out of his way to memorialize his disdain for the project, "Alas, Poor Richard" stages the epistemological struggle between Baldwin, presented here as a younger, clear-eyed thinker, and Wright, an aging mentor toying with his "fanciful" "notions of society, politics, and history." Here, for instance, is Baldwin's initial questioning of Wright at the Royal St. Germain: "How, I asked him, in the first place, could one find out how many American Negroes there were in Paris? Richard quoted an approximate, semi-official figure, which I do not remember, but I was still not satisfied. Of this number how many were looking for jobs? Richard seemed to feel that they spent most of their time being turned down by American bigots, but this was not really my impression" (616). Of course, Baldwin notes that he did not disagree with Wright's belief in, or knowledge of, the racial biases of government hiring. No one did. "I did not know anyone who doubted that the American hiring system remained in Paris exactly what it had been at home," Baldwin continues (616–17). Rather, he questions the haphazard anecdotal evidence, the solipsistic thinking, that Wright gravitates toward in order to justify his alliance and to persuade himself that it was, in fact, a worthwhile pursuit. "But who was one to prove this with a handful, at best, of problematic Negroes, scattered through Paris?" Baldwin wonders. "Unlike Richard, I had no reason to suppose that any of them even *wanted* to work for Americans—my evidence, in fact, suggested that this was just about the last thing they wanted to do. But even if they did, and even if they were qualified, how could one *prove* that So-and-So had not been hired by TWA *because* he was a Negro?" (617, italics in original). Evidence, proof, causality—this is the language that Baldwin emphatically invokes to measure the distance between Wright and the rest of the black American community in Paris. It is a language of empiricism that does not unsettle Wright's plans, as his plans are not, and never have been, based in reality. "One could certainly not, on the basis of our findings, attach a policy or evolve a strategy—but this did not seem to surprise Richard, or even to disturb him," Baldwin concludes.

Focused only on exposing his idiosyncratic sense of racial oppression, Richard's paranoid flailings present Baldwin with an "object lesson" in black American internationalism, a warning for what can happen when someone "cut[s] himself off from his roots." His insistence on organizing his "Alliance" against Baldwin's clear-headed and rational assessment of the true political desires of black Americans in Paris presents the most powerful example of what Baldwin identifies as Richard's desire to "hold himself against everyone else." This attitude is all-consuming and nonspecific. It seemed to him, Baldwin suggests, as much as it "seemed to apply, with great rigor, against a great many others. It applied against old friends, incontestably his equals, who had offended him, always, it turned out, in the same way: by failing to take his word for all the things he imagined, or had been led to believe, his word could cover" (614). Richard's attitude "applied, in short, against anyone who seemed to threaten Richard's system of reality. As time went on, it seemed to me that these people became more numerous and Richard and fewer and fewer friends" (614). What is so canny about the essay is how Baldwin's alignment of Wright with the paranoiac—the writer consumed by his own "system of reality," angered by friends who failed "to take his word for all the things he imagined," beholden to the white French intellectuals who were, for many black Africans, political persecutors—is offered as an attempt to defend Richard from the charges others had leveled against him. "I defended Richard when an African told me, with a small, mocking laugh, I believe he thinks he's white," Baldwin reports. "I could not fail to begin, however, unwillingly, to wonder about the uses and hazards of expatriation."

Participating in FAF, then, required ignoring the evidence and unequivocally aligning oneself with Richard's system of reality. "Alas, Poor Richard" enacts this alignment by slowly reconfiguring Baldwin's helpless, creeping insinuations into a controlled mockery of Richard's paranoia, brandishing many of the tropes and figures that would recur in *Island of Hallucination*. "We were in too deep to be able to turn back now," Baldwin writes ominously—"in too deep" a cliché familiar from psychological thrillers—"and, accordingly, there was a pilot meeting of this extraordinary organization, quite late, as I remember, one evening in a private room over a bistro" (617). Setting the scene for FAF's first meeting, Baldwin populates it with a "disorganized parade" of thirty or forty black writers who, he claims, have no way of "defeating detection" from either the "ever-present agents of the CIA, who certainly ought to have had better things to do, but who, quite probably on the other hand, didn't." The shadowy omnipresence of the agents is pointedly juxtaposed to the spectacular presence of Wright, who "stood on a platform above us," basking "in his glory." The father figure, the lone genius, the orator, the paranoiac, standing above the crowd he addresses—it all suggests that he, and only he, is capable of perceiving and remedying the problems of black Americans in France.

Yet more alarming, Baldwin reports, was "Richard's speech," which "frightened me," beginning with its unusually elevated footing, both literally and metaphorically, and ending with a shocking "revelation" that the FAF meeting minutes failed to report. "I do not remember how his speech began, but I will never forget how it ended," Baldwin relayed. "News of this get-together, he had told us, had caused a great stir in Parisian intellectual circles. Everyone was filled with wonder (as well they might be) concerning the future of such a group. A great many white people had wished to be present, Sartre, de Beauvoir, Camus—'and,' said Richard, *'my own wife*. But I told them, before I can allow you to come, we've got to prepare the Negroes to receive you!'" "This revelation," which prompted a "strained, stunned, uneasy silence" among the meeting's attendees, was hardly the revelation—the common-place, really—we as readers might have expected based on Lacroix's meeting minutes: that black Americans in Paris were subject to the same discrimination by the US government that they had experienced at home. Rather, the revelation Baldwin describes is one of the deepest betrayal and the most profound alienation: that Richard Wright, the most cherished writer of African American protest fiction, had so intimately aligned himself with white intellectuals that he believed it was his responsibility to "prepare the Negroes" to receive them. Both in its footing and its grammar, the statement seemed to substantiate the charge that Baldwin claimed to have defended Wright from earlier in the essay: that he thought he was white.

Wright's speech act, which Baldwin describes as both "terribly funny" and "not funny at all," thus reads as a spectacularly failed performative attempt, insofar as his announcement of preparation did not enact the preparation it intended. Instead, the humorous and awful infelicity of Wright's utterance only drew attention to the particular circumstances that made such an utterance possible in the first place—not just the general fact of Wright's expatriation, as Baldwin had suggested earlier, but the asymmetries endemic to any kind of counter-institution that sought to pursue the same cultural "appreciation" of and "orientation" to French values that the white institutions of politics did. "I rather wondered what the probable response would have been had Richard dared make such a statement in, say, a Negro barbershop; rather wondered, in fact, what the probable response would have been had anyone else dared make such a statement to anyone in the room, under different circumstances," Baldwin mused. Imaging the space of the barbershop, or any number of nonpolitical spaces or circumstances, prompts Baldwin to ventriloquize a response to Wright that rejects his overture to preparation. "Nigger, I been receiving white folk all my life—prepare *who*?" he asks. "Who do you think you going to *prepare*?" (618, italics in original).

One wonders what to make of the fact that none of the performative drama that Baldwin stages in "Alas, Poor Richard" is present in Lacroix's meeting minutes. Indeed, the only trace we have of Baldwin's presence at the meeting is a short and seemingly genial note from Lacroix: "Mr. Jimmy Baldwin to approach personnel officers of government agencies to talk informally with them in regard to job possibilities in their agencies." (Elsewhere, Baldwin is described as showing up giggly drunk with a date, leaving abruptly, and never coming back.) Yet the most interesting question for my purposes is not whether the specific events Baldwin describes in the essay actually happened—they almost certainly did not. Rather, it is the way in which paranoia, when conjoined to bureaucratic hubris, facilitates a betrayal of one's historical conditions, one's race, and one's chances for achieving solidarity. (Never mind that Baldwin's reading of Wright is strangely paranoid itself, insofar as every one of Wright's actions, no matter how minor, becomes symptomatic of everything that conspires against black Americans.) Perhaps the most damning transformation of the entire essay takes place through Baldwin's final series of questions, in which his hailing of Wright ("Who do you think you going to prepare?") converts Wright from the paranoid truth seeker—the solitary man who asks "Who is after me?"—into a mediating figure of systemic oppression: the bureaucrat who wonders "How should I prepare the people I wish to rule over?" Or as Baldwin puts it, "It seemed, indeed, that Richard felt that, with the establishment of this club, he had paid his dues to American Negroes abroad, and at home, and forever; had paid his dues, and was off the hook, since they had once more proved themselves incapable of following where he led." To follow Wright into the political fray would have meant institutionalizing the same hatred of other blacks and the same self-hatred that Baldwin ultimately diagnoses as Wright's tragic flaw, both as a writer and as an aspiring bureaucrat.

"Alas, Poor Richard," then, gives us a fictionalized pragmatic account of how and why Wright's paranoid imagination marked FAF for failure, even though the archive contains nothing specific about its final days or failed projects—nothing, that is, like Faulkner's spectacularly inebriated incarnation of pluralist failure in PTPI's final meeting. Yet the lack of epiphenomenal fireworks surrounding its dissolution is, in and of itself, more telling than Hazel Rowley's appropriately paranoid claim in her biography of Wright that the organization's failure resulted from its infiltration by writers and artists turned State Department informants.[32] I suspect, however, that the truth is far more mundane than Rowley's conjectures. As any organizational theorist could have predicted from even a cursory reading FAF's meeting minutes, the emphasis on racial separatism had to be abandoned after FAF's first two meetings in favor of the now commonplace rhetoric of transnationalism that Maxwell and others have ascribed to "Paris Noir." The final draft of FAF's constitution thus called on its sixty or so members "to reaffirm the common identity and destiny of humankind, and the internationalism of the human spirit" by rising above all "racial, class, social, religious, and national divisions between men."[33] Ironically, the constitution's resplendent vision of unbounded international communication proved even less specific in its purpose and plans than the imperative to expose American racism abroad. While we know that FAF would go on to protest the American Hospital in Paris for its discriminatory hiring practices, and while we also know that FAF would sponsor speeches by American Civil Liberties Union (ACLU) founder Roger Baldwin, French intellectual Claude Bourdet, and jazz musician Charles Delauney, all this activity seems incidental to the axiom that Baldwin proffered at the end of "Alas, Poor Richard." "The Franco-American Fellowship Club," he stated, "ceased to exist because it had never had any reason to come into existence" (284). To understand what it might look like for paranoid reading and the knowledge that results from it to have a reason to exist—what it might look like for paranoia to serve as an impetus to social action—we must now turn from FAF's failure to the successful reception history of Williams's roman à clef of Wright's life: *The Man Who Cried I Am*.

PARANOID RECEPTION HISTORY

What does it mean for a work of literary fiction to enjoy a "successful reception history"? While critics have approached this question from the perspective of authorial intention or market performance, in the case of Williams's *The Man*, a successful reception history meant something else altogether: a causal link between literary discourse and social action. Consider as a point of comparison the tragically unsuccessful scene of reception staged in the final chapters of the novel itself, in Max's attempt to transmit the contents of the King Alfred Plan from Amsterdam to New York over a transatlantic telephone line. Although he spends more than fifty minutes carefully reading "notes, names, addresses, things" to Minister Q, the self-proclaimed revolutionary leader who picks up Max's call in his Harlem office, Max does not know that the line is gravely compromised (390). Listening in on Max and Minister Q's call are two employees of an unnamed intelligence agency equipped with the "delicate recording machinery" that taps into the line and intercepts the call. "The subject of the call was an organization called Alliance Blanc—that means White Alliance," explains one of the eavesdropping agents to agency headquarters once Max has hung up (391). "And something called King Alfred that sounds really crazy, about race riots and emergencies and the President and the Army." Textual and telephonic reception merges in what appears to be a moment of communicative triumph for Max. Even the agents are surprised and suspicious. The word is out on the King Alfred Plan. The jig is up.

In a second scene of proliferating communication, the agents' recording machinery transmits Max's message through a literal underground network of telephone wires to a metaphoric underground network of federal spies. "The call had traveled beneath the sewers and subways through one wire which was bound tightly to a thousand others," Williams details (391). "From the Federal office which the first call reached, still another call was made, this one traveling out of the city, southward to Washington where, in a matter of minutes, the top secret vaults were opened and cross-indexed files traced back upon the other." "Washington," in turn, sends an upper-echelon bureaucrat, Ted Dallas, and his suspiciously quiet assistant to listen to the tape recording of Max's call in a different room in Harlem, this one populated by two agents known only as Barney and Tom: "The man called Tom pressed a lever and the voices of Max and Minister Q, along with telephone cable noises, filled the room" (392). The white noise accumulated across multiply mediated acts of technological transmission disappears when Max brings up the King Alfred Plan. "Suddenly the larger than life voices, Max's cold and tired, Minister Q's quick and angry, were talking about something called King Alfred. Dallas spun and stared at the loudspeaker. The voices boomed on" (393). As Max's voice reading the text of the King Alfred Plan clarifies, Dallas realizes that "his assistant had known about King Alfred all along." He realizes, too, that his assistant, the man called Barney, and the man called Tom, are all operatives of the Alliance Blanc, and that they will soon murder him, Minister Q, and Max so that the King Alfred Plan may never see the light of day. The communications circuit that began so hopefully with Max's telephone call is now definitively closed. Systemic oppression is trapped within a feedback loop of death that will prevent any future actions against the alliance and their plans for advancing a whitewashed version of American internationalism.

The short-circuiting of international communication proves all the more damning because Max, who has hung up the phone in Amsterdam with no knowledge of the cascade of calls placed in the United States, has burned all the King Alfred Plan dossiers. He assumes that Minister Q's oratorical delivery of the King Alfred Plan to his audiences in Harlem will ignite the race revolution he has long desired. "Now if something really happened," Max reasons, "there would be no papers and their absence would be a sword of Damocles over the head of the Alliance and King Alfred. No papers and therefore no end; the Alliance and King Alfred, whatever happened, would always know that someone else knew" (392). Implicit in Max's thinking is an assumption about the relative felicity of paranoid knowledge when transmitted through two distinct and competing media forms: speech and text. The proof of paranoia that is concretized in the form of a text can always be disavowed, misinterpreted, edited, erased, or simply ignored by an ungenerous or illiterate reader. By contrast, Minister Q's speech provides the ideal medium not only to preserve and transmit knowledge of the plan but also to convert that knowledge into social action. Marked by the prophetic testimony of a man of God, who is, in turn, flanked by a group of protestors desperate for change, Minister Q's speech emerges at the medium for revolution. And yet once all the major players in Max's scene of communication are killed off, their voices silenced forever by an untraceable network of international institutions, neither the transmission of the plan nor revolution will come to pass. Like Wright's FAF organizing, *The Man* ends with a mission statement that ultimately fails to achieve the ends that Max or Harry or Minister Q desire: "The secret to converting *their* change to *your* change was *letting them know that you knew*" (386, italics in original).

Although the post-protest narrative of *The Man* closes on this rather bathetic note, the same could not be said for the reception of the novel itself, which Williams revised assiduously to assure that readers would engage with the King Alfred Plan as proof of institutionalized racism. The novel's publication history provides the most direct evidence for a meticulously crafted relationship between *The Man*'s paranoid aesthetics, its spaces of literary reception, and its desire to catalyze social action, beginning with a series of letters that Williams wrote to his agent Carl Brandt and his editor at Little, Brown and Company, Harry Sions. In the first draft of the novel that Williams had submitted to Brandt and Sions, Max had learned of the existence of the Alliance Blanc not through the mimeographs of classified government documents but through a long letter that Harry had written to Max just before his death. Yet after reading the draft, neither Brandt nor Sions had approved of the genre of the letter as the vehicle for exposing the Alliance Blanc. "The more I think about it, the more I am convinced that [the letter] is wrong," Brandt argued.[34] Sions, who had previously worked as an editor at *Holiday* and was thus exceptionally well trained in the art of fusing documentary texts and visual objects, concurred with Brandt's assessment. Harry's "James Bondish note" to Max was "not quite convincing," he observed, and tonally out of step with the rest of the novel, which "up to now" "had been sharply realistic."[35] "The <u>nature</u> of the plot must be more convincing," Sions urged Williams. "The reader must feel that it damn well could be true and indeed may well come true." With the aim of converting a fictive document into an institutional fact for a great number of disparate and distant readers, Sions offered the following editorial suggestion to Williams for revising the end: "I wonder if you would consider the possibility of the existence of an operating plan devised by some special task force of the United States government, even some division of the National Security Council, the Department of Defense, or of the FBI and CIA, which would describe in detail plans for the control or isolation, or even the deportation, of all or even certain elements of the negro population in the United States. Such a plan would contain . . . detailed information about leaders of various negro organizations in every important town and city in the United States, as described in Harry Ames's letter."

In contrast to the "somewhat fuzzy" exposure of the Alliance Blanc in the letter, the "operating plan" that Sions imagined was "sharply focused," "believable and convincing"—something that would tap into recognizable genres of political authority. Such a plan, he proposed to Williams, "would create not one Watts, but hundreds." Sions's reference was to the 1965 Watts rebellion in Los Angeles just one year earlier, in which the arrests of two black American brothers had incited six days of civic unrest against the Los Angeles Police Department, thirty-four deaths, and more than $40 million in property damage. The idea of hundreds of Watts uprisings spurred by the novel's fictional plan represented nothing short of a total revolution in American race relations—not to mention a staggeringly ambitious goal for a novel's desired reception. But the plan had to have the right textual and visual packaging in order to achieve its desired ends. Sions concluded his letter by suggesting that Williams design the plan so that it resembled "a pamphlet outlining in clear detail steps to be taken by the security forces of our government to preserve law and order and so forth against a negro revolution." While the pamphlet had served as the privileged genre for fomenting American revolution since the 1776 publication of Thomas Paine's *Common Sense*, Williams's pamphlet was unique in that it aimed to galvanize social action not by advocating for revolution explicitly, but by merely committing to textual form proof of the oppression he believed his readers would have known about all along.

Nowhere is the performativity of paranoid reading—the idea of "converting *their* change to *your* change"—more strikingly contested than in Brandt's skeptical response to the plan that Sions and Williams had discussed. While Brandt agreed that a pamphlet would ensure that the novel appeared "as absolute reality with no sense of either science fiction or paranoia," he expressed doubts about the institutional setup of the Alliance Blanc and its interest in black oppression.[36] "I simply do not believe that representatives of fifteen or twenty governments formally sit around discussing" "the horrible details in the life of the Negro around the world," he confessed to Sions. "No international organization is required to deal with this kind of thing." Brandt's privileged disbelief piqued William's ire. "Why in the hell would Carl have reason to discount such an organization, such a uniform evil?" Williams asked Sions in a subsequent letter.[37] "His reality is not mine. But more important, he will not even _imagine_ my reality." Brandt's resistance to Williams's reality was precisely what convinced Williams to revise not only the pamphlet's typography and pagination, but also its forms of address, so as to reflect the generic forms that Brandt, a white literary agent, trusted to convey his reality.[38] "The positiveness of Carl's reaction—'I simply do not believe, etc.'—makes me sure I'm on the right track," Williams wrote to Sions. Wittingly or not, Brandt's readerly hesitation had the effect of further tightening the causal logic that Williams imagined could link the plan's textual forms to its material effects, first on its individual readers and then on national institutions and ideologies at large.

Importantly, however, Williams's textual conversion of paranoia into knowledge was also positioned in direct opposition to the public and self-reflexive communication of racist exposure undertaken by "Negro organizations" like FAF. In contrast to the staged performances of orality undertaken by spokespeople like Wright, his fictional counterpart Harry Ames, and Minister Q, the textuality of the pamphlet imbued it with the bureaucratic anonymity that Williams believed was key to the production of belief among its readers. "The ineffectiveness of Negro organizations," Williams wrote to Sions, "is because the leaders can't keep their mouths shut. They don't have to give interviews; they don't have to talk to reporters; they don't have to create slogans that they know will be misinterpreted. The loss of power is equal to the amount of publicity they secure for themselves. The programs are undercut before they can get underway, because they have big mouths."[39] The effectiveness of the King Alfred Plan, by contrast, derived from the fact that it appeared to have no identifiable source—no creator, no author, no representative with a "big mouth" giving interviews, talking to reporters, making up slogans, or seeking publicity. It seemed to have sprung from a self-documenting institutional setting. Revising his work in the crosshairs of mass-market publishing and the inadequacies of black American institutions of political representation, Williams thus drafted the King Alfred Plan as an additional seven-page insert into the novel.

Far from embracing the post-protest ethos of *The Man*'s narrative trajectory, the text of the King Alfred Plan represents Williams and Sion's shared commitment to creating a formidable performative relationship between a fictive paraliterary text and revolutionary social action. For Williams and his publisher, there existed a very real possibility that a fictionalized document—when crafted with the necessary aesthetic precision, circulated through the proper media forms, and read by an appropriate audience—could mobilize readers against the structural conditions of racial oppression: police brutality; housing and hiring discrimination; lack of access to health-care services, public transportation, schooling, and more. From a formal point of view, then, what is crucial to appreciate in Sions's suggestions, Brandt's skepticism, and Williams's revisions is how the "pamphlet" mimicked certain generic features they believed a contemporary reader would recognize in the text of a plan devised by an institutional consortium of the US government, the National Security Council, the Department of Defense, the FBI, and the CIA. If we recall some of the bureaucratic aesthetic features of the plan that I highlighted in the beginning of this chapter (e.g., its typography and pagination, its impersonal tone), we can see now how some of the more obvious aspects of its visual design (e.g., the crude map of the US geographic regions designed by the Department of the Interior, the list of black organizations put together by the attorney general) respond directly to Sions's editorial request for something that "looked like" it "could be true and indeed may well come true." And crucially, in contrast to what happens to the plan within the plot of the novel—Max burns it, Minister Q's mouth is shut forever, and thus King Alfred is lost to the world due to the failures of orality—the textual layout of the plan in the object of the novel suggests its imminent and eternal detachability from its written genre of origin. Williams's pamphlet design aggressively courts the possibility that a reader, any reader, at any point in time, could mistake the plan as a government document rather than a chapter excerpted from a novel. (To wit: in discussing rights and permissions for this book, one of my editors assured me I would not need to secure permissions for figure 6.1 as it came from a government document and was thus covered under fair use.)

In this sense, Williams's paranoid textual aesthetic recalls another para-prefixed concept that my broader argument about the paraliterary has flirted with in previous chapters but has not invoked explicitly: the "paratext" of a novel, which, as Gerard Genette has argued, functions as its "privileged place of pragmatics" by suggesting a strategy of "influence on a public; an influence that—whether well or poorly understood and achieved—is at the service of a better reception for the text and a more pertinent reading of it (more pertinent, of course, in the eyes of the author and his allies)."[40] Unlike the paratext of a work of literary fiction, which announces its generic status as a work of fiction for the outset, the paratext of the King Alfred Plan proclaims its status as a bureaucratic institutional product—a paraliterary text par excellence. The pamphlet's strategy of influence, which we find embedded in its genre markers, is to offer tangible and replicable proof that the Alliance Blanc can and will override any efforts that black Americans may make to establish political recognition or equality. As such, it imagines and enacts a "better reception" in which the pamphlet is read not with the suspicious protocols of the literary critic but with the outraged credulity of a protestor, an activist, a revolutionary—in short, a reader committed to creating a more just world.

The question of the paratext more explicitly directs our attention to questions of *The Man*'s audience, both addressed and intended. Who served as Williams's "allies" in his quest for a better reception of his text? What kinds of readers made up the public that Williams—and perhaps separately and somewhat distinctly, Sions and Brandt—imagined the novel might influence with its presentation of the King Alfred Plan? One answer, which weds the desire for expansive social action to the crass realities of the predominantly white publishing house's bottom line, is that any individual who Little, Brown and Company's publicity team could persuade to buy the book might be spurred to anger, protest, rioting, and revolutionary action by the plan. As such, Little, Brown and Company first released the plan to the public as a promotional pamphlet for *The Man*, but a pamphlet that was deliberately evasive about what the plan was and where it came from. Ensconced in a manila cover with "CLASSIFICATION: TOP SECRET" stamped on it, the pamphlet's bright purple sidebar announced the text as "King Alfred" from "*The Man Who Cried I Am*" by John A. Williams" "to be published on October 25, 1967," but it never specified what King Alfred or *The Man* actually were.[41] The pamphlet simply presented readers with the first sentences of the plan—"In the event of widespread and continuing and coordinated racial disturbances in the United States, KING ALFRED, at the discretion of the President, is to be put into action immediately"—followed by its list of participating federal, state, and local agencies. The text was completely detached from the novel's narrative framing of Max's discovery of the plan in

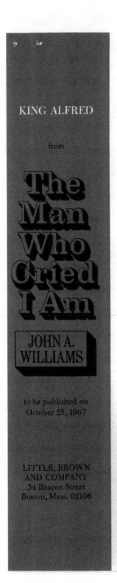

KING ALFRED

from

The Man Who Cried I Am

JOHN A. WILLIAMS

to be published on
October 25, 1967

LITTLE, BROWN
AND COMPANY
34 Beacon Street
Boston, Mass. 02106

KING ALFRED*

In the event of widespread and continuing and coordinated racial disturbances in the United States, KING ALFRED, at the discretion of the President, is to be put into action immediately.

PARTICIPATING FEDERAL AGENCIES

National Security Council	Department of Justice
Central Intelligence Agency	Department of Defense
Federal Bureau of Investigation	Department of Interior

PARTICIPATING STATE AGENCIES
(Under Federal Jurisdiction)

| National Guard Units | State Police |

PARTICIPATING LOCAL AGENCIES
(Under Federal Jurisdiction)

| City Police | County Police |

Even before 1954, when the Supreme Court of the United States of America declared unconstitutional separate educational and recreational facilities, racial unrest and discord had become very nearly a part of the American way of life. But that way of life was repugnant to most Americans. Since 1954, however, that unrest and discord have broken out into widespread violence which increasingly have placed the peace and stability of the nation in dire jeopardy. This violence has resulted in loss of life, limb and property, and has cost the taxpayers of this nation billions of dollars. And the end is not yet in sight. This same violence has raised the tremendously grave question as to whether the races can ever live in peace with each other. Each passing month has brought new intelligence that, despite new laws passed to alleviate the condition of the Minority, the Minority still is not satisfied. Demonstrations and rioting have become a part of the familiar scene. Troops have been called out in city after city across the land, and our image as a world leader severely damaged. Our enemies press closer, seeking the advantage, possibly at a time during one of these outbreaks of violence. The Minority has adopted an almost military posture to gain its objectives, which are not clear to most Americans. It is expected, therefore, that, when those objectives are denied the Minority, racial war must be considered inevitable. When that Emergency comes, we must expect the total involvement of all 22 million members of the Minority, men, women and children, for once this project is launched, its goal is to terminate, once and for all, the Minority threat to the whole of the American society, and, indeed, the Free World.

Chairman, National Security Council

* 849-899 (?) King of England; directed translation from the Latin of the *Anglo-Saxon Chronicle*.

FIGURE 6.2 Publicity materials for John A. Williams's *The Man Who Cried I Am* (1967). John A. Williams Papers (box 84, folder 6), Rush Rhees Library. Photograph: Courtesy of the Department of Rare Books, Special Collections and Preservation, University of Rochester River Campus Libraries.

Harry's suitcase. The same detachment held true for the novel as a whole; indeed, the pamphlet betrayed no relation, at least semantically, to the purple sidebar with the name of the author who created it and the novel in which it appeared. Yet when distributed at book parties in New York and mailed to "some 2,000 bookstores and jobbers," the publishing company's primary intention (and the effect of the pamphlet) was to drum up interest in the book, rather than spur its readers to action.[42]

Even the relatively unobtrusive presence of Little, Brown and Company's insignia threatened to muddle the generic identification (or misidentification) in which Williams wanted his readers to engage. Initially, he had requested that the book's title, author's name, and the publisher appear only on "the rear of the last page and in small print."[43] When the publishers failed to heed his request, Williams suggested to his publicity manager Pat McCaleb that the plan be replicated as a stand-alone piece in the *New York Times* and other nationally syndicated newspapers. But this scheme was set aside by Little, Brown and Company "in favor of a letter asking readers to open the novel to page such and such" in order to read the plan.[44] As Williams explained in an "enormously distressed" letter to publicity director Robert H. Fetridge, he worried that his revolutionary intentions for the plan's reception did not align well with his publisher's economic incentives. "I told Sions that if Little, Brown didn't want to [print the plan], to let me know and I would do it at my own expense," Williams wrote to Fetridge. "That is exactly how much confidence I have in the section as a publicity piece. And I don't believe it is cheap publicity. McCaleb discovered that the concentration camps do exist. I have since learned that the Federal government does have such a contingency plan. We know that the Army and National Guard as well as local police are undergoing riot training. What in the hell is cheap about the truth?" For Williams, no publishing expense was too great to communicate the truth to the broadest audience possible, both in the United States and abroad. "McCaleb and I talked about the value of the foreign press in this matter as well and in this regard, I can through contacts at the UN, if you get me a batch, get some circulation," he told Fetridge, enclosing a memo outlining a timetable for how the plan would be distributed through the United Nations. First, it would be sent to "representatives of the Soviet bloc nations," then "perhaps 48 hours later" to "the embassies of every nation mentioned in the plan," then another "48 hours later, copies should go in some mysterious fashion to Dick Gregory, James Meredith, Claude McKissick, and Stokely Carmichael," the civil rights activists who Williams believed would "make the most noise."[45] Across all the distinct audiences Williams targeted—attendees of book parties, book distributors, readers of the *New York Times*, UN delegates, civil rights leaders—Williams's insistence that the copies arrive in "some mysterious fashion," divorced from the institution of the publishing house, reaffirmed his commitment not just to the fantasy of the plan's self-authorship but also to the fantasy of its self-transmission. The truth ought not to require mediation of any kind.

Judging by the silence of the historical record, Little, Brown and Company did not sign on to Williams's scheme to infiltrate the UN with the plan, prompting Williams to abandon the sphere of political institutions and wage his own grassroots publicity campaign. In what undoubtedly ranks as one of the boldest authorial interventions into the reception of one's own novel, Williams took "one hundred copies of the King Alfred piece" he requested from Little, Brown and Company—no narrative frame, no promotional paratext, no page numbers—and, as he later told journalist Herb Boyd, "left copies in subway car seats all over Manhattan."[46] As photocopies of the fictive government dossiers circulated virally throughout the New York City subway system and the city at large, readers began to register their reflexive attunement to the document's generic conventions. "The ploy worked so well," Boyd recalled, "that soon after, black folks all over New York City were talking about 'the plan'—a fictitious plot that many thought was true." Readers started editing the plan's visual presentation to make it appear even more institutionally authoritative. Portions of the plan were redacted with black boxes; the maps were enhanced to include color coordinated keys and specific city names; and patterned code names like "REX-84," short for "Readiness Exercise 84," were affixed to the documents and retroactively attributed to various government agencies. It stands as a testament to the endurance of paranoid reading that REX-84, formerly King Alfred, would resurface more than twenty years later in another paranoid text: Thomas Pynchon's 1990 novel *Vineland*, in which Oliver North, Ronald Reagan, and the National Security Council secretly create "REX-84 Bravo," a Federal Emergency Management Agency (FEMA) "readiness exercise" designed to "test civilian mobilization, civil security emergency and counterterrorism plans."[47] If the textual strategies Williams and Sions deployed to transform paranoia into truth were stylized to condition a highly regulated reader response, it is not surprising that their responses would be reflected in the paranoid literary texts of the future. And it is even less surprising that historicist literary critics, the most dutifully suspicious readers of all, would accept REX-84's well-documented and "extensively footnoted" existence as the historical reality influencing Pynchon's paranoid literary imagination.[48]

As the plan's textual and epistemological contours evolved through its readers' active editing and replication of its documents, so too did its spaces of reception, its modes of circulation, and its protocols of interpretation in the late 1960s. In accounts by critics Keith Gilyard and Cheryl Wall, the Black Topographical Societies of both Chicago and Boston hosted three-hour-long political awareness sessions in which members took turns reading aloud and interpreting the plan. As Gilyard recounts the reading response and discussion that took place, the plan was used as the representative document through which to contextualize all forms of institutionalized racism, from the hiring practices of American firms to how "super highways such as the Dan Ryan Expressway in Chicago were always routed through black ghettoes to facilitate eventual military operations against those communities."[49] Reported coverage of the Topographical Society meetings helped the plan wend its way out of the underground subway system and the meeting halls of major cities into a more widely circulated, geographically diffuse, and replicable medium of literacy: the oppositional black newspaper. By January 1971, the *Chicago Defender* reported, "Every black newspaper in the United States has, at one time or another, received copies of such a plan," even though "their inability to check such items through government sources" had made it difficult for newspapers to confirm or deny its reality to their national and international readerships.[50] Here we can see a key discursive shift in the burden of proof from the paranoiac, who must work tirelessly to justify his suspicions, to the institutions he accuses, which must acknowledge his suspicions in order to deny them. Like the deafening silence that Williams had faced after his fellowship to the American Academy in Rome was withdrawn, the silence that haloed the plan's circulation seemed only to confirm the reality of its existence. Why else would government sources simply not deny it?

If the plan's multiyear transformation from a novel excerpt into a distinctly paraliterary text did not exactly bring out the hundreds of Watts rebellions that Sions had imagined, it did help to initiate a mass-mediated social movement that played out within the same political institutions that Williams fingered as the plan's architects. Unlike Wright's formation of a counter-institution as the answer to systemic oppression, the plan's paranoid aesthetics allowed it to circulate within the white institutions of politics through local performances of reading, many of which wed individual readers' personal testimonies of racial oppression to the generic forms of the plan. Through their performances of reading, they demanded government accountability; the attempt to compel speech in place of silence. In

October 1970, a former leader of the Black Panthers, Clive DePatten, described the King Alfred Plan to the House Internal Security Committee as "a secret white establishment plan to do away with all black people within 24 hours if revolution erupts."[51] Although he was assured by multiple congressmen that "the FBI had checked out the King Alfred Plan last year and found it to have been lifted from a novel, *The Man Who Cried I Am*, by John A. Williams, a black himself," DePatten resisted the committee's assertion of the plan's fictionality as a convenient strategy for dismissing the truths it had brought to light. "Even if it actually is fictional," he replied to the congressmen, "events in the black community are paralleling those set out in the King Alfred Plan." Urban renewal projects, in particular, he argued, had had the effect of isolating black Americans "into the ghettos," where they occupied the physical and subjective positions of interned Japanese American during World War II or Jewish prisoners in concentration camps. In the pages of the *Hartford Courant* and the *Chicago Tribune*, Representative Richard H. Ichord denied the international comparison by insisting that the plan was created by "Communist front organizations" intent on "spreading literature about the revival of concentration camps."[52] "It is a plan of fear," echoed Representative William J. Scherle. "If you want to believe it, sure, it will scare the hell out of you."[53] Yet none of these competing assertions about the plan's fictional origins affected the epistemological operations of its paranoid reception. DePatten's testimony only reaffirmed that if paranoid reading could not singlehandedly incite revolution from the ground up, it could infiltrate the white institutions of politics that already existed, mobilizing a black counterpublic in protest against systemic oppression.

We can see an even more elaborate overlay of paranoid reading and the demand for accountability just several months after DePatten's defiant response to the House, when an active duty military officer offered a similar testimonial presentation of the plan—this time within the judicial branch of the US government and aided by the publicity of an oppositional newspaper. "The so-called King Alfred plan does exist, according to testimony of Thomas Filkins, civilian chief of the special operations section of the 113th Military Intelligence Group in Suburban Evanston," reported the *Chicago Defender* on January 2, 1971, in its coverage of a Chicago federal court trial in which the ACLU had challenged the constitutionality of the government's invasions into civilian privacy.[54] Filkins, who presented evidence in the courtroom that the Reverend Jesse Jackson was one of the black leaders under surveillance by order of the King Alfred Plan, had his testimony corroborated not only by the plan's text but also by the anonymous journalist who had written the article for the *Defender*. "Filkins' statement fits the King Alfred plan which, according to copies seen by this writer, placed all civil rights leaders under surveillance and rated them according to their ability to control the black community under stress," wrote the *Defender*. "The King Alfred plan was first circulated, usually by the more militant black organizations, in 1964," and it had remained in circulation through the early 1970s even though "the validity of such a plan as a riot control method has never been established." More believable because of its unwillingness to attribute knowledge of the plan to one identifiable, and thus fallible, writer but to "this writer," whoever he or she may have been, the *Defender*'s backdating of the plan's entry into public circulation—three years before the novel was published—had the effect of doubly occluded both the plan's origin point and its author. The refusal to attribute the plan to anyone other than "the more militant black organizations" seemed to elevate it from a deliberate production into a widely acknowledged truth that had just happened to make its way into textual form.

The erasure of the plan's origins was a strategy that Williams continued to pursue when asked point blank about its fictionality. Using the uncertainty surrounding the plan's emergence into the public sphere to bolster its claims to truth telling, Williams never outright denied the plan's status as fiction. Rather, he asserted that the underlying truths made legible by the plan had always existed in the public sphere in one form or another. As such, the novel was simply another generic form through which to present what was already known; neither the author himself nor his representational forms mattered except as corroborating sources. "We all know that practically every city government has announced a contingency plan for dealing with rebellion, i.e. Black people in rebellion, and not only city governments but the federal government," Williams told National Educational Television's (NET's) news program *Black Journal* in an October 1971 episode titled "Genocide."[55] While refusing to address the specific status of his plan as reality or fiction, implicit in Williams's claim that "We all know" about the existence of such government contingency plans is the same universalizing profession of truth we see in the examples of DePatten, Filkins, and the *Defender*—a foregone conclusion that, in this case, received additional support from *Newsweek* correspondent Samuel Yette, who also appeared alongside Williams on "Genocide." Prompted by Williams's statements, Yette revealed to viewers that a division of the Justice Department, the Law Enforcement Assistance Administration (LEAA), "is right now building what they call regional detention facilities which, in fact, are concentration camps in virtually every state in the country. That's going on now." In a 1976 profile in the *Washington Post*, when asked by reporter Hollie West if he continued to think that "such a plan is probable," Williams replied with the same discretion that characterized his testimony on *Black Journal* almost ten years earlier.[56] Note the deflection in West's account of Williams's response to her query: "'The Germans never admitted that they were carrying out a plan of genocide. Why the hell should the Americans admit it? I think there is general agreement that people think that America's problems could be solved if there were no black people here.'" By shifting his answer first to the Holocaust, and then to his sense of a "general agreement" that the genocide of blacks would solve Americans problems, Williams dodges the question by invoking the government's lack of admission: the same awful silence that "made his paranoia real" in "We Regret to Inform You . . ." and the same "absence" that Max banked on in *The Man*.

Where the King Alfred Plan circles back to the specifically international dimension of communication is in Williams's subsequent use of the plan's textual reception to organize a transnational black counterpublic constituted not by political institutions but by literary forms. To organize the "censure of the world" that he alluded to in his *Post* profile, Williams began to plan "a new Black magazine": a "political-literary publication" he called *Amistad*, which borrowed "its name from the Spanish slave vessel which revolutionary African slaves took over and turned right around back to Africa."[57] As Williams explained it to an unnamed reporter at London's leading black newspaper *The Crusader*, *Amistad*'s mission was "to underpin, enrich, and enlarge the scope of Black history courses" by presenting "penetrating analytic and interpretive essays, and new fiction that will also serve as a systematic cohesive body for a basic material for these history courses." To explain the apparent genre slippage between "new fiction" and a proposed syllabus for worldwide black history courses, the reporter pointed to *The Man Who Cried I Am*'s revelation of the King Alfred Plan. Capitalizing on Williams's discourse of paranoid reading as merely a different form of historical truth telling, the reporter described the plan as "a new idea to certain cloistered bookish types, uninformed about Nazi Germany, American slavery, the CIA, a certain section in the McCarran Act and the massive wrecking force within the soul of exploiting, bestial white America." Operating outside of official political spaces, the plan had "supplied a lot of people with lecture money, some teaching posts, and even research centers," which were now slowly consolidating their efforts to resist "the potentially repressive nature of the Nixon administration." "For the first time there is a genuine coming together of the Black masses and the Black middle class," Williams noted. Indeed, it was to further this coalition building that he had come to London "on the final phase of a sojourn to contact Black writers scattered through-out the world in small bunches or in literary colonies to inform them of the enterprise" of *Amistad*. In the formation of *Amistad*, we can see how Williams's discourses of paranoid reading reach their performative apogee, insofar as he imagines the magazine as a medium for communication in which literary fiction can exist on its own terms as historical truth tell-ing. It need not mime institutional genres in order to produce social action. Sadly, that claim must remain pure speculation for now, because Williams never managed to get *Amistad* off the ground. That *Amistad* failed is perhaps indicative of Williams's overly ambitious claim to literature's autonomous ability to mobilize action. But then again, maybe that is being too paranoid for our own good.

"THE WHITE BOY'S PLAN IS BEING READIED"

While tracing the discourses of paranoid reading, paraliterary genres, and race could take us from Williams to our present day, I want to conclude by examining one final form through which the reading of the King Alfred Plan addresses and instantiates a black counterpublic: spoken word poetry. Con-sidered alongside the other communicative forms I have discussed in this chapter, both spoken and written, spoken word poetics, sometimes identified as a kind of proto-rap or hip-hop, offers an intriguing cross-pollination of oral performance and textual iterability. Nowhere are the resonances between vocal testimony and text more apparent than in spoken word poet Gil Scott Heron's song "The King Alfred Plan," which he released on his 1972 album *Free Will* and which his recording company, Flying Dutchman Records, re-issued in 2012 for Heron's posthumous compilation album *The Revolution Begins*.[58] Given Williams's eagerness to have the plan distributed far and wide, it is interesting that on hearing Heron's LP, he asked Little, Brown and Company's copyright lawyers to "write the Flying Dutchman people about their use of 'The King Alfred Plan.'"[59] Comparing Williams's text to Heron's spoken word poem allows us to speculate as to why Williams wanted credit where credit was due—a strange demand given his insistence on the plan's self-authorship throughout its reception history—as well as how Heron capi-talized on the plan's lack of an author to shape his style of reading aloud.

Clocking in at just under three minutes, Heron begins the recording of his poem "The King Alfred Plan" by orienting his listeners to his recording's time and place of production. "Uh, it's 1972, an election year, and once again black people are running [*pause*] for their lives," he says. Overlaying the year of the poem's production ("1972") with the institutional temporality of American politics ("an election year"), Heron hammers home the irony of this overlay by punning on the idea that "black people" are "running"—"running" not for political office, as a listener may initially expect from Heron's pause, but "running for their lives." "Reasons are things like the King Alfred Plan," he continues. "The concentration camps that were used during the Second World War to house Oriental Americans are now being refurbished to, uh, confine their new residents, i.e. Black people. Brothers and sisters, there is a place for you in America. This is the King Alfred Plan." Aligning the concrete institutional space of the World War II "concentration camp" with the more metaphorical sense of black people's social "place" in the United States, Heron's hailing of his "brothers and sisters" invites his listeners to experience with—and through—his voice what it might be like to live in such a "place."

The call to "brothers and sisters" provides the refrain that Heron will use to pivot from his framing of the poem to the recitation that initiates the poem's lyric address, accompanied by an ominous percussive beat, a shrill flute, and bells: "Brothers and sisters there is a place for you in America / Places are being prepared and readied night and day, night and day / The white boy's plan is being readied night and day, night and day / Listen close to what rap says bout traps like Allenwood P.A." Extending the frame's equation of the physical spaces of the internment camps to blacks' social place in the United States, the first lines of "The King Alfred Plan" then uses this equation to offer the listener a potent double meaning of Heron's prophecy that the "white boy's plan is being readied." While the institutional sites of the camps "are being prepared and readied" to receive blacks, black listeners are also "being readied" by Heron to read the plan—or more accurately, to hear the text of the plan read to them by Heron. This is first hinted at in Heron's imperative to his audience that they must "listen close to what rap says," but only fully realized after a short caesura in Heron's otherwise breathless recitation. Pausing for the slightest beat, he asks his audience, "What you think 'bout the King Alfred Plan? / You ain't heard? Where you been, man?" Not waiting for an answer to his hypothetical question, he launches into the scene of reading that prompted Williams's legal inquiry to his record label: "If I may paraphrase the government notice reads: / 'Should there at any time become a clear and present danger initiated by any radical element threatening the operation of the government of the United

States of America, members of this radical element shall be transported to detention centers until such time as their threat has been eliminated—code KING ALFRED.'"

What is extraordinary about Heron's recitation here is how the rhythm of his speech and his poly-vocalization conspire to create the effect of textual citation and bureaucratic anonymity through the aesthetics of sound. To listen to Heron read the excerpt from Williams's plan is to hear the following simultaneous changes in vocal quality: the drums, the flute, and the bells cease as soon as Heron begins paraphrasing the "government notice"; Heron's voice speeds up dramatically and loses all inflection; the addition of reverb adds both distance and flatness to his already robotic tone. It is as if Heron is speaking not as himself, but from the faraway and acoustically dead space of a state institution—or rather, as if he is speaking as a bureaucratic document might if such a document could speak. Beyond whatever historical or intertextual interest we may have in this version of "The King Alfred Plan," then, Heron's remediation of Williams's fictional text through sound technology reveals a new strategy for amplifying the authoritativeness of the plan (and loosening Williams's claim to copyright) through the performance of reading. Unlike the stark distinction between orality and textuality that Williams's takes as a starting point for his dissemination of the plan, Heron's sound markings of citation reveal the plan as an open secret, available for public reading and recitation to anyone who wants to speak the truth.

Of course, the point of amping up the plan's publicly recognized truth value is precisely to encourage social action, which, for Heron, involves the banding together of black people outside of political institutions before the government physically brings them together in the institutions of the concentration camps. After Heron finishes reciting Williams's text, the musical accompaniment resumes, louder than before, and Heron returns to his earlier speaking rhythm, but now with an added sense of urgency as he shouts above the drums, bells, and whistles. "There must be black unity, there must be black unity / For in the end unity will be thrust upon us and we upon it and each other," he intones, before turning to a long description of the physical carnage he imagines will take place in the camps: the "stench of unwashed bodies and unsanitary quarters," "concrete and barbed wire, babies screaming," "blood oozing from cracks and wooly heads." After detailing the horrors of the camps for the final minute of the song, he ends by resurrecting his call for solidarity but this time in a more collaborative, rather than imperative, rhetorical register: "Let us unite because of love and not hate / Let us unite on our own and not because of barbed wire death / You dare not ignore the things I say / Whitey's waiting night and day, night and day, night and day, night and day." The request that blacks unite "on our own" rather than through Williams's "white institutions of politics" takes on even greater importance now that the white institutions are explicitly institutions of genocide. The only riposte to the government's coercive monopoly on power is "love," which, as we have seen throughout this book, seems to exceed institutionality in its capacity to bring people together. To end on "love," then, is to end with a social, rather than political, demand for solidarity.

From the American Academy in Rome to FAF to the various iterations of the King Alfred Plan we have encountered in subways, meeting houses, courtrooms, government buildings, and now spoken word poetry, the shift from assimilation to separation to revolution entails a corresponding aesthetic shift away from literary realism to paranoid experimentalism—or rather, a muddling of those two categories so that they are no longer stable aesthetic forms, but beholden to local reading practices. This is a bold inversion of what most literary critics and historians of African American literature have seen as the traditional relationship between social activism and realist literary form. Yet to conclude on this upheaval in social and aesthetic codes is also to claim for the imaginative work of literary fiction an unprecedented felicity: the ability to take social action by prompting large masses of readers, through the painstaking lamination of formal techniques and institutional discourse, to transcend the analysis paralysis of paranoid reading.

If Heron's "The King Alfred Plan" represents a fitting terminus for this chapter, both in its historical end point and its performance of paranoid reading, it also offers a fitting end point for this book's exploration of the relationship between reading, communication, and social structure. Insofar as the previous chapters have treated acts of resistance to institutional practices as sociologically or politically important, these acts have always been limited in their scope, ambition, and affective posturing. Indeed, none of the examples of reading and writing practices I have presented so far—from McCarthy's literary impersonation to Plath's sadomasochistic publicity, the Beats' literary branding, O'Connor's anti-sight reading, or Faulkner's bureaucratic illiteracy—aspire to overthrow so radically the norms of the institutions in which such acts occurred. In this sense, "The King Alfred Plan" imagines a truly revolutionary alternative to the interplay between texts, people, and the processes of institutional formation that this book has placed at the heart of the postwar period's ethos of liberal internationalism. Aptly, then, the vision Heron projects of a community uniting out of "love," free from "Whitey waiting" with "hate," offers us a utopian world—a world that exists outside the "barbed wire" of regimented sociality, but perhaps even more evocatively, a world in which a reader or listener "dare not ignore the things I," the writer or speaker, "say." While we know all too well these days that such a utopian order does not exist, our knowledge of its historical failings does not weaken the claim that Heron, Williams, and their thousands of readers and listeners made by engaging the King Alfred Plan: that almost nothing can rival the reality instituted by literature when it calls on its bad readers to do good work.

Retracing One's Steps

This is the way I name or accuse the fearful reader, the reader in a hurry to be determined, decided upon deciding. . . . Now, it is bad, and I know no other definition of the bad, it is bad to predestine one's reading, it is always bad to foretell. It is bad, reader, no longer to like retracing one's steps.

JACQUES DERRIDA, *The Post Card* (1987)[1]

If it is possible to insist on the operation of the reactivation of the sense objectified in institutions, one should not neglect the converse operation of the reactivation of the embodied past by institutions.

BERNARD LAHIRE, *The Plural Actor* (2011)[2]

It once was a truth universally acknowledged, that among a professional class of literary critics, there are good and bad ways to read a work of literature. Like many other categories of human behavior, it is far easier to praise the good than it is to appreciate the bad. Bad reading takes many forms, and I do not want to suggest that I have exhausted all the models of reading applicable to American social and political institutions at the midcentury. Rather, I have wanted to lead my reader through various theories of bad reading in order to think about how reading of any kind—good or bad, autonomous or instrumental, detached or passionate, deep or shallow, artistic or technocratic—depends on the historical convergence of aesthetic forms, textual artifacts, social practices, and human actors. Since my claim is that the valorization of certain practices of reading over others is not only a historically contingent process, but also a limitation for literary criticism, I have tried to overcome that limitation by placing postwar literature alongside the institutions of literary reception that restore some agency to bad readers as reflexively speaking, feeling, consuming, perceiving, and socializing subjects. The best way to understand the class of readers I have termed paraliterary, then, is through their systematically organized scenes of literary reception, as well as the discourses about reading that proliferate around their professions of identification, action, and interaction.

Given how important bad reading is to the history of literature and American literary study in the twentieth century, it is surprising that scholars have been reluctant to explore its logics of action—to seek out the sites and spaces in which it survives and thrives. While my approach to the problem of bad reading is distinctly historical and sociological, a methodology enabled by the richly specified texts and well-curated archives that chronicle the bad reading of the past, I want to conclude by speculating about our present and future. What is the proper way to study bad reading today as a distinctly contemporary phenomenon? Must we become bad readers ourselves? What would we read? How would we read? Where would we read? Who would teach us to read? As questions that seem to privilege the empirics of literary activity over attention to literary form, perhaps these queries sound too much like an ethnographer's hobby horse for scholars of literature to devote much thought to it. The closest anyone has come to a direct consideration of these questions is in debates over "critical reading": a second cousin of sorts to Nabokov's sense of good reading as aesthetic appreciation. Critical reading also prides itself on the cultivation of aesthetic distance, reflexivity, and even a healthy dose of paranoia, but posits as its end the production of a reasoning subject who, in the words of Michael Warner, is "oriented to freedom and autonomous agency against the background of a modern social imaginary."[3] Yet critical reading, and by extension, the readerly disposition it aspires to create, have come under considerable scrutiny over the last several decades from all sorts of quarters: not just from figures outside of literature departments—who, as Nancy Easterlin points out, question the "usefulness of literature" to further buttress their purportedly anti-elitist and "practical notion of the university's mission"—but figures within literature departments as well.[4] The two fronts in contemporary attacks on reading are not unrelated to one another. Too often, it seems that the more vociferously university administrators, state politicians, employers, and others decry how people in literature departments read (without joy, without purpose, without utility, perpetually on the brink of "crisis"), and the kinds of people they become as a result (joyless, purposeless, useless, unemployable), the more people in literature departments labor to prove their detractors wrong by altering what they do, rather than doubling down on their strengths.

Is it any small wonder, then, that the tactics critics have devised to shake the legacy of close, critical, or useless reading as the sine qua non of literary culture betray a whiff of desperation? As we saw in the chapter on scientific and ethnographic reading, the shallowness of sight reading emerged as an epistemological alternative to the uselessness of literary writing, banking on the quiescence of the human consciousness as its distinguishing attribute—no "deep study" or "reasoning" required. Today, as the humanities have continued to cede cultural prestige and funding to more avowedly scientific fields, we have witnessed a similarly anti-interpretive mode of cognition find expression in the rise of methods like "surface" reading, along with its attendant terminologies of shallow aesthetics, thick description, New Formalism, and weak theory. These practices have sought to move away from reading as seeking a "depth model of truth" and toward a reading subject capable of "accepting texts" for what they are—a subject who insists on her "epistemological humility" as a corrective to the elitism of interpretive literary study's strong claims.[5] But are these practices of reading really as non-normative, as radical, or as bad as their practitioners want them to be? Do they offer any techniques of textual engagement that are at all distinct from close or critical reading? Do they produce anything other than complex readings of difficult texts? Indeed, the literary critics who have branded themselves as the bad readers of today seem to have a difficult time describing their methodologies in anything other than metaphors and abstractions, promises and aspirations. This is precisely because they have skipped straight from reading techniques to the fantasy of the kinds of literate subjects and textual objects they want to normalize: critics who are "susceptible," "just," and "physically intimate"; texts that are "friendly, frank, generous, self-conscious, auto-critiquing, and unguarded."[6] And if the subjects of critical reading were keyed to liberalism's pillars of freedom and autonomous agency, the friendly surfaces and infinitely flexible subjects of bad reading today seem to be oriented to what Jane Elliott and Gillian Harkins have described as the neoliberal political and economic order's "attempt to rule without penetrating interiority": a system premised on the incontestability of individual interests, a tolerance for critical disagreement, and the maximization of usefulness.[7] The badness of readers today inheres not in their radicalness vis-à-vis literary reading, which I take to be a category error, but in their happy self-delusion about which technocratic masters they are serving.

Whether it is a practice as familiar as critical reading or as in vogue as surface reading, the critic's commitment to one form of reading over another often ensures that the empirical, historical, and institutional practices of reading go unnoticed. This book has argued that attending to reading requires expanding the institutions we consider beyond the college classroom, the graduate seminar, and the rapidly shrinking field of professional literary study; beyond the normalized forms of reading that literary critics practice; and beyond the textual objects that individual writers and readers have produced within the narrow logics of what counts as properly literary. But I have not wanted to find and champion an alternative to literary reading; I have wanted to make inroads into distinct forms and genres of textuality (lectures, elocution primers, conduct books, advertisements, consumer guides, financial instruments, magazines, journals, intelligence reports, bureaucratic files) and the institutions in which they are read alongside literature as alternatives to a single model of reading, or to an idea of the literary as institutionally singular. To round up such miscellaneous objects under the rubric of the paraliterary is to suggest both the capaciousness of the world outside of professional literary study, as well as the messy, fraught, and contradictory uses to which different textual forms can be put.

Today, however, I believe it is impossible to consider these questions of reading practices without also reevaluating how we gather and analyze our evidence—indeed, what we even count as our evidence. What materials can we draw on to make claims about the uses of literature outside of the institutions that we—as critics—inhabit right now? Literary critics are fond of pretending that old reading habits die easily. There appears to be some secret, subversive thrill to casting off disciplinary protocols so effortlessly, so willfully, whenever one pleases. But is the foray into phenomenological make believe either the most intellectually ambitious or intellectually honest way to broaden our critical methods? Would it not be better to venture outside of ourselves, to witness how readers with limited or no exposure to the protocols and habits of criticism read? In the case of the historical work this book has undertaken, the answer to these questions begins and ends with what Bernard Lahire identifies as "the embodied archive": a microsociological record of how readers within institutions of literacy can form constitutive relationships between literature and historical schemes of action like speaking, feeling, perceiving, seeing, and interacting. But what do we do when no such archive exists to demonstrate how schemes of actions are transmitted from writer to reader? As critics, can we—and should we—begin to build our own embodied archives by inhabiting new and strange contemporary institutions of our own? For the answer to these questions, a more appropriate guide than Lahire might be Jacques Derrida, whose epigraph to my conclusion interpellates as the "fearful reader" the reader who "predestines" her reading by predestining not just her methods but also her objects of study. Derrida's chiding of the bad reader thus doubles as an invitation to projects of archival construction, ethnographic description, biography, physical and mental immersion into the world of living readers, and other literate activities we can pursue to analyze writers and readers with little to no social value to the institutions of literature and the guardians of literary culture.

A similar double impulse can be found in my attempt to locate the history of bad readers at the intersection of literary criticism, reception history, book history, sociological theory, and communications theory, where it can speak to the disciplinary concerns of literary scholars while accounting for literature's capaciousness and capacity in the world. The various methodologies this book has drawn together have been designed with eye to outward expansion, to thinking big and bigger, so that the core of a thing called literature is no longer merely what people in literature departments do. Rather, literary texts can range alongside a vast spectrum of human beings and human behaviors, rooted in contingent scenes of political, cultural, economic, and emotional actions with tremendous material consequences for everything from individual relationships to national alliances to global revolutions. It is thus with an abiding conviction in the expansiveness of reading literature, and our ability to comprehend and appreciate many different forms of self and social production as aesthetically motivated and socially consequential, that I ask, and invite others to answer: what can't literature and its bad readers do?

Acknowledgments

This book has its roots in New Haven, Connecticut, where the faculty and graduate students in Yale's English Department made my years there a time of extraordinary happiness, growth, and productivity. I owe a great debt to Jane Patch Bordiere, Wai Chee Dimock, Sam Fallon, Len Gutkin, Langdon Hammer, Margaret Homans, Matt Hunter, Jonathan Kramnick, Palmer Rampell, Glyn Salton-Cox, Erica Sayers, Anna Shechtman, Justin Sider, Caleb Smith, Joe Stadolnik, Michael Warner, Ruth Yeazell, and, above all, Sam See. I am especially grateful to Amy Hungerford, whom I have had the privilege of knowing first as a mentor, then as a friend. I thank her for everything she has done, and continues to do, for me.

This book was revised and expanded in Cambridge, Massachusetts, through a generous postdoctoral fellowship from the American Academy of Arts and Sciences. Lawrence Buell and Amanda Claybaugh offered their wisdom and guidance at a pivotal moment in my career. I am thankful to the academy's administrative staff, especially John Tessitore, for helping me secure five months of undisturbed writing time and four months of fully paid parental leave. My life in Cambridge would have been very dull without the unruly women of 17 Stanford Terrace: Maggie Doherty, Annie Wyman, and Hannah Rosefield provided me with a home away from home, and I am beholden to them for their care, their wit, and their excellent conversations. My life in New York would have been unthinkable without the daily company of Sarah Chihaya, Ming-Qi Chu, Anna Dubenko, Marcel Przymusinski, and, from a distance, Eve Fine, Daniel Larremore, Pete Manning, and Sarah Rose—my brilliant friends.

This book has profited immensely from the many smart and kind people who have taken the time to respond to my writing in its early stages. My sharpest and friendliest readers have always been the members of the Post45 Collective: J. D. Connor, Florence Dore, Mary Esteve, Loren Glass, Kate Marshall, Deak Nabers, Debbie Nelson, and Richard Jean So. Sean McCann's intelligence, generosity, and good humor will not soon be forgotten. Nor will Mark McGurl's spirited criticism. I am thankful for the diligent editorial labors of Alan Thomas, Randolph Petilos, Christine Schwab, Katherine Grimes, and Steven Blevins, and the intellectual camaraderie of Evan Kindley and Donal Harris. Portions of some of the chapters in this book appeared in quite different forms in *American Literature*, *American Literary History*, and *REAL: A Handbook of American Studies*. I thank Priscilla Wald, Gordon Hutner, and Gunter Leypoldt for their enthusiasm for my ideas.

This book is dedicated to my family, whom I have been waiting a long time to thank: my mother, Umit Emre, whom I love for her stylish and practical and opinionated ways; and my father, Sukru Emre, whose passion for his work is only outstripped by his devotion to his family. My sisters, Gulus and Melis, are my best friends and allies. I cannot imagine who I would be without them—a terrible only child, I suppose. Finally, I am grateful beyond measure to my two guys: Christian Hart Nakarado, my best bad reader, and Aydin Berk Nakarado, who, true to his name, has filled my world with light.

Notes

INTRODUCTION

1. Vladimir Nabokov, *Lectures on Literature* (New York: Harcourt, 1982), 3.

2. *Dear Bunny, Dear Volodya: The Nabokov-Wilson Letters, 1940-1971* (New York: Harper & Row, 1979), 182.

3. See James F. English, "Literary Studies," in *The SAGE Handbook of Cultural Analysis*, ed. Tony Bennett and John Frow (Los Angeles: Sage, 2008), 126-44; Gerald Graff, *Professing Literature: An Institutional History* (Chicago: University of Chicago Press, 2007), 1989; John Guillory, *Cultural Capital* (Chicago: University of Chicago Press, 1993); Frank Lentricchia, *Criticism and Social Change* (Chicago: University of Chicago Press, 1985); and Jane Tompkins, *Sensational Designs: The Cultural Work of American Fiction, 1790-1860* (New York: Oxford University Press, 1986).

4. Heather Love, "Close but Not Deep: Literary Ethics and the Descriptive Turn," *New Literary History* 41, no. 2 (2010): 371-91; Michael Warner, "Uncritical Reading," in *Polemic: Critical or Uncritical*, ed. Jane Gallop (New York: Routledge, 2004).

5. Edouard Roditi, *Oscar Wilde* (New York: New Directions, 1947), 2.

6. William York Tindall, *A Reader's Guide to James Joyce* (Syracuse, NY: Syracuse University Press, 1959), 126.

7. Kenneth Burke, *Counter-Statement* (Berkeley: University of California Press, 1968), 70.

8. Walter Kaufmann, *The Future of the Humanities* (New Brunswick, NJ: Transaction, 1977), 65, and *College Teacher* (Ann Arbor: Macmillan Professional Magazines, 1973), 79.

9. Conrad Aiken to William Faulkner (October 3, 1956), Papers of William Faulkner, People-to-People Program (PPP), accession #7258-l, Special Collections Department, University of Virginia Library, Charlottesville, VA.

10. See Brett Gary, *The Nervous Liberals: Propaganda Anxieties from World War I to the Cold War* (New York: Columbia University Press, 1999); Evan Kindley, "Big Criticism," *Critical Inquiry* 38 (2011): 71-95.

11. See Beth Driscoll, The New Literary Middlebrow: Tastemakers and Reading in the Twenty-First Century (New York: Palgrave Macmillan, 2014).

12. See John B. Hench, *Books as Weapons: Propaganda, Publishing, and the Battle for Global Markets in the Era of World War II* (Ithaca, NY: Cornell University Press, 2010).

13. Jeffrey Williams, *The Institution of Literature* (Albany: State University of New York Press, 1995), 1.

14. Bernard Lahire, *The Plural Actor* (New York: Polity, 2011), 92.

15. See Wai Chee Dimock, *Through Other Continents: American Literature across Deep Time* (Princeton, NJ: Princeton University Press, 2006); Rachel Adams, *Continental Divides: Remapping the Cultures of North America* (Chicago: University of Chicago Press, 2009).

16. See Rita Felski, *Uses of Literature* (New York: Wiley-Blackwell, 2008); Dorothy Hale, "Aesthetics and the New Ethics" (*PMLA* 124.3 [May 2009]: 896-905); Blakey Vermeule, *Why Do We Care about Literary Characters?* (Baltimore: Johns Hopkins University Press, 2010).

17. Radio Free Europe, *Radio Free Europe: Situation Report*, vol. 3 (Washington, DC: Radio Free Europe, 1976), 265.

18. Sebastian Barker, *London Magazine*, vol. 1 (London: London Magazine, 1954), 94.

19. University of Michigan, *Official Bulletin* (Ann Arbor: University of Michigan, 1974), 32.

20. *Qualitative Research with Text, Image, and Sound*, ed. Martin Bauer and George Gaskill (London: Sage, 2000), 148.

21. See Catherine Gallagher and Stephen Greenblatt, *Practicing New Historicism* (Chicago: University of Chicago Press, 2000). The word *trace* appears no fewer than ten times in the brief introduction. In this sense, my project expands Barbara Ryan and Amy Thomas's "simple yet radical premise" that "when scholars start from documents left by readers deemed 'ordinary,' long-standing questions undergo sea changes and assumptions are put in doubt" (*Reading Acts* [Knoxville: University of Tennessee Press, 2002]).

22. Catherine Gallagher, "The Rise of Fictionality," in *The Novel*, vol. 1, ed. Franco Moretti (Princeton, NJ: Princeton University Press, 2006), 359. See also John Frow, *Character and Person* (New York: Oxford University Press, 2014).

23. Mary Poovey, *Genres of the Credit Economy: Mediating Value in Eighteenth and Nineteenth Century Britain* (Chicago: University of Chicago Press, 2008). In this vein, see also John Guillory, "The Memo and Modernity," *Critical Inquiry* 31, no. 1 (2004), 108-32.

24. Deidre Lynch, *The Economy of Character: Novels, Market Culture, and the Business of Inner Meaning* (Chicago: University of Chicago Press, 1998), 132.

25. UNESCO, *Cultures*, vol. 6 (New York: UNESCO, 1979), 15.

26. Warner Berthoff, *A Literature without Qualities: American Writing since 1945* (Berkeley: University of California Press, 1979).

27. Leslie A. Fielder, "Literature as an Institution: The View from 1980," *English Literature: Opening Up the Canon* (Cambridge, MA: English Institute, 1981), 81.

28. See Samuel Delaney, *Shorter Views: Queer Thoughts and the Politics of the Paraliterary* (Hanover, NH: Wesleyan University Press, 1999); Rosalind Krauss, "Poststructuralism and the Paraliterary," *October* 13 (1980): 36-40; and Gerard Genette, *Palimpsests: Literature in the Second Degree* (Reno: University of Nevada Press, 1997).

29. Pierre Bourdieu, *Distinction: A Social Critique of the Judgment of Taste* (London: Routledge, 1984), 499.

30. Armando Petrucci, "Reading to Read: The Future of Reading," in *A History of Reading in the West*, ed. Guglielmo Cavallo and Roger Chartier (Amherst: University of Massachusetts Press, 2003): 345-67.

31. Henry Luce, "The American Century," *Life*, February 17, 1941.

32. Christina Klein, *Cold War Orientalism: Asia in the Middlebrow Imagination, 1945-1961* (Berkeley: University of California Press, 2003), 41.

33. State Department, *Department of State Bulletin* (Washington, DC: Office of Public Communications 1953), 253.

34. For a thorough overview of scholarship in this vein, see Amanda Claybaugh's "Government Is Good," *Minnesota Review* 70: 161-66.

35. Michael Walzer, "On the Role of Symbolism in Political Thought," *Political Science Quarterly* 82, no. 2 (1967): 194.

36. Frances Stonor Saunders, *The Cultural Cold War: The CIA of Arts and Letters* (New York: The New Press, 2000). For recent studies in this vein, see Hugh Wilford, *The Mighty Wurlitzer: How the*

CIA Played America (Cambridge, MA: Harvard University Press, 2009); Greg Barnhisel, *Cold War Modernists* (New York: Columbia University Press, 2014); and Eric Bennett, *Workshops of Empire: Stegner, Engle, and American Creative Writing during the Cold War* (Iowa City: University of Iowa Press, 2015).

37. See Cecilia Konchar Farr and Tom Perrin, "Introduction: Inventing the Middlebrow," *Post45 Peer Reviewed* (July 2016). http://post45.research.yale.edu/2016/07/introduction-inventing-the -middlebrow/.

38. *Globalizing American Studies*, ed. Brian Edwards and Dilip Gaonkar (Chicago: University of Chicago Press, 2010), 14.

39. See Love; Caroline Levine, *Forms: Whole, Rhythm, Hierarchy, Network* (Princeton, NJ: Princeton University Press, 2015); and Dorothy Hale, "Fiction as Restriction: Self-Binding in New Ethical Theories of the Novel," *Narrative* 15 (2007): 187–206.

40. See *Cultures of U.S. Imperialism*, ed. Amy Kaplan and Donald Pease (Durham, NC: Duke University Press, 1993); Donald Pease, *The New American Exceptionalism* (Minneapolis: University of Minnesota Press, 2009); and Donald E. Pease and Winfried Fluck, *Reframing the Transnational Turn in American Studies* (Hanover, NH: Dartmouth University Press, 2011).

CHAPTER 1

1. National Association of Elocutionists, *Proceedings of the National Association of Elocutionists*, vol. 13–14 (New York: National Association of Elocutionists, 1905), 91.

2. Jean-François Revel, "Miss McCarthy Explains," *New York Times*, May 16, 1971.

3. Mary McCarthy, "A Guide to Exiles, Expatriates, and Internal Émigrés," *New York Review of Books*, March 9, 1972.

4. Mary McCarthy, "Language and Politics," *Occasional Prose: Essays* (New York: Harcourt, 1985), 94.

5. See Arthur and Barbara Gelb, "Culture Makes a Hit at the White House," *New York Times*, January 28, 1962.

6. See Margaret Leslie Davis, *Mona Lisa in Camelot: How Jacqueline Kennedy and Da Vinci's Masterpieces Charmed and Captivated a Nation* (New York: Da Capo, 2009).

7. See Tina Chen, *Double Agency: Acts of Impersonation in Asian American Literature and Culture* (Stanford, CA: Stanford University Press, 2005); Lara Langer Cohen, *The Fabrication of American Literature: Fraudulence and Antebellum Print Culture* (Philadelphia: University of Pennsylvania Press, 2012); and Harry Berger, *Situated Utterances: Texts, Bodies, and Cultural Representations* (Bronx, NY: Fordham University Press, 2005).

8. Benjamin Lee, *Talking Heads: Language, Metalanguage, and the Semiotics of Subjectivity* (Durham, NC: Duke University Press, 1997), 12.

9. The phrase *experiments in international living* comes from Helene Cattanes, the administrator of Smith College's inaugural Junior Year Abroad (JYA) program, in 1924. See "*Le voyages forment la jeunesse,*" *Smith Alumni Quarterly*, February 1951.

10. *The New Guide to Study Abroad* (New York: Harper & Row, 1977).

11. John A. Garraty and Walter Adams, *A Guide to Study Abroad* (New York: Harper & Row, 1962), 12.

12. John A. Garraty and Walter Adams, *Is the World Our Campus?* (East Lansing: Michigan State University, 1960).

13. Henry James, "The Question of Our Speech," in *Henry James on Culture: Collected Essays on Politics and the American Social Scene*, ed. Pierre A. Walker (Lincoln: University of Nebraska Press, 1999), 42–57.

14. For an overview of the connection between James and aesthetic autonomy, see Ross Posnock, "Affirming the Alien: The Pragmatist Pluralism of *The American Scene,*" in *The Cambridge Companion to Henry James*, ed. Jonathan Freedman (Cambridge: Cambridge University Press, 1998).

15. Jessica Berman, *Modernist Fiction, Cosmopolitanism, and the Politics of Community* (Cambridge: Cambridge University Press, 2001).

16. Mary McCarthy, "Ideas and the Novel: Henry James and Some Others," *London Review of Books*, April 3, 1980.

17. Henry James, *Letters: 1895-1916*, ed. Leon Edel (Cambridge, MA: Harvard University Press, 1984), 492.

18. James, *Letters*, 352.

19. William Dean Howells and Elizabeth Jordan, *Howells and James: A Double Billing* (New York: New York Public Library, 1958), 35.

20. Elizabeth Long, *Book Clubs: Women and the Uses of Reading in Everyday Life* (Chicago: University of Chicago Press, 2003), 36.

21. Millicent Bell, "Nineteenth-Century Europe (1843-1900)," in *Henry James in Context*, ed. David McWhirter (Cambridge: Cambridge University Press, 2010), 14.

22. James, *Letters*, 492.

23. Henry James, "The Manners of American Women," *Henry James on Culture*, 89.

24. "The Lady and the Hoax," *Chicago Record-Herald*, March 11, 1905.

25. "Henry James in Chicago," *Chicago Daily Tribune*, March 10, 1905.

26. Henry James, *What Maisie Knew* (New York: Penguin, 2009), 122.

27. T. S. Eliot, "The Aims of Education," *To Criticize the Critic and Other Writings* (Lincoln: University of Nebraska Press, 1965), 83.

28. Mary Bennet Poppenheim, *Southern Women at Vassar* (Columbia: University of South Carolina Press, 2002), 165.

29. Tirzah Snell Smith, "Point of Honor," *Smith College Monthly* 8 (1900): 74.

30. H.D., *Hermione* (New York: New Directions, 1981), 58.

31. Mark McGurl, *The Novel Art: Elevations of American Fiction after Henry James* (Princeton, NJ: Princeton University Press, 2001), 2.

32. Florence Brooks, "Henry James in the Serene Sixties," *New York Herald*, October 2, 1904.

33. Christopher Looby, *Voicing America: Language, Literary Form, and the Origin of the United States* (Chicago: University of Chicago Press, 1996), 14.

34. Erving Goffman, "The Lecture," in *Forms of Talk* (Philadelphia: University of Pennsylvania Press, 1981), 163.

35. J. W. Strout, "How to Write in English," *The Editor*, July 1905. Strout's account is corroborated in "Our Speech Untidy, Says Henry James," *New York Times*, June 9, 1905.

36. Mrs. Humphrey Ward, *A Writer's Recollection* (New York: Harper & Brothers, 1918), 336.

37. Gertrude Stein, *Fernhurst* (New York: Liveright, 1971), 3.

38. See Kelley Wagers, "Gertrude Stein's 'Historical' Living," *Journal of Modern Literature* 31 (2008): 22-43; and Anne Raine, "Science, Nature Work, and the Kinaesthetic Body in Cather and Stein," *American Literature* 80 (2008): 799-830.

39. *Chicago Record-Herald*, January 22, 1910.

40. "Editorial Jottings," *Philadelphia Dispatch*, June 8, 1905.

41. "Letters," *New York Times*, June 10, 1905.

42. "Untidy Speech," *New York Times*, June 10, 1905.

43. "A Movement to Reform," *New York Times*, December 16, 1906.

44. National Congress of Parents and Teachers, *Proceedings of the Annual Meeting* (Washington, DC: National Congress of Parents and Teachers, 1908), 165.

45. "Society for the Study of Spoken English," *New York Sun*, November 22, 1906.

46. *The First International Congress for the Welfare of the Child* (Washington, DC: National Congress of Mothers, 1908), 156.

47. "All about Henry James," *New York Times*, June 4, 1907.

48. Eric Hayot, "Against Periodization: or, On Institutional Time," *New Literary History* 42 (2011): 739.

49. Henry James, *Selected Letters* (New York: Doubleday, 1960), 100.

50. Henry James, "Manners of American Women," *Henry James on Culture: Collected Essays on Politics and the American Social Scene*, 82-114.

51. "The Absence of the Musical Voice," *New York Times*, November 1, 1908.

52. "Manners of Our Women," *New York Times*, April 19, 1908.

53. Alfred Emmanuel Smith, *New Outlook* (New York: Outlook Publishing, 1908), 612.

54. "Henry James's First Interview: Noted Critics and Novelist Breaks His Rule of Years to Tell of the Good Work of the American Ambulance Corps," *New York Times*, March 21, 1915.

55. Jean Bethke Elshtain, *Women and War* (Chicago: University of Chicago Press, 1987), 141.

56. Henry James, *The Portrait of a Lady*, ed. William Allan Neilson (New York: P. F. Collier, 1917), iv.

57. William Allan Neilson, *The Inauguration of William Allan Neilson* (Concord, NH: Rumford Press, 1918), 48.

58. See *The American Ethical Union*, vol. 8 (1921) and *Ethical Culture School*, vol. 3 (1922). Although he did not exude the same star power as James or attract the same fanfare, "The Need for Better English" received widespread attention when it was reprinted in Harold Garnet Black's popular self-improvement book *Paths to Success* (1924).

59. Emma Hart Willard, "Journals and Letters, from France and Great Britain," in *Telling Travels: Selected Writings by Nineteenth Century American Women Abroad*, ed. Maria Suzanne Schriber (DeKalb: Northern Illinois University Press, 1995), 24.

60. See Alice Kaplan, *Dreaming in French: The Paris Years of Jacqueline Bouvier Kennedy, Susan Sontag, and Angela Davis* (Chicago: University of Chicago Press, 2012); and Whitney Walton, *Internationalism, National Identities, and Study Abroad: France and the United States, 1890-1970* (Stanford, CA: Stanford University Press, 2009).

61. William Allan Neilson to Mr. Rhodes S. Baker (Dallas, TX, March 28, 1925), Smith College Archives (SC), box 49, folder 3.

62. Sally Goodell to William Allan Neilson (Northampton, MA, February 28, 1928), SC, box 49, folder 5.

63. Hubert Herring, *Neilson of Smith* (Brattleboro, VT: Stephen Daye Press, 1939), 64.

64. Henry James, *The Portrait of a Lady* (Oxford: Oxford University Press, 2009), 292.

65. Cattanes, *Le voyages forment la jeunesse*.

66. Elizabeth Murphy, "Ten Years Ago the Juniors Went to France," SC, box 49, folder 12.

67. Hilda Donahue to Mr. David A. Robertson (Northampton, MA, February 4, 1927), SC, box 49, folder 5.

68. Alice Ross Colver, *Adventure for a Song: Sheila's Junior Year Abroad* (New York: Dodd Mead, 1938), iv.

69. Norman Mailer, "The Mary McCarthy Case," *New York Review of Books*, October 17, 1963.

70. Mary McCarthy, "The Vassar Girl," *Holiday*, May 1951.

71. Mary McCarthy and Hannah Arendt, *Between Friends: The Correspondence of Hannah Arendt and Mary McCarthy*, ed. Carol Brighten (London: Secker and Warburg, 1966), 174; McCarthy, "Ideas and the Novel."

72. Slava Gerovitch, *From Newspeak to Cyberspeak: A History of Soviet Cybernetic* (Cambridge, MA: MIT Press, 2002).

73. Charles Frankel, "The Role of Government," *Diversity and Interdependence through International Education* (Washington, DC: Board of Foreign Scholarships, 1967), 35.

74. Talcott Parsons, "Certain Primary Sources and Patterns of Aggression in the Social Structure of the Western World," *Psychiatry: Interpersonal and Biological Processes* 10 (1947): 171.

75. John Arthur Garraty and Walter Adams, *From Main Street to Left Bank: Students and Scholars Abroad* (East Lansing: Michigan State University Press, 1959), 194.

76. *Esquire* 2 (1961), 59.

77. Bernard Lahire, *The Plural Actor* (New York: Polity Press, 2011).

78. Helen Vendler, "Mary McCarthy Again Her Own Heroine—Frozen Foods as New Villain," *New York Times*, May 16, 1971.

79. Hilton Kramer, "Mary McCarthy's Valentine to Fanny Farmer," *Chicago Tribune*, May 23, 1971; Dale McConathy, "All Mom and Frozen Apple Pie: Mary McCarthy's Latest," *Vogue*, July 1971.

80. *The Sopranos*, Home Box Office, season 4, episode 2.

81. Anthony Giddens and Christopher Pierson, *Conversations with Anthony Giddens: Making Sense of Modernity* (New York: Wiley, 1998), 90.

CHAPTER 2

1. Sylvia Plath, *The Unabridged Journals of Sylvia Plath*, ed. Karen V. Kukil (New York: Anchor Books, 2000), 313.

2. Robert Spiller, "American Studies Abroad: Culture and Foreign Policy," *The Annals of the American Academy of Political Science* 366 (1966): 1.

3. Ted Hughes, *Birthday Letters* (New York: Faber & Faber, 1998).

4. Lytle Shaw, *Fieldworks: From Place to Site in Postwar Poetics* (Tuscaloosa: University of Alabama Press, 2013), 4.

5. An excellent overview of this tendency in sociolinguistic scholarship is provided in the introduction to James Wilce's *Language and Emotion* (Cambridge: Cambridge University Press, 2009).

6. The New Critical antipathy to feeling is best observed in the work of T. S. Eliot and Cleanth Brooks. More recent work in affect theory and literary ethics includes the writings of Ruth Leys, Dorothy Hale, Blakey Vermeule, and Rita Felski.

7. Raymond Williams, *Marxism and Literature* (Oxford: Oxford University Press, 1977), 132.

8. Arlie Hochschild, *The Managed Heart: Commercialization of Human Feeling* (Berkeley: University of California Press, 1983).

9. Wilce, *Language and Emotion*, 8.

10. Sylvia Plath, *Letters Home: Correspondence, 1950–1963* (New York: Harper Collins, 1992), 283.

11. William J. Fulbright, *Freedom and Union*, vol. 4–5 (1948).

12. For an excellent history of the Fulbright's political and economic foundation, see Sam Lebovic, "From War Junk to Educational Exchange: The World War II Origins of the Fulbright Program and the Foundations of American Cultural Globalism," *Diplomatic History* 37 (2013): 280–312.

13. Walter Johnson and Francis J. Colligan, *The Fulbright Program: A History* (Chicago: University of Chicago Press, 1965), 17.

14. Richard T. Arndt and David Lee Rubin, *The Fulbright Difference* (Washington, DC: Transaction, 1996), 30, 43, 49–51, 54, 84, 91, 105, 119, 124–29, 148–50, 193, 213, 231, 240, 259, 272–75, 324, 407, 422, 435, 447. Arthur Power and Russell Rowe Dynes, *The Fulbright Experience* (New Brunswick, NJ: Rutgers University Press, 1987), 21, 26, 69, 73, 76, 150, 212, 298.

15. See Leonard Cassuto's *Hard Boiled Sentimentality: The Secret History of American Crime Stories* (New York: Columbia University Press, 2009); Shameem Black's *Fiction across Borders: Imagining the Lives of Others in Late-Twentieth-Century Novels* (New York: Columbia University Press, 2010).

16. Lauren Berlant, "A Properly Political Concept of Love," *Cultural Anthropology* 26 (2011): 676.

17. Donald E. Pease and Winfried Fluck, *Reframing the Transnational Turn in American Studies* (Hanover, NH: Dartmouth College Press, 2011), 30.

18. Dana Nelson, "Consternation," in *The Future of American Studies* (Durham, NC: Duke University Press, 2002), 579.

19. Dana Heller, "*Salesman* in Moscow," *The Future of American Studies*, 189.

20. Gene Wise, "Paradigm Dramas in American Studies," in *Locating American Studies*, ed. Lucy Maddox (Baltimore: Johns Hopkins University Press, 1999), 179.

21. Russell Nye, "Robert E. Spiller and the ASA," *American Quarterly* 19 (1967): 291-92.

22. Sigmund Skard, "Robert E. Spiller: Bridge Builder and Image Maker," *American Quarterly* 19 (1967): 299.

23. Louis D. Rubin, "Spiller of 'Spiller et al.,'" *American Quarterly* 19 (1967): 302.

24. Malcolm Cowley, "U.S. Books Abroad," *Life*, September 16, 1946.

25. John Guillory, *Cultural Capital* (Chicago: University of Chicago Press, 1993).

26. Christina Klein, *Cold War Orientalism: Asia in the Middlebrow Imagination, 1945-1961* (Berkeley: University of Berkeley Press, 2003).

27. I take this definition of middlebrow reading from Janice Radaway's *A Feeling for Books: The Book-of-the-Month Cub, Literary Taste, and Middle-Class Desire* (Chapel Hill: University of North Carolina Press, 1997).

28. See George J. Stein, "Information Warfare—Words Matter," in *InfoWar*, ed. Gerfried Stocker and Christine Schöpf (New York: Springer, 1998), 51-59. In this sense, the ASA's work with communications parallels Wilbur Schramm's more diligently researched consideration of the relationship between communication and affect.

29. Power and Dynes, *The Fulbright Experience*, 19.

30. Alfred Kazin, "The Function of Criticism Today," in *Modern Criticism*, ed. Walter Sutton and Richard Foster (New York: Western Publishing, 1963), 336.

31. Stanley Cavell, *Philosophy the Day after Tomorrow* (New York: Belknap Press, 2006), 173.

32. F. O. Matthiessen, "The Responsibilities of the Critic," in *The Responsibilities of the Critic: Essays and Reviews by F. O. Matthiessen* (New York: Oxford University Press, 1952), 13.

33. Alfred Kazin, *Alfred Kazin's Journals*, ed. Richard M. Cook (New Haven, CT: Yale University Press, 2011), 81.

34. Irving Howe, "The Sentimental Fellow-Travelling of F. O. Matthiessen," *Partisan Review* 15 (1948): 1127.

35. For an extensive discussion of Matthiessen's political posturing relative to the conservative and radical thinkers of his time, see William E. Cain, *F. O. Matthiessen and the Politics of Criticism* (Madison: University of Wisconsin Press, 1988).

36. F. O. Matthiessen, *American Renaissance: Art and Expression in the Age of Emerson and Whitman* (New York: Oxford University Press, 1941), 524-26.

37. Walt Whitman, *Democratic Vistas* (London: W. J. Gage, 1888), 26.

38. Alfred Kazin, *A Lifetime Burning in Every Moment* (New York: Harper Collins, 1996), 85.

39. Few critics today read *From the Heart of Europe*. Those who do, most notably Arthur Redding and Donald Pease, have linked Matthiessen's canon-building exercises to the biographical fact of his queerness, which I want to resist here. See Arthur Redding, "Closet, Coup, and Cold War: F. O. Matthiessen's *From the Heart of Europe*," *boundary 2* 33 (2006): 171-201.

40. Frank J. Lewand, "*From the Heart of Europe* (Book Review)," *Annals of the American Academy of Political and Social Science* (1948): 183.

41. John K. Hutchens, "Books and Things," *New York Herald Tribune*, September 9, 1948.

42. See Jo Gill, *The Cambridge Introduction to Sylvia Plath* (Cambridge: Cambridge University Press, 2008), 20; and Laura Frost, *Sex Drives: Fantasies of Fascism in Literary Modernism* (Ithaca, NY: Cornell University Press, 2002).

43. In one of the only comprehensive historical studies of sadomasochism, Romana Byrne tracks how, over the course of the twentieth century, "sadomasochism would evolve from a means of articulating social critique to a more inward-pointing query." See *Aesthetic Sexuality: A Literary History of Sadomasochism* (New York: Bloomsbury, 2013), 73. For the literary theorization of sadomasochism, see Lynda Hart, *Between the Body and the Flesh* (New York: Columbia University Press,

1998) and Elizabeth Freeman, *Time Binds: Queer Temporalities, Queer Histories* (Durham, NC: Duke University Press, 2010).

44. "Misfortunes with Iko" most likely refers to a night Plath spent with Isaac Meshoulem (Iko) and confessed to him her affair with Richard Sassoon, American cousin of poet Siegfried Sassoon; St. Botolph's night references the February 25, 1956, launch party for the Cambridge journal *Saint Botolph Review*. This is the party where Plath met Hughes, the party she would later memorialize in "Stone Boy with Dolphin."

45. David Buck, Mallory (Joseph Mallory Wober), Iko (Isaac Meshoulem), Hamish (David Hamish Stewart), Ted (Hughes), Tony Gray, and M. Boddy were all men whom Plath dated at Cambridge.

46. Christopher Isherwood's character Sally Bowles of his 1937 novella *Sally Bowles* is known for her social crudity, or "not caring a curse what people thought of her."

47. Krook is Dr. Dorothea Greenberg Krook, Plath's Fulbright supervisor in 1954–55.

48. See *Cold War Constructions: The Political Culture of U.S. Imperialism*, ed. Christian G. Appy (Amherst: University of Massachusetts Press, 2000).

49. Oxford English Dictionary, "Publicity," *Oxford English Dictionary* (Oxford: Oxford University Press, 2015).

50. Edward Shils, *The Torment of Secrecy* (New York: Free Press, 1956), 226.

51. There are, of course, echoes here of Jürgen Habermas's notion of "communicative rationality." See "Communicative Rationality and Theories of Meaning and Action," in *On the Pragmatics of Communication*, ed. Maeve Cook (New York: Wiley, 2014).

52. Sylvia Plath, "Stone Boy with Dolphin," in *Johnny Panic and the Bible of Dreams* (London: Faber and Faber, 1977).

53. Johnson and Colligan, *The Fulbright Program*, 126.

54. Herbert Nicholas, "The Education of an Americanist," *Journal of American Studies* 14 (1980): 24.

55. Johnson and Colligan, *The Fulbright Program*, 130.

56. Eileen Gillooly, *Smile of Discontent: Humor, Gender, and Nineteenth Century British Fiction* (Chicago: University of Chicago Press, 1999).

57. John Ashbery and James Schuyler, *A Nest of Ninnies* (New York: Dalkey Archive Press, 1969), 116.

58. James Schuyler, *Just the Thing: Selected Letters of James Schuyler, 1951–1991* (New York: Turtle Point Press, 2004), 137.

59. Ben Lerner, *Leaving the Atocha Station* (Minneapolis, MN: Coffee House Press, 2011), 181.

CHAPTER 3

1. Gregory Corso, "The American Way," in *Elegiac Feelings American* (New York: New Directions, 1961), 73.

2. F. Scott Fitzgerald, *Tender Is the Night* (New York: Scribner, 2003), 231.

3. F. Scott Fitzgerald, *The Crack-Up*, ed. Edmund Wilson (New York: Scribner, 1945), 218.

4. Erving Goffman, "On the Characteristics of Total Institutions," in *Asylums: Essays on the Social Situations of Mental Patients and Other Inmates* (Chicago: Aldine, 1961), 6–7.

5. Ibid., 63.

6. Michel Foucault, *"Society Must Be Defended": Lectures at the Collège de France, 1975–1976*, trans. David Macey (New York: Picador, 2003), 46.

7. Henry Miller, *The Tropic of Cancer* (New York: Grove, 1961), 48.

8. Ibid., 16, 17, 67, 70, 310–12.

9. Corso, "The American Way," 69.

10. For examples of the counterculture's alleged resistance to mass culture, see James Campbell, *This Is the Beat Generation: New York, San Francisco, Paris* (Berkeley: University of California Press,

1999); Ann Charter, "Introduction," in *The Portable Beat Reader* (New York: Penguin Books, 1992); and Thomas Frank, *The Conquest of Cool: Business Culture, Counterculture, and the Rise of Hip Consumerism* (Chicago: University of Chicago Press, 1998).

11. Michael Clune, *American Fiction and the Free Market: 1945–2000* (New York: Cambridge University Press, 2010), 89.

12. Francis J. Colligan, *Americans Abroad* (Washington, DC: US Department of State, 1956), 3.

13. Huntington Smith, "Tourists Who Act Like Pigs," *Saturday Evening Post*, May 22, 1954.

14. Grace S. Yaukey, "Responsible International Behavior," *Washington Post*, October, 8, 1946.

15. John M. Morahan, "Tourists' Spending Outstrips Point 4 Aid: 'Point 5' Plan, More Travel Abroad, Urged," *New York Herald Tribune*, March 11, 1956.

16. Dean MacCannell, *The Tourist: A Theory of the Leisure Class* (Berkeley: University of California Press, 1976).

17. Ibid., 40.

18. "Beatniks Lose in Europe," *Christian Science Monitor*, August 23, 1966; "Glamorous Coastline," *New York Herald Tribune*, March 4, 1962; "Paris Splits Hairs over Beatniks," *Globe and Mail*, May 7, 1966; and "End of an Era," *Baltimore Sun*, December 31, 1959.

19. William Burroughs, *Naked Lunch* (New York: Grove, 2009), 182.

20. Roger Warner, "Advertising Travelers Checks," *Bankers Magazine* 103 (1921): 673.

21. Quoted in Webb B. Garrison and Ray Abel, *Why Didn't I Think of That? From Alarm Clocks to Zippers* (New York: Random House, 1979), 98.

22. Warner, "Advertising Travelers Checks," 673.

23. Ibid., 676.

24. William S. Burroughs and Allen Ginsberg, *The Yage Letters Redux* (San Francisco: City Light Books, 2006), 37.

25. Ralph Reed, *American Express, Its Origin and Growth* (New York: Newcomen Society in North America, 1952), 11.

26. Elaine Tyler May, *Homeward Bound: American Families in the Cold War* (New York: Basic Books, 1988).

27. Bruce McConachie, *American Theater in the Culture of the Cold War: Producing and Contesting Containment* (Iowa City: University of Iowa Press, 2003), 126.

28. Reed, *American Express, Its Origin and Growth*, 21.

29. Michael Warner and Lauren Berlant, "Sex in Public," *Critical Inquiry* 24 (1998): 550.

30. Jack Halberstam, *In a Queer Time and Place: Transgender Bodies, Subculture Lives* (New York: New York University Press, 2005), 5.

31. For a more detailed discussion of gender and space in midcentury tourism, see Christopher Endy, *Cold War Holidays: American Tourism in France* (Chapel Hill: University of North Carolina Press, 2004).

32. James Baldwin, *Giovanni's Room* (New York: Delta, 2000).

33. See Valerie Rohy, "Displacing Desire: Passing, Nostalgia, and *Giovanni's Room*," in *Passing and Fictions of Identity*, ed. Elaine K. Ginsberg (Durham, NC: Duke University Press, 1996).

34. Jack Kerouac and Allen Ginsberg, *Jack Kerouac and Allen Ginsberg: The Letters*, ed. Bill Morgan and David Stanford (New York: Viking Penguin, 2010).

35. Allen Ginsberg, *The Letters of Allen Ginsberg*, ed. Bill Morgan (Philadelphia: Da Capo, 2008), 146.

36. Gregory Corso, *Accidental Autobiography: Selected Letters* (New York: New Directions, 2003), 20.

37. Ibid., 21.

38. Ibid., 22.

39. Ibid., 294.

40. For theories of the coterie based on kinship and family structures, see Lytle Shaw, *Frank O'Hara: The Poetics of Coterie* (Iowa City: University of Iowa Press, 2006).

41. Penelope Moffet, "Poet Gregory Corso: Beat Goes on for Survivor of '50s," *Los Angeles Times*, February 20, 1985.

42. Loren Glass, *Counterculture Colophon: Grove Press, the Evergreen Review, and the Incorporation of the Avant-Garde* (Stanford, CA: Stanford University Press, 2013).

43. Gregory Corso, *The American Express* (Paris: Olympia Press, 1961), 3.

44. Corso, *Accidental Autobiography*, 260.

45. William Burroughs, "The Cut Up Method," in *The Moderns: An Anthology of New Writing in America*, ed. Leroi Jones (New York: Corinth Books, 1963).

46. For an overview of this critical response, see Michael Davidson, *Guys like Us: Citing Masculinity in Cold War Politics* (Chicago: University of Chicago Press, 2004).

47. Ginsberg, *The Letters of Allen Ginsberg*, 250.

48. Art Buchwald, "So This Is Literature?" *Palm Beach Post*, May 7, 1961.

49. Thomas Frank, *The Conquest of Cool: Business Culture, Counterculture, and the Rise of Hip Consumerism* (Chicago: University of Chicago Press, 1997).

50. Owen Edwards, "In Athens, Greeks Don't Have a Word for Beats," *Nevada Daily Mail*, March 19, 1967.

51. Corso, *Accidental Autobiography*, 286.

52. Erica Jong, *Conversations with Erica Jong* (Jackson: University Press of Mississippi, 2002), 34.

53. Erica Jong, *Fear of Flying* (New York: Signet, 1973), xii.

54. Paul Theroux, "Hapless Organ," *New Statesman*, April 19, 1974.

55. John Updike, "Jong Love," in *Picked-Up Pieces: Essays* (New York: Random House, 2012), 395.

56. Rita Felski, *Beyond Feminist Aesthetics* (Cambridge, MA: Harvard University Press, 1989), 14.

57. Lauren Berlant, "The Female Complaint," *Social Text* 19 (1988): 237.

58. Erica Jong, *The Devil at Large* (New York: Random House, 1993), 91.

59. Maria Farland, "Sex Oppression, Systems of Property, and 1970s Women's Liberation Fiction," *Yale Journal of Criticism* 18 (2005): 385.

60. Larry McCaffery, "The Artists of Hell," in *Breaking the Sequence: Women's Experimental Fiction*, ed. Ellen G. Friedman and Miriam Fuchs (Princeton, NJ: Princeton University Press, 1994), 217.

61. Jong, *Conversations with Erica Jong*, 46.

62. Jennifer Wicke, "Celebrity Material: Materialism Feminism and the Culture of Celebrity," *South Atlantic Quarterly* 93 (1994).

63. Ira Galtman, American Express Corporate Archivist, e-mail to author, August 29, 2014.

64. "T&L Editor-in-Chief Nancy Novogrod Adjusts for War," *Media Industry Newsletter* 54 (September 2001).

65. Erica Jong, "My Italy," *Travel and Leisure* 61 (September 1996).

66. Diana G. Lasseter, "New Jersey's Most Powerful Network," *Business News*, February 21, 1996.

67. Erica Jong, *Parachutes and Kisses* (New York: Penguin, 1984), 90.

68. Quoted in Joan Schnekar, *The Talented Miss Highsmith: The Secret Life and Serious Art of Patricia Highsmith* (New York: St. Martin's, 2009), 448.

69. Graham Greene, "Foreword," in *The Selected Stories of Patricia Highsmith* (New York: Norton, 2001), x.

CHAPTER 4

1. Ernest Hemingway, "Homage to Switzerland," in *The Complete Short Stories of Ernest Hemingway* (New York: Simon & Schuster, 2007), 329.

2. Flannery O'Connor, *The Habit of Being*, ed. Sally Fitzgerald (New York: Farrar, Straus, and Giroux, 1979), 164.

3. Janice Carlisle, *Common Scents: Comparative Encounters in High Victorian Fiction* (New York: Oxford University Press, 2004), 3.

4. Frank Sibley, *Approach to Aesthetics*, ed. John Benson, Betty Redfern, and Jeremy Roxbee Cox (Oxford: Clarendon Press, 2001), 248.

5. The *National Geographic* Collector's Corner reveals that many subscribers have made it a habit of smelling the magazine. While some complained about the mustiness of the smell, others reveled in it. "I have come across a very nice collection of Nat Geo Magazines," wrote one collector. "They are all very yellow, very rich looking. They smell nice. They smell wonderful." Derek Buentello, "Wish to Sell," http://ngscollectors.ning.com/profile/DerekBuentello, September 10, 2013.

6. A Google n-gram of the two terms shows a tenfold increase in the use of both terms after 1937. *Library Journal* 74 (1949).

7. Otis W. Caldwell, "Why the Society for Visual Education?" *Visual Education*, vol. 1–2 (Chicago: Society for Visual Education, 1919).

8. *Communication and the Communication Arts*, ed. Francis Shoemaker (New York: Columbia Teachers College, 1955).

9. *The Princeton University Library Chronicle*, vol. 20 (Princeton, NJ: Princeton University, 1958), 5.

10. John Ball and Frances Bynes, *Research, Principles, and Practices in Visual Communication* (Greenwich, CT: IAP, 1960), 107.

11. Roland Barthes, *Camera Lucida* (New York: Hill & Wang, 1960); and Susan Sontag, *On Photography* (New York: Farrar, Straus, and Giroux, 1977).

12. See Sara Blair, *Harlem Crossroads: Black Writers and the Photograph in the Twentieth Century* (Princeton, NJ: Princeton University Press, 2007); and Sara Blair and Eric M. Rosenberg, *Trauma and Documentary Photography of the FSA* (Berkeley: University of California Press, 2012).

13. O'Connor, *The Habit of Being*, 532.

14. Ibid., 534.

15. See Barthes, *Camera Lucida*; and Walter Benn Michaels, *The Beauty of a Social Problem: Photography, Autonomy, Economy* (Chicago: University of Chicago Press, 2015).

16. Pierre Bourdieu, *Photography: A Middlebrow Art* (Stanford, CA: Stanford University Press, 1990), 75.

17. See Michael North, *Camera Works: Photography and the Twentieth Century Word* (New York: Oxford University Press, 2005); and W. J. T. Mitchell, *What Do Pictures Want? The Lives and Loves of Images* (Chicago: University of Chicago Press, 2013).

18. Elizabeth Bishop, "In the Waiting Room," in *The Complete Poems, 1927–1979* (New York: Farrar, Straus, and Giroux, 1983).

19. This is assuming that no quantitative tools are used in the analysis.

20. See Lawrence Rainey, *Institutions of Modernism* (New Haven, CT: Yale University Press, 1998); and Donal Harris, *On Company Time: American Modernism and the Big Magazines* (New York: Columbia University Press, 2016).

21. Marianne Moore, *Selected Letters* (New York: Penguin, 1997), 143.

22. Elizabeth Bishop and Robert Lowell, *Words in Air: The Complete Correspondences between Elizabeth Bishop and Robert Lowell*, ed. Thomas Travisano with Saskia Hamilton (New York: Farrar, Straus, and Giroux, 2008), 630.

23. John Oliver LaGorce, *The Story of the Geographic* (Washington, DC: National Geographic Society, 1915), 3.

24. Walter Ong, *Orality and Literacy* (New York: Routledge, 2015), 7.

25. Quoted in Stephanie L. Hawkins, *American Iconographic: National Geographic, Global Culture, and the Visual Imagination* (Charlottesville: University of Virginia Press, 2010), 14.

26. Quoted in Linda Steet, *Veils and Daggers: A Century of National Geographic's Representation of the Arab World* (Philadelphia: Temple University Press, 2000), 19.

27. "Editor's Foreword," *National Geographic Magazine* 68 (1935): 107.

28. Quoted in Tamar Y. Rosenberg, *Presenting America's World: Strategies of Innocence in National Geographic* (Aldershot, UK: Ashgate, 2007), 169.

29. Robert Poole, *Explorers House: National Geographic and the World It Made* (New York: Penguin, 2006), 185.

30. Gilbert Grosvenor, *National Geographic Society and Its Magazine* (Washington, DC: National Geographic Society, 1957), 24.

31. Quoted in Jonathan Nashel, *Edward Lansdale's Cold War* (Amherst: University of Massachusetts Press, 2005), 140.

32. Quoted in ibid., 141.

33. For an excellent history of the R&A, see Trevor J. Barnes, "Geographic Intelligence: American Geographers and Research and Analysis in the Office of Strategic Services, 1941-45," *Journal of Historical Geography* 32 (2006).

34. "Intelligence Photographic Documentation Project: Memorandum for Field Teams" (undated), box 4, folder 10, National Archive and Record Administration (NARA).

35. *Secret Reports on Nazi Germany: The Frankfurt School Contribution to the War Effort*, ed. Raffaele Laudani (Princeton, NJ: Princeton University Press, 2013), 199.

36. Richard Hartshorne, "Draft of Proposed Guide to Preparation of Political Reports" (undated), box 5, folder 3, NARA.

37. *Secret Reports*, 7.

38. Robin Winks, "Getting the Right Stuff: FDR, Donovan, and the Quest for Professional Intelligence," in *The Secrets War: The Office of Strategic Services in World War II* (Washington, DC: NARA, 1992), 26.

39. Lt. Col. Ilia Tolstoy, "Across Tibet from India to China," *National Geographic* 90 (1946).

40. Joseph Heller, *Conversations with Joseph Heller*, ed. Adam J. Sorkin (Jackson: University of Mississippi Press, 1993), 120.

41. Joseph Heller, *Catch-22* (New York: Simon & Schuster, 1999), 18; Kurt Vonnegut, *Slaughterhouse-Five* (New York: Random House, 1991), 2.

42. Beverley Bowie, *Operation Bughouse* (New York: Dodd, Mead, 1947), 2.

43. Jerome D. Ross, "Dizzy Doings in the Bewildered Balkans," *New York Herald Tribune*, September 21, 1947.

44. Orval Hopkins, "The Magazine Rack," *Washington Post*, October 22, 1950.

45. John Godfrey Morris, *Get the Picture: A Personal History of Photojournalism* (Chicago: University of Chicago Press, 2002), 283.

46. Ibid., 124.

47. Mark Collins Jenkins, *National Geographic 125 Years: Legendary Photographs, Adventures, and Discoveries That Changed the World* (Washington, DC: National Geographic Books, 2012), 185.

48. C. D. B. Bryan, *National Geographic Society: 100 Years of Adventure and Discovery* (Washington, DC: National Geographic Society, 1997), 294.

49. Catherine Lutz and Jane Collins, *Reading National Geographic* (Chicago: University of Chicago Press, 1993), 142.

50. Quoted in ibid., 142.

51. Walter Abish, *Alphabetical Africa* (New York: New Directions, 1974), 53.

52. Maynard Owen Williams, "Adventures with a Camera," *National Geographic* 40 (1921): 87.

53. O'Connor, *The Habit of Being*, 273.

54. Ibid., 283.

55. Flannery O'Connor, *The Violent Bear It Away* (New York: Farrar, Straus, and Giroux, 1960), 15.

56. Ibid., 29.

57. Flannery O'Connor, "Living with a Peacock," in *Mystery and Manners: Occasional Prose* (New York: Farrar, Straus, and Giroux, 1969), 3.

58. *"Holiday* Is Here," *Tide,* October 15, 1945.

59. O'Connor, *The Habit of Being,* 408.

60. Ibid., 411.

61. Ibid., 433.

62. *Ten Years of Holiday* (New York: Simon & Schuster, 1956), viii.

63. O'Connor, *The Habit of Being,* 165.

64. Flannery O'Connor, "The Displaced Person," in *The Complete Stories* (New York: Farrar, Straus, and Giroux, 1971), 194.

65. O'Connor, *The Habit of Being,* 118.

66. Ibid., 157.

67. *The Correspondence of Flannery O'Connor and the Brainard Cheneys,* ed. C. Ralph Stephens (Jackson: University Press of Mississippi, 1986), 53.

68. O'Connor, *The Habit of Being,* 206.

CHAPTER 5

1. Dwight D. Eisenhower, "Remarks to the Staff of the U.S. Embassy and the American Community in New Delhi," in *Public Papers of the Presidents of the United States* (Washington, DC: National Archives and Records Service, 1959), 835.

2. William Faulkner, "Undergraduate Writing Class, Tape 2," in *Faulkner at Virginia* (Charlottesville: Rectors and Visitors of the University of Virginia, 2010).

3. "Circular Letter" (September 15, 1956), Papers of William Faulkner, People-to-People Program (PPP), accession #7258-l, Special Collections Department, University of Virginia Library, Charlottesville, VA.

4. Joseph Blotner, "William Faulkner. Committee Chairperson (An Excerpt, Part I)" (1969), PPP.

5. Joseph Blotner, "William Faulkner. Committee Chairperson (An Excerpt, Part II)" (1969), PPP.

6. "Circular Letter," PPP.

7. E. B. White to William Faulkner (October 5, 1956), PPP.

8. Conrad Aiken to William Faulkner (October 3, 1956), PPP.

9. Shelby Foote to William Faulkner (October 6, 1956), PPP.

10. Committee on Armed Services, "Military Cold War Education and Speech Review Policies" (Washington, DC: United States Congress, 1962), 3148.

11. Jonathan Turner, *The Institutional Order* (New York: Longman, 1995).

12. Max Weber, "Bureaucracy," in *From Max Weber: Essays in Sociology* (New York: Routledge, 1948).

13. Katherine Anne Porter to William Faulkner (September 26, 1956), PPP.

14. Lionel Trilling to Harvey Breit (October 8, 1956), PPP.

15. Robert Lowell to William Faulkner (September 25, 1956), PPP.

16. Donald Hall to William Faulkner (October 2, 1956), PPP.

17. John Dos Passos to William Faulkner (October 9, 1956), PPP.

18. Allen Tate to William Faulkner (October 6, 1956), PPP.

19. "Undergraduate Writing Class, Tape 2," in *Faulkner at Virginia.*

20. Lisa Gitelman, *Paper Knowledge: Toward a Media History of Documents* (Durham, NC: Duke University Press, 2014), 24.

21. "Circular Letter," PPP.

22. Blotner, "William Faulkner. Committee Chairperson (An Excerpt, Part I)," PPP.

23. Marianne Moore to William Faulkner (October 11, 1956), PPP.

24. John Berryman to William Faulkner (November 26, 1956), PPP.

25. Donald Hall to William Faulkner (November 21, 1956), PPP.

26. Thorstein Veblen, *Absentee Ownership: Business Enterprise in Recent Times: The Case of America* (Piscataway, NJ: Transaction, 1923), 142.

27. William Faulkner, *The Town* (New York: Vintage Books, 2011), 296.

28. See Anna C. Hunter, "Snopes Again Corrupt Morals of Small Southern Community," *Savannah Morning News*, April 28, 1957; Margot Jackson, "Family Seeks Power and a Town Changes," *Akron Beacon Journal*, May 5, 1957; and Robert Johnson, "Faulkner's Revolting Snopeses in New Novel," *St. Paul Sunday Pioneer Press*, April 28, 1957.

29. Joseph Blotner, *Faulkner: A Biography* (Jackson: University Press of Mississippi, 1974), 619.

30. "Report of Writer's Committee" (November 1956), PPP.

31. John Steinbeck to William Faulkner (January 11, 1957), PPP.

32. Thornton Wilder to William Faulkner (January 4, 1957), PPP.

33. Saul Bellow, "Alone in Mixed Company," *Boston Globe*, May 19, 1996.

34. Blotner, "William Faulkner. Committee Chairperson (An Excerpt, Part I)," PPP.

35. William Faulkner, *Requiem for a Nun* (New York: Vintage Books, 2011), 39.

36. Blotner, *Faulkner: A Biography*, 643.

37. Joseph Blotner, "William Faulkner. Committee Chairperson (An Excerpt, Part II)" (1969), PPP.

38. William Faulkner, "A Word to Young Writers" (April 24, 1958), in *Faulkner at Virginia* (Charlottesville: Rectors and Visitors of the University of Virginia, 2010).

39. Robert Penn Warren to William Faulkner (October 19, 1956), PPP.

40. "Report of Writer's Committee," PPP.

41. Wilder to Faulkner, PPP.

42. Robert Van Gelder, "Interview with a Best-Selling Author: Thornton Wilder," *Cosmopolitan* 124 (April 1948): 122.

43. Horst Frenz, "The Reception of Thornton Wilder's Plays in German," *Modern Drama* 3 (1960): 125.

44. Frenz, 127.

45. Bob McCoy, "Thornton Wilder in Our Town," *San Juan Star*, January 2, 1974.

46. Thornton Wilder, *Our Town* (New York: Perennial Classics, 1998), 15.

47. Donald Haberman, *The Plays of Thornton Wilder* (Middletown, CT: Wesleyan University Press, 1967), 103.

48. Art Buchwald, "Accept Crisis and Enjoy It, Advises Famed Author," in *Conversations with Thornton Wilder* (Jackson: University of Mississippi Press, 1992), 82.

49. Stephen E. Ambrose, *Eisenhower: Soldier and President* (New York: Simon & Schuster, 1990), 70.

50. "Review of *Our Town*," *Die Welt*, December 18, 1947.

51. *Die Welt*.

52. Wilder to Faulkner, PPP.

53. Ibid.

54. "Undergraduate Writing Class, Tape 2," in *Faulkner at Virginia*.

55. "A Word to Young Writers," in *Faulkner at Virginia*.

56. Saul Bellow, *Letters*, ed. Benjamin Taylor (New York: Penguin, 2009), 248.

57. Nina Steers, "Successor to Faulkner?" *Show*, September 1964.

58. James Atlas, *Bellow: A Biography* (New York: Modern Library Paperbacks, 2000), 248.

59. *Letters*, 163.

60. Saul Bellow to William Faulkner (January 7, 1957), PPP.

61. Saul Bellow, *Herzog* (New York: Penguin, 2003), 176.

62. *Letters*, 165.

63. *Letters*, 396.

64. *Letters*, 178.

65. Saul Bellow, *Henderson the Rain King* (New York: Penguin, 1996), 7.

66. Toni Morrison, *Playing in the Dark: Whiteness and the Literary Imagination* (Cambridge, MA: Harvard University Press, 1992).

67. Laurence Leamer, *The Kennedy Men, 1901–1963* (New York: Harper Collins, 2002), 337.

68. Frances Kelly, "Henderson the Rain King," *Review* 1 (1965).

69. Senate Committee on Appropriations, "Foreign Assistance and Related Agencies Appropriations for 1964" (Washington, DC: United States Congress, 1964), 541.

70. Dennis L. Carlson, *Volunteers of America* (Rotterdam: Sense, 2010), 88.

CHAPTER 6

1. John A. Williams to Harry Sions (August 4, 1966), box 1, folder 12, Papers of John A. Williams (JW), Rare Books, Special Collections, and Preservation, University of Rochester.

2. Eve Sedgwick, *Novel Gazing: Queer Readings in Fiction* (Durham, NC: Duke University Press, 1997), 5.

3. John A. Williams, *The Man Who Cried I Am* (New York: Little, Brown, 1967), 371.

4. Richard Wright, "Franco-American Fellowship: First Meeting Minutes," Richard Wright Papers (RW), box 115, folder 1834, Yale Collection of American Literature, Beinecke Rare Book and Manuscript Library.

5. John A. Williams, "We Regret to Inform You That . . ." *Nugget*, December 1962.

6. John A. Williams, *The Most Native of Sons: A Biography of Richard Wright* (New York: Doubleday, 1970), 93.

7. Patrick O'Donnell, *Latent Destinies: Cultural Paranoia and Contemporary U. S. Narrative* (Durham, NC: Duke University Press, 2000), viii.

8. *Bay State Banner*, September 25, 1969.

9. Rita Felski, *The Limits of Critique* (Chicago: University of Chicago Press, 2015), 34.

10. "We Regret to Inform You That . . ."

11. "Memorandum from Haussermann, Davison & Shattuck" (January 31, 1967), box 1, folder 9, JW.

12. Chester Himes and John A. Williams, *Dear Chester, Dear John: Letters between Chester Himes and John A. Williams*, ed. John and Lori Williams (Detroit, MI: Wayne State University Press, 2008), 216.

13. Ibid., 94.

14. Emily Apter, "On Oneworldedness: Or Paranoia as a World System," *American Literary History* 18 (2006): 366.

15. For examples of literary theory's absorption and rejection of Paul Ricoeur's "hermeneutics of suspicion," see Stephen Best and Sharon Marcus, "Surface Reading: An Introduction," *Representations* 108 (2009).

16. Sedgwick, *Novel Gazing*, 22.

17. Kenneth Warren, *Black and White Strangers: Race and American Literary Realism* (Chicago: University of Chicago Press, 1995), 75.

18. Richard Wright, *Island of Hallucination*, box 34, folder 472, RW, 236.

19. William Maxwell, *F. B. Eyes: How J. Edgar Hoover's Ghostreaders Framed African American Literature* (Princeton, NJ: Princeton University Press, 2015), 247.

20. See *Paris, Capital of the Black Atlantic: Literature, Modernity, and Diaspora*, ed. Jeremy Braddock and Jonathan P. Eburne (Baltimore: Johns Hopkins University Press, 2013).

21. Wright, *Island of Hallucination*, 235.

22. Richard Wright, "Rough Notes," box 115, folder 1825, RW.

23. Colette Lacroix to Richard Wright (June 23, 1950), box 115, folder 1826, RW.

24. Mme G. L. Huezé to Richard Wright (June 1950), box 115, folder 1826, RW.

25. Richard Wright, "Provisional Preamble to Constitution and Statement of Aims," box 115, folder 1825.

26. "Franco-American Fellowship: First Meeting Minutes."

27. Stanley Patrick to Richard Wright (undated), box 115, folder 1826, RW.

28. "Franco-American Fellowship: First Meeting Minutes."

29. "Franco-American Fellowship: Second Meeting Minutes," box 115, folder 1834, RW.

30. "Franco-American Fellowship: Second Meeting Minutes."

31. James Baldwin, "Alas, Poor Richard," *The Price of the Ticket: Collected Nonfiction, 1948-1985* (New York: St. Martin's, 1985), 269; William J. Weatherby, *James Baldwin: Artist on Fire* (New York: D. I. Fine, 1989), 124.

32. Hazel Rowley, *Richard Wright: The Life and Times* (New York: Henry Holt, 2001).

33. "Franco-American Fellowship Constitution and Aims," box 115, folder 1825, RW.

34. Carl Brandt to John Williams (August 1, 1966), box 1, folder 8, JW.

35. Harry Sions to John Williams (July 29, 1966), box 1, folder 12, JW.

36. Carl Brandt to Harry Sions (September 8, 1966), box 1, folder 8, JW.

37. John Williams to Harry Sions (August 4, 1966), box 1, folder 13, JW.

38. Initially, Williams resisted the idea of "another Watts," insisting that he did not want to alter people's actions but "touch sensibilities." John Williams to Harry Sions (July 28, 1966), box 1, folder 13, JW.

39. Ibid.

40. Gerard Genette, *Paratexts: Thresholds of Interpretation* (New York: Cambridge University Press, 1997), 2.

41. "King Alfred Plan," box 1, folder 11, JW.

42. Robert H. Fetridge Jr. to John Williams (September 21, 1967), box 1, folder 11, JW.

43. John Williams to Harry Sions (April 2, 1967), box 1, folder 13, JW.

44. John Williams to Robert H. Fetridge (October 10, 1967), box 1, folder 13, JW.

45. John Williams, "King Alfred Memo," box 1, folder 13, JW.

46. Herb Boyd, "The Man and the Plan: Conspiracy Theories and Paranoia in Our Culture," *Black Issues Book Review* 4 (March 2002), 39.

47. Thomas Pynchon, *Vineland* (New York: Penguin, 1997), 353.

48. See Niran Abbas, *Thomas Pynchon: Reading from the Margins* (London: Dickinson University Press, 2003).

49. Keith Gilyard, *Let's Flip the Script: An African American Discourse on Language, Literature, and Learning* (Detroit, MI: Wayne State University, 1996), 101.

50. "King Alfred? Army Spy Confirms Black Control Plan," *Chicago Defender*, January 2, 1971.

51. "Ex-Panther Reveals Do-Away-With Plan," *Hartford Courant*, October 9, 1971.

52. Ibid.

53. Ibid.

54. "King Alfred? Army Spy Confirms Black Control Plan."

55. "Black People May Face Extermination in America," *Atlanta Daily World*, October 24, 1971.

56. Hollie I. West, "Writing in Black and White: Novelist John A. Williams, 'The Man Who Cried I Am,'" *Washington Post*, October 3, 1976.

57. "Author John A. Williams Plans New Black Magazine," *The Crusader* (undated).

58. Gil Scott Heron, vocal performance of "The King Alfred Plan," by Gil Scott Heron, recorded 1972, on *Free Will*, Flying Dutchman Records.

59. Llewellyn Howland III to John Williams (December 5, 1972), box 1, folder 11, JW.

CONCLUSION

1. Jacques Derrida, *The Post Card: From Socrates to Freud and Beyond* (Chicago: University of Chicago Press, 1987), 4.

2. Bernard Lahire, *The Plural Actor* (New York: Polity, 2011), 67.

3. Michael Warner, "Uncritical Reading," in *Polemic: Critical or Uncritical*, ed. Jane Gallop (New York: Routledge, 2004), 19.

4. Nancy Easterlin, "The Functions of Literature and the Evolution of Extended Mind," *New Literary History* 40 (2013): 661.

5. Stephen Best and Sharon Marcus, "Surface Reading: An Introduction," *Representations* 108 (2009): 16.

6. Emily Apter and Elaine Freedgood, "Afterword," *Representations* 108 (2009): 139.

7. Jane Elliott and Gillian Harkins, "Introduction: Genres of Neoliberalism," *Social Text* 31 (2013): 10.

Index

Page numbers in italics refer to figures.